From England to the American West

A Social History

Covering Six Generations

A
Gurr
Family
Odyssey

Paul Magel and Ted Robert Gurr

Special Note: First Edition of this book printed at McNally Robinson Booksellers, ISBN: 9781927533819
Address: 1120 Grant Avenue, Winnipeg, Manitoba, Canada R3M 2A6

SECOND EDITION: Printed in the United States by CreateSpace, an Amazon.com Company

ISBN-13: 978-153700 1579   ISBN-10: 153700 1574

Categorical information:

    1) History – Sussex, London commercial 19th Century, United States homesteading

    2) Immigration – to the United States

    3) Social history – Sussex – London – Chelan, Washington – Merced, California

    4) Genealogy – Gurr family

The list price of this book is $24 US.

Copies may be ordered from Amazon.com and other bookstores.

Dedication

In memory of

three brothers

each of whom

dared seek a better life

for himself

and his children.

Acknowledgements

It must be acknowledged that much of the information used in the preparation of this manuscript has become available to the public in general, thanks to the introduction and expansion of genealogical sites on the growing internet. Co-author Paul Magel has filled several notebooks with data from his research on Gurr family history, with most of the citations for that data having been obtained from Family Search.org and Ancestry.com. The authors have commented more on these and other sources in Chapter 21.

Both authors were fortunate enough to have grown up in families that encouraged education and broadening one's outlook by reading, and to this end materials such as encyclopedia, geographical globes and classical and scientific books were made available in the home to promote interest in a variety of subjects. Internet sites are bringing this information into the world of our children at no cost and we believe that these sites should receive acknowledgement and support. In fact, a great deal of the general historic and geographic content for this manuscript was developed by referring to Wikipedia.com and other free internet sites.

Many individuals have also helped provide the information used here. David Gurr (brother of co-author Ted Robert Gurr) of Los Angeles loaned photo albums and his substantial collection of papers relating to Reverend Henry J. Gurr and provided notes on their father's reminiscences about growing up in Chelan. Then ninety-six year old Dorothy Gurr (aunt of co-author Paul Magel) of Winnipeg rather reluctantly sat for an interview on her life and her knowledge of the Gurrs from London and in the end provided photos and documentation that advanced our understanding of family relationships. Colonel Hugh Stott (3rd cousin of Paul Magel and 2nd cousin of Ted Robert Gurr) of Surrey has provided enlightenment on one family extension with his unpublished manuscripts on Stott family members.

Elizabeth Watson Perry, Chelan's local historian, compiled information on the Gurrs for her own writings and passed on many of them, especially items from the Chelan Valley Leader from 1902 through 1921. Gloria Lund, archivist of the Episcopal Diocese of Spokane, passed on copies of documents from the Diocesan records. Thanks also are due to comments and information from Michael Link of the Episcopal Diocese of Nevada, Suellen Pirages of Las Vegas, researcher Len Barnett of London, and Jennie Rathbun of Harvard's Houghton Library. Joanne Gilbert, a genealogist and author in Las Vegas, gave detailed editorial guidance in preparation of the first edition of this manuscript. Lorie Zorbes (artistlz.aol.com), also of Las Vegas, restored several old photographs.

Especially, we thank our spouses Beryl Magel and Barbara Harff for their patient indulgence of our preoccupation with the Gurr family's past.

Table of Contents

List of Tables, Maps and Sketches

List of Photos

Name	Description	Ref. Page
Photo 15.4a	Mary Amanda Lucas	199
Photo 15.6.2a	Launch 'FJ'	203
Photo 16.1a	Edwin Robert Gurr, Chelan 1919	211
Photo 16.3a	Gravestone of Reverend Henry J. Gurr	213
Photo 16.3b	St. Andrews Episcopal Church, Chelan 2006	213
Photo 16.3c	Reverend Henry Jonathan Gurr, Juneau c.1900	213
Photo 17.2a	Celia Spur Frost Gurr, c. 1882	218
Photo 17.2b	Alf and Will, c. 1886	218
Photo 17.4a	Alf and Will in Alaska, c. 1898	223
Photo 17.4b	Will, Studio Portrait, c.1906	225
Photo 17.6a	Lake Chelan from War Creek Trail	227
Photo 17.6b	Lake Chelan from a point near Goat Mountain	228
Photo 17.7a	Will's Jewellery Store	229
Photo 17.7b	Will and Friends c. 1918	230
Photo 17.8	Chelan's 1916 Pennant Winning Baseball Team	231
Photo 17.9	Chelan Volunteer Fire Department, Late 1920's	232
Photo 17.11a	Will and Maude	236
Photo 17.11b	Will and Maude, 1940's	236
Photo 17.11c	Will and Gladys, late 1950's	237
Photo 17.12	Will on Bicycle, 1977	237
Photo 18.4a	Alfred Richard Gurr's Son, Ted	244
Photo 18.8.2a	Nell Gurr in Nurses Uniform	250
Photo 18.8.2b	Frederick Craik Dewar Jr., Nell's Son c. 1952	250
Photo 18.8.2c	USS Breese - Minelayer	250
Photo 19.3.1a	Father Jack, Father John Edwin Gurr	259
Photo 19.4.1	Mabel Gurr with Eileen, Learning to Walk	263
Photo 19.4.2	Gurr Family on Porch in Spokane, late 1920's	265
Photo 19.4.3a	Group of Boys at Chelan Farmhouse	267
Photo 19.4.3b	John Bennett Gurr and Family, 1950's	267
Photo 20.5.1	George Herbert and father Edwin Robert Gurr, Chelan 1919	277
Photo 20.9.1a	George Edgar Gurr, c. 1930	280
Photo 20.9.1b	George Edgar Gurr, c. 1970	280
Photo 20.9.1c	Dorothy (Dot) Gurr, 1938	280
Photo 20.9.1d	Constance (Connie) Elizabeth Gurr, c. 1940	280

Foreword

Surnames and Kinship

The study of a family's history usually starts with the family's last name, so an understanding of "surnames" in general can be both interesting and helpful. Surnames for common people appeared in China as early as 2,800 BCE, in parts of Western Europe during the Roman Empire, in Britain during the Middle Ages, and as late as 1933 in Turkey. The emergence and evolution of surnames are topics that have long intrigued historians, sociologists, linguists, and genealogists. The history and kinship systems that are delineated by surnames provide scholars with complex fields of study and debate.

Kinship systems have helped people negotiate daily life and understand themselves and their place in society and time. Historically, kinship networks provided the first line of support for emergencies, sick-care, death, and mourning. They also offered connections for personal and family development, child-raising, and shared celebrations. They are still the fundamental social building-blocks in most developing societies, augmented by connections via the workplace, religious communities and friendships.

In the more developed and complex societies of today kinship networks have been expanded by, and in some cases given way to, the abundant associations of modern commerce, professional life, community activism, sports and hobbies. Now ranging beyond membership in families, clans and tribes, these contemporary modes of "belonging" can diminish the importance of kinship networks—and for some people may make them obsolete. Despite sociological sophistication and extraordinary technological advances, surnames still designate the social systems that shape people's sense of family, place, history and purpose. And for contemporary people, who share surnames, and whose interest is therefore subjective rather than academic, personal investigations into their own kinship networks can produce very profound results.

On a Personal Note

The search for their family history brought two cousins (the authors) together. [1] By chance they were searching for a common ancestor in the same place at the same time. Ted Robert Gurr was preparing for publication the memoirs of his uncle Will Gurr of Chelan, whose father, the Reverend Henry Jonathan Gurr had once been Rector at St. Andrew's Episcopal Church in Chelan as well as a service priest for the Spokane Diocese. Paul Magel, recalling that his mother (nee Gurr) once told him that she had lived in Chelan when she was five, wondered whether there were any Gurrs in that locale and, on searching the 1910 and 1920 United States Federal Censuses, found a Henry Gurr and an Edwin Gurr listed as living in Chelan. Independently, the two cousins approached the archivist at the Spokane Diocese for information on the Reverend Gurr within days of one another. It was that archivist who re-united two branches of the extended Gurr family.

---

[1] Ted Robert Gurr and Paul Magel (whose mother was Constance Gurr), both authors being descendants of a branch of Gurrs traced back to Sussex, England.

This chance reunion led the authors on a journey that combined their personal interest with an academic perspective. In the course of this odyssey, they discovered how a seemingly simple four-letter surname can be used to trace relationships and events encompassing centuries of world history. Not satisfied with conventional genealogical lists of names with dates of birth, marriage and death, they wanted to attempt to reconstruct the lives, times and travels of their common ancestors. In search of this history they ended up with hundreds of pages of documentation, well researched, but understandably incomplete. For, while one can gather evidence of historical events and document important incidents concerning kin, one can seldom be certain about the human elements that motivated their behaviour in another time and place.

The Importance of Sharing

With so much accumulated data, the question naturally arose: What to do with it? Ultimately the authors decided to put their findings into a book that would allow others to follow 200 years of history through the experiences—both unique and universal--of one extended family, and so we have produced: *A Gurr Family Odyssey, From England to the American West, A Social History Covering Six Generations*.

The authors originally embarked on a personal genealogical investigation in search of kinship. Not only did we manage to find evidence of our own direct lineage, but in doing so we encountered others with similar aspirations, and in sharing data with them saved many hours of independent research. The authors and readers of this book are members of the restless and ambitious species of *homo sapiens* who from small beginnings in eastern Africa populated the world and built its civilizations. The larger dimensions of this movement, over 25,000 years, are reasonably well known. Yet we have far too few accounts of how and why specific individuals participated in this long migration. The hundreds of hours we have spent in our genealogical research has rewarded us with knowledge of our personal lineage back to the mid-18th century. We have found records of other Gurrs, probably kin, as far back as the 14th century. We are prepared to share this data with our readers, confident that those searching for kinship in our extended family will benefit, and hopeful that by sharing we may establish family connections not yet realized.

The Scope of A Gurr Family Odyssey

This book outlines the lives and times of our more recent Gurr ancestors and their migration from rural England to the new communities of the North American West. We tell their story, and show how we went about reconstructing it, so that others can follow our paths to better understand their own families' histories. We provide a glimpse of the British and American social history of one Gurr family spanning two centuries and two continents. Successive generations of that family migrated from farmlands in Sussex and Kent to London, and from Victorian London to the Americas. Many ancestors of contemporary American and Canadian Gurrs followed similar paths - paths that are well worth reconstructing by their descendants – for our study clearly shows that the vast majority of North American Gurrs are of English ancestry and that, like the authors, their lineage can be traced back to individuals from Sussex or Kent.

Authors' Introduction

Between 1841 and 1890 over 12,000,000 people emigrated from Western Europe and the British Isles to settle in North America. [2] Among those immigrants to the United States were a small number of individuals with the surname Gurr, most of them from England, a few from Germany. Among the roughly 1,600,000 immigrants from England were three Gurr brothers from London. They typify the European immigrants who helped settle and build the towns of the American West, and in part, this is their story.

This book is not a conventional family history or genealogy, although the three brothers are direct ancestors of the authors. We began our search for our Gurr ancestors not knowing the names of the parents of the three brothers nor where they came from, though family tradition said they were English. The family name is uncommon. A search of city and phone directories estimates that there were about 1300 Gurr households in the English-speaking world in the late 20th century. [3]

Where did the name Gurr originate? We know not where or when, but perhaps twenty or thirty generations ago, some historical person, somewhere in Europe, was given or took upon himself the appellation that would evolve into the surname Gurr of our English ancestors. We do have a theory about the name origin. Chapter 1 of this work follows demographic, linguistic, and geographic evidence to one possible conclusion; that the "earliest Gurr" in our line of descent may have been a soldier, likely Norman (Guerrier), who was granted the use of land in England for service to a feudal lord, sometime after the Norman Conquest. We have concluded that the majority of Gurr immigrants to the Americas, Australia and other English speaking countries came from the counties of Sussex and Kent or from Metropolitan London. Supporting this conclusion is the fact that the censuses for the years 1841 to 1891 show that about 95% of the Gurrs enumerated for England and Wales lived in those three regions. Moreover, available documentation covering births, baptisms, marriages, deaths, wills and other records for individuals with the surname Gurr between the year 1349 and the mid 19th century are almost exclusively from the same three regions.

The authors have been able to trace their Gurr lineage back to a family living in the village of Salehurst, Sussex in the latter part of the 18th century. Over a hundred Gurr families have been identified as living in Sussex, Kent or London between the 16th and 19th centuries and it is possible that all are descended from the same individual, though we have been unable to establish any direct linkage between these early families and our more immediate ancestors.

---

[2]   See Appendix A, Tables A4a and A4b.

[3]   From *The World Book of Gurrs, Halbert's Family Heritage*, (1990). Section V. Like other Halbert's publications on family names this contains no Gurr-specific information other than the list of names and locations gleaned from directories.

Our personal family narrative begins in Part I with the birth, in 1800, of Jonathan, the second son of John Gurr, farm worker, and his wife Hannah (nee Chainey) of Salehurst, Sussex. Under-aged Jonathan fathered an illegitimate son George in 1820, but did not marry Mary Barham, George's mother, until 1823. A year or so later, Jonathan and Mary moved to London with George and son Alfred James and there Jonathan spent his working life as a Licensed Victualler or Publican, a prosperous and growing trade. The couple had eight children, but only four are known to have survived childhood.

Alfred James Gurr, the second son of Jonathan, became a servant and then the butler for a prestigious Paddington family. In 1861 Alfred was encouraged and assisted by his mother's nephew, George Barham, in establishing a retail dairy close to newly built Paddington Station, where Gurr and Son's milk supplies could be easily brought in by rail from outlying farms. We trace the development of the 19th century dairy industry in London that enriched the Gurr and Barham families – and led to the knighting of George Barham for his many accomplishments.

London was a densely settled, polluted, and disease-ridden city with few safe water supplies in the early Victorian era, although herculean efforts were being made to remedy these conditions at the time the Gurr and Son dairy was established. Alfred James and his wife Mary Ann had eight children, at a time when many children died in childhood. Alfred James's family was no exception, for one son died within a year of birth and one daughter died at the age of five. The three sons and three daughters who did survive were all well schooled (in this regard the family was exceptional) and each child worked for the dairy firm at one time or another during their lives.

Of the three sons, the second, Henry Jonathan, was the most adventurous and the first to leave home. He went to sea as a cabin boy when he was 13 or 14, in training as a prospective ship's officer. He returned from the India trade a few years later, worked briefly in the family firm, and then immigrated to the United States in 1874. He became an Episcopal clergyman who served some 20 parishes in the upper Midwest, California and gold-rush Alaska before settling down in 1903 to a homestead and parish on Lake Chelan at the eastern edge of Washington State's Cascades Mountains Range. His adventuresome life, and the stories he relayed to his brothers in London by letter and on visits, prompted his older brother Alfred Richard, who was married and had 12 children, to leave the relatively prosperous family dairy business (he was the son in Gurr and Son) to immigrate to Merced in California's Central Valley in 1889. There he established a successful market farm. The road that lead to the Gurr farm is, to this day, named Gurr Road. It is probable that the Reverend Henry Gurr also persuaded his younger brother, Edwin Robert, to leave London and join his two brothers in Merced in 1892, for Edwin became a landed immigrant in 1893. When Edwin's wife died in Merced in 1894, he returned to England but he finally found his way back to America, where he and his second wife homesteaded in Washington in 1906, on land adjacent to his brother Henry. The brothers' homesteads atop Bear Mountain, overlooking the spectacular Chelan Valley, became known as Gurrland.

Over four generations our Gurr ancestors evolved from field workers and servants, who typified much of European population of the 18th century, into the growing middle class of 19th century London, then the world's largest city, where they became publicans, servants and businessmen. Though successful in England they chose to immigrate to the Pacific states of America, where they homesteaded and became landowners, giving their descendants the opportunity to live the American dream. *A Gurr Family Odyssey* is a social history of the lives and times of one family of Gurrs spanning two centuries and two continents.

In Part II we are able to reconstruct in some detail the lives of the three Gurr brothers and their children in North America. Three of Alfred Richard's twelve children became nurses and one son an engineer. Others farmed or found other work, and most had children of their own. We have especially rich documentation about Reverend Henry Jonathan in early 20th-century Chelan, thanks to family narratives, diaries, memoirs and news accounts. These records illuminate the life and daily activities of a small, raw western town – now a resort region in which apple orchards are giving way to viniculture. Although Edwin Robert followed his brother Henry Jonathan to Chelan, his two surviving sons did not, for the eldest decided to remain in Canada while en route to Washington while the younger eventually returned to England, where he served in the British army during WWI.

Six generations of Gurr families provide the thread that ties this book together and thus should intrigue anyone connected to that extended clan. But it is more than a family history. It provides a glimpse of the social worlds in which successive generations moved from farm villages to London, and from London to the Americas. The three Gurr brothers from London exemplify the settlers who helped build the towns of the American West. They were adventurers, preachers, businessmen, farmers, and in the case of the Reverend Gurr all four at once. None became famous or rich but they lived challenging and rewarding lives. Their children and grandchildren are among their legacies, and we give some attention to those connections in the final chapters in Part III.

And how are the authors connected to the three brothers?

Paul Magel is the great-grandson of Edwin (Teddy) Robert Gurr. Edwin's eldest son, George Herbert, settled in Winnipeg after waiting there for several months for permission to enter the United States as a landed immigrant. He eventually decided that there were greater opportunities in Winnipeg, then known as the Gateway to the Canadian West, than in the wilderness that was Chelan at the beginning of the 20th century. Paul was born and raised in Winnipeg, where he established an engineering firm that designs and manufactures electrical equipment that is incorporated in hydro equipment built by other electrical manufacturers and shipped to all parts of the globe.

Ted Robert Gurr is the son of Robert Lucas Gurr, one of the six children that the Reverend Gurr fathered with his third wife, Mabel Lucas Gurr, and raised at Gurrland. Ted was named for his father's favorite uncle, Edwin (Teddy) Robert Gurr. Ted is a professor and author, widely known for his studies of protest and rebellion, retired now after a career at Princeton and Northwestern Universities and the University of Maryland.

Paul Magel is principally responsible for the research and writing that have gone into Part I, while Ted Robert Gurr has done much of the work on Part II, especially on the Chelan years. Both have worked on tracing the lives of the descendants of the three brothers. Early versions of Chapter 11 on the Reverend Henry Jonathan Gurr and of Chapter 15 on "Daily Life in Chelan in

1911" were published in *The Lake Chelan Historical Society History Notes.* Chapter 17 on Will E. Gurr is excerpted from Will E. Gurr and Ted Robert Gurr, *Coming of Age in the West 1883-1906, A Memoir by Will E. Gurr* (2011), edited and annotated by Ted Robert Gurr.

Part I
England

Chapter 1
Contemporary Clans of Gurrs

1.1   Three Contemporary Clans of Gurr

Where are the Gurrs in the contemporary world, and what claims do they have to membership in families descended from common ancestors? We can identify three contemporary clans of people who share the name Gur(r), though we cannot present a shred of evidence of any historical connection among them, yet!

1.2.1   The German Clan

There is a clan of German Gurrs that seems to have originated as a separate family in Bavaria by the 13th century. The earliest German reference to a bearer of the name Gurr can be found in German archives c. 1200 regarding a "Heinrich Gurre" of Bavaria. In 1367, an Ulrich Gurr was a leading citizen of Ingolstadt, Bavaria and other "Gurrs" were recorded in Bavaria and Austria at later dates.

With 15.2% of all Americans reporting themselves as having German ancestry, it is not surprising that the second largest number of Gurrs who immigrated to North America claim German origin. [4] The US census records from 1790 to 1900 include the list of individuals, known to be, or probably of German origin, shown in **Table 1.2.1a**. [5] There are contemporary Gurr households in the United States and Canada headed by men with the common Germanic given names of Wolfgang, Conrad and Erich. Gurrs with the Germanic first names of Anna, Amalie and Gottlieb reportedly arrived in Halifax, Nova Scotia in 1899. [6]

Table 1.2.1 designates the birthplace of those individuals listed as born in Germany, but does not indicate the German state from which they came. In considering what German state the American immigrants might have come from, the authors conducted a limited study of German phone books for 2008. That study found 197 listings for Gurr living in central or northern Germany, with almost none in Bavaria, and it is worth noting that the spelling of Gurr in German phone books is exactly the same as the spelling in English phone books. Also found were 27 listings for Gur and 37 for Gore, though there was not one Gurre or Guerre, and no other names with similar spelling in significant numbers.

Few of the Gurrs residing in England, Australia and New Zealand are of German descent. The majority of Australian and New Zealand Gurrs trace their ancestry back to England, and many Australians will confirm that their ancestors arrived "down under" when it was primarily

---

[4] According to the 2000 United States Federal Census those who claimed descent from European immigrants included German (15.2%), Irish (10.8%), English (7.7%), Italian (5.6%), Scandinavian (3.7%) and Polish (3.2%).

[5] 1850 was the first year a birthplace was required on a U.S. Federal Census, so the 1800 listings for George, Jacob and Lorentz are speculative.

[6] According to a July 1992 phone conversation between Ted Robert Gurr and a Mr. Waffle who was tracking the ancestry of his family, one of whom had married one of the 1899 Gurr immigrants.

serving as a penal colony. [7]   The major colonies were Tasmania (originally Van Diemen's Island), Norfolk Island and New South Wales, to which over 165,000 English convicts were transported between 1787 and 1868. There is evidence that suggests that New Zealand may have

Table 1.2.1a [8]		**Gurrs of German Origin in all United States Federal Censuses to 1900**			
Year	County, State	Name	# in Fam	Birthplace	Year
1800	Northampton, Pennsylvania	George Gurr	10	Unlisted	?
1800	Northampton, Pennsylvania	Jacob Gurr	5	Unlisted	?
1800	Northampton, Pennsylvania	Lorentz Gurr	3	Unlisted	?
1860	New York Ward 3, New York	Charles Gurr	1	Wurttemberg	1830
1870	New York Ward 19, New York	Margaret Gurr	1	Germany	1847
1870	Marshall, Kansas	Frederic Gurr	6	Prussia	1830
1870	Marshall, Kansas	Mary Gurr	wife	Prussia	1835
1880	Cook, Illinois	William Gurr	5	Prussia	1819
1880	New York, New York	Charles Gurr	1	Prussia	1848
1880, 1900	Jefferson, Wisconsin	Godfried Gurr	5	Prussia	1833
1880	Jefferson, Wisconsin	Anne Gurr	wife	Prussia	1837
1900	New York, New York	Frank Gurr	2	Germany	1842
1900	New York, New York	Maria Gurr	wife	Germany	1848
1900	Nebraska City, Nebraska	A. P. Gurr	2	Germany	1867
1900	Nebraska City, Nebraska	Sophia Gurr	wife	Germany	1880
1900	Port Huron, Michigan	Charles Gurr	2	Germany	1845
1900	Port Huron, Michigan	Wilhemena Gurr	wife	Germany	1847
1900	South Bend, Nebraska	Christian Gurr	3	Germany	1850
1900	South Bend, Nebraska	Augusta Gurr	wife	Germany	1851
1900	Cook, Illinois	Charles Gurr	7	Germany	1856
1900	Cook, Illinois	Johanna Gurr	wife	Germany	1861
1900	Columbia, Wisconsin	William Gurr	4	Germany	1861
1900	Columbia, Wisconsin	Fredericka Gurr	wife	Germany	1861
1900	Hobart Lake, Indiana	Julian Gurr	5	Germany	1861
1900	Hobart Lake, Indiana	Bertha Gurr	wife	Germany	1868
1900	Wayne, Michigan	G.A. Gurr	1	Germany	1864

---

[7]   See Chapter 10. The British used North America as a form of penal colony (indentured servitude for convicts) during the 17th and 18th centuries. Following the American Revolution, several penal colonies were established in Australia. One-quarter of the immigrants to the American colonies from England before the Revolution were penal transports. Between the first arrival of convicts at Botany Bay in 1787 and the Australian gold rush of 1850 the majority of the Australian population were penal transports or their descendants, or military personnel sent to keep the peace among the transports.

[8]   Table composed by Paul Magel from census data retrieved from http:www.search.ancestry.com.

received a few convicts for rehabilitation, or as parolees from the Australian penal colonies, but there is no evidence of a penal colony ever being established there.

There is a slight possibility that the very first Gurr to set foot in England came from Bavaria, or some other part of the Holy Roman Empire. However, there was little regular intercourse between the Duchy of Bavaria and England in medieval times, and there were open hostilities between France and England for much of the 13th to 15th centuries. It is interesting, however, that Louis I, Duke of Bavaria, participated in the 5th Crusade and became the guardian of Henry III in 1225. The Bavarian Duke served in that capacity until the young English king reached the age of majority in 1228. Henry was the father of Edward I (nicknamed Longshanks, because of his height) and during the 13th century there is at least some evidence of cooperation between the Duchy of Bavaria and the Kings of England.

1.2.2   The Jewish Clan

The second contemporary clan of Gur(r)s is Jewish-Israeli, and the spelling of the family name is almost invariably Gur. The 1985 Jerusalem phone directory contains 70 listings for Gur. Several factors coincided in the adoption of the Gur name among Jewish people. First gur is Hebrew for lion cub. Second, it may be derived from the old Jewish family names of Gurion or Gorren. [9] Third, many Eastern European Jews had surnames that began with Gur, as in Gurowitz or Gourevitch. When emigrating to Israel many used just the first syllable - one which had social and linguistic significance in their new homeland. One of the most prominent Israeli Gurs was Mordecai Gur, whose paratroop battalion led the capture of East Jerusalem from the Jordanians during the Six-Day War of 1967, and who went on to become chief of staff of the Israeli armed forces. At least one 19th century Jewish family in the United States seems to have simplified their family name to Gurr, rather than Gur, the parents of 20th century American artist Lena Gur, whose Jewish origins are evident in her parents' given names. [10]

In tracing any Jewish Gurrs in England it is important to understand the history of Jews there. The first Jewish community recorded in England dates from 1070, during the reign of William I, although individual Jews had lived there from Roman times. When King William encouraged Jewish merchants and artisan from northern France to move to England, German Jews came as well. The first incidence of blood libel against Jews in England occurred in 1144. [11] The Jews of Norwich were accused of ritual murder after a boy (William of Norwich) was found dead with stab wounds. The story was turned into a cult, William acquiring the status of martyr and subsequently being canonized. The cult of St. William attracted large numbers of pilgrims

---

[9]   Goreen is a Sephardic Jewish name documented in 15th century Spanish sources, according to computerized records at the Nahum Goldmann Museum of the Jewish Diaspora in Tel Aviv. David Ben-Gurion, the first prime minister of Israel took his Hebrew name from a 9th century Jewish historian, Joseph ben Gorian. In Hebrew, Ben means "son of", so Ben-Gurion may have been taken from the historian, or alternatively means "son of a lion."

[10]   Born in Brooklyn in 1897, Lena was the daughter of Hyman and Ida (nee Gorodnick) Gurr and became the wife of Joseph Biel, Jewish artist and photographer, born 1891 in Grodno Poland, then under Russian occupation.

[11]   Blood Libel is the false accusation or claim that religious minorities, usually Jews, murder children to use their blood in certain aspects of their religious rituals and holidays.

and brought wealth to the local church, but led to continuous, increasing violence against Jews. On 6 February 1190, all the Jews of Norwich were massacred except for a few who found refuge in the castle. Violence against Jews in England continued throughout the following century.

In 1290, the crusading King Edward I expelled all Jews from England. They were forced to leave with only what they could carry and with few exceptions were not even allowed to sell what they owned. After the *Edict of Expulsion of 1290*, there were no Jewish communities in England. In fact, there were few, if any, individuals who would have dared to call themselves Jews. This is because of the *De Judaismo* statute, passed by Edward I, which imposed severe penalties for practicing Judaism or even for helping anyone who was Jewish. The statute, which also required Jews to wear special dress that identified them, was not repealed until 1846, although by then Britain had acquired a reputation for religious tolerance.

That tolerance may have begun under Oliver Cromwell (1599-1658), the English military leader who became Lord Protector of the Commonwealth of England, Scotland and Ireland following England's Civil War which resulted in the beheading of Charles I in 1649. The Civil War arose from Charles' claim to absolute power and his refusal to negotiate with Parliament, but there was also an underlying conflict between Catholics and Protestants.

When Cromwell, himself an independent Puritan, became Lord Protector, he recognized the need to restore order and bring the various religious factions together and he called for "healing and settling" as the first goal of the new Parliament. There were those who were insisting on radical constitutional reforms, but Cromwell's second stated goal was "spiritual and moral reform", and rather than deal with the constitutional radicals who were in the majority, he eventually dissolved Parliament in 1655. His objective was to restore liberty of conscience and promote both outward and inward godliness throughout England. A definite sign of this growing tolerance of religious diversity occurred when a small colony of Sephardic Jews was identified in London in 1656. [12] Under his authority, they were allowed to remain there.

The fact that Jews were unwelcome in England during the 12th century and banned there before the end of the 13th century makes a Jewish origin for the Gurrs of England improbable. Still, we suggest the reader keep an open mind on the subject for, curiously, the earliest records of the Gurr name in England include a 1459 will, that of William Gurre of Fransham Parva in Norfolk (a few miles west of where the Jews of Norwich were slaughtered), a 1508 will, that of Richard Gur of Rottingdean, Sussex, and a 1515 record of a William Gurr of York. The earliest

---

[12] Sephardic Jews are Jews of Spanish and Portuguese descent with an Iberian style of liturgy. Following the expulsion of Jews from Spain in 1492, and Portugal in 1497, and the establishment of the Spanish Inquisition, banished Sephardim settled in other parts of Europe, many ostensibly Catholic but ready to convert back to Judaism. In 1656, Rabbi Menasseh ben Israel, from Amsterdam, where a community of Sephardic Jews had established itself and reverted back to Judaism, paid a visit to England to try and persuade the English Government to allow the Jews to once again settle in England. He met Oliver Cromwell, who was favourably disposed to the idea, and after a Commission had deliberated on the problem, it was announced that the Deed of Expulsion in 1290 was a Royal decree, and no longer had any relevance (England was part of a Commonwealth and no longer a monarchy). Sephardic Jews immediately established a Synagogue in London and attracted others to openly revert to Judaism. Excerpts sourced from the website: Foundation for the Advancement of Sephardic Studies and Culture.

Gurr record of all is a Chancery Court document dated 1349 designating a Richard Gurre of Belton, Lincolnshire as the attorney for the executors of a 14th century will.

1.2.3 The English Clan

The largest contemporary clan with the surname Gurr is of English origin. The name with this exact spelling (there are other records for Gur, Guere and Gurre) is recorded as early as 1515 for a William Gurr of York. Another record exists for a Willyam Gurr of Hove, Sussex, who married Joanne Jenerton in October, 1544. Data compiled from the England and Wales census of 1891 indicates a total of 1179 families with the surname Gurr residing in England and Wales, almost ninety percent of them concentrated in Kent, Sussex and Metropolitan London. [13]

The authors have compiled a Master List of Gurrs, which includes 2335 UK Gurr records dating from AD 1349 up to the end of 1841 (including the 1841 census). Ninety-five percent of all the records referenced individuals living in southeast England and, more specifically, Sussex, Kent or Middlesex, including London. The 2335 records (summarized by County in Table 1.2.3a) were found by searching Ancestry.com, the International Geological Index and other sources. They include Chancery and church archives (weddings, baptisms and deaths), probate and various other records. Records include duplication of individuals, as individuals may be recorded for birth, marriage, probate, apprenticeship, etc. **Table 1.2.3a** on the following page is structured to show the percentages of records by county from 1349 to 1600, from 1349 to 1700 and from 1349 to 1841. The data indicates a migration of Gurrs from Sussex to Kent during these five centuries.

The earliest records of families of Gurrs (rather than of individuals) are almost all from Sussex. **Table 1.2.3b** on the following page shows the location of the earliest Sussex records found. Hove, Broadwater and Rye are along the coastal plain on what is known as the South Downs, while each of the other towns is on the Weald. During the 1500s, the majority of Gurr families in England resided within a twenty mile radius centered at Lewes in the low Weald, an area whose low-grade iron ore supported mining and smelting from early Roman times onward.

The Weald is a broad shallow valley in the counties of Kent and Sussex, between a series of rolling chalk hills known as the North and South Downs. Once heavily forested, the Weald was known for its oak (used in shipbuilding), its iron foundries and its gunpowder factories. The region became depressed during the 18th century as the forests were depleted and coal became the fuel of choice for iron smelting. This depression and the Industrial Revolution probably led many Gurr families to migrate north and east to Kent and beyond. References to Gurr families in Kent did not become significant in numbers until the mid-18th century. By the 1840s, the majority of Gurr records found are from northwest Kent (Maidstone, Rochester, Dartford).

---

[13] Compiled by Ancestry.com from the 1891 England and Wales census records.

Table 1.2.3a [14]	Gurr Records 1349 to 1841 Distribution by County or Country From Author's Master List of Gurrs		
British County or Country	Dated 1349 - 1841	Dated 1349 - 1700	Dated 1349 - 1600
Sussex	1118 (48%)	235 (66%)	95 (69%)
Kent	802 (35%)	61 (17%)	9 (7%)
Middlesex, London	280 (12%)	38 (11%)	16 (12%)
Other Counties of England	103 (4%)	18 (5%)	17 (12%)
Scotland, Ireland, Malta, United States and Abroad	14 (< 1%)	1 (< 1%)	0
Undetermined UK Locations	18 (<1%)	4 (< 1%)	0
Total Number of Records	2335	357	137

Table 1.2.3b	Location of Earliest Sussex Gurr Records From Author's Master List of Gurrs	
Town	Location	Dating
Lewes, Rottingdean	East Sussex, The Weald	1508
Steyning, Hove	West Sussex, South Downs	1544
Lewes, Beddingham	East Sussex, The Weald	1552
Battle, Westfield	East Sussex, The Weald	1555
Cuckfield, Ditchling	East Sussex, The Weald	1562
Worthing, Broadwater	West Sussex, South Downs	1570
Rye	East Sussex, Rye Estuary	1574
Lewes, Alciston	East Sussex, The Weald	1576

Map 1.2.3c and Map 1.2.3d on the following pages show the approximate outlines of Registrations Districts for Kent and Sussex, respectively, as of 1837. [15] The number in each district indicates the number of records for individuals in that district found in the Author's Master List of Gurrs gathered from various sources.

---

[14] Tables 1.2.3a and 1.2.3b are by Paul Magel composed from data from the Author's Master List of Gurrs based on records found dated between 1349 and 1841. Note: There are deliberate as well as unintentional duplications of records for many individuals, especially for birth date. The argument for keeping duplicate records is that the database was developed over time, with records being added as found. When a marriage record was first found, the birth dates for the individuals involved may have been estimated (listed as Birth), where no age or birth date was found on the marriage record. Later a birth or baptism date for a corresponding individual of that marriage might be found and recorded as Child. Unless absolute evidence of a match was found, both Birth and Child records appear in the database, the argument being that no record should be lost by possible mismatching.

[15] Both Maps 1.2.3a and 1.2.3b are by Paul Magel prepared from the Author's Master List of 2335 Gurr Records dated between 1349 and 1841.

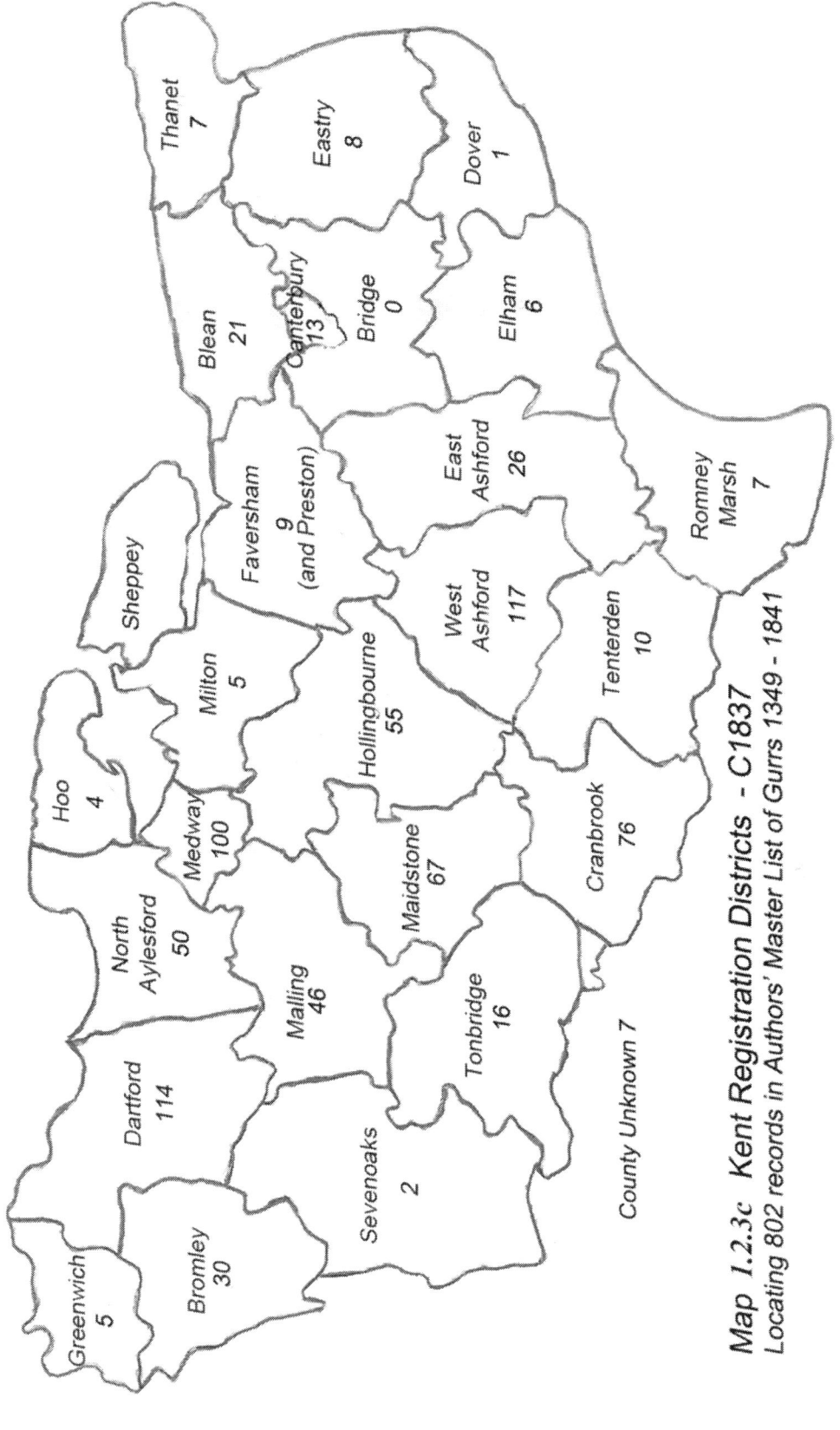

Map 1.2.3c Kent Registration Districts - C1837
Locating 802 records in Authors' Master List of Gurrs 1349 - 1841

Thanet 7

Eastry 8

Dover 1

Blean 21

Canterbury 13

Bridge 0

Elham 6

Faversham 9 (and Preston)

East Ashford 26

Romney Marsh 7

Sheppey

West Ashford 117

Tenterden 10

Milton 5

Hollingbourne 55

Hoo 4

Medway 100

Maidstone 67

Cranbrook 76

North Aylesford 50

Malling 46

Tonbridge 16

County Unknown 7

Dartford 114

Sevenoaks 2

Greenwich 5

Bromley 30

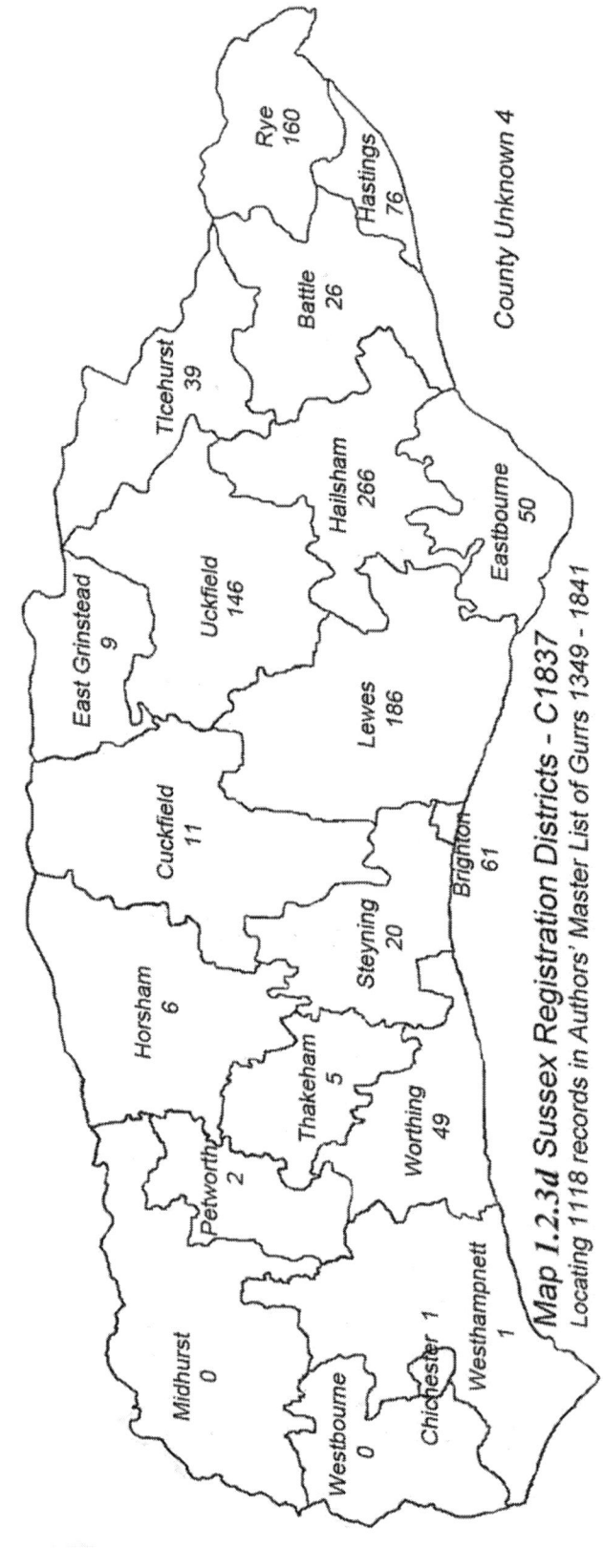

Map *1.2.3d* Sussex Registration Districts - C1837
Locating 1118 records in Authors' Master List of Gurrs 1349 - 1841

Chapter 2
Origin and History of the Surname Gurr
in Southeast England

Chapter one demonstrates that except for North America and Australia, the highest concentration of individuals with the exact surname Gurr (or of individuals acknowledging Gurr ancestry) inhabited the Sussex-Kent-London region of the United Kingdom, while a smaller concentration was found in Germany. Subsequently, considering the history of north-Western Europe, it might well be that the original Gurr (or some variation of Gurr) is of Celtic, Gallic, Anglo-Saxon, Viking or Norman origin.

There has been much speculation on possible origins of the Gurrs who now inhabit Sussex-Kent-London, some much less plausible than others. Following are a few of those suggested geographic and demographic possibilities.

2.1   Geographic

Gur in Welsh signifies a man or husband. [16] This Welsh reference gives no indication of the age of the word or its origin, and does not appear to be used as a surname in Wales.

A contemporary Flemish scholar (not a genealogist) named John Goormaghtich suggested that the Gurr name might be of Dutch origin. His family name is rare and derives from an old Dutch word for moor. There is a town near Antwerp named Goor. We know of no migratory connection between medieval Holland and Sussex, and consider this suggestion unlikely.

One 19th century English source says the name is "probably from Gueres, a village in Normandy near Dieppe. A Peter Gyrre, apothecary from Dieppe, a Protestant refugee arrived at Rye, County Sussex 1572." [17]   The name Gyrre is rare (two families are listed in Normandy and Brittany in the 2008 phone book for France, and no Gyrres appear in existing records between 1515 and 1837, nor in the 1841 to 1891 UK censuses), but this is one possible source of at least some of the English Gurrs (assuming the name was anglicized after Peter Gyrre's arrival in Rye).

Another suggested origin is that the (Gûr, Gurr) family name is Anglo-Norman from the Old French "guerrier" meaning warrior or foot soldier [18], and that William I may have granted captured land to one or more of the Norman guerriers who served him in the battle of Hastings. Some of those so rewarded may have remained in Sussex after the Conquest, and the name guerrier, by which they were commonly known, was gradually anglicized to Gurr.

---

[16]   Source: Arthur, William, M.A, (1857). *An Etymological Dictionary of Family and Christian Names with an Essay on their Derivation and Import*; New York, NY: Sheldon, Blake, Bleeker & Co., 1857.

[17]   Mark Antony Lower, (1860) *Patronymica Britannica, A dictionary of the family names of the United Kingdom.* Thanks to David Gurr, Los Angeles, for the citation.

[18]   Thanks to Carlos K. Gurr, see Gurr.org However, although we believe that this is a possibility, it seems more probable that the guerriers who may have become Gurrs fought in later wars as suggested in the Authors' Introduction and documented below.

One genealogical service says that "The surname "Gurr" originated in Bavaria as a nickname (ubername) and was adopted by the original individual, or one of his descendants, as a surname. [19] This service states that the surname "Gurr" arose from the Middle High German word "gurre" which can be translated as "old mare", and describes an aged or infirm horse."

2.2   Demographic

We know that, following the Norman Conquest of Britain, the Anglo-Norman language (Old French) of the invaders was gradually intermingled with the Anglo-Saxon (Old English) spoken by the conquered people. As the Norman aristocracy took over positions of authority from the old aristocracy, Norman names replaced Saxon names. Archers, infantry and cavalry who followed their Norman lord into battle often had names associated with that lord.

Following the conquest it was prestigious to have a Norman French name in England. But, Many of the invading Normans that stayed on in England, as well as the Norman settlers that followed them were of a lower class and their Old French names were gradually anglicized. This did not happen overnight and not always intentionally. Since few members of the population were literate, when an illiterate person gave his or her name for whatever record was being kept, it might well be listed according to the sound. Thus, the name Guernon (a Norman Knight listed in the Battle Abbey Roll, who was from Montifiquet near Guernay), or a Gyrre, Gore, Garr, Gurry, Guere, Guerre, or Guerriere might well become Gur or even Gurr. [20]

The use of surnames gradually became necessary to distinguish one person from another in the more heavily populated areas of Britain during the 12th and 13th centuries, because there were so few given names in use. About half the male population carried the names Thomas, William, John, Richard or Henry. Surnames were developed by using variations of first names (e.g. Williamson, Johnson, Richards, Richardson), of occupations (e.g. Smith, Cook, Knight, Woodman, Baker), of place names (e.g. Hill, Lake, Fields, London), of religious names (e.g. Abbot, Priestley, Bishop), or of derivations from many other categories.

Although surnames were not in common use at the time of the Norman conquest, by the 14th century hereditary surnames had been formally adopted, first by the aristocracy and then gradually by the middle class and the common people. By about 1430 when the Chancery Standard was being implemented, most people in England and Scotland had acquired a surname. [21] In the reign of Henry VIII (1509-1547) it was decreed that all marital births be recorded using the surname of the father, descent in England being traced through the male line at a time when gender equality was not imagined.

---

[19]   Historical Research Center Inc. and also *The Dictionary of American Family Names.* Oxford University Press, ISBN 0-19-508137-4

[20]   The Battle Abbey Roll(s) (several versions have appeared during past centuries) are claimed to be lists of those who crossed the English Channel in support of William the Conqueror in 1066. The authenticity and accuracy of the Rolls have always been questioned. The earliest Roll, a copy dating from the 14th century, is supposedly from a memorial at Battle Abbey erected by William following the Conquest.

[21]   The Chancery Standard was a clear and unambiguous written form of English used by government bureaucracy and for other official purposes from the late 14th century.

2.3   Language Considerations

Is it possible that the origin of the surname Gurr can be traced backward through language studies? The English language of today is of Germanic origin traceable to the "Old English" of the Anglo Saxon era as well as to the "Old French" spoken by the Normans at the time of their conquest of England. [22] Following the invasion of 1066, the language of the indigenous population changed from the standardized "Old English" (of the Anglo Saxon, with its distinctly Scandinavian or Viking influence) into a *patois* which included much of the standardized "Old French" of the Normans (with its distinctly Gallo-Roman influence). [23] This *patois* is now identified as "Middle English" and, over a period of more than three hundred years, several dialects of the language developed in different regions of the British Isles, without there being a standard system for writing any of them.

In medieval England scholars spoke and wrote in Latin, which was still a living language at the time. When they tried to express themselves in English those scholars, trained only in Latin and with no defined writing system, wrote English using Latin vowels and consonants to represent English sounds. There weren't enough letters in the Latin alphabet to accomplish this and so different combinations of letters were often used to represent English sounds that did not have a Latin equivalent. [24] To complicate matters even more, different scholars often used different letters of the alphabet in writing English because they interpreted the English sound differently, and as a result, many of these early writings were inconsistent.

Standardization of the English language began in the reign of Henry V (1413-1422). Up until the 1400s, although "Middle English" was the spoken language of the common people, most of the church, the nobility and the aristocracy spoke French, and almost everything written was either in French or Latin. Henry V was able to read and write in English, and it is probable that he did so in order to appeal to the common people. In 1417, he ordered his Chancery to use English rather than French or Latin and, by 1430, the Chancery Standard, based on the dialect then used in London, was established. For the first time matters of the court and of law, business and even literature began to be recorded in "Middle English", while spoken French and Latin gradually became less and less prevalent. For the leaders of the Church, for scholars and for the nobility, it remained essential to be able to speak French, and this continued to be the language of European courts, and of "polite" society. By the 1470s, the Chancery Standard was in general use and, with the advent of the printing press (Gutenberg, c 1440), what we now call early modern English (Elizabethan English) became the standardized language of the British people.

---

[22]   Hypothetically, it is believed that all Germanic languages developed from a Nordic language spoken some 4500 years ago in the region of South Sweden and Jutland, while that early language is considered to have Indio-European roots.

[23]   *Patois*; a regional dialect, not standardized, and without a defined writing system.

[24]   The "gh" in through is one example of this, as there is no Latin letter to represent the English sound "huh." One might think of the words "threw" and "through" and how you would differentiate the two words in writing, noting that phonetically the word "threw" is cut short while the word "through" is elongated, much like adding the "huh" ending.

One of the earliest pieces of literature written in "Middle English" is the *Canterbury Tales,* produced by Chaucer in the late 14th century. Chaucer wrote in a combination of dialects that had developed by that time, and the *Canterbury Tales* precedes standardization. Table B1 in Appendix B is an excerpt from that work, presented as an example of early English, and as one that illustrates some of the subtle changes that can take place during the evolution of a language.

2.4   Gurr from Guerrier – A Reasonable Possibility?

The origin of the English word "war" is guerre (from Old French). [25] The related word guerrier means "warrior" or "foot soldier" in both the old and modern French. One language dictionary provides the following explanation for the origin of the word "war." [26]

> The word "War" can be traced back to the Indo-European root *wers*, "to confuse, mix up." In the Germanic family of the Indo-European languages, this root gave rise to words having to do with confusion. One was the noun *werza*, "confusion," which in a later form *werra* was borrowed into Old French, probably from Frankish, a largely unrecorded Germanic language that contributed about 200 words to the vocabulary of Old French. From this Germanic stem came both: the form *werre* in North Old French, borrowed into English in the 12th century; and the form *guerre* (the source of "guerrilla") in the rest of the Old French-speaking area. Both forms meant "war."

Remembering that it was uncommon for those of the lower classes to have surnames, it is possible that some were identified as (for example) Edward the guerrier, and that guerrier became anglicized to Gurr during the next three or four centuries. The Norman-French conquerors granted land in the Sussex-Kent-London region of England to their supporters, so it quite possible some of their foot soldiers or guerriers settled amongst the Anglo-Saxons soon after the Norman Conquest. Of course, the same scenario may have taken place much later than the Conquest, for there were several periods of war between England and France between 1066 and the 15th century dates of the earliest records for individuals with the surname Gurr (or a variation of Gurr).

For example, one of the Field Commanders in Normandy from 1430 to 1435 was John Fitz Alan (1408-1435), the 14th Earl of Arundel (the oldest extant earldom and the oldest extant peerage in the Peerage of England today). [27] In 1433, while serving under the Duke of Bedford he had in his service a crossbowman by the name of Peter de la Guerre. [28] Crossbowmen were the elite of the archers and usually led ground forces into battle immediately prior to an attack by mounted knights. The commander of crossbowmen was one of the highest ranks in the military

---

[25]   *Compact Oxford Dictionary*

[26]   William Morris, editor 1st edition (1969). *The American Heritage Dictionary of the English Language.* Boston: Houghton Mifflin Company.

[27]   One branch of the Fitz Alan family would become the Stuarts who ruled Scotland in later years.

[28]   From The National Archives muster rolls for the years 1369-1453 which contains 128,525 records of those in service for the English crown in the occupation of Normandy 1415-1453. The rolls for the Normandy period include 24 archers and 1 crossbowman, all 25 with the surname Guerre (or de la Guerre), as well as the Earls of Huntingdon, Dorset, Somerset, Beaufort, Suffolk and a number of lesser commanders from the nobility.

during the 100 Years war. Some early records of Gurrs in England are found in the region of Sussex that were the lands of the Earl of Arundel. Alciston lying about thirty-four miles east of the Castle of Arundel is part of the land holdings of the Earl, and it is there that we find records of Gurr families in the late 15th century. It is possible that the Earl of Arundel provided land in Sussex for those who had supported him in Normandy, perhaps including Peter de la Guerre, or another of the Earl's many followers who may have adopted the surname Guerre.

Earl John Fitz Alan, by all reports an outstanding commander, returned to England from Normandy to raise troops in May of 1434, then returned to France as joint commander of all forces in Normandy. In a battle for the fortress at Gerberoy in May of 1435 the earl was wounded in the foot and captured by the French. He eventually lost his leg and died in June of that year. His body was returned to Arundel Castle and he was buried there. He was a courageous and popular commander, and it is likely that most of his retinue and some of his followers returned to England with his body. In the years that Fitz Alan was in Normandy, the English held almost half of France, but following his death English fortunes began to decline and by 1453 they were driven out of France (except for Calais).

2.5   Early Records in England for Gurr

As previously outlined, there is considerable evidence to suggest that the name Gurr evolved from Old French to modern English and through the Middle Ages the spelling may have been Guerre, Gurre, Gur or Gurr and we are inclined to accept any of these variations as probable members of the Gurr family. With this in mind, we offer the following early records.

The earliest record of a Gurr found in England is dated 1349, a Chancery record involving a land claim that refers to a Richard Gurre as the attorney of note residing in Lincoln. [29] There is no other information provided about Richard or his family.

An all-England search of Ancestry.com records led the authors to records for two *individuals* with the surname Gurr (Gur, Gurre), one for a John Gurre and another for a William Gurre, both residents of Norfolk. [30]

A third record for William Gurre (possibly the same individual as the earlier record) was found in an online search for details on Fransham Parva. [31] The details in order of date follow:

- Demise by William Gurre, clerk, Rector of Crownthorpe church, Thomas Sayve of Carleton Forehoe, Thomas Baly of Wicklewood and John Smyth of Brandon to Thomas Lawes, Eustace Lawes his brother, Edmund Bryghteve and Henry Schrympelyng, all of Barnham Broom, of a messuage and land in Barnham Broom. KIM 2N/37 5 April 32 Henry VI (1454).

- Conveyance by John Portman and Agnes his wife to John Gurre and John Wedyrby of 69.5 acres of land in Wicklewood. KIM 2C/18a 2 March *1465*.

---

[29]   Chancery Record Ref: C 131/8/7 Land Claims

[30]   The Norfolk locations specified (Wicklewood, Barnham Broom and Fransham Parva) lie several miles west of Norwich.

[31]   Francis Blomefield, (1808) 'Launditch Hundred: Fransham Parva', *An Essay towards a Topographical History of the County of Norfolk*: volume 9, pp. 500-503

- 1482: Gurre, Gurr, William, rector of St. Mary, Fransham Parva 126 A. Caston Norfolk: Norwich – 1. Index To Wills, Consistory Court of Norwich, 1370-1550, 2. Wills Among The Norwich Enrolled Deeds, 1286-1508.

As we show below, almost all other early Gurr names are from Sussex, and there are very few later records of Gurr(e)s in East Anglia. [32] We suspect there was a Norfolk clan of Gurr(e)s that were not connected with the Gurrs of Sussex and Kent. Rather, the name may be a variant of Gower or Goher, a prominent Norman-descended family in Yorkshire.

The earliest Gurr *family* identified held land in the vicinity of Lewes, of the Manor of Falmer, according to the following data from the National Archives UK. Copies of the court roll of a messuage (later described as a barn) and 3 virgates of land in West Street, Rottingdean held of the Manor of Falmer BRD/1/2 *1508-1701*. Contents are as follows:

- In 1508 Isabel Gur, widow of Richard Gur was admitted to the property (BRD/1/2/1).

- In 1579 John Gurre admitted on the death of Richard Gur forty years before, was readmitted because a fire in his house at Christmas 1575 had destroyed his evidence of title (BRD/1/2/2-3).

- In 1588 his wid., Margaret, was admitted for life, remainder to son, Richard (BRD/1/2/4).

- After Margaret's death the property passed in 1602 to William Gurr, brother of Richard, because Richard had died (BRD/1/2/5).

- In [1622] William Gurr's widow was admitted (BRD/1/2/6).

- In 1665 Isaac, youngest son of Richard Gurr, was admitted on Richards's death, Elizabeth Gurr his mother being appointed guardian (BRD/1/2/7-8).

- In 1682 Isaac Gurr sold to Samuel Beard, son of Nicholas Beard, sen. of Falmer, the latter acting as guardian during his minority (BRD/1/2/9).

- In 1701 Samuel surrendered the property to Daniel Beard of Rottingdean, yeo., his bro. (BRD/1/2/10).

These early Sussex records bearing the name Gurr (Gur, Gurre) concern an Isabel Gur of West Street in Rottingdean (east of Brighton, south of Lewes and about 12 miles southwest of Chiddingly). [33] In 1508, on the death of her husband Richard Gur, Isabel was admitted (by the Lord of the Manor) to three virgates (about 90 acres) of land held of the manor of Falmer. Since the eldest son normally inherited from his father, the fact that Isabel inherited could have meant that the eldest son was not yet of age, or that Richard had no children. However, it is more likely that Richard's heir was not yet of age, for the land remained in the family until the late 1600s when it (the tenancy) was sold to the Beard family, major leaseholders in the region. The record is interesting in that it tracks the hereditary transfer of property from one heir to the next over a period of almost 200 years, and the family name gradually changes from Gur, to Gurre, to Gurr.

---

[32] Less than 1% of records in the Master List of Gurrs come from East Anglia and almost all of those are post 1770.

[33] National Archives of the UK, documents held at East Sussex Record Office in Lewes, Sussex.

According to *Wikipedia* the archaic term messuage was a term used in legal conveyances that was "nearly synonymous with dwelling house. A grant of a messuage with the appurtenances will not only pass along a house but all of the buildings attached or belonging to it, as also its curtilage[34], garden and orchard, together with the close on which the house is built."

The Manor of Falmer originally covered a large tract of downland (grasslands of southeastern England) in a valley that runs to the sea east of Brighton. Its lands extended south to include the Gur(r) messuage in Rottingdean, which meant that the Gurrs owed annual rents to the Lord of the Manor. Falmer was part of the lands granted by William the Conqueror to Earl William of Warenne, passed on to his successors, and later held by a priory in Lewes. After the dissolution of religious establishments by Henry VIII in the 1530's, the Manor and its rents were conveyed to a succession of absentee earls and lords who enjoyed royal favor. Change of the Lord of a Manor did not normally result in change of the Manors tenants or of grant agreements.

The village of Rottingdean lies at the southern end of the valley that opens out onto a low chalk cliff overlooking the sea. By chance we can pinpoint the exact location of the Gurr holding in the modern village. West Street is scarcely 100 yards long, a shortcut as it were from High Street, opposite the post office, to the coastal highway. The Gurr messuage was almost surely on the north side of West Street, because the chalk cliffs begin not far to the south. Ninety acres is a substantial area so the holding may have extended the full length of West Street. The area with the 16th c. dwelling would have been close to the street – a dirt lane then, not a neatly cobbled way –and was very likely cultivated and included a barn and small outbuildings. Beyond that lay pasturage that extended north into the hills, for the sheep that were a major source of income for the Manor of Falmer and no doubt for the Gurr family as well. Several hundred yards further west is a lane called Sheep Walk that comes down from the pastures to the coastal highway. Its name suggests it was the route by which sheep were driven seasonally from the pastures at higher elevation to the coastal farmsteads.

West Street today has an odd configuration: it divides into two streets that surround a bubble. Google Earth shows that the bubble is a car park, just opposite a Tedesco supermarket. Small shops and private homes, and a bus stop, take up the rest of the West Street frontage.

The Gurrs' messuage of 90 acres on West Street was relatively large and in a prosperous area – when the Rev. Henry J. Gurr established his homestead outside Chelan in 1902 (Chap. 14) it had about 160 acres of far less arable land. The messuage may have originated in a grant of land to a French soldier, a Guerre, in the service of one of the English lords who fought in Normandy late in the Hundred Year's War (1337-1453). That is speculation for there are no records linking the holdings of any of those lords to the Manor of Falmer or to Rottingdean. Yet the fact that from 1508 onward the Gur(r)s for nearly two centuries were successful in keeping their hereditary legal rights to the farm suggests a strong family attachment and tradition. Moreover the legal records show that four generations of Gurrs named their sons Richard, a given name common in England, France, Germany, and many other European countries at the time.

---

[34] Immediately adjacent land and buildings

This may have been the given name of the first person to hold the messuage, and it would be interesting to search the 15th century muster rolls from Normandy for a Richard Guerre.

Can we connect the Rottingdean Gurrs to our own line, traceable to the birth of John Gurr of Salehurst in 1765? Only by inference. The geographic dispersion of 1,118 Gurr names in surviving records, from 1349 to 1841, is centered on south Sussex, as shown on Map 1.2.3d.[35] The Rottingdean Gurrs are the earliest recorded Sussex family of that name and over time the name spreads along the East Sussex coast, north into the Weald, then to London and its environs. The distance from Rye in the east to Broadwater in the west is about 50 miles. The Lewes registration district, which includes Rottingdean, is near the epicenter of the dispersion. Even more numerous are Gurrs in the Hailsham district in the Weald, to the immediate northeast.

At the eastern end of the dispersion, in the Battle area, where many later Gurrs are recorded including immediate ancestors of the authors, the earliest record is of a Jone Gurr found at St. John the Baptist Anglican Church in Westfield. [36] The record is dated October 7, 1555 confirming the marriage of one John Harre to a Jone Gurr. No other information on Jone Gurr or her parents is recorded, nor have Jone Gurr or the Gurrs of Rottingdean been genealogically linked, except by name, to our more recent ancestors. However, it is remarkable that it is at St. John the Baptist Church in Westfield that the authors' direct ancestors Jonathan Gurr and Mary Barham were married in 1823.

2.6 Summary

The most likely founder of the Sussex Gurrs, and our remote ancestor, was a Norman soldier in the service of an English lord during the Hundred Years' War. There are other possible sources of the name, as suggested at the outset of this chapter, but only this one is wholly consistent with the linguistic, legal, geographic, and genealogical evidence. The linguistic evidence is apparent in the drift in pronunciation and spelling of the Norman French word for "warrior" from Middle English to Chancery English. Granted a farm on the south Sussex coast, we can trace the gradual diffusion of his presumed descendants along the south coast and northward along the ancient Roman routes towards London and Rochester in the period from the 15th to the 19th century. By the end of the 20th century there were Gurr households in every English-speaking country, with large concentrations in southern England and North America.

The earliest documented ancestor in the authors' line of descent is John Gurr of Salehurst (born c. 1765). Salehurst is a village about five miles north of Battle, the actual site of the major battle of the Conquest of 1066, and about seven miles northwest of the village of Westfield. We know little of John and his wife Hannah, but we have learned a great deal about their son, Jonathan Gurr and his descendants, as will be outlined in later chapters.

---

[35] Of the total 95% are in Sussex. This does not mean there were 1,118 individuals named Gurr during this period because some appear multiple times in the records, whereas many more left no traces in the surviving documents.

[36] Ruth Carter. Retrieved from records at http://www.westfieldhistory.co.uk.

Chapter 3
Geography, History and Customs
of the Gurr Homelands in Sussex and Kent

3.1   Geographic and Pre-Historic

Studies show that, at the turn of the 20th century, the highest concentrations of Gurr families in the world were in the southeast of England, specifically in Sussex and Kent. Moreover, the next highest concentrations of Gurr families, those that lived in the Americas or Australia-New Zealand, invariably claimed their ancestors came from Sussex or Kent.

Most of the land making up the counties of Sussex and Kent lies on the southern side of a geological feature of lower England known as the Wealden Anticline. The southern portion of the Anticline consists of two ridges of high lands with a valley between them. The upper ridge is the Weald itself, while the lower ridge is called the South Downs. The valley between them is the Vale of Sussex. The Weald is a forested area with soil consisting mainly of clays and sands.[37] Beneath the thin topsoil of the South Downs lies a sub-soil which is predominantly chalk. East of Sussex, in the county of Kent, the white chalk cliffs of Dover are a prominent feature of the southern coast of England. The lower valley between the two ridges is made up of undulating fields formed by the erosion of the higher ridges to either side. Several rivers flow from the Weald across the Vale and through the Downs to the sea. There is a fertile coastal plain stretching from Chichester to Brighton, and a few sandy beaches from Chichester to Rye, while all along the southern coast are marsh lands bordering the bays that make up the river outlets.

At the glacial maximum of the most recent ice age, the polar ice cap covered almost all of the British Isles and much of Europe. However, there is a great deal of evidence suggesting that the southernmost region of England was clear of ice, as illustrated in **Map 3.1a** on the following page.[38]

Because sea levels were considerably lower than today, it is probable that what we call lower England was actually connected to the European land mass. It was not until c. 6,500 BC that melting polar ice had resulted in a rise in sea level, forming the English Channel and the Irish Sea, and dividing the British Isles from the rest of Europe. There is evidence that the southern regions of England were inhabited as early as 10,000BC. These early people were nomadic and lived by hunting, fishing and gathering. We know of their existence only from the flint arrowheads and other debris they left behind at the sites where they congregated to feast and intermingle.

There is later evidence of a more advanced but still stone-age people living on the islands dating back to c. 2,000BC. They are easily identifiable from their pottery, but they are notable

---

[37]   Weald is Old English for 'forest'.

[38]   Map by Paul Magel. Extent of glaciation based on data retrieved from http: www.metatech.org.

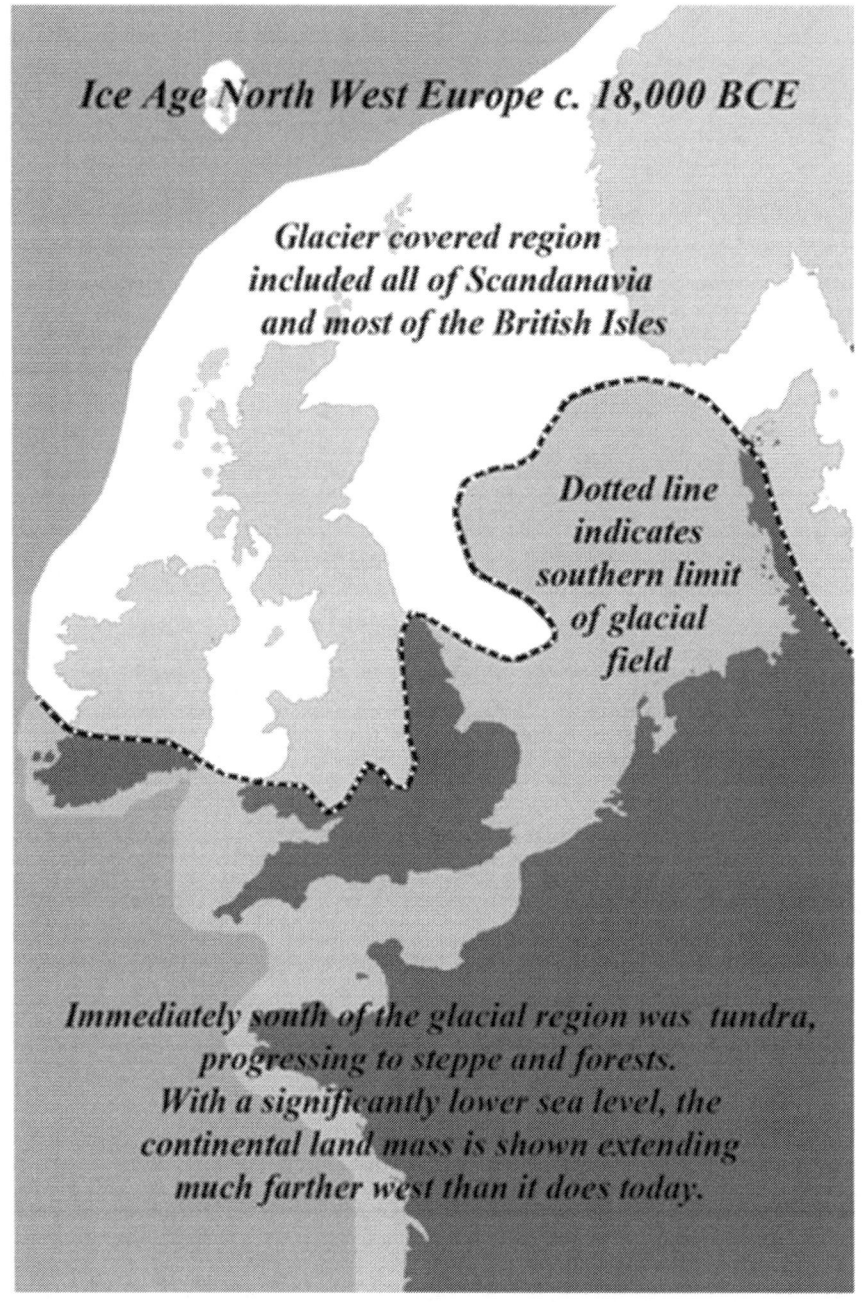

Map 3.1a Ice Age Europe

primarily for having constructed Stonehenge, and there is still much speculation as to who they were and where they came from. The earliest iron-age peoples to inhabit the island were fierce, independent and warlike Celtic tribes who appear to have arrived from mainland Europe c. 500BC. The Celts dominated the islands until the Romans encountered them at the beginning of the first millennium.

Is it possible that the first of the Gurrs in England is a descendant of one of these early nomadic peoples or the more recent Celts? Throughout this manuscript you will find references to the antiquity of the region from which our immediate forefathers came, as well as some details and some speculation about that region's history. The reader may be inclined to ask about their relevance, for those references and details might seem to be totally unrelated to the six generations of the family Gurr who are the immediate subject of this work.

The answer to this question is that, not only do we not know the origin of the name Gurr, we do not know the origin of the line of human beings that took on that appellation. In a previous chapter we have postulated a theory about who the first individual was who took on the name Gurr (or the name from which the name evolved) and where he came from. A Peter de la Guerrier may well have been the first to use the name from which the English Gurrs are descended. But that possible ancestor would have lived in the land we call south England or more narrowly in Sussex or Kent. Was he married when he came to that land? Or, as is more likely. did he or his children inter-marry with the existing population?

Although we can speculate that a person of foreign origin was the first Gurr, it is also clear that the first to call himself Gurr might have been a member of the native population. If so, his origin may have been Anglo Saxon, Roman, Celtic or even another race. So, it is possible that the Gurr progenitors built Stonehenge or that they walked across solid ground that later became the English Channel.

Knowing the history of the region from which we come is important, but knowing our genomic history can also provide us with surprising information as was the case with Robert Ballard who discovered the resting site of the R.M.S. Titanic.[39]

Our genealogic studies have taken us back a few hundred years, but evaluating our DNA can provide a roadmap back to our human origins. National Geographic's Genographic Project has used advanced DNA analysis and worked with indigenous communities to help answer fundamental questions about where humans originated and how we came to populate the Earth. As one National Georgraphic internet site suggests, that project may be able to discover the migration paths our ancient ancestors followed thousands of years ago, providing a view of our ancestral journey, telling us what percentage of our genome is affiliated with specific parts of the world and may even give us an indication of whether we have Neanderthal or Denisovan ancestry. [40]

3.2.1   History, The Roman Era

The earliest recorded history concerning the British Isles dates back to Roman times. Under the command of Julius Caesar, Roman legions completed their conquest of Gaul in 55BC. Caesar described Gaul as that vast area that is essentially modern day France, and the conquered

---

[39] A *National Geographic* advertisement confirms that Ballard's genealogy traces back to the British Isles and Holland. While most of his DNA agreed with this linkage, he also learned that his genome is about 2% Oceanian, connecting him to the first seafarers who settled the islands off the coast of southeast Asia around 50,000 years ago.

[40] Detail for this paragraph were retrieved from https://genographic.nationalgeographic.com/.
Neanderthals and Denisovans (a body of the latter was discovered in 2008 and its finger bone DNA analysed) are genetically distinct extinct species of genus Homo, to which modern humans belong.

people of the region as the Belgae in the north, the Aquitani in the south, and the Galli (Celtae, in their tongue) in between. Each group had its own language, laws and customs. [41]

North of Gaul, protected by a wide channel, were the islands that Caesar named Brittania, and the same year he subdued Gaul, he made an unsuccessful campaign to invade those islands. The Celtic population that had called the islands home since the fifth century BC were considerably more militarily advanced than the Romans anticipated. The Romans underestimated the tactical capability of the highly territorial Celtic population and the effectiveness of their war chariots, and after some initial successes the Roman legions were repulsed. A second attempt the following year was a success, but the Romans were again forced to withdraw their legions, this time in order to deal with uprisings in Gaul.

In 43AD Rome launched a more determined and ultimately successful attack on the Kentish coast, and for the next four hundred years the Romans consolidated their control of the Roman province of Brittania. Roman influence in Brittania endured until the fifth century, when attacks on Rome dramatically weakened the Romans and their hold on their territories. The last Roman legions departed Brittania in 407AD, and by the middle of the fifth century, groups of Angles, Saxons and Jutes (collectively the English, with a common language) began invading Brittania.

3.2.2 History, The Anglo Saxon Period, The Dark Ages

The Anglo Saxons established settlements on the south-eastern seaboard of the islands, and forced the Celtic population to withdraw to the west and north. Many of these displaced Britons also crossed the channel into north-western Gaul (now Brittany) and relative safety. Angles and Saxons crossed the channel in large numbers, Saxons establishing themselves in the south, and the Angles moving more to the north. At the beginning of the seventh century, Anglo-Saxons also still controlled a large part of what today is Northern Germany and Denmark.

During the middle of the fifth century, the Franks, a group of West German tribes living east and north of the Rhine, and first identified as an ethnic group in the third century, began moving westward into Gaul, following the Roman legions' withdrawal. They completely conquered all of Gaul, including most of modern day France during the sixth century.

Anglo-Saxons dominated and controlled the British Islands until the beginning of the ninth century when the islands came increasingly under attack by Vikings, primarily Norse, Svear (Swedes) and Danes. One Viking leader by the name of Rollo also conquered an area of northern Gaul belonging to the Franks. In exchange for his fealty he was granted a fiefdom over the conquered territory by treaty with the Franks after he had placed a siege on Paris. The territory was given the name Normandy, reflecting the Norseman's origin. Rollo, his followers and their descendants intermarried and adopted the local language. The descendants of Rollo and his followers became the Normans. The language of the Normans evolved into what we refer to as Old French, a mixture of Scandinavian, Anglo-Danish and the language of the indigenous Franks and Gauls of the conquered territories.

---

[41] Julius Caesar, *De Bello Gallico*, retrieved from Microsoft Encarta Encylopedia.

Despite the ever increasing influence of Viking invaders, Saxons were able to maintain a foothold on English soil until the reign of Alfred the Great (871-899). That part of England known as Wessex appears to have survived from the fifth to the late ninth century as the only continuously Saxon controlled territory. Under Alfred the Great and his successors Saxon domination of England was expanded and consolidated and the English "kingdom" became unified. The language of the Anglo Saxons evolved into what we refer to as Old English, a mixture of the languages of the Celts, the Angles, the Saxons and the Scandinavian invaders.

Alfred the Great ordered many fortified towns built during his reign (c871-899), including what are now Hastings, Lewes and Chichester in Sussex, and Canterbury in Kent. Alfred's policy was to encourage the building of fortified burhs (the later boroughs) such that no place in Wessex was more than 20 miles from a town. Under the feudal system of the times, settlers were given free plots of land within the towns in exchange for providing a defence force. The Saxon burhs were usually built along, or on top of, old Roman roads both for convenience, and for transportation and communication reasons. They were also located on the sites of Roman settlements where there where existing fortifications, such as stone walls, or on hills or other prominent points of land that provided some protection. Often a ditch or moat (derived from the Old French "motte") was dug and earthwork defences were built around the burhs. The burhs became centres of commerce and local government, and for defensive reasons were located primarily along the coast and along the borders of Alfred's lands.

In Anglo-Saxon England regal authority was shared between the King and the Earls that he appointed and from whom he demanded allegiance. The Kingdom was divided into four earldoms prior to the Conquest. Earls had full authority over their earldoms. They were judges and tax collectors, and they led the king's armies into battle in wartime. Earldoms were further divided into shires. At the death of Edward the Confessor there were four earldoms, as shown on **Map 3.2.2a.**

The Vice-Regal Earldoms of England at the Conquest.

The Godwines controlled most of Wessex and East Anglia. The Leofrics Northumbria and Mercia

Map 3.2.2a Earldoms Pre Conquest

The four earldoms were Wessex, Mercia, East Anglia and Northumbria. Earls were royal governors, with powers that were in some ways equal to those of the dukes on the continent, though earls were never absolute rulers as were some other European dukes at the time.

Scattered throughout Sussex and Kent at the end of the Anglo-Saxon rule were many of the roads, walls and ruins left by the Romans and other occupiers The Roman fort at Pevensey, built in 290AD (**Photo 3.2.2b**), as well as the medieval castle within the fort and the moat surrounding it are standing to this day. On the beaches near Pevensey William, Duke of Normandy landed his invasion force, camping within the walls of the Roman fort, then marching his army to Hastings, and on to the final conflict on the fields of Battle. A new kingdom was launched on the South Downs of Sussex.

Photo 3.2.2b Roman Ruins at Pevensey
Paul Magel Collection

3.2.3 History, The Conquest and Its Aftermath

At the beginning of the second millennium, under Edward the Confessor, the Saxons once again had the southern regions of Brittania secured. But, in January of 1066, Harold Godwinson, was crowned king. William, Duke of Normandy, of Scandinavian descent, firmly believed that it was he who had legitimate claim to the English throne and in September of 1066, he launched an invasion force of almost 700 ships. [42] Although the Normans were heavily outnumbered, the

---

[42] Upon the death of the childless Edward the Confessor, three individuals claimed the English throne: Harold Godwinson (Earl of Wessex), Harald III (Viking King of Norway) and William. In 1064 Harold Godwinson was aboard a ship wrecked on the coast of Ponthieu. He was captured by Count Guy of Ponthieu and imprisoned at Beaurain. William demanded that Count Guy release him into his care. Guy agreed and Harold went with William to Rouen. Later the two men went into battle against Conan of Brittany. For his role in the capture of Dinan, Harold was knighted by William at Bayeux, and pledged allegiance to him. During the ceremony (William claimed), Harold

circumstances of battle favoured them, and in less than a month King Harold was dead and England was under Norman rule. The conquest of England was complete, but because the Old French-speaking Normans were unpopular, there was great unrest for the next twenty years, and many uprisings were brutally put down. William became king of England in 1066, but he retained the fiefdom of Normandy for himself and his descendants. [43] At the time of the Norman invasion, Wessex (the southern third of England which includes Sussex and Kent) was heavily forested, although there were many scattered farms and hamlets and a few larger settlements or villages.

The Conquest turned into a gigantic land grab. There was wholesale confiscation of all landed estates throughout the conquered territories, and all rights to the conquered lands passed from the original Anglo Saxon landholders to the new king. Under the Norman feudal system, William, the landowner king and lord of all, loaned fiefs to those aristocrats (or nobles) who had supported him in his campaign, while they promised allegiance and homage, and became his vassals. These nobles, in turn, became lords to their own vassals, and these lesser nobles or knights were in turn lords of the manor to those peasants who worked the land.

So it is that all rights of most of the original Saxon landowners were abrogated and any commitments or liabilities they had outstanding were generally ignored by the new Norman lords. There was much confusion, dissatisfaction and great resentment as the Normans ruthlessly suppressed any opposition. Since William did not know the extent of his new holdings, and was probably concerned that his Norman followers might be evading the taxes he imposed, he ordered a reckoning, which was completed in 1086.

The Domesday Book, as it came to be called, listed the names of the king's vassals (landowners) and the assessments on which their tax was to be paid. It also listed the vassals of the landowners (Christian names only) and while this was important for military reasons, it also allowed him to enforce allegiance of the under-tenants and their vassals. Because the Domesday Book listed all the assets of the kingdom, the king now knew where he could look should he need to raise money, but it also allowed him a reference point should there be any future dispute about the disposition of any of his holdings.

3.3.1 Law and Government, Sussex after the Conquest

The county of Sussex was of great importance to the Normans; The Ports of Hastings and Pevensey were on the most direct route to Normandy. William I divided Sussex into five Baronies (Rapes), each with at least one town and one castle, assigning them to loyal followers.

After the Norman conquest 353 of the 387 Sussex manors that had been in Saxon hands were confiscated and assigned to just 16 heads of manors (chief tenants) who held their land directly from the crown. These included the five barons and only two Saxons.

---

took an oath to help William become king when Edward died, and also to marry William's daughter. In return, William promised Harold half the realm of England.

[43] Exerpts from Richard Cavendish and Pip Leahy, (2006). *Kings and Queens*. Cincinnati:David and Charles

The baronies were further divided into hundreds and boroughs. [44] Each barony had a hundred or borough court as illustrated on **Map 3.3.1a**. [45]

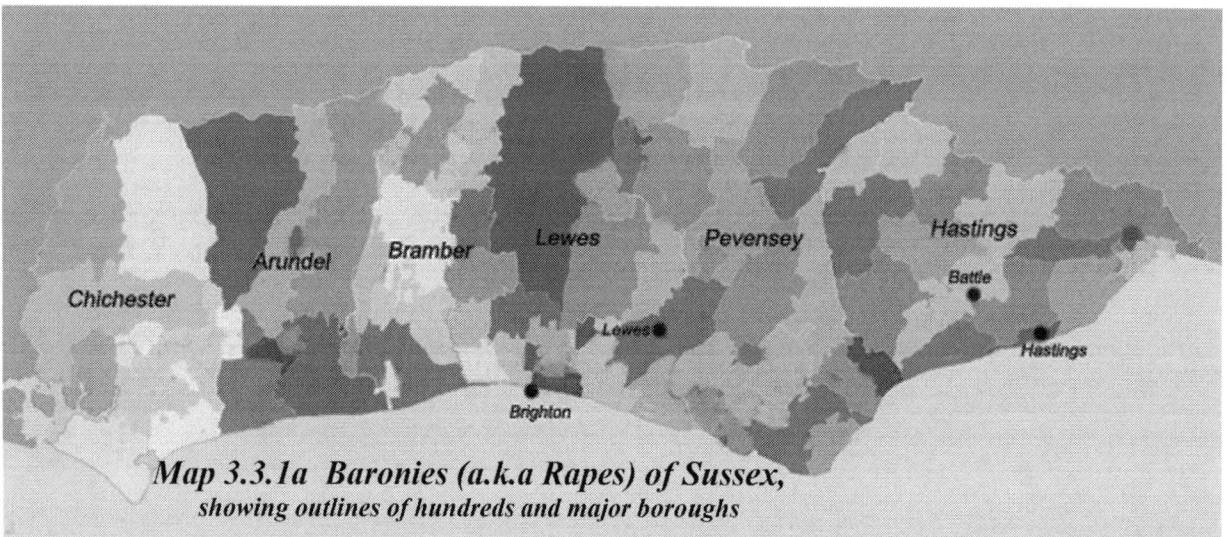

Map 3.3.1a Baronies (a.k.a Rapes) of Sussex,
showing outlines of hundreds and major boroughs

There were 59 hundreds at the time of the Domesday Book, but the number grew to 63 by the 19th century, with 38 retaining their original names. Since 1504 the county court has been held at Chichester for West Sussex and Lewes for East Sussex. Details of the five Barons' holdings are shown in **Table 3.3.1b** on the following page.

3.3.2   Law and Government, The Administration of Justice

The Anglo-Saxon manor system was continued under William I's rule, and the global English society of today, with all its traditions and institutions has its roots in the English Manorial System. [46] It is there that the first judge-made laws and the concept of precedent were established. English common law is based on the feudal legal system with its origins going back to Anglo Saxon and Norman times, and especially to the Magna Carta. [47]

---

[44] A hundred was considered the amount of land needed to support one hundred families.

[45] Map 3.3.1a was developed by Paul Magel from historic documents corrected to 1832.

[46] Notes from History of the Manorial System. Retrieved from http://www.historyworld.net

[47] Retrieved from http://www.Wikipedia.org Constitutionally, Britain is feudal, based on the contract theory of government as first set forth in the Magna Carta, a document that guaranteed "that the English Church shall be free, and shall have its rights undiminished, and its liberties unimpaired." Signed by King John at Runnymede in 1215, it was an agreement between the king and the lords who served him setting limits to the king's rights and protecting the privileges of his nobles. It was so written that it applied to all the king's subjects, whether free or not, and it forbade unlawful imprisonment and provided for courts and judges to interpret the law based on precedent. It became the basis of common law throughout the English-speaking world, and it is still the cornerstone of English law today. Even the American Declaration of Independence was an act of feudal defiance by the people who claimed that the king had tyrannically broken his contract with them and subsequently they were no longer bound to their allegiance to him.

Table 3.3.1b The Five Barons of William I [48]			
Baron	**Barony**	**Castle**	**Manors**
Roger of Montgomery	**Arundel**	**Arundel c1068**	**83**
William de Braose	**Bramber**	**Bramber c1070**	**38**
William de Warenne	**Lewes**	**Lewes c1066**	**43**
Robert, Count of Mortain	**Pevensey**	**Pevensey c400**	**81**
Robert, Count of Eu	**Hastings**	**Hastings c1065**	**108**
Others			**34**

In the manorial system (unlike the European feudal system), the peasants were not serfs. They were free to leave their employment, if and when they wished, although this was usually impossible for economic reasons. The lord of the manor employed peasant families whose members worked the fields of the manor. These workers benefited by being allowed to work a portion of the fields for their own sustenance, as well as from being under the protection of the feudal lord. The lord was responsible for the health and well-being of his peasants, and for dispensing justice for crimes committed on the manor, for hearing civil disputes between tenants, and for all financial matters.

As the power of a manorial lord grew, he might acquire more than one manor and these manors made up the Lord's "estate." As an estate grew, its operations became more complex and a manorial court was set up to address problems and to administer justice. The manor lords were entitled to compensation for operating these courts, and it became common practice for them to levy taxes on the peasants. Essentially, the manorial system was an employer/worker system, but in a society that demanded and rewarded the ability to work. There were abuses on both sides. A manorial lord might abuse his peasants and overtax them, while a peasant might be lazy or make trouble. The ideal arrangement would be one in which the master treated his productive subjects fairly and there was mutual respect. The reality is that there were always some peasants who did not measure up and the deaf, blind, handicapped, psychotic or lazy within a manor were often simply cast out. The manorial system rewarded those who worked hard. There was no expectation of "entitlement", by the peasants (free or otherwise), though that was not necessarily true of the lords of the manors or members of their families, nor of the nobility.

While the lords of the manors held power over the peasants and landholders in their manors, it was the kings of England who decided what the laws were and who administered those laws. While Britain's manor lords might appoint judges and magistrates, who generally adhered to Roman law in administering justice, the manor lords, freemen and those accused of more

---

[48] Map composed by Paul Magel by combining historic maps of East and West Sussex. Arundel Rape was divided into Chichester and Arundel about the year 1250.

serious crimes were ultimately judged by the king or by the ecclesiastical courts which were part of the Roman judicial system.

The struggle for supremacy between Church and State, between Popes and Kings continued throughout the middle ages. In England, the power of the ecclesiastical courts began declining under William I, was openly opposed by Henry II and eventually ended during the reformation with Henry VIII's dissolution of the Roman Catholic Church.

During his reign, Henry II (1154-1189) instituted judicial reforms including the establishment of a centralized system of justice that was available to all freemen. It was administered by judges who travelled around the country, serving the royal court. One of Henry's decrees was that priests accused of crimes must be tried in his royal courts. [49] Henry's judicial reforms were of great significance and produced lasting results. [50] Modern court procedures are the result of the process that Henry began, and ecclesiastical court practices such as trial by ordeal and trial by princes of the church (bishops, archbishops, cardinals and popes, many of whom were also powerful landowners with conflicting secular interests) were gradually eliminated.

English Law is the legal system of the United Kingdom and the basis of the common law legal systems in Ireland, all British Commonwealth countries and the United States. It has its origins in the judicial royal courts of Henry II instituted early in his reign. By the middle of the 13th century the concept of precedent was established with secular judges justifying their court decisions by reference to previous decisions. [51]

Formulated around the end of the 13th century and separate from the common law courts was the Chancery Court, a so called court of equity, a Royal Court established by the Crown and administered by the Lord Chancellor (the Keeper of the King's conscience) and his Chancery staff. [52] The Chancery Court was intended as a means of correcting perceived errors made by the common law courts and of ensuring that justice was dispensed equitably. The Chancery Court had significantly more power than the common law courts and could overrule their decisions, at least up until 1875 when it was essentially abolished (although some of its responsibilities went to the new Chancery division of the High Court of Justice).

---

[49] Thomas Becket, the Archbishop of Canterbury who had been appointed by Henry II, claimed that such cases should be handled by ecclesiastical courts which had preceded the royal courts. The controversy ended in 1170 with Becket's murder by four of Henry's knights, after which the king rescinded his decree.

[50] The Magna Carta also played a part in the development of English Law, but it was essentially a charter of rights and did not in any meaningful way limit the power of the king. However, it inherently created a need for educated advocates and ultimately contributed to the development of the legal profession in England.

[51] Common law is also known as case law or precedent law. It is law developed by judges through court decisions, as opposed to civil law which is based on statutes adopted through legislative/parliamentary acts.

[52] The Chancellor was usually, but not always, a man of the church. St. Thomas More, an English lawyer and author was an advisor to Kind Henry VIII and was his Chancellor from 1529 to 1532. He was tried for treason, found guilty under perjured testimony, and executed in 1535 for his opposition to the dissolution.

Today, the High Court of Justice in England and Wales decides cases (rather than appeals) and is divided into three divisions: Queen's Bench, Chancery and Family. Queen's Bench deals with civil matters (contracts, torts, actions against government). Chancery deals with disputes over land, wills and trusts (charitable and non-charitable). Family deals with matrimonial, child and ethical issues.

3.3.3   Law and Government, Parish System and Settlement

Local governance and responsibility for the care of the poor continued to be the responsibility of the manors, supported by the Christian Church, until the dissolution of the monasteries in 1536. Thereafter, responsibility was irregular and undefined until the Poor Law Act of 1601 was passed, when there was a shift of responsibility for support to the civil parish in which the unfortunate had resided for one month. [53]   Under this act, the poor were classed as "impotent", "able bodied", or "idle." The "impotent" included the ill, the infirm, the elderly and orphans, the "able bodied" were those who were capable of work, but unable to find employment, while the "idle" were those who were able bodied but refused to work, and had a reputation for begging and vagrancy.

The Settlement Act of 1662 entitled the poor to claim relief in their parish of settlement. A child was legally settled if that child was born in the parish of a settled father, and until a child was seven it took the settlement of its father. Illegitimate children took the parish of their birth as settlement. Thus, almost everyone born in England & Wales began with a settlement in their place of birth, and taxes were imposed on property owners in the various settlements, to provide relief for the poor. Workhouses were created and those refusing to work could be placed in houses of correction. The rules of settlement to determine to which parish a person properly belonged and to ensure that the appropriate parish would bear responsibility if that person, or his or her dependents, fell on hard times, would change from time to time over the next three centuries, but the "workhouse system" was not abolished until 1930.

3.3.4   Law and Government, Marriage in England, Scotland and Wales

In England and Wales there was no statutory legislation requiring a formal ceremony of marriage until the Marriage Act of 1753 was passed by Parliament. The only legal requirement prior to that was that the marriage be performed by an Anglican clergyman according to the canon law of the Church of England. In the years before the Church of England was established only mutual consent was required for a couple to marry, while under the Church of England, mutual consent was only a binding contract to marry, not a legal marriage.

In Scotland, the only requirements for marriage were mutual agreement by the couple and a witness to that agreement. That witness could be anyone, although a person of some note, such as a blacksmith was preferable. Surprisingly, the acceptable marriage age in Scotland was 14 for boys and 12 for girls. The Marriage Act of 1753 was prompted by a practice that was known as a Gretna Green Marriage, named for the fact that under age English couples eloping to Scotland to

---

[53]   *The Columbia Encyclopedia*, (2008) Sixth Edition. Copyright Columbia University Press.

marry, generally followed the most travelled road to Scotland, on which the first Scottish village reached was Gretna Green.

The Marriage Act of 1753 was intended to end clandestine marriages (those that took place in a parish other than the parish of the couple, or not according to canon law) in England and Wales and to demonstrate that Gretna Green marriages were socially unacceptable. An earlier *Marriage Duty Act of 1695* had put an end to clandestine marriages at parochial churches by penalizing clergymen who married couples without banns. By a legal quirk, however, clergymen operating in the Fleet prison could not be prosecuted, and the clandestine marriage business carried on there, with over half of all London weddings taking place in Fleet Prison, whenever any couple simply wanted to get married quickly.

Under the Marriage Act of 1753 a marriage was valid only if it took place in an Anglican church in accordance with church canons, or by obtaining a licence (Jews or Quakers were exempt). It prevented individuals under the age of 21 from having the banns read without parental consent. However, in practice a marriage by banns that that took place without parental *dissent* was considered valid. The 1753 Act did not apply to marriages celebrated elsewhere in the growing British Empire, nor to those in Scotland.

3.4 The Roman Catholic Church

One of the legacies left by the Romans in England when they withdrew their legions in 407AD was Christianity. Although the Western Roman Empire collapsed in 476AD, Rome rebounded as the center of the Christian West. The Christian church in England survived the Anglo Saxon invasions, and in 597 AD a monk by the name of Augustine was sent to England by Pope Gregory I, to evaluate the situation of the church. Augustine is credited with converting the Anglo Saxons to Christianity and became known as St. Augustine of Canterbury. Meanwhile, the Eastern Roman Empire, centered at Constantinople withstood the onslaught of the invading Germanic tribes. The church of the Christian East at Byzantium continued to grow and to prosper, unequivocally resisting Roman interference and Roman authority. Its final collapse came at the hands of the Ottoman Turks in 1453AD.

The question of separation of church and state and of which had ultimate authority, led to arguments and conflict throughout the Christian world for centuries. In the British Islands, following the Norman conquest, the Christian church was closely aligned with the Roman Catholic Church. In fact, William the Conqueror's claim to the throne of England had been backed by Pope Gregory VII, and William had come to England armed with a papal Bull. Because of the Pope's support, William's expedition was identified with the cause of church reform, and throughout his reign William always showed the greatest respect for the Holy See.

However, King William did not consider himself a vassal of the pope. While he recognized the pope's spiritual supremacy, he did not recognize any pope's supremacy over a king. [54] King William personally selected all bishops for the Roman Church in his Kingdoms.

---

[54] When the Pope appeared to call upon the new King of England to pay Romescot (Peter's Penny) and do homage for his kingdom, William was quite clear in his response. "One claim (Peter's Penny, or tribute to the Pope) I admit", he wrote in Latin, "the other I do not admit. To do fealty, I have not been willing in the past, nor am I

Although William is credited with making good choices for his bishops, it is undoubtedly true that many bishops throughout Western Europe were licentious and corrupt. Bishops were responsible for the selection and education of men for ordination, so there was a filtering down effect that made the entire church morally corrupt. Worldly minded men were appointed bishops by sovereigns and they in turn appointed like-minded individuals to some of the most important positions in the church, many of them obtaining that promotion by the payment of a sum of money, or by some other worldly compact. The lower clergy were as a rule ignorant and in many cases unchaste, but under such corrupt bishops they enjoyed almost complete immunity from punishment.

During the next five centuries many good bishops would attempt to improve the leadership and ultimately the moral situation of the church. Henry II chose his friend and Chancellor, Thomas Becket as Archbishop of Canterbury, but that choice would result in a confrontation between church and state that the King had not foreseen, though Thomas surely had. Thomas Becket's respect for the dignity and the rights of the Church would lead him to accept martyrdom rather than submit to the King's will in matters concerning the right of the king to use tax money (including taxes on church lands) as he saw fit. Becket was canonized just three years after his death and Canterbury became a center of pilgrimage.

John Wycliffe (c1320-1384) was an early dissident in the Roman Catholic Church and one of the earliest opponents of Papal interference with secular authority. He and his followers are also credited with translating the Holy Bible from Latin to vernacular English at Oxford. Wycliffe felt that the Scriptures should be the sole rule of faith, that the word of God should be accessible to all men, and that each man should be free to interpret the word. He insinuated that maintaining the Bible in Latin was a Church policy intended to withhold the scriptures from the English speaking laity to prevent free thought.

The German monk Luther (1483-1546), the father of Protestantism, also challenged papal authority by insisting the Bible is the only infallible source of religious authority, and proposing that salvation is a gift of God received through repentance and faith in Jesus Christ, unmediated by the church. He went a step farther than Wycliffe and confronted the Holy Roman Emperor Charles V with his beliefs, refusing to submit to his authority. These acts resulted in his excommunication, but by his actions he changed the course of Western Civilization. He translated the Holy Bible from Latin into German, wrote hymns that inspired congregational singing and his marriage served as a model for clerical marriage within Protestantism.

3.5 The Church of England, Reformation

The Protestant Reformation that spread across Europe during the early 16th century was essentially a Christian reform movement which proposed to correct ecclesiastic malpractices within the church hierarchy. Among these sinful practices were the buying and selling of church

---

willing now, inasmuch as I have never promised it, nor do I discover that my predecessors did it to your predecessors."

offices, the sale of indulgences and other worldly transactions carried on by church officials. [55] The reformists believed that these transactions, done for profit, were sins of greed, and unworthy of God's representatives on earth. While the Christian reform movement eventually brought about fundamental reforms within the Catholic Church, the desire by some sects in England to distance themselves as far from any sign of the "worldly" led to Puritanism and eventually to civil war in Britain, ushering in the Protectorate under Cromwell. [56]

Henry VIII took great pains to suppress the support for reformation in his realm that dated back to Wycliffe in the 14th century, but during the early 16th century the acceptance of the need for reformation throughout Roman Catholic Western Europe was gaining momentum. In 1534, more for personal motives than any dissatisfaction with the Catholic Church, Henry VIII imposed reformation on all his subjects, named himself the head of the Catholic Church in England, and refused to recognize Papal authority. The Church of England so created became subject to, and part of the state, and it would survive the efforts of Mary Tudor and loyal Papists to reverse her father's decrees and restore the Papacy.

When Henry VIII passed the Act of Supremacy in 1534 which led to the dissolution of monasteries, it allowed him to gradually seize and redistribute the wealth of the Catholic Church. He proclaimed himself the Supreme Head of the Church of England, refusing to acknowledge the authority of the Catholic Pope. He saw himself as the head of a "Catholic" Church of England, and those "Papists" who dared to continue their loyalty to the Roman Pope were considered traitors to the King and therefore to England. The persecution of Papists began during, and continued throughout the balance of Henry's reign, but was somewhat relaxed during his son Edward's short time on the English throne (when, incidentally, for the first time ordained priests were allowed to marry). When the Papist Mary Tudor ascended the throne it was the Reformists turn to be persecuted, and Bloody Mary did so with a vengeance (she also revoked the right of priests to marry, which led to the separation of the 25% or so of priests who had married during Edward's reign, from their families). Elizabeth I's approach to reconciliation was characterized by an effort to find a "middle way." She consolidated her position as Supreme Leader of the Church, but allowed many reforms while adhering to many church traditions (although she did restore a priest's right to marry).

3.6.1 Education and the Christian Church

Up until the imposition of Reformation, in medieval England, Scotland and Wales the Roman Catholic Church had provided all education for all classes of society in monasteries,

---

[55] A practice that included even the position of pope. During the 15th century, a series of events resulted in both a pope and an antipope being selected by the same governing body. Different countries recognized one or the other of the two popes, resulting in what has been called the Great Schism within the Catholic Church, and led to growing dissension among the clergy, with calls for reform from Wycliff, Martin Luther and others.

[56] The Council of Trent convened between 1545 and 1563, condemning what it defined as Protestant heresies, defining Church teachings and issuing numerous reform decrees, intended to address and answer Protestant disputes with counter-reformation precepts.

schools, orphanages, charity foundations, or by chaplains tutoring in private households. The first sign of state involvement in education had come in 1496 with the passing of the Education Act, requiring compulsory education of the eldest sons of nobles. One important aspect of these events was that the Church of England took over responsibility for all education thereafter.

From medieval times there was no place for well-educated women in affairs of church or state, with the possible exception of women from the nobility or upper classes who often had obligations that required some degree of literacy. Since all education came from the church, it was the church's view of women that was predominant, and as a result, the limited education some women did receive was with a view of what was necessary in their roles as wives and mothers. This attitude towards the education of women persisted in England well into the 19th century. While education was deemed essential for men who wished to improve their position in life, and thus encouraged in all classes, education of women in other than the basics and a few womanly arts (music, cooking and sewing) was unseemly and subject to ridicule.

Even at the level of royalty, women in line of succession were usually poorly educated. Elizabeth I was fortunate that her father Henry VIII showed her great affection, and although she was not always in his favor, he allowed his precocious daughter to be educated as a potential heir to his throne. She was allowed to join her brother Edward's and sister Mary's tutoring sessions, and was found to be a gifted student with a great curiosity for learning all things, but being especially proficient in languages. This remarkable woman became fluent in Latin, Greek Spanish, French and Italian and it is said that she could carry on conversations with three different ambassadors at the same time speaking to each in his own language.[57]

During her long reign, Elizabeth I stood strong against attempts by the Pope and European powers, including Spain (the Armada), to depose her as Queen of England and as the Supreme Head of the Church of England. Civil strife continued between extremists in both the outlawed Catholic Church and the Reformists throughout the 17th century but such was the power of the Church of England that, as late as the 19th century, all university fellows and many school-masters were expected, or required, to be in holy orders, and the Church of England was able to resist all attempts by the state to be involved in public education.

3.6.2   Education in Scotland, An Interesting Exception

The reformation also reshaped the national Church of Scotland with John Knox and a small supporting group of clergy setting up a program of universal education in 1561. Unlike England, the Scottish crown was not involved in the reformation of the church and for the next few decades progress in education was slow as tensions rose over matters of church and state. But, in 1633, after years of debate, the Parliament of Scotland ratified an act that required every Church of Scotland parish to establish a school and introduced a tax on landowners to provide the necessary funds. The Education Act of 1696 further regulated Scottish elementary education and ensured funding to pay the salaries of schoolmasters, and remained the law until revised in 1872. For over two centuries, Scotland led all European nations in literacy. While never free, the cost

---

[57]   Maureen Waller, (2006). *Sovereign Ladies.* London: John Murray.

of education was kept exceptionally low, with funding for the very poor provided by taxes and charity, in an atmosphere of recognition of the importance of literacy for all God's people. Scotland's universities even attracted students from England including many who could be excluded from Oxford and Cambridge for refusal to adhere to the Anglican faith.

3.7   The Modern Era

While the Reformation is sometimes cited as the beginning of the "modern era" in Western Civilization (and the extended reign of Elizabeth I did allow time for consolidation of Protestant control of the United Kingdom), most believe that it is with the restoration of the monarchy in 1660 that Britain's "modern era" begins. In fact, following the death of Elizabeth I, the relationship between church and state continued to be hotly debated in the three kingdoms of England, Scotland and Ireland well into the 17th century. The polarization between those loyal to Catholic traditions and those who conspired to undertake radical Protestant reform would eventually lead to civil war and the abolishment of the monarchy.

The events that took place between 1649 and 1660 were revolutionary. Oliver Cromwell was the leader of the army that defeated the Royalists, dissolved the House of Lords, and dethroned and beheaded Charles I. He dominated the short-lived Republican Commonwealth and in what became known as the War of the Three Kingdoms, he united England, Scotland and Ireland. He might have crowned himself king, but instead took on the mantle of Lord Protector of the British Isles (a virtual dictatorship) until his sudden death from malaria in 1658. His treatment of Catholics was so extreme that it bordered on genocide and he was so hated by Catholics and Royalists that after the monarchy was restored by the army, with the crowning of Charles II in 1660, his body was exhumed and he was ritually executed, his head left hanging on a pole outside Westminster Hall for almost twenty-five years.

The struggle between Protestants and Catholics in some regions of the British Isles has continued even to the present day. Still, the "Three Kingdoms" have formed a union of one kind or another since James VI of Scotland inherited England and Wales from Elizabeth I. The United Kingdom of Great Britain and Ireland was not actually created until 1800, while dissension over Irish Home Rule in staunchly Roman Catholic Ireland would lead to partition in 1921. The United Kingdom of Britain and Northern Ireland became the official name of the Union in 1927.

Chapter 4
Jonathan and Mary Gurr,
From the South Downs to London [58]

At the turn of the 19th century, a son Jonathan was born to Hannah and John Gurr of the Civil Parish of Salehurst and Robertsbridge. A few miles south of Salehurst, in the village of Mountfield in Battle Parish, a daughter Mary had been born to Mary and Robert Barham just three years earlier. This region of East Sussex has been designated an "Area of Outstanding Natural Beauty" by the UK government. [59] It was in this environment that Jonathan Gurr and Mary Barham would come of age, meet and marry. [60] We do not know where or how they met, but it may have been in Westfield, a village seven miles south-southeast of Mountfield, because that is where they eventually married. At the time of their marriage, Jonathan was settled in Westfield and his occupation was servant, probably at an Inn, as will be shown later. We also have evidence suggesting that related Barham families worshiped at the church in Westfield.

4.1 East Sussex

Sussex, when Jonathan and Mary were born, was rural and agrarian, with that part of it known as East Sussex having no large cities, few towns, and a relatively small population residing primarily in its many small villages and hamlets. **Photo 4.1a** on the following page illustrates the Southeast England landscape. In those days a typical East Sussex village consisted of a compact cluster of houses, entirely surrounded by farmlands, always a church, and perhaps an alehouse or pub, a few specialty shops and a blacksmith. A hamlet was typically a small group of houses, and might include a shop or two, but never a church.

Natives of East Sussex did a lot of walking, and walking in Battle parish would have been a pleasant outing for Jonathan and Mary in mild weather. Paths and roadways are lined with hedges of hawthorn, blackthorn, evergreen holly and rambling dog rose and these are adorned with flowering climbers such as honeysuckle and wild hops. Wild bluebells, daffodils, primroses and purple rampion might be seen everywhere, but especially alongside the quaint farmhouses that dotted the area, and beyond the hedges there were cleared open fields where sheep and other livestock grazed, and stretches of forest with many brooks and streams, where wild deer came to drink.

---

[58] The authors acknowledge that although no text has been copied verbatim, many of the non-familial details in this chapter have been sourced from http://wikipedia.org. Where these appear there may be no citation, although there may be footnotes for clarification. Details from Non-Wikipedia sources are always cited.

[59] An Area of Outstanding Natural Beauty (AONB) is an area of countryside considered to have significant landscape value to the United Kingdom. There are now 35 AONBs designated by Natural England in the United Kingdom.

[60] See family details in Part III , where Chapters 18, 19, 20 provide family trees for Jonathan's and Mary Barham Gurr's son Alfred James Gurr's male descendants and their spouses.

Photo 4.1a Typical Sussex-Kent Landscape
The Gurr homelands, looking south towards the sea

Paul Magel Collection

The southern downs surrounding Westfield are made up of forest, farmland and marsh flats. Two miles south of the center of Westfield is a ridge extending east to west overlooking Hastings. Today there is a roadway along that ridge, known simply as The Ridge from which one can look southward towards Hastings and the open sea. From that wooded ridge Jonathan and Mary would have been able to see the fields and gardens below, the ancient castle of Hastings and look out across the multi-colored blues of the English Channel.

The parish church of St. John the Baptist in Westfield **(Photo 4.1b** on the following page**)** is a Norman structure built in the early 12th century and one that has had few structural changes made to it during the past nine centuries. It is in the parish church at Westfield, five miles east of Battle, that Jonathan and Mary were wed. Today that churchyard is still large and there are many marked graves, though the stone used as markers has not weathered well. There are several gravestones engraved with the names of Barham family members, but on a recent visit to the graveyard by one of the authors, not one was found bearing the Gurr family name.

Photo 4.1b   St. John the Baptist Church

In April of 1823,
Jonathan Gurr and Mary Barham were married in this
12th century Norman church in Westfield, Sussex.

Paul Magel Collection

The Barhams of Wadhurst were ironmongers during the 16th, 17th and 18th centuries and their success in that industry allowed them to flourish. Barham families spread throughout this region of the Weald, notably from Wadhurst southerly along the well-travelled turnpike that ran a distance of 21 miles through Salehurst, Robertsbridge, Mountfield and Battle to Hastings. **Map 4.1c** by Paul Magel shows the major turnpikes of East Sussex as they existed c.1820.

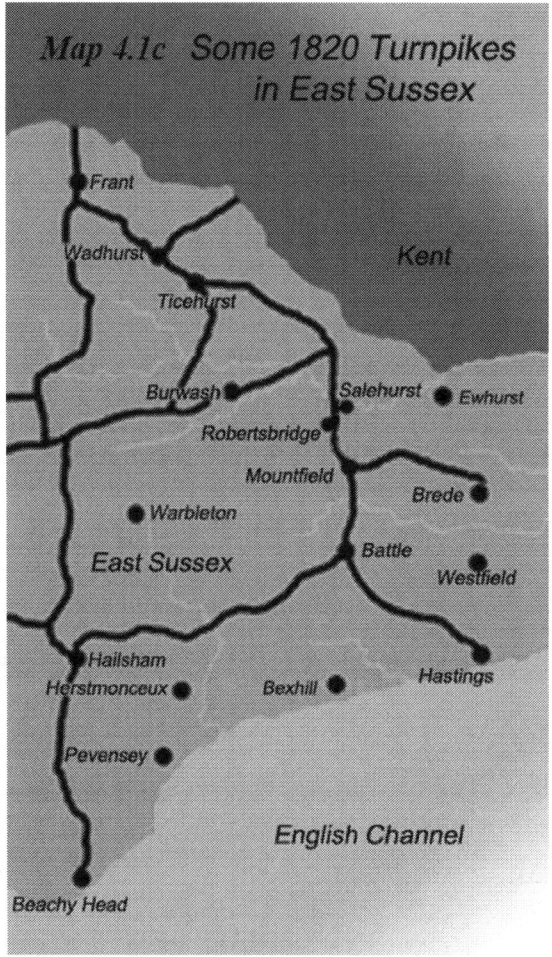

4.2   Life In East Sussex

Job opportunities in East Sussex were limited for young men like Jonathan. Neither the sands and clays of the Weald, nor the chalk of the Downs are suitable for intensive farming. There are few areas in Sussex that can be used for growing vegetables or cereals profitably, and only the coastal plain has ever been extensively utilized by market gardeners. Various sources estimate that at the beginning of the 19th century more than half of the population of the County of Sussex was employed in farming, the wool trade, or fishing. For centuries, farming centered on raising livestock, and by 1800 large herds of Sussex cattle were common, a specific breed considered one of the finest in the world. Sheep and pigs were raised by virtually every landholder. As early as the 13th century, South Down sheep wool was considered among the finest in the world, while weaving and "fulling" were home industries well into the industrial revolution. The Sussex fisheries were extensive, and from Norman times the salt pans along the south coast produced salted herring which was shipped to all parts of the British Isles and abroad on English ships. Hastings, where William the Conqueror landed his invasion fleet in 1066, has been a major fishing port in East Sussex for over a thousand years.

There were other industries that Sussex natives engaged in, many of which offered job opportunities for lower class male workers such as Jonathan. Since clay lies just below the top soil of the Weald, it is not surprising that clay became a focus of industry, with pottery, tile and brick works springing up throughout the region. Also, the chalk (limestone) of the southern downs was used in making cement for the construction industry. Large deposits of gypsum discovered in the Mountfield-Robertsville region in the 18th century are still being mined for use in construction materials. As late as 1847 black gunpowder, long considered the finest in Europe, was being manufactured in Battle with sulphur from the region, charcoal from the wood of the Weald forests, and pure saltpeter (potassium nitrate) as the oxidizer.

Although early 19th century England was a relatively civilized nation, and its people considered themselves among the most sophisticated in the world, for the majority of its citizens day to day living was not easy. This was especially true in farming regions such as East Sussex where the population was so scattered that communities where essentially isolated from one another by expanses of open fields and forest. This isolation meant that finding work could be a challenge, especially for young workers like Jonathan, whose only way to and from work was to walk the distance. For the poor, there were few job opportunities other than agricultural field work, shepherding or domestic service. Any illness could lead to loss of employment and this could mean catastrophe for poor families, for there were few safety nets other than the poorhouses that were administered by the parish councils. We know almost nothing of the circumstances specific to Jonathan and the other members of John Gurr and Hannah's family, but we believe that they were a farming family with John probably working as a labourer for the local manor or one of its tenants. It was customary for most workers to be on the job six days a week for twelve to fourteen hours a day. Since the majority of children of the lower classes received little or no education, and idleness was frowned upon, many children were employed as early as eight or nine years of age. Ordinarily, girls would be hired on for household duties and boys would be hired out as labourers, or apprenticed out by their parents, by the age of eight to twelve years. Large and small landholders employed agricultural labourers from the local population, with the larger farms employing as many as five to ten workers. Occasionally, the largest landholders provided their best workers with a cottage on or near the farm to house their families, the men in the family helping in the fields and the women performing household duties for the landlord and his family.

In the largest villages and in the towns, wealthy families employed both men and women as servants while the specialty shops employed the better educated as clerks. In these larger communities there were opportunities for employment of those with limited education as barmen or barmaids, cellar-men and potboys at the many local taverns, and horse handlers and boot cleaners at the coaching inns.

We have reviewed the types of employment that were available to young men such as Jonathan Gurr at the beginning of the 19th century. As the younger son of John and Hannah Gurr, in keeping with the practices of the time, Jonathan was second in line to inherit his father's estate, whatever that consisted of. While we have assumed that Jonathan's father was a farm laborer, he may also have had the right to farm land belonging to his employer. The marriage banns of Jonathan Gurr and Mary Barham record Jonathan as a servant settled in Westfield, and in light of the fact that he eventually became a publican, it seems probable that Jonathan was working in a coaching inn or tavern in Westfield. Since Jonathan was likely employed from the age of about ten, it is possible that by the time of his marriage to Mary he had worked his way up to some level of responsibility. He may even have become a member of the licensed victualler trade when he married at the age of twenty-three. It is certain that he was a member of that profession a few years later.

4.3   The Barhams of Wadhurst

Mary Barham's family in Mountfield are descended from the Barhams of Wadhurst. Court records indicate that between the mid-15th and early 19th centuries Barham family members included yeomen [61] and tradesmen (ironworkers), and some were feoffes [62] or Seneschals [63]. Several Barhams held property rights from manors between Wadhurst and Battle in East Sussex. Although none of the Barhams were members of the nobility (until George Barham was knighted in 1904) many did achieve positions of authority and respect, and the Barhams appear to have been "of the lower gentry" in the highly class-conscious English society.

One early record of interest, concerning the Barhams, is this reference to a manor that eventually came into the family's possession: Snape [64], c.1200 is in the Battle Abbey cartulary recording the gift of *"all my lands of Snape, in the parish of Wadehurst to the Abbot and Convent of Battle."* The Abbey owned Snape until the dissolution; then for almost three hundred years it was a part of the Glynde holdings, some of which were in the care of one of the Barham families. David Barham appears to have inherited Snape in the 1590s, while still a ward of his uncle, William Courthope of Whiligh. [65] In 1617 David Barham built a new house on the property, and in 1721, his great grandson, also named David, sold the property, and with that transaction Snape passed out of Barham ownership for over 160 years.

Mary Barham's great-grandfather Arthur Barham (b1693, Salehurst Kent) held a lease on 90 acres of farmland in Mountfield, which included barns, an oast-house, stables, buildings, gardens and orchards. [66] The property was known as Darvill Beech Farm, and was part of Darvill Forest, which had been a major iron-working area until the end of the 17th century. Arthur Barham leased this property from Thomas Snepp, the son of Thomas Snepp, the elder, a renowned iron master of the 17th century. Following in his father's footsteps, Thomas Snepp,

---

[61] Yeoman: A farmer with a small freehold = a member of a former class of English commoners who owned and cultivated their own land (medieval: a servant or minor official employed in a royal or noble house).

[62] Feoffe: a fief holder, usually a vassal holding land granted him by a feudal lord.

[63] Seneschal: the medieval steward of a manor (one who managed the staff of a nobles house)

[64] This paragraph with original data thanks to Brian Yates: Snape, February 2001 has been edited for this volume. The original text can be seen on the website http://www.wadhurst.info/whs/newsletters/whs02/page4.htm.

[65] The Courthope family were landholders in the Wadhurst area from 1272AD (Battle Abbey Cartulary).

[66] An oasthouse is a structure used to store and dry hops.

the younger was one of the last iron masters of Sussex. In 1707 he took a lease of the famous Robertsbridge Ironworks, from the Earl of Leicester.

While the Romans were the first to smelt and forge iron in Sussex, ironworking remained the primary industry of the county for centuries. The iron foundry in Robertsville, north of Mountfield where the Barhams held land, was operational until the 1770s. There were many Sussex towns with foundries, although from the year 1729, the industry gradually moved northward as coal began to replace wood as fuel in blast furnaces. There is evidence that the Barhams of Salehurst were once ironworkers, and it is possible that Arthur Barham worked for the younger Thomas Snepp at the Robertsbridge foundry. It would appear that when the younger Thomas died in 1729, Arthur may have been rewarded for his family's service to the Snepps with the opportunity to lease one of Thomas Snepp's holdings from his heirs. In any case, the year after the younger Thomas Snepp died, his son John sold the Darvill Beech Farm to William Cranston of London (brother-in-law and partner of the celebrated John Collier, Mayor of Hastings). Arthur's lease was renewed by the new, absent landlord. When Arthur Barham died, the lease on Darvill Beech Farm passed to his son, Thomas Arthur Barham and eventually to his grandson Robert Barham, the father of Mary Barham. For almost one hundred years, the Barham family had prospered at Darvill Beech farm. Although Arthur Barham had only one son (Thomas Arthur), this son had six sons and five daughters, including Mary's father Robert, who also fathered five sons and five daughters.

It appears that four of the five male members of Robert Barham's family were entrepreneurial and successful in diverse endeavors (the third son died at the age of two). There is some evidence to indicate that the family were in the dairy business and raised other livestock. The youngest son, and Robert's namesake, would become a London dairyman of some account after leaving Mountfield in the 1820s. This younger Robert Barham was the dairyman father of George Barham of Express Dairies fame, who was knighted in 1904, not only for his many technical contributions to the development of the dairy industry, but also his philanthropy.

John Barham, later of Gloucester, was another of Robert's sons, and he, as well as George Mills, the husband of Mary's eldest sister, Elizabeth, were curriers, a much respected trade throughout Europe from medieval times until the early 20th century. The job of a currier was to take tanned leather hides such as ox, cow, calf, goat, sheep, pig, deer and rabbit, stretch and soften them, then shave and massage the leather with tallow and oil till it was pliant and workable for the craftsman who would use it. Like most rural trades, currying skills were often passed down from one generation to the next and the finished product was frequently taken by other members of the family and used for making shoes and boots, gloves, belts and saddles and other fine leather products (cobblers and saddlers). The eldest of Robert's sons (Thomas) had a son James who would serve in the British army, and is listed as a shoemaker in the 1871 census. It is also possible, since different family members raised livestock and ran a currier business, that the Barham family did the tanning as well, but we have been unable to establish this with certainty.

We do not know how the children of Robert Barham Sr. interacted with one another, but there is concrete evidence that he loved his children and treated them well. In Georgian England and throughout the British isles married women walked in the shadow of their husbands and, with few exceptions, were excluded from participating openly in the principle activities of men, specifically in the military, politics, business, science, religion and the arts. On a man's death, his property passed to his eldest son and unless the man had made specific provisions for her, a wife might find herself without the means to support herself. Spinsters were also dependent upon their fathers for support, or on his death upon the male sibling who inherited from that father. For all women in 19th century England, there were limitations on what they could do and say, and there was always a great deal of uncertainty about their future financial security. Many women who had enjoyed comfortable lives found themselves and their children suddenly forced to enter Union Workhouses when their husbands died or abandoned them.

One can assume that, raised in such an environment, the Barham girls were treated fairly (if unequally) by their father and brothers. In any case, both of Mary Barham's elder sisters married well: the eldest as previously stated, became the wife of a currier, while the second eldest (Sarah) became the wife of a surgeon from Hastings (she and her doctor husband would raise two sons, one of whom would take on Holy Orders). Of Mary's two younger sisters (Janet and Harriet) we know little.

We know nothing definitive about Jonathan and Mary's education, but certain assumptions can be made. Since Mary was the daughter of a land-leaser in the Parish of Mountfield, she probably received some formal education and would certainly have learned to read and write. In the class-conscious society of Georgian England it is doubtful that Mary Barham would have given Jonathan Gurr encouragement of any kind had he not had some redeeming qualities, and probably an equivalent social status and education. Considering this, as well as the fact that Jonathan would eventually become the operator of a prestigious public house in London, we can assume that he also received some formal education in his early years, and that he was competent in reading, writing and arithmetic.

Where might Mary and Jonathan have received their education? Until the 19th, and for most of that century, there was no law to prevent anyone from opening a school and, as a result, elementary education was in the hands of many different groups no matter how unqualified. There were *Dame Schools:* small fee-paying schools managed by women in which poorer children could learn to read and, possibly, to write. There were *Factory Schools:* some factories attracted workers by opening part-time schools where both boys and girls were taught reading, writing and arithmetic, with the possible addition of knitting and sewing for girls. There were *Workhouse Schools:* schools where boys were trained as blacksmiths, carpenters and shoemakers, while girls learned housework, laundry work and cookery. *Sunday Schools* taught basic literacy so that pupils could read the Bible, and these offered many girls their only chance of education. *Charity Schools (also called Ragged Schools)* were those set up by wealthy benefactors for children too poor to be accepted into other schools.

By the beginning of the 19th century, religious schools had begun offering education to the poor. These were full-time schools and for the majority of poor children these were the only educators. The religious schools of early 19th century England were run by two rival religious groups: the National Society Schools organized by the Church of England; and the Lancasterian Schools (soon to become the British and Foreign School Society) set up by non-conformists.

Both of these schools used the monitorial system of teaching, which used older children who had some education (monitors) to teach the younger children. There were many who objected to this method because the monitors were usually poorly qualified and, of course, had no teaching experience. However, from these early beginnings, a progression of education reforms would gradually result in the government subsidized education of all children by the early 20th century. It is probable that Mary and Jonathan were beneficiaries of a religious school education.

4.4 Jonathan and Mary

I wish we could tell you how and when Jonathan and Mary met. It may be that as youngsters the couple attended the same school or church or, more romantically, they were childhood sweethearts, perhaps a Romeo and Juliet whose families held one another in disdain. But, the fact is, we know so little about Jonathan's history that we can only speculate about such possibilities The couple's first meeting must have been sometime before the autumn of 1819, when Jonathan was barely nineteen years old, because their first child, George, was born out of wedlock in June of 1820. [67]

Considering the attitude towards unmarried mothers at the time Mary's pregnancy must have been looked upon as a family tragedy by the Barhams, and at best scandalous conduct on the part of Jonathan by those who knew him. The Rother District Parish Council proceeded to issue bastardy papers citing Jonathan as the father of Mary's newborn son. [68] That there was no subsequent warrant issued against Jonathan by the Rother Council probably means that either he paid support for the child, or that Mary's father accepted the liability of supporting his daughter and child. It should be noted that Jonathan was not of age when the Rother Council issued their initial warrant, and the Barhams may have refused to allow their daughter Mary to marry. The Rother Council in issuing their order defined Westfield as the settlement of baby George. [69] Although we know that Mary and her newborn were resident in the home of her father Robert Barham immediately following the child's birth, we do not know anything of the relationship

---

[67] East Sussex Records Office, Bastardy papers Ref. DR/D/111/1/39

[68] Parish councils (parish courts) were required to issue bastardy orders which identified the settlement of the child. Where the father was known, an order would be issued to the father of the illegitimate child compelling him to support the child and the mother financially. The law changed from time to time. In the early 1700s a pregnant woman with a bastard was required by law to declare the fact and name the father, and the named father was made responsible for child maintenance. Failure to comply made the father subject to jail time, and while the father was in jail the parish supported the mother and child until the father was able to. From 1743, a bastard took the settlement of its mother, no matter where the child was born, while prior to that date a bastard took the settlement of its birth and the mother was publically whipped.

[69] The Settlement Act of 1834 required paternity claims to be corroborated in some material particular, though this was usually impossible to achieve. The child took the settlement of the mother until it was sixteen or until it acquired settlement of its own. It also made the mother solely responsible for the bastard child until it was sixteen, and if unable to support herself and the child the mother was forced to enter the parish workhouse. The Act of 1834 was intended to make the consequences sufficiently unattractive to deter women from risking extra-marital pregnancy. The Act was softened by changes in 1844 that allowed an unmarried mother to apply for an affiliation order against the father for maintenance of the mother and child, regardless of whether she was in receipt of poor relief

between Jonathan and the Barham family. However, it is evident that the family did not expel their daughter in an effort to distance themselves from scandal, but showed her love and respect by accepting her and the child into their lives.

While one might consider the attitude towards bastards as harsh in pre-Georgian and Georgian England, there was actually a progressive relaxation of the laws regarding illegitimacy during the 19th century, and an increasing social acceptance of illegitimate children. [70] In Victorian times the percentage of illegitimate births per capita increased, almost doubling in comparison to the previous century in some regions of England. This increase is probably related to population growth as well as population movement from close-knit rural communities to densely populated urban areas where one might remain relatively inconspicuous amongst a plethora of strangers. Undoubtedly, the larger cities offered an escape for those who felt any shame about their birth or their previous indiscretions. Jonathan and Mary were married in Westfield, Sussex (the settlement of Jonathan Gurr) on April 2, 1823. [71] Sometime that fall, Alfred James was born to the couple and later census records record his birthplace as Battle, where he was baptized on October 26th, 1823. Jonathan's occupation at the time is listed as servant. Although we have no information as to where and by whom Jonathan was employed up to this date, we speculate that he was probably working as a servant in an inn or an ale house. He would soon pack up his wife and two children, and with a third child on the way the growing family would head north to the sprawling metropolis of London, where Jonathan would soon be accepted as an accredited member of the Licensed Victualler's Society.

4.5   London

The Industrial Revolution peaked during the first half of the 19th century, bringing railroads, steamships, the telegraph and a host of other technological changes that created a snowball effect on the economy of Britain. The British Empire expanded to encompass almost one quarter of the world population, and London became the largest city in the world, growing from less than one million in 1801 to about 2.25 million in 1851 and 6.5 million by 1901.

Technological change created an unprecedented demand for workers. Men, women and children were drawn into London's labor market, attracted by job opportunities, increasingly higher wages and gradually improving working conditions. The new factories that sprang up produced goods that were cheaper and this brought an end to many cottage industries, with the result that women also began looking for paid employment. Many occupations became obsolete as machinery replaced manual workers, but new job opportunities were also created for

---

[70]   As outlined in Chapter 2, it was not until the Marriage Act of 1753 that statuary legislation required a formal ceremony of marriage in England and Wales for that marriage to be recognized. Jonathan and Mary appear to have lived as man and wife outside the bonds of marriage until Mary became pregnant with her second child.

[71]   An unconfirmed submission by a member of the LDS Church resulted in the generation of an IGI Individual record (Family Search International Genealogical Index v5.0) for the marriage of Jonathan Gurr and Mary Barham in Westfield, Sussex. This led the authors to the Archives in the East Sussex Record Office in Lewes where they found the confirming Parish Document PAR 504/1/3/1 recording said marriage at the Westfield Church on April 2nd, 1823 with the consent of parents, witnessed by Thomas Gurr and Harriet Barham.

individuals with skills required to build, operate and maintain that machinery. Gas lighting was introduced and this not only allowed factories to work longer hours, but also to operate two shifts per day, which increased production, and also increased the demand for more workers.

A less obvious reason for the rural to urban migration were new laws introduced after the war with France ended in 1815. The Corn Laws and the Law of Enclosure both had the effect of forcing small farmers and many farm workers off the land. The Corn Laws imposed tariffs on cereal grains which caused food prices to rise dramatically making the poor poorer while benefiting the larger landholders. The Law of Enclosure required all properties to be fenced, a cost the smallest farmers could not afford, but it also prevented the poorer farmers from grazing on the fields of large estates, traditionally unfenced for that very purpose.

The rapidly expanding economy drew workers from rural areas into England's larger cities, and at the same time dramatically increased commercial activity and the flow of goods and services. Service-related job opportunities began to appear in the fields of transportation and in the feeding and housing of the more mobile population. There was a growing need for coachmen for transportation services, and for servants and domestic help for the inns that housed travelers at the many stops along the major roads. Many village ale houses became public houses and barmen and barmaids were needed to serve and entertain weary travelers.

Jonathan Gurr was one of those who took advantage of the new opportunities that the Industrial Revolution offered. He brought his wife Mary and his sons, five year old George and two year old Alfred James, to London from Sussex and began a career that would allow him to support and educate the two brothers and their siblings in a fashion that would not have been possible in rural Sussex. They moved to Dockhead, Bermondsey, Southwark, Surrey sometime between early 1824 and December of 1825. The couple's third son, John, was born in Dockhead on December 5th, 1825 and baptized on January 4th, 1826 at St. Mary Magdalene Church where he was buried on July 7th of the same year. Baby John's baptismal record shows that by the end of 1825, Jonathan was employed as a Victualler in Dockhead and he and his family spent their first year in London in that rough wharf district, noted for its many taverns and prisons. They lived just east of where the oldest prison in London for men and women was located until it was burned to the ground by rioters in 1780. That prison had stood in the area since the twelfth century and was notoriously known as the Clink. [72]

4.6   Jonathan's Profession - Licensed Victualler

Ale made from malted cereal grain had been part of the diet of the indigenous peoples of the British Isles even before the Romans arrived, and alehouses were common in every Anglo Saxon village before and after the Conquest. When hops were introduced in the early 15th

---

[72] The Clink was a jail, located in the Liberty of the Clink which housed both men and women. The Liberty of the Clink was the dock area in north-east Southwark which during the 12th century was under the jurisdiction of the Prior of Bermondsey who sold it to the Bishop of Winchester. A Liberty is a place exempt from the jurisdiction of the County Sheriff, and which for all practical purposes is allowed to make its own laws. In 1161, the Bishop of Winchester was granted the power to license prostitutes and brothels in the Liberty of the Clink.

century, the beer that resulted from adding them to the malted mash became even more popular than ale, and the number of ale houses multiplied even further.

There had been some local regulation of beer and ale houses under the earlier manorial system, but a perceived increase in drunkenness and social disorder led the brilliant young King Edward VI to propose action in 1551 (he was 14 at the time). The Alehouses Act of 1552, approved by Parliament, required alehouse keepers to obtain a license, renewable on a quarterly basis by local Justices of the Peace, and they were required to enter into a bond ensuring that good behavior would be maintained on their premises. That same year, by royal edict, young King Edward also authorized the use of hops in making beer. By the end of the 17th century alehouses and beer-houses had proliferated and the demand was so great that most of the ale and beer had to be produced by commercial breweries. In 1729 licensing was changed to allow annual approval, while the Licensing Act of 1753 stated that only those persons who could produce certificates of good character and who attended church regularly could be licensed.

Gin was introduced to the British Isles in the late 17th century and because it was cheaper than ale or beer it became popular among the poorer classes. Gin houses sprang up everywhere and, by the middle of the 18th century, gin was outselling beer and ale by about six to one. Drunkenness and lawlessness resulting from the "gin craze" was considered to be leading to ruination and degradation of the working classes, and authorities tried to bring the situation under control by passing the Gin Act of 1751. Drinking establishments were required to be licensed to sell gin, and control of licensing and of drunkenness was brought under the jurisdiction of local magistrates. The new Act didn't work and by 1800 "gin palaces" numbered about ten thousand in London alone, most of them operating with no licence. Public outcry was such that the government felt forced to take action and it came up with the Beer Act, based on the concept that public drunkenness and related offences would be reduced by allowing home-owners to brew, sell and consume beer and ale in their homes.

Changes in the regulations relating to the public and private consumption of alcohol took place in the late 1820s and these would have a direct impact on the Gurr family. The Beer Act of 1830 made the licensing and operation of a public house easier than it had ever been, and with the industrial revolution underway, with railways beginning to change the mobility of the population, and the urban populations exploding, workers were looking to public houses as places to relax and unwind and meet new friends. [73] The new Act was about to make the expression "merry old England" a very appropriate appellation and the demand for barmen, barmaids and brewer help was increasing throughout England, especially in the larger cities.

_____

[73]   The Beer Act of 1830 was an ill-conceived attempt to convert gin drinkers to beer drinkers. The Act was a revolutionary event which dramatically affected the lives of the lower and middle class in England, because virtually any homeowner could brew and sell ale or beer on his premises by paying a modest licensing fee. They were not allowed to sell gin or other spirits and they were not allowed to open on Sundays. New beer-houses sprouted up everywhere in the British Isles (an estimated 46,000 between 1832 and 1840). This growth continued for the following three decades, until eventually it had to be checked, by introducing new magisterial controls and licensing laws in the Wine and Beerhouse Act of 1869.

As previously stated, though raised in a small hamlet by a father who was almost certainly an agricultural laborer, it seems probable that Jonathan sought work in a beer-house as a barman when he was a young man. We know that by the mid to late 1830s he had become a pub manager. This transition from barman to publican is interesting in itself. The public houses employed barmen and barmaids, cellermen, and potboys and the coaching inns, ostlers. Barmen were usually young men who worked for a few years and then moved on to other occupations. A barmaid was often the wife or a family member of the publican, and only in the better class of pubs were they commonly seen, because in Victorian times it was considered unseemly for women to be serving men in public places. The cellermen handled barrels of beer and ale, and did maintenance. Potboys (and sometimes potmen) kept the pewter mugs clean and shiny. Ostlers were employed to handle the horses in coaching inns which were still common in rural areas until the late 19th century. The publican was the person who held the licence to run the pub, and it was his job to ensure its financial success. Some publicans were tenants of breweries, that is, they held the licence and operated the pub which was owned by the brewery, and they paid an annual rent.

The expansion of the pub industry changed the manner in which business was conducted, as the larger breweries turned more and more to owning and leasing their pubs, rather than just supplying existing houses with their products. The advantage of owning was that they now controlled the products their houses were allowed to purchase. This practice of pub ownership by breweries eliminated many of the smaller breweries as they gradually lost market share. These pub-owning breweries also began hiring and training workers for their public houses, and eventually they increased their profit margins by using salaried employees as publicans. One outcome of this practice was that many pub workers now worked only for the incorporated brewery, and not for any one pub. The possibility of promotion within the trade, and of the better workers being offered transfers to new or existing locations operated by the brewery became a reality.

Jonathan Gurr received his Freedom of the City of London license, and at the age of 26 was formally admitted into the Company of Innholders (Victuallers), beginning the 6th day of March 1827. [74] Jonathan was one of those publicans who seems to have accepted relocation quite willingly, for we have concrete evidence that he was employed in the industry in at least three different locations: Dockhead (Bermondsey), 23 Addle Street in the heart of the City of London, then Tottenham about 7 miles north of the City, then as the publican of 23 Addle Street. [75]

---

[74]   Freedom of the City Admission Papers, 1681-1925, Record 1324 retrieved from Ancestry.com.

[75]   The City of London is a small, separate entity at the heart of the Greater London metropolitan area, which now has 32 boroughs in addition to the City of London. It encompassed the original Roman settlement, and is now the home of the financial district. At the time Jonathan arrived in London the City was already dwarfed by its surroundings. The Freedom of the City was the right to trade, enabling members of a guild or livery to carry out their trade or craft in the square mile that encompassed the City. The guilds who granted this Freedom guaranteed that the goods or services their members provided would be of the best possible quality. Before the mid-19th century, the Freedom of the City of London was a practical necessity for those who plied a trade or made their living in the City

It is certain that he worked for the brewery that owned the Cheshire Cheese chain of pubs (Ye Old Cheshire Cheese and City Cheshire Cheese were related operations). [76]   A reasonable assumption is that this brewery moved him from one pub to another as circumstances demanded. We know that he was listed in the 1839 Pigot's directory as the Publican of the City Cheshire Cheese Pub at 23 Addle Street off Fleet Street. He used the same Addle Street address during most of his years in metropolitan London, indicating that he may have lived at or near that pub and may have been a licensed manager for the Cheshire Cheese chain for a period of thirteen years (1827-1839). Author Paul Magel visited Ye Olde Cheshire Cheese Pub of Fleet Street in the late spring of 2011 with his grandson (**Photo 4.6a** on the following page). The pub is now a tourist attraction and some of the history of the Wine Office Court were the pub is located is listed on a sign hanging near the pub entrance. Mention is made of the famous who have visited there, including Voltaire, Pope, Dickens, Mark Twain, Teddy Roosevelt, Yeats and others.

Jonathan and Mary had eight children. As previously outlined, the two eldest, George and Alfred James were born in Battle, while a third son, John, was born in 1825, soon after the couple's arrival in Dockhead, but died in infancy. Two daughters, Mary Ann and Emily, were born while Jonathan worked at the Cheshire Cheese Pub at 23 Addle Street between 1829 and 1833.   A third daughter, Mary, and two sons, Jonathan and Robert, were born in Tottenham, between 1834 and 1838. Robert was born in Tottenham, but was baptized in Bromley, Kent, after which Jonathan and Mary moved to Bromley.   The Gurr children would have been educated at the Licensed Victuallers' school, with the two eldest, George and Alfred James, completing their education in the 1830s, and the two youngest, Jonathan and Robert, attending the school during the 1840s and early 1850s. The Licensed Victuallers were a prosperous and growing profession in Victorian England that operated schools for their members' children, asylums for their widows, and published a widely-circulated newspaper. Mary and her children would reside in the Licensed Victuallers' Asylum after Jonathan's death.

In the mid 1830s Jonathan and his family apparently resided in Tottenham. Tottenham, situated about seven miles north of the City of London, has been a settlement for over a thousand years, one which developed along an old Roman road. In Tudor times, and until it became part of urban London in 1894, Tottenham was considered a popular recreation and leisure destination by the wealthy and the nobility, and even Henry VIII is known to have hunted there. The area became noted for its large Quaker population and its school, Rowland Hills at Bruce Castle, and it remained an upper middle class area until the 1870s. In the 1830s Tottenham was one of the northern suburbs of London and was still quite rural. It had no train service until the 1840s.

---

of London. Indeed, certain groups of people were compelled, on pain of prosecution, to be Free of the City, including Licensed Victuallers (Publicans). In 1835 the Freedom of the City was extended to any guilds doing trade in the city.

[76] We found seven Cheshire Cheese pubs in an 1841 Trades Directory for London. Five were Cheshire Cheese and two were Old Cheshire Cheese. The Pub at 23 Addle Street was named the City Cheshire Cheese Pub under Jonathan Gurr, Publican in 1839, the Old Cheshire Cheese Pub under John Jones in 1841 and Ye Old Cheshire Cheese under John Hay in 1902.

Photo 4.6a Ye Olde Cheshire Cheese Pub

*London off Fleet Street at Wine Office Court
where Jonathan Gurr may have worked in the 1830's.
Jonathan's Gt-Gt-Gt Grandson, co-author Paul Magel
is shown, with his grandson Ryan in the pram.*

Paul Magel Collection

We do not know where Jonathan was employed during his Tottenham years, though it may have been at one of the area's coaching inns, probably operated by the same brewery that controlled the Cheshire Cheese Pub on Addle Street. Tottenham was a series of small villages and there was little in the way of industry in the area. One village named Tottenham Hale boasted an inn and some 125 houses, containing over 600 people. However, the entire population of Tottenham in 1831 was less than 7,000. [77] Many inns in suburban areas such as Tottenham were coaching inns, but the advent of railways would soon end coaching in England, and these inns no longer needed ostlers and stables. Still, the railways also brought new traffic and many inns and public houses managed to survive.

Sometime in late 1838, Jonathan and Mary and family re-settled on Kender Street in Hatcham, Surrey, a small western portion of Deptford, Kent which borders Lambeth. Deptford is rich in history as the administrative centre for the British Navy, where most English ships were built or outfitted for sea duty. Francis Drake, the first Englishman to circumnavigate the globe, returned to England and a hero's welcome at Deptford, where he was knighted by Queen Elizabeth aboard *The Golden Hind*. It is at Deptford, legend says, that Sir Walter Raleigh gallantly laid down his cape for Queen Elizabeth. Peter the Great came to Deptford to study shipbuilding, and it is from Deptford that Captain Cook set sail on the Endeavour to chart the south seas and lay claim to New Zealand and Australia for England. Deptford is where the first ocean steamships were built and where the first urban rail stations were constructed (1836-1838) as part of the London and Greenwich Railway. In the late 1830s, with its wharfs and naval dockyards, its many fine houses built for the Navy staff and skilled shipbuilders, Deptford was a beehive of industry, awash with workers, traders and naval personnel, most of whom frequented the many inns and public houses in the area. It was one of three districts where publican Jonathan Gurr is known to have been employed.

4.7 Family Reunion

It was fortunate for the Gurr family that another of those attracted to London from East Sussex in the late 1820s, was Mary's youngest brother, Robert Barham. While it is possible that Jonathan and Robert had established a brotherly relationship before they left Sussex, it is more probable that Robert Barham and his sister Mary supported one another, and maintained contact before and after Mary left Sussex for London. Robert arrived in London around 1828 and it seems likely that Jonathan Gurr as a freeman of the Licensed Victuallers would have assisted his brother-in-law in his move and in obtaining employment. It is not surprising then that Robert found work at one of the London Inns. Historically, British Inns were licensed public houses, also offering bed and board for travellers. Jonathan, with his contacts in the industry, would have known where the opportunities for work in a pub or inn might be found. The locations at which Jonathan was employed in London and Environs during the 1820s and 1830s are illustrated in **Map 4.7a** on the following page, composed by Paul Magel.

---

[77] Excerpts from: 'Tottenham: Growth before 1850', *A History of the County of Middlesex: Volume 5: Tottenham.* Oxford University Press pp. 313-317.

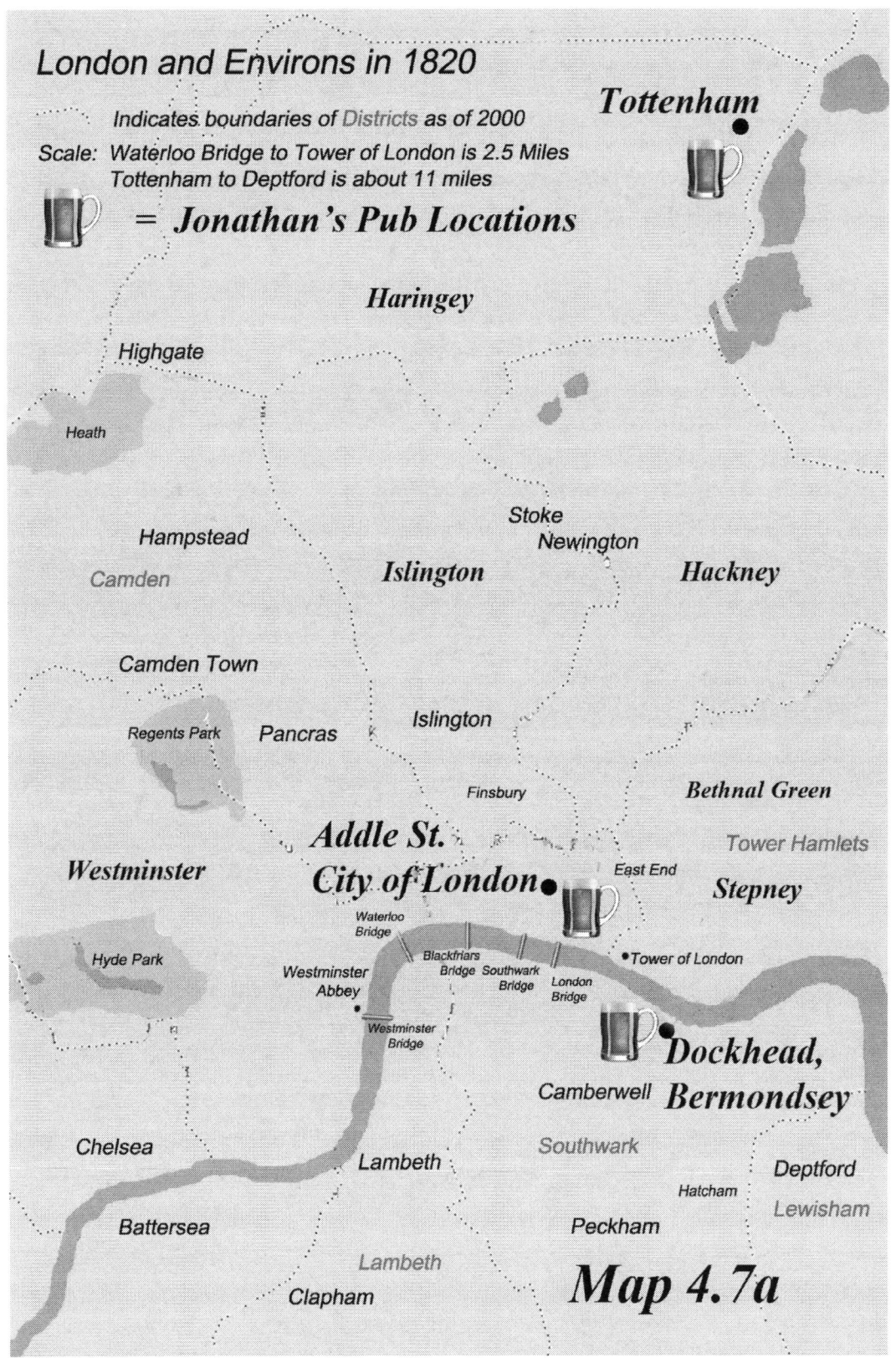

London and Environs in 1820

.... Indicates boundaries of Districts as of 2000

Scale: Waterloo Bridge to Tower of London is 2.5 Miles
Tottenham to Deptford is about 11 miles

= *Jonathan's Pub Locations*

Tottenham

Haringey

Highgate

Heath

Hampstead
Camden

Stoke
Newington

Islington

Hackney

Camden Town

Regents Park   Pancras   Islington

Finsbury

Bethnal Green

Addle St.   *Tower Hamlets*
City of London   East End   *Stepney*

Westminster

Waterloo
Bridge

Hyde Park

Westminster
Abbey

Blackfriars
Bridge Southwark
Bridge   London
Bridge

• Tower of London

Westminster
Bridge

Dockhead,
Camberwell *Bermondsey*

Chelsea

Lambeth

Southwark

Deptford

Hatcham
Lewisham

Battersea

Lambeth

Peckham

Map 4.7a

Clapham

Robert was twenty three when he married Altezeera Henrietta Davey, a Middlesex girl barely 20, at St. Edward the King and Martyr, Lombard Street, London, in March of 1830. Their first child was born in the fall of that year. In 1832, at the age of twenty-five, Robert became a freeman of the Worshipful Company of Innkeepers. [78]

Thus, during the early 1830s, Robert and Jonathan were Guild members in related trades. The brothers-in-law would have had much in common as freemen of related and respected liveries, so it seems very likely that they would have had a tendency to exchange confidences and assist one another in advancing their respective stations in life, though we have no evidence that they became fast friends. Any loneliness that Mary and Jonathan experienced after leaving their family and friends behind in Sussex would be mitigated by the arrival of a sibling, and it appears that Mary Barham Gurr and Robert Barham did have a close relationship. It is likely that the Gurr and Barham children played together and got to know one another on those special occasions that brought them into one another's company. However, it must be acknowledged that unless they lived in close proximity those special occasions would have been rare because, for most of the first half of the 19th century, public transportation was in its infancy, and costly, and walking any distance in London took time and was not safe after dark. Moreover, it was customary for tradesmen and most workers to spend 12 to 14 hours at their jobs, six days a week, and taking time off for personal reasons was not generally acceptable.

In fact, the concept of rewarding good workers with time off to spend with families only began to take hold as the industrial revolution increased the wealth of the population as a whole. Traditionally, the practice of taking a day away from work had been limited to Sundays and other holy days, but the sense of the word "holiday" that had referred specifically to holy days changed as individuals and organized trade groups sought more time to enjoy their new found prosperity. [79] One example of the trend towards holidays began in the late 1830s when, greatly influenced by Queen Victoria and her German consort Prince Albert, Christmas began taking on new meaning. Out of the distant past, pagan and Christian festivals had evolved into Christmas celebrations, and in England it had become customary to bedeck houses and churches with mistletoe, holly and ivy, while most people went on working as usual. When Charles Dickens wrote Christmas Carol in 1843, it encouraged the wealthier to give to the poor and gradually these radical middle class ideals spread their way down to the lower classes as well. The wealth that was being generated by new factories and industries allowed middle class families to take time off work and celebrate Christmas over two days, Christmas Day and Boxing Day. Boxing Day earned its name as the day servants and working people opened the boxes in which they had received gifts (usually of money) from their "rich" employers.

---

[78]   Barham Family History: Robert Barham admitted a Freeman of the Innholders Company, 21 April 1832. The Innholders received their first charter, setting out their rights and privileges, from Henry VIII in 1514. Seven years later they were occupying a hall on the present site held by the Company since its initiation, below which are the foundations of the Roman quay which lay in the angle between the north bank of the Thames and the east bank of the Walbrook.

[79]   From the Old English Haligdaeg (or holy day)

We can conjecture that the Gurrs and Barhams spent their Christmas Holidays together in London, enjoying plum pudding and rabbit or perhaps a fat goose on such a special occasion. It was Victoria's reign that introduced Santa Clause [80], Christmas crackers [81], Christmas cards [82], Christmas carols [83], Christmas trees and turkey dinners. Both chicken and turkey were very expensive at the time, so a goose dinner was more likely what the Gurr family would have enjoyed. By the Christmas of 1839 Jonathan had died. Mary and her five surviving children would have needed Robert and Altezeera and their two children for support on their first Christmas without husband and father. George and Alfred were already young men at nineteen and sixteen, while little Mary was only five, and Jonathan's youngest sons Jonathan and Robert were toddlers: Robert's children, Robert and George were nine and three years of age. The two families were relatively prosperous, so there might have been a Christmas tree adorned with colored paper, candy, fruit or nuts and perhaps beneath it a small doll, a game, a book or other gifts. Gurrs families always made the most of the Christmas holidays, using the occasion to renew family ties, resolve differences, and thank God and one another for the many blessings bestowed upon them.

When the 1841 census was taken, Robert Barham and his family were living at 12 Water Street, just a few houses north of the Thames, between Waterloo and Blackfriars Bridges, two short blocks south of St. Clements Danes Church and a few blocks east of Hungerford Market. [84] As mentioned earlier, the Barham men were notably entrepreneurial and Robert was no exception. In the same year that his father died (April, 1842; his mother passed away a few months later) Robert became the proprietor of a dairy business at 272 The Strand in London (reputed to be the oldest in London). The now "Barham dairy" was situated in one of the busiest locations in London, between Waterloo Bridge and Hungerford Market. The Savoy Palace once occupied the entire area between The Strand and the Thames River. A fire in 1864 destroyed much of the area, but in 1881 the Savoy Theatre was built there and the Savoy Hotel in 1889. In 2010 the site of the Barham dairy on The Strand was occupied by an upscale clothing store.

Sometime after 1842, following Robert's purchase of the dairy farm on The Strand, the family may have taken up residence on that site, for we could find no record of them during the

---

[80] St. Nicholas (or Sinter Klaas from the Dutch).

[81] Christmas Crackers: Invented by Tom Smith, a London sweet maker in 1846. The sweets were wrapped in a fancy coloured paper, but he later added love notes, paper hats, small toys and made them go bang.

[82] Christmas Cards; The Penny Post was introduced in Britain in 1840. A penny stamp paid for the postage of a letter or card to anywhere in Britain. This idea paved the way for the sending of the first Christmas cards and in 1843 Sir Henry Cole tested the market printing a thousand cards for sale in his London art shop.

[83] 1843 O Come all ye Faithful; 1848 Once in Royal David's City; 1868 O Little Town of Bethlehem; 1883 Away in a Manger

[84] St. Clements Danes Church dates back to the ninth century, when seafaring Danes occupied a large part of England. None of the original structure remains, but the church was rebuilt on the same site several times, with the structure we see today designed and built by Christopher Wren in 1682. Heavily damaged during the blitz in 1941 the church was restored a few years later with funds raised by the Royal Air Force.

1851 census, although it is known that they were then operating their dairy in the heart of London. It was not unusual for London dairies to have living quarters above their store, and in the case of the Barham dairy the storefront faced The Strand with the cowshed behind it. The air in the loft above the dairy and much of the surrounding area would be pungent with odours from hay, manure and the cows themselves.

The Barhams and perhaps the Gurrs would have bought food at Hungerford Market (on land originally owned by the Hungerford family since 1425, and usually referred to as Hungerford Inn after 1444) which sold meat, vegetables and other produce. [85] There was a suspension bridge (designed by Isambard Brunel) built between Lambeth and the market in 1845, and it is possible that Mary Gurr crossed that bridge to shop and visit her brother on many occasions.

Hungerford Market was on the same site from the late 17th century, but in 1830, it was sold to a group of businessmen who called themselves the Hungerford Market Company, and many improvements were made. It was a popular shopping area for the next twenty-two years, and boasted many specialty shops, including one that sold pastry and ice cream in 1851 (reputed to be the first ever to sell ice cream on a pastry shell). Fire destroyed much of the market in 1854 and it was sold to the South Eastern Railway company in 1862. The site became the Charing Cross Rail station and the Hungerford suspension bridge became a railway bridge to Lambeth and points south. The atmosphere of Hungerford Market is captured in the artistic illustrations **Sketch 4.7b** [86] **and Sketch 4.7c** [87] on the following page.

4.8   Mary Barham Gurr - Alone

The 1841 census records Mary Gurr as the head of the house on Kender Street in the Hamlet of Hatcham, the Civil Parish of St. Paul in the Deptford district of Greenwich, with four of her children George, Alfred, Jonathan Junior and Robert, while the whereabouts of daughter Mary is unknown. The last evidence of Jonathan being alive was his listing as the publican for the City Cheshire Cheese Public House at 23 Addle Street in Cheapside in 1839. [88] He was also listed in the Post Office Trades Directory of that year, but in that directory in 1841, Jonathan has been replaced at the Addle Street Pub by a John Jones.

---

[85]   Sir Walter Hungerford (later Baron Hungerford), Speaker of the House of Commons and Steward of the Household of Henry V acquired the land in 1425. Members of this colorful family were in and out of favor with their sovereigns for the next three hundred years. Sir Edward Hungerford was licensed to operate a market at Hungerford Inn before he died a pauper in 1711, at which time the Wise family purchased it. Christopher Wren owned a portion of Hungerford Inn in the late 1600s.

[86]   From a print of a painting by Thomas H. Shepherd c. 1830

[87]   From a print of a painting by George Sydney Shepherd c. 1810

[88]   Pigot's Directory, London 1839

Sketch 4.7b Hungerford Market
View from the Strand c. 1830

Sketch 4.7c Hungerford Market
View from the Thames c. 1810

The authors conducted many searches for Jonathan Gurr in researching our family line, but initially were unable to find any evidence of Jonathan's death, although it seemed probable that he died before 1841 and after 1839 from what records we did have. As it happens, Jonathan's death occurred in Bromley Kent in 1839 and his burial took place on Oct 2, 1839 at St. Mary Magdalene, Bermondsey in Southwark. We found this record by searching for all Jonathans (regardless of last name) whose deaths in England were recorded by Ancestry.com. We finally found a Jonathan Gun (transcription error) which proved to be our Jonathan Gurr. The cause of his death is not known, but during the 1830s and early 1840s there were two massive waves of contagious disease: first, from 1831-1833 there were two influenza epidemics and the first appearance of Asiatic cholera; second, from 1836-1842 major epidemics of influenza, typhus, typhoid and cholera.

Mary and Jonathan's eldest son George lived with his mother until at thirty-three he married twenty-eight year old Harriet Butcher, the daughter of Benjamin Henry Butcher and Harriet Cole at St. Botolph without Bishopsgate. [89] The couple were married by licence on August 2nd, 1853, less than three months before Harriet bore them a son, George Benjamin. George has given his age as thirty, probably to avoid any embarrassment over the fact that he was born out of wedlock a full three years before his parents married. He is listed as a railway clerk on the marriage certificate and his father is correctly recorded as Jonathan Gurr, Licensed Victualler. In both the 1841 and the 1851 censuses George is listed as a clerk, but living with his mother, though it is probable that he was a clerk with the railroad during both censuses. We have no further concrete information regarding George, his life or death. However, we can confirm that Harriet was alive and well during the 1871 census, living in St. Paul Deptford with her son George Benjamin (a law clerk at the time) and a daughter Fanny (born 1863). Little Fanny was probably named after Harriet's sister, Fanny Butcher. George Benjamin married Emma Webb c. 1878 and during the 1911 census was widowed and living in Lewisham with his daughter Frances and William Thomas Webb, Emma's brother. Both men were politically active, with George Benjamin serving as the clerk for an unnamed political organization and his brother-in-law as a clerk for the London County Council.

Mary and Jonathan's second son, Alfred James, born in October of 1823, married Mary Ann Bennett at St. George Church in Hanover Square, Bloomsbury in 1846. Their marriage certificate provides the detail that Alfred James was a servant, his father Jonathan Gurr a publican and his new father-in-law Henry Bennett, a coachman. It was quite customary for marriage registers to list the occupation of the bride and grooms fathers whether they were living or not, although a later practice was to list a father as deceased, should he have passed away at the time of his child's marriage. Chapter 5 traces the lives of Alfred James Gurr and Mary Ann Bennett ands the lives of their eight children.

Mary Barham Gurr lost at least two (and more probably three) of her eight children in childhood. John, born in December of 1825 and baptized in January, 1826 died at seven months of age and was buried in July, 1826, while Mary Ann, born in December of 1829, and baptized in January of 1830 died at ten months of age in October, 1830. Of Emily, born in 1832 we have not been able to find any documentation, and we assume she died at birth, or soon after.

Mary Gurr, the sixth child and third daughter of Mary and Jonathan was born in February of 1834. In 1856, she married Edwin Morgan, a clerk for the Courts of Justice, and the couple had four children: Charles Henry, Edwin Alfred, Emily Mary and George Percy. Mary and

---

[89] Benjamin Henry Butcher married Harriet Cole on July 9th, 1818 at St. Mary Lambeth Surrey and he was a fish salesman at the time his daughter Harriet married George Gurr.

Edwin Morgan are listed in the 1901 census. Living with them is their unmarried son Edwin Morgan.

Jonathan , the eighth child of Mary and Jonathan, married Mary Milton in Islington in 1856 and became a letter carrier (porter) for the post office. He and his wife Mary had five children (Henry Milton, Ellen, Frederick Jonathan, Alice Mary and Robert A). Jonathan was enjoying retirement from the civil service by the 1891 census, passing away in Lambeth in 1910.

Robert, the youngest of Mary and Jonathan's eight children married Julia Annie Drury of Dover, the daughter of George Drury, ironmonger at St. George Camberwell in September of 1866, with Edwin Morgan and Harriet Gurr as witnesses. Edwin was the husband of Jonathan's sister Mary (Gurr) Morgan, while Harriet (Butcher) Gurr is the widow of Jonathan's brother George Gurr. The couple are listed in the 1871 census with one son, Walter, but are residing on Oxford St. in Chelsea. During the 1881 census the family are living in Peckham, Lambeth and Robert is living on an annuity. In the 1891 census, Robert (incorrectly transcribed as Garr, no profession listed) and Julia are recorded along with one child (Walter Gurr) who's occupation at the time is listed as a barman in an inn. In both the 1901 and 1911 censuses, widowed Julia is living with her son Walter and his wife Annie Elizabeth in Wandsworth, where Walter is a tobacconist. Julia died in 1924, and Robert was not located in the 1901 census and is believed to have died in 1900.

At the time of the 1841 census Mary was living with four of her sons, George, Alfred, Robert and John on Kender Street in St. Paul, Hamlet of Hatcham in Deptford, Greenwich, Kent. We speculate that the family used the nickname John for the younger Jonathan while his father was living and that this is Jonathan Junior. Daughter Mary is not recorded as living there with them, but it is probable that she was boarding at the licensed Victuallers School at the time.

In the 1851 census, Mary Gurr is listed as a widow and as a "nurse" at the Licensed Victuallers' Asylum in Lambeth while George and John (now listed as Jonathan) are still with her, and again her daughter Mary is not resident with them (she would have been 17 and may have been employed elsewhere).

Mary Barham Gurr is listed as an almswoman at the Asylum in both the 1861 and 1871 censuses. [90] She died there in 1872 at the age of seventy-five years. Mary Barham Gurr lived for her children and was instrumental in ensuring a close relationship between the Jonathan Gurr and Robert Barham families, despite the fact that she lived alone during her later years.

The original Asylum, which sat on six acres of land, was damaged during World War II, but was partially restored. However the Licensed Victuallers decided that there was not enough space available to continue their operations there and a new and larger building was constructed

---

[90] Asylum meant 'sanctuary' to the founders of the Licensed Victuallers' Asylum, rather than having the connotation of psychiatric hospital or 'madhouse' that the term Asylum took on during the 20th century. There was a hospital for the insane in Lambeth several miles to the west of the Licensed Victuallers' Asylum, that is described on maps of the time as a lunatic hospital. This was St. Mary's of Bethlehem in Lambeth, commonly known as 'Bedlam'. Bedlam was one of a few locations that took its water from an underground source rather than from the Thames. During the cholera epidemics of the 19th century it was noted that cholera was virtually non-existent at Bedlam, although a connection between this fact and the water supply was not made until many years later.

in Denham, Buckinghamshire. In 1960, the original structure in Lambeth was turned over to the Camberwell Council and was subsequently converted to residential housing, now Caroline Gardens.

4.9 The Licensed Victuallers' Asylum, off Old Kent Road [91]

There is little doubt that Jonathan Gurr's membership in the Licensed Victuallers' Guild had a profound effect on the lives of his children. The Guild was enlightened and progressive and its strong leaders provided a school, a hospital and a home for the aged in Lambeth to benefit its members.

The Licensed Victuallers' Asylum was founded, on six acres of freehold land lying just off the Old Kent Road. It consisted of a group of one-storied houses, a chapel, a chaplain's residence, board and court rooms, a library, and other structures set round two green lawns. The Duke of Sussex was its first patron in 1827, and he was succeeded by the Prince Consort, on whose death the Prince of Wales assumed the office. The idea of establishing an institution, wherein any distressed members of the licensed victuallers' trade and their wives or widows might be enabled to spend the latter part of their days in peace and quietness, was conceived by the late Mr. Joseph Proud Hodgson, in the year 1826, when he called a meeting of several influential gentlemen in the trade, and ventilated his views; there it was decided that a society should be formed under the title of the Licensed Victuallers' Asylum.

Subscriptions were solicited, and the hearty response that was accorded to the scheme by those most deeply interested in its success enabled the committee to purchase the land above mentioned, upon which it was resolved to erect an asylum, to consist of one hundred and one separate houses, containing three rooms each, with all the requisite conveniences. In May, 1828, the foundation-stone was laid, with full Masonic honours, by the Duke of Sussex, in the presence of a distinguished company, many of whom, in later years, exhibited a sincere attachment to the institution. Promoters of the institution decided to first erect the central portion of the building, consisting of forty-three houses, which were soon completed and speedily became the abode of as many deserving individuals.

The applicants for admission being numerous, it was deemed advisable to complete the asylum as early as circumstances would permit, and consequently, in the year 1831, the south wing was erected, and in 1833 the north wing, thus completing the original design of the institution. The friends of the society, being relieved of the anxiety of erecting additional houses, in the year 1835 turned their attention to the advisability of granting weekly allowances of money to the inmates of the asylum, in order to provide them with the necessaries of life, and, as might be imagined, the proposal met with cordial approval, and allowances began, since which period they have been increased from time to time, until they have reached the sum of twelve shillings per week for

---

[91] This section is taken almost word for word from: 'The Old Kent Road', *Old and New London: Volume 6* (1878), pp. 248-255, http://www.british-history.ac.uk?report.aspx?compid+45729. The original text refers to the building of houses (there were originally 27 in all), but an early sketch and subsequent photos of the structure suggest that they might more appropriately be called flats or apartments. By the early 20th century there were some 200 houses built on the site.

married couples and eight shillings for single persons—members of the Incorporated Society of Licensed Victuallers receiving one shilling per week extra. In addition to allowances, a weekly supply of coal was granted to each inmate, besides being supplied with medical attendance, medicine, and wine, when recommended by the medical officer. In 1842 a charter of incorporation was granted to the institution, and the following year, on the death of the Duke of Sussex, Prince Albert became patron. **Sketch 4.9a** [92] is an artist's impression of the Licensed Victuallers' Asylum c 1845. [93]

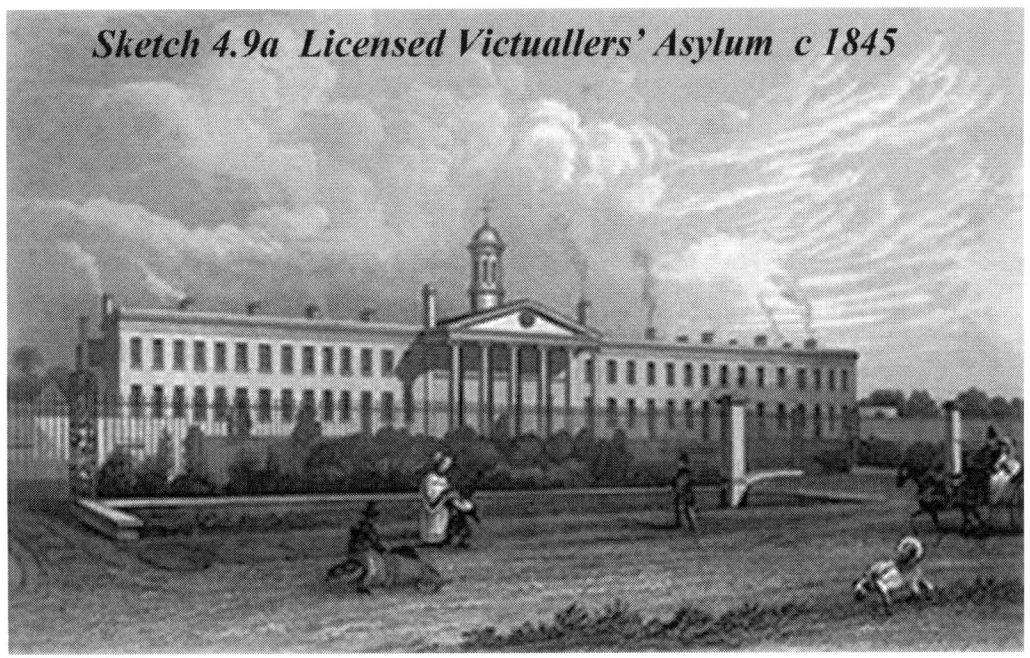

Sketch 4.9a Licensed Victuallers' Asylum c 1845

In 1849 construction of the "ladies' wing" comprising twenty-three habitations began, the foundation-stone being laid by H.R.H. the Prince Consort, and was completed in the following year. Several years having elapsed since an addition was made to the asylum, this important subject was considered, and so readily approved of by those who had the management of the institution, that in the year 1858 a new wing was commenced, the asylum being again honoured by its royal patron condescending to lay the foundation-stone. The thirty-four new houses were designated the Albert Wing, in compliment to his Royal Highness.

A donation of one thousand guineas having been made to the institution in 1866, by a Mr. William Smalley, it was resolved that the only remaining space on the asylum grounds available for building purposes should be utilised. This was accordingly carried out, and ten additional

---

[92] From a print of painting by George Virtue c. 1830.

[93] Taken from the book: John Lane, editor (1917) 'Victorian London – Charities'. *Herbert Fry's Royal Guide to the London Charities*. The original buildings (albeit with many additions and improvements, including restoration from bomb damage in WWII) along with the original property was sold to the Camberwell Borough Council in 1960, and renamed Caroline Gardens.

houses built, which were named the Smalley Wing, the foundation-stone being laid by the Duke of Edinburgh. This addition completed the asylum as a building, and it now (that is, in1878) consists of one hundred and seventy separate and distinct houses.

The beautiful little chapel is enriched with stained-glass memorial windows, and also several handsome marble tablets, in memory of donors to the institution; whilst upon the grounds in front of the building, and facing the Asylum Road, is erected a marble statue of the late Prince Consort, which was unveiled in 1864 by the Prince of Wales. The expenses attending the institution are about £7,000 annually, which is met by the subscriptions among the members of the trade, by bequests, by the proceeds of a ball given annually at Willis's Rooms or the Freemasons' Tavern, and also by the proceeds of the anniversary festival.

4.10   The Licensed Victuallers' School, Lambeth

Another of the Licensed Victuallers' charities was the Licensed Victuallers' School founded in 1803 by the Licensed Trade Charity. It's original objective was to educate the children of those working in the licensed drinks trade, and a school was founded in Kennington in Lambeth, where the children could be educated in a "wholesome and airy environment." [94] As industrialisation increased and London spread outward, the school moved to another green area in Slough in 1921, then to Ascot in the late 1980s, where it continues serving that community today. Queen Elizabeth II is now patron of the school.

The Licensed Victuallers' School at Upper Kennington Lane was founded in 1803 for the education and care of the children of licensed victuallers. The present building was constructed in 1836, renamed Imperial Court and in 1921 taken over by the NAAFI. [95]   Today Imperial Court is an apartment complex.

4.11   St. John's Naval School ?

The authors once found a reference that suggested the existence of a St. John's Naval School, Kennington which was reportedly partially funded by the Licensed Victuallers' Society. Although further research has shown that there was a school established in Upper Kennington in the mid 1860's by a missionary curate (the Reverend Daniel Elsdale) wherein church services were held (this led to the establishment and eventually to the construction of St. Johns the Divine Church in Upper Kennington) we have found no conclusive evidence that this St. John's school had a naval connection, nor that it was funded by the Licensed Victuallers. We mention this because Henry Jonathan Gurr, a grandson of Mary and Jonathan may have attended a naval school before he went to sea circa 1867 and the family association with the LVS would likely have made him eligible for admission to such an LVS supported school.

---

[94]   ibid: Licensed Victuallers' Permanent Fund and School; 1794; 127, Fleet Street. School at Kennington Lane, Lambeth; To relieve poor members, their wives and widows, and to educate their children.

[95]   The Navy, Army and Air Force Institutes (NAAFI) is an organisation that exists to this day. It was created by the British government in 1921 to run recreational establishments needed by the British Armed Forces, and to sell goods to servicemen and their families.

Chapter 5
The London Lives of Alfred James and Mary Ann Gurr

This chapter is devoted to Alfred James and his wife Mary Ann, the authors' direct ancestors, and to the early years of the couple's lives together with their young family. It is unfortunate that we know few details about the upbringing and education of these two parents, and that we know nothing about how they met and fell in love. Although their story really begins with their marriage in 1846, we can speculate about their separate childhoods and provide a few details about the world in which they grew to young adulthood.

5.1 Alfred James Gurr

Alfred James Gurr was an infant when his parents, Jonathan and Mary migrated from rural East Sussex to urban Bermondsey, transferring him and his older brother George into a world far different from that of the south downs farming community in which they were born. Alfred and his siblings were raised in one of the most densely populated cities in the world and unlike their parents, would never experience the solitude of the wooded Downs nor the darkness and quiet of a starlit night in a rural setting. For London was a noisy, crowded city of close to two million souls, a city that was vibrant with commerce during the day, and bustling with activity at night along newly lamp-lighted streets with thousands of pubs. [96] It also had a steadily increasing number of prostitutes and brothels. [97] London was not necessarily a sinful city, but one that was changing rapidly, not only because of technological advances, but also because of a growing social consciousness among its people. New technology brought wonders such as gas lighting, telegraphy and the steam engine, the latter spawning railways, steam-ships and steam-driven machinery to power the new factories that were proliferating in cities throughout the United Kingdom. Meanwhile, science and a new social awareness were bringing about changes in health care and education and in attitudes towards the care and education of the poor.

The migration of workers from rural to urban areas in search of work at the new factories led to overcrowding and pollution on an unprecedented scale. This was especially true in London

---

[96] Public Houses. British Parliament's Beer Act of 1830 allowed licensing of 'beer only' houses, by virtually anyone, for a small fee. The act was intended to make beer more readily accessible in order to combat the immorality, drunkeness and crime associated with the 15,000 or so drinking establishments in London, the majority of which were 'gin palaces'. It was believed that freely available beer would wean drinkers off the evils of the higher alcoholic (and cheaper) gin. Instead, with thousands of new workers streaming into the city from rural areas, it led to a massive increase in the number of public houses. In the 1830s, beer was viewed as harmless, nutritious and even healthy. Young children such as Alfred James and George, were often given what was described as small beer, brewed to have a low alcohol content, because the local water was unsafe. Even the evangelical church and temperance movements of the day viewed the drinking of beer very much as a secondary evil and a normal accompaniment to a meal.

[97] In 1839, in London, a city of two million inhabitants, there were estimated to be up to 80,000 prostitutes, according to A brief cultural history of sex, The Independent. September 23, 2008.

which by the 1840s had become the largest, most densely populated city in the world. The wealthier upper and middle class residents of London soon found themselves surrounded and pressed upon by ever-increasing numbers of lower class workers. Rather than rub shoulders with the multitudes, or suffer through the increasing stench from the growing number of cesspits and the increased volume of garbage, it soon became preferable to those who could afford it to move out of the city. The wealthy escaped the developing slums and exposure to the miasma of the poor by moving into the surrounding countryside. [98] Suburban London became a reality as villages such as Paddington, Kensington, Ealing and Chelsea began to develop. In his forty-nine year journey through life, Alfred James would elevate himself in class-conscious London society, moving out of the wharf-side slums of Dockhead, Bermondsey into the flourishing community of Lambeth and eventually into the middle class environment of Paddington where he and his wife Mary Ann would raise their children.

It was in London, this city of dramatic change, that Alfred James grew to maturity. Alfred's father Jonathan was associated with the Cheshire Cheese chain of pubs. As suggested in an earlier chapter, he was probably employed by the brewery that ran this chain, and he spent most of his years in London using 23 Addle Street (the location of the Cheshire Cheese Pub) as his home address. The Gurr family invariably lived at or near the public house in which Jonathan Gurr worked. Public house hours were variable, but none were allowed to open on the Sabbath. In London they were the busiest in the evenings and late into the night, though there was always a public house available to serve a passer-by during the day.

Because Jonathan Gurr was a licensed victualler in 1836 when the Society of Licensed Victuallers received its Royal Charter, one of the benefits his children were entitled to was admission to the charity school the Society sponsored. The Society of Licensed Victuallers was well organized and well funded. Prior to receiving the Royal Charter there was a group of prominent victuallers who had founded the *Morning Advertiser* in 1794, as well as the Licensed Victuallers' School in Lambeth in 1803, and the Licensed Victuallers' Asylum in 1827, as trade charities. [99]

---

[98] It was a common belief that the lower classes, who bathed infrequently or not at all, and could not afford the expensive perfumes that the higher classes often used to cover up body odors, had a higher prevalence of disease among their kind because of the bad air (miasma, Greek for pollution) emanating from their filthy environment and bodies. The air along the foggy banks of the River Thames in London, which year after year became more and more polluted from the human waste dumped into it, was considered particularly miasmatic. The widely accepted 'miasmatic theory' of disease was a step in the right direction in the control of disease, in that it made a connection between disease and pollution, but it was limited in that it suggested that it was only polluted air that somehow spontaneously generated diseases such as the plague, typhoid and cholera. During the cholera epidemics of the mid-19th century new ideas about disease, such as that cholera might be water-borne or that some unknown organism (germ theory) that humans couldn't see might cause people to get ill, were completely discounted, and even ridiculed, in favor of the miasmatic theory.

[99] The *Morning Advertiser* was first published in 1794 by the London Society of Licensed Victuallers. It was devoted to trade interests. Its circulation in the middle of the 19th century was second only to that of *The Times*. Charles Dickens was an early contributor to the paper.

The Licensed Victuallers' School's designated objective was to educate the children of those working in the licensed drinks trade. The Asylum was intended as an institution where distressed members of the licensed victuallers' trade, and their wives or widows, might spend the latter part of their days in peace and quietness, and where inmates would receive a weekly allowance for food and other necessities of life, as well as medical services without charge. We showed in the previous chapter that Jonathan Gurr's wife and children benefitted from both of these charities, for his children attended the school and his wife and children were residents of the Asylum for many years following Jonathan's early death in 1839.

Although we have no specific details regarding Alfred James education, knowing that he attended the Licensed Victuallers School and that he was employed as a butler later in life we can make certain assumptions. We can assume that he received at least a complete primary education, which in the 1820s and 1830s meant four years of reading, writing and arithmetic. The Licensed Victuallers' School was rather progressive and supposing that Alfred James was a good student and received encouragement from his relatively well educated mother (meaning she could read and write) he probably continued his education until the age of about twelve. If this is true, he would have received some of the tutoring that was usually reserved for the upper classes. This seems likely, for as the butler to a prestigious lawyer throughout the 1850s, Alfred must have had some understanding of how an upper class gentleman thought and behaved.

In the 19th century, well bred gentlemen of the English upper classes attended public schools (we call them private schools today) or were privately tutored. The most prominent public schools were Eton and Westminster which provided a pre-university education which might include one or more European languages as well as Latin, Greek, arithmetic, writing, history and antiquities. Private tutors might teach reading, writing, Greek and math, but they would also assist the family in teaching the young gentlemen manners, social graces, and proper decorum with servants. Conversely, Alfred James must have been trained in what was proper decorum for a servant involved with the upper classes. It also seems likely that he was exposed to Latin and Greek, the classics and was taught good manners and social graces. Alfred James would insist upon good manners and gentlemanly behaviour from his own three sons during his lifetime.

The first London record of Alfred James Gurr that we have found was in the 1841 census at which time he was seventeen years of age. According to that census, he lived with his mother and three brothers, George, John (Jonathan b 1836) and Robert (b 1839) in Deptford. [100] At this point in our research we had no knowledge of his brother John (b 1825), nor of his three sisters Mary Ann (b 1829), Emily (b1832) and Mary (b 1834). We would discover their births in archival records much later in our ancestral search. We notice that young Jonathan (b 1836) was being called John in the 1841 census. Of Alfred James's three sisters, the first born Mary Ann died the year following her birth, while the whereabouts of the other two siblings Emily and

---

[100]   They lived on Kender Street in the Parish of St. Paul Deptford, the Hamlet of Hatcham, Greenwich. Kender Street was about one-half mile east of the Licensed Victuallers' Asylum, which was in a rural part of London noted for its market gardens (northeast part of Peckam, Camberwell).

Mary during the census is not known, though we have later records of them. Based on the 1841 census and a few other records we had at the time, we could only assume that Mary and Emily were still alive and of school age, and may have been boarded out at the Licensed Victuallers School.

The 1841 census does not specify the occupation of Alfred James, but it is probable that he was a servant somewhere in Deptford. But for the fact that Jonathan Sr. was a member of the Licensed Victuallers' Trade, his early death would have placed his wife Mary in an extremely desperate situation, with at least five children still alive and no means of support. Mary may have been housed on Kender Street in Hatcham by the LV trade charity, awaiting admission to the Licensed Victuallers' Asylum, for from the 1851 census record, we know that Mary eventually became a resident (and served as a practical nurse) at the Asylum, where she remained for the remainder of her life, listed as an almswoman there during the 1861 and 1871 censuses.

5.2   Mary Ann Bennett

How little information we have about Mary Ann Bennett's early life! We know that she was born in London, England in 1819 and had at least three younger siblings, Hannah Sophia (b 1821), Sophia Ann (b 1824) and Thomas (b 1827). Mary Ann's father Henry Bennett's occupation was recorded as coachman in the baptismal records of all four children, and also in the marriage certificate of Mary Ann and Alfred James.

As a London coachman in the first half of the 19th century, Henry Bennett had about the same social status as a chauffeur would in England today. A coachman drove a carriage, and there were many different types of carriage ranging from a simple horse drawn two wheeled rig to an enclosed four wheel conveyance with a matched team of horses. The coachman rode atop an elevated perch at the front of the vehicle. Those who kept carriages were usually upper class persons of wealth and social position, with the wealthiest also employing footmen or even outriders to protect them and to clear a path through crowded streets. The status of a coachman among his peers was relative to the carriage that he drove and therefore to the wealth and power of his employer. London coachmen usually resided in the servant's quarters of their employers' residence, although in some cases they lived in nearby lodging with their families, for they had to be available on short notice, day and night, to serve their masters' households.

From medieval times most lower class families in England gave their daughters no education except that which might attract a husband and girls were almost exclusively educated at home. Around 1800, a few "religious schools" began offering education to the poor and to lower middle class children. These "religious schools" were full-time schools and, for the vast majority of children, these were the only educators. The schools were run by the Church of England (or by a non-conformist religious group, the Lancasterians) and used the monitorial system of teaching. The monitorial system used older children, who had some education, as monitors to teach the younger children. Though this system was flawed, it was a beginning and it was probably here that Mary Ann received her education, for we know that she could not only read and write, but she was a major player in the Gurr family business during the 1860s and up until her death in 1884. It was not until 1833 that Parliament and the municipal governments began to participate in education, and not until the 1870s that educational reforms required that all children be educated, so if it were not for the religious schools Mary Ann might never have received any formal education.

There is an interesting comparison that can be made between two girls born at about the same time in England, less than two miles apart. Mary Ann was born in Bloomsbury in 1819, the daughter of a coachman and a mother, neither of whom, in all likelihood received any formal education. "Drina", the little princess who would become Queen Victoria of England was born in Kensington in May of 1819, the daughter of Prince Edward, Duke of Kent and German-born Princess Victoria. Alexandrina Victoria received an upper class education appropriate for ladies of her age, but since she was sixth in line to the throne at her birth, she did not receive any education that would prepare her to be the Queen of England, and almost none of the classical education that men of the ruling class were entitled to. The emphasis of her education was on the feminine accomplishments - dancing, music and drawing. In most respects the basic education of the two girls was not so different, except perhaps in the quality of the educators.

Bloomsbury, where Mary Ann grew up, is a district that has historically been associated with the arts, education and medicine. St. George, Bloomsbury Church where she was baptized and nearby Grenville Mews where she spent her early childhood are a few hundred yards from the British Museum (established 1753) and are also close to the University of London (established 1836). Bloomsbury was considered one of the finer districts of London in the first half of the 19th century and many wealthy and influential families lived there. Both Charles Darwin and Charles Dickens were residents of Bloomsbury during their lifetimes. To avoid confusion, it is important to note that there were two other "St. George" churches in the same district of London. They were St. George, the Martyr and St. George, Hanover Square, the latter being the church were Mary Ann and Alfred James would take their vows of marriage in 1846.

5.3   Marriage of Alfred James and Mary Ann

We do not know when or how Alfred James and Mary Ann met, but we would like to believe that their romance was akin to another of the years 1845-1846 - that between Elizabeth Barrett and Robert Browning. "How Do I Love Thee" was one of the many poems Elizabeth wrote to Robert when he was courting her. Written in 1845, it was not published until 1850, but it represents the thoughts of a young lady of the time totally in love with a younger man. This simple but elegant poem became a memorable expression of one romantic relationship that transcended all others, for Elizabeth's father forbade the couple to marry, and when they eloped he disowned his daughter and never spoke to her again.

In considering how Alfred James and Mary Ann met: is it possible that Alfred James accepted employment with the same family that employed Henry Bennett as a coachman? Alfred James's and Mary Ann's marriage certificate records his occupation as "servant." Their marriage certificate suggests that Mary Ann is unemployed, but they both reside on Maddox Street (though not necessarily at the same address). Employment of Alfred and Henry by the same household would have provided the opportunity for the couple's first meeting.

In the 1851 census Alfred James is recorded as a butler, living in, at the residence of Henry James Wheeler, a prominent and very wealthy proctor, who at that time employed a domestic staff of ten to serve him, his wife and six children. Henry Bennett is not listed in the census as one of Wheeler's staff, but the fact that Alfred James was employed by such a household in such a highly respected servant capacity, makes us wonder if Henry might not have been one of the Wheeler's staff at an earlier date.

Whatever brought Alfred James Gurr and Mary Ann Bennett together, their marriage took place at the Parish Church of St. George Hanover Square in Bloomsbury, with Richard Shaw and Maria Poole as witnesses, following the reading of the Banns. On the couple's marriage certificate, the late Jonathan Gurr, Publican is recorded as the father of Alfred James and Henry Bennett, Coachman as the father of Mary Ann.

The Anglican Church of St. George, Hanover, which is located at St. George St. and Maddox St. in the Mayfair district just north of Buckingham Palace was completed in 1724 and has been a fashionable place for high society weddings in London for generations. It is a noted landmark, built in Roman style, with a statue of King George I in Roman dress atop the steeple, and its portico supported by six Corinthian columns. Many famous people have worshipped or been married there since its foundation. [101]

During the year 1846, in which Alfred James and Mary Ann were married events were taking place across the Atlantic that would impact the lives of the couples unborn male children. California broke away from Mexico and began seeking statehood. President Polk and the Congress of the United States, by threatening war with the United Kingdom over the disputed northern Oregon boundary, finally negotiated a settlement. [102] The 1846 Treaty of Oregon defined the border between the United States and British North America as the 49th parallel, from the Lake of the Woods to the Strait of Juan de Fuca. Little did our newly wedded couple know how significant these events were to their future children, for their three sons would one day immigrate to America with one settling in California and the other two in the once disputed part of the Oregon Territory that became the State of Washington. Some of the couple's grandchildren and great grandchildren would live within a hundred miles of one another on opposite sides of the 49th parallel, never knowing the existence of their cousins to the north or south of that Canada/United States boundary.

5.4   The Butler Father

The census of 1861 shows Alfred James and Mary Ann in separate residences, he a butler in the Wheelers' upper middle class family home at 27 Hyde Park Gardens with six servants, and she in a small lower middle class family residence at 488 Stanley Street with their five children and no servants. It is significant that none of the Gurr neighbors have servants, while all of the

---

[101]   George Frederick Handel composed the Messiah while a parishioner at St. George Hanover during the later years of his life. Theodore Roosevelt married Edith Carow at St. George Hanover in 1886 before he became President of the United States and she the First Lady. On a light note: St. George, Hanover was the church that Alfred Doolittle asked his friends to "get me to the church on time" in My Fair Lady, the musical based on Shaw's Pygmalion.

[102]   Coined during Polk's presidency was the slogan "fifty-four forty or fight", referring to the geographic parallel. That boundary would have included much of what is now the Canadian province of British Columbia and all of Vancouver Island.

neighbors of the Wheelers have five to ten servants, even those couples who are childless. The two residences are less than half a mile apart physically, but in social terms the distance is enormous. The Gurrs live in the older area of Paddington near the wharfs serving the Paddington Basin Canal, surrounded by lower class workers, while the Wheelers live in one of the new homes of the very wealthy, built facing onto Hyde Park, surrounded by bankers, landowners and professionals.

Alfred James Gurr was in household service throughout most of his adult life. He held the position of butler in the Wheeler household for at least a dozen years, for he is recorded as a butler in the same residence in 1851. Alfred James, as a live-in butler, garrisoned his family as close to his place of employment as possible, permitting him to spend the little time off allowed him with his growing family.

To serve as the butler in any upper class Victorian home meant that Alfred must have been well brought up and reasonably well educated, of high moral character, impeccable in dress and manners, able to lead, train and manage the household staff, and absolutely trustworthy. A butler of that time was essentially the overseer of the household staff, including the cooks and kitchen maids, the lady's maid, the housekeeper and her housemaids, and the carriage-men and footmen. The Victorian butler's duties were extensive. While he had to know the planned schedule of his master and the other family members well ahead of time, to be sure that household arrangements were made to suit those schedules, he also had to be capable of adapting to sudden changes in that scheduling. He would ensure that the household was awakened at the proper time each morning and he would be the last to go to bed once the family had settled down for the night. He carried the household petty cash, purchasing food and overseeing it's preparation by the cook. He served the family members and their guests at table, saw to the security of the premises, the safety of the wine, the silverware and other household valuables.

But the best butlers had many personal responsibilities for the families they served. Each butler knew a great deal about family members, was often inadvertently privy to delicate family secrets, and even had some knowledge of the affairs of the friends and others who visited that family. It was the valued butler who, as the front line contact with the outside world, mirrored the standards set by the master of the household.

In their early years, the children of Alfred James would have seen their father only rarely, and they probably would have considered him in the same way they would an occasional visitor to their dwelling in Paddington. The average live-in butler of the mid 1800s had only parts of days off during each week, unless the master and his family were vacationing or abroad. In the larger households such as that of Alfred's employer it may have been possible to occasionally arrange to be away overnight by assigning responsibility to another member of the household staff, but this might be considered an abrogation of responsibility were it to become a habit. Thus, during their very early years their butler father probably had little day to day influence on the development of his children, though he would still have set the standards as master of his household. Those standards, influenced by his station in life, would alter the development of his offspring. His three sons, and later generations of Gurrs showed signs of that upbringing, exhibiting polished manners and speech, cleanliness, fastidiousness and concern for one another.

5.5   Raising a Family in London

By the year 1850, Alfred James and Mary Ann had their first child, Sarah Sophia (born 13 May, 1849 and baptized June 10, 1849), while living on Pitt Street in Peckham, Surrey. Pitt Street was off Kent Road and slightly more than a mile north-west of the Licensed Victuallers' Asylum (on Asylum Road, also off Kent Road) where Alfred's mother Mary was a resident. Alfred James is listed as a butler on the baptismal record, and may have been living-in at his employer's residence (probably the Wheeler residence) when Sarah Sophia was born. The year 1848 in which Sarah Sophia was conceived was remarkable for the number of deaths in England from Asiatic cholera, a disease that up to the end of the 19th century was second only to the black death for its impact around the globe. [103]

Asiatic cholera appears to have originated in the Indian subcontinent. [104] The British first became aware of the disease during a cholera outbreak that began in India and spread throughout south-east Asia between 1816 and 1826. This, the first recorded cholera pandemic, resulted in the deaths of millions in Asia, including some 10,000 British troops who were stationed in India. Cholera then spread along land and sea trade routes from India to other parts of south-east Asia, Russia, Western Europe, including Great Britain, and eventually to the Americas, where as many as 150,000 are believed to have died of the disease by the late 1840s (including President Polk, three months after his presidency ended).

The first cases of Asiatic cholera in Britain were diagnosed in late 1831 and the disease reached epidemic proportions in 1832, when an estimated 6,536 died of the disease in London alone. Cholera continued to be a major problem in Britain for the next 40 years, with the disease reaching epidemic proportions in greater London in 1848 (14,137 deaths), 1854 (10,738 deaths) and 1866 (5,596 deaths). [105]

The theory of germ disease had not yet been proposed, and the cause of the scourge was unknown, but it was assumed that "bad air" (miasma) had something to do with its spread. The fact that the disease was rampant among the foul-smelling poor of India gave credence to that assumption. Authorities were at a loss to explain the epidemics, but it became apparent that something had to be done. Finding a solution was finally deemed urgent after the "Great Stink of

---

[103]   Bubonic Plague or the "black death" appears to have originated in China during the early 14th century reducing the population there by 30%. It spread along the silk route to the Crimea, and on merchant ships to western ports, carried by fleas that lived on black rats. The Plague had a devastating effect on Europe and Great Britain reducing populations by up to 60%. An estimated 30,000 died in London in 1603, another 35,000 in 1625, 10,000 in 1636, and about 100,000 during the Great Plague of London in 1665-66. Data from historylearningsite.co.uk

[104]   Cholera is a severe bacterial infection spread through contaminated drinking water or infected food, with symptoms including profuse watery diarrhea and vomiting which leads to dehydration and electrolyte loss. The cholera bacterium produces a toxin that causes the human body to move fluids from the blood stream into the intestines. Symptoms start within a few days of infection and dehydration can be so severe that death can occur within hours of onset. In most cases cholera can be treated by replacing the water and electrolytes lost. If cholera patients are treated quickly, the mortality rate is one in a hundred, but left untreated it rises to over fifty percent.

[105]   Excerpts from the article 'Cholera epidemics in 19th-century Britain'. Published by The Institute of Biomedical Science .

1858." Until the mid1850s most London basements functioned as waste storage areas, not only for ashes and other household refuse, but also for the storage of human waste in cesspits under the house, with overflow channels from the basement area into the streets. Most homes had attached outdoor privies at the back of the house with waste accumulation beneath the scullery and kitchen at the rear of the house, and the offensive odors from the basement permeated the walls and the rooms of the ground floor, the stench becoming overpowering during the summer months.

Beginning in 1848, all houses built in greater London had to, by law, have enclosed drains connected to the public sewers, and a ban was put on emptying cesspits into the street forcing homeowners to have the waste hauled away. These two actions did nothing to alleviate the problem because there were still hundreds of thousands of cesspits that had no outlet other than the overflow culverts running from the basements to the open or partially covered storm sewers that ran down London's city streets. Eventually the ban on dumping waste from the cesspits into the storm sewers had to be lifted, for there was no way to haul the massive amount of waste material out of the city. Within a few years some thirty thousand cesspits were emptied.

It gradually became obvious that the draining of the cesspits was somehow related to disease, although the mechanism by which this took place was unknown. The public sewers drained into the Thames, as did the storm sewers, and the volume of human waste reaching the river increased dramatically between 1848 and 1858. The "Great Stink of 1858" finally stimulated action but it was not until the mid-1870s that modifications to the sewerage system began to alleviate the problem.

The solution to the health problem is attributed to a private physician by the name of John Snow who came to the conclusion that cholera had something to do with an unidentified agent in the water supply. Snow began arguing his "water borne cause" theory in 1848, but it was not given any credence until 1854, when he demonstrated that his theory might indeed have merit. Snow examined water samples under a microscope, but he was never able to see or identify what it was in the water that was killing people. However he established his credibility by plotting the location of cholera related deaths in 1853 and 1854. At this time London was supplied with water by two water companies. One company drew its water from the Thames River upstream of the main city. The second company drew its water from the river downstream from the city. More cases of cholera occurred in the London area supplied by the water company that drew its water from the downstream location. Snow concluded that water from the second company might be contaminated by the sewage deposited in the Thames as it flowed through the city.

This conclusion was actually ridiculed and might not have been accepted as fact had not Snow made another discovery. He studied weekly statistics on cholera deaths in London and noted that there was a higher incidence of cholera the closer you were in walking distance to the intersection of Cambridge and Broad Street in the Soho district. As many as 500 deaths from cholera occurred within 10 days in the immediate area of that intersection. This area was one of the poorest and most overcrowded areas of London, and at that intersection there was a "free-to-the-public" water pump. Snow's argument was convincing, and the local Board of Governors ordered the Broad Street pump closed. Soon afterward the epidemic abated.

In spite of this dramatic outcome, Snow could still not convince the majority of his colleagues that cholera was water–borne and not air-borne. Proponents of the miasmatic theory dominated the fields of medicine and public health. Fortunately, British authorities inadvertently made the right decision (for the wrong reasons) following the Great Stink of 1858. In the unusually hot summer of that year, the stench from the Thames was so overwhelming that it spurred the London agencies that were responsible for health and welfare into action. The decision was made to clean up the Thames and almost immediately great undertakings began to rid Londoners of the "bad air" that most experts believed caused cholera and other diseases such as typhoid and plague.

Early in 1859, the Metropolitan Board of Works finally accepted a scheme proposed in 1858. An extensive underground sewerage system was designed to divert waste downstream of the main population of London to the Thames Estuary. Almost one hundred miles of main diversion sewer was constructed between 1859 and 1865, fed by another 450 miles of main sewers, in turn fed by some 13,000 miles of smaller local sewers. The extensive excavations for this massive project took place at the same time as the construction of new rail lines, including the new underground Circle Line and Paddington station in 1863. New embankments and excavations throughout the city allowed new roads to be built to reduce traffic congestion, along with new public gardens to beautify the landscape. In the early years gravity was relied upon for the sewage to flow eastwards, but eventually pumping stations were built to provide sufficient flow. Deborah Cadbury describes the engineering feats of the 19th and early 20th century in her book *Seven Wonders of the Industrial World*, and the London Sewers are one of those seven wonders.

It was between 1848 and 1864 that Alfred James and Mary Ann brought their eight children into the world, six of whom would reach maturity. Life expectancy and particularly infant mortality rates improved dramatically in London during this period because of the measures taken to get rid of the stink, and the growing awareness of the public that *"bad air"* should be avoided.

The couple's second child, Alfred Richard was born in Paddington on the 13th of March 1851 and baptized on the 20th of April, 1851. Alfred James and Mary Ann were living on Conduit Street, a few hundred yards northwest of Henry Wheeler's Hyde Park Garden home. They moved to 488 Stanley Street in Paddington, where their third child Henry Jonathan was born on 22nd January, 1853. For some reason Henry Jonathan was not baptized until November, 1853 and then at St. George the Martyr, in Southwark. He was baptized alongside George Benjamin Gurr, the first born son of Alfred James's elder brother George. Baptisms were traditionally performed within three to six weeks of birth, so it appears likely that Mary Barham Gurr, who lived in Southwark at this time, influenced the timing and setting of the event.

Chapter 6
All About Milk, 1861 - 1903

6.1   Dairy Industry

One of the oldest industries of man is the distribution and sale of dairy products. Changes in the dairy industry in 19th century England would alter the lives of Alfred James and Mary Ann and would dramatically alter the future of their children, for the family's eventual participation in the distribution and sale of milk and milk by-products would raise them from the lower to the middle class.

The earliest human settlements that might be called towns or cities date back to 8000-9000 B.C. There is evidence that an agriculture industry had developed by this time, that is, that grains and other produce were being processed by some of the population for distribution to others. Moreover, domestication of animals had begun and goats' milk and sheeps' milk were part of the population's diet, which raises the possibility that some of the inhabitants were involved in dairy industry. Clay tablets discovered in Mesopotamia contain details of dairy industry, with direct reference to herds of goats, sheep and cattle and the production of milk and cheese some 5000-6000 years ago. A copper frieze was discovered in Iraq decorated with bulls and cows, and there were other objects found in the same region, one depicting a cow being milked, another butter being churned. [106]

The Romans most certainly had herds of cattle, sheep and goats and their dairy industry flourished with milk, butter and cheese being distributed and sold throughout the Empire. Meat, milk and cheese were a mainstay of the diet of the Roman soldier and the legions travelled with their herds as part of the rearguard. [107] The art of turning perishable milk into its portable and durable by-product, cheese, was well developed, for the Romans knew to use fresh milk in making cheese and heated the milk to speed up fermentation and the production of lactic acid. They knew to add rennet to precipitate the curds in which the milk fat is trapped. They knew that the whey had to be separated from the curd and that different types of cheese would result by varying the quantity of rennet, the type of bacteria added for fermentation, and the time taken in the processing. They also used other additives during processing to modify the cheese to satisfy different tastes.

Clearly, dairy industry has been a major pursuit of man from the earliest civilizations, and the basic methods of production had varied only slightly from Roman times until the mid-19th century. But then came the railroads, germ theory and pasteurization. The ingenuity of entrepreneurs such as George Barham in recognizing the opportunities provided by these new

---

[106]   In the Temple of Ninhursag, Tell al-'Ubaid, southern Iraq, dating around 2600 BC. Ninhursag was a mother goddess. Her name means 'lady of the steppe land' where herds would have been kept, making the frieze appropriate to her temple. Retrieved from British Museum.org website.

[107]   Marco Polo described a kind of paste that the Mongolian Tatar troops of Kublai Khan carried for nourishment made from sun-dried skimmed milk.

developments, and taking advantage of those opportunities, changed the London milk industry forever, and ultimately redirected the lives of members of the Gurr and Barham families.

6.2   London Dairies

From early days milk had been distributed to consumers in cities such as London by milk maids, and by milk men who carried buckets or pails of milk on a wooden yoke. Most of these vendors worked for a local cowshed, though some operated independently, usually contracting with an urban or suburban supplier for the milk produced by a number of cows, which they often milked themselves. They measured out the milk for buyers using a metal ladle on a long handle, and could deliver about 20 gallons a day. It was not until around 1860 that wheeled pull carts, or perambulators, were introduced, enabling a milk man to deliver milk in churns instead of pails, and increasing the amount he could distribute to about 30 gallons a day. Some men began using horse drawn carts and these roundsmen could distribute perhaps 40 gallons per day. [108] Milkmaids began to disappear by the mid-19th century, probably because girls were finding opportunities in shops called "dairies" which retailed milk to their customers as well as other dairy items such as butter and cheese. [109] Increasingly, as the century progressed, men were taking over established routes using prams and horse drawn carts with churns, although until as late as the 1870s a man or a women might still be seen transporting milk using the yoke.

Because it was not uncommon for vendors to water down the milk they sold in order to increase their profit, many customers would only buy milk drawn directly from a cow in their presence. [110] In London this was only possible at a cowshed, and as a result there were cow-keepers throughout the city. Some cow-keepers even went door to door with their cows and goats, or hired servants to do it for them, so the customers could see the animal being milked in front of them. This concern for freshness is one of the reasons why the number of cowsheds within London proliferated during the city's tremendous growth in the 1800s.

It seems contradictory to think of cowsheds existing within the thriving metropolis of London, at a time when it was the largest urban population in the world, with upwards of two million people residing in an area of only about sixty square miles. London was arguably the wealthiest city in the world in the 1840s, but it was also a city of overcrowding and poverty. It was dotted with unsanitary slums, thousands of cesspools, and surprisingly an estimated 1000

---

[108]   Around the middle of the century the term roundsman was applied to any individual who delivered milk using a pram or cart, following a regular route serving his customers. It gradually evolved to milkman to differentiate from other roundsmen (ice man, bread man).

[109]   Cow-keepers produced milk for local delivery, and most cow-keepers could not be classified as dairy farmers because their only product was raw milk. However, some cow-keepers had shops at their cowsheds, and in the early 1800s these became known as dairies. By the mid-19th century, retail outlets that did not keep cows, such as milk houses or shops that sold milk and other dairy products, became known as dairies. Some grocers who sold milk and milk products might have a dairy section on their premises. By the 1870s, dairies were being supplied by wholesalers who brought milk in by rail from distant points, and the number of cow-keepers in London gradually diminished, as regulation became more intensive.

[110]   The water used to water down London milk had to come from the Thames. Water from the Thames was responsible for tens of thousands of deaths in London from epidemics of typhoid and cholera until about 1865.

dairies and cowsheds. [111] The cowsheds were a necessary evil if Londoners were to have access to fresh milk in an age when there was no refrigeration and where the crowded streets and lack of transport did not allow milk to be transported economically, or in a timely fashion, from dairy farms outside the city. [112]

As previously mentioned, Robert Barham, the brother of Mary Gurr and the uncle of Alfred James Gurr, operated a cowshed at 272 The Strand from 1842, that was reputed to be the oldest in London. The Barham cowshed was situated a few hundred yards north of St. Clements Danes, and although the Barhams may have been known for the quality of their milk and their cleanliness, they were definitely one of the major contributors of waste and air pollution to the immediate area. The Barham dairy business prospered under Robert and was eventually taken over and expanded by Robert's son George Barham who, in the last four decades of the 19th century, would build a multi-faceted milk empire that would bring great wealth and recognition to the Barham family, and a knighthood for George in 1904.

6.3   Opportunity Knocks

In the early 1860s, two unrelated happenings took place that would dramatically alter the lives of Alfred James Gurr, his wife Mary Ann and their children. The first was the death of his employer. The second was the success of his cousin George Barham in his dairy business. These two events and the responses they generated in others would lead Alfred into making a critical career change. At almost forty years of age, he would walk away from a life of service as a butler and embark on a new career - as a milkman.

When Henry James Wheeler passed away in late 1860, Alfred James's situation took a reversal that probably cost him many nights sleep. [113] The future of his employment was suddenly in doubt. The despondent widow made it clear to him that she would continue to need him for the foreseeable future. With three unmarried daughters and one son between the ages of eleven and eighteen, it would not have been appropriate to make too many changes in the family's situation until she and her family had recovered from the loss of her husband. But Alfred must have seen the writing on the wall. The mansion had been a hive of industry with visitors coming and going day and night. The busy solicitor had needed a capable butler to keep his household organized, but with his death there would be far less for Alfred to do. Alfred must have sensed that eventually he would have to find another position. Not that this would be too

---

[111]   Post Office, London and Suburbs Directories.

[112]   Cows produce milk twice a day, sometimes three times a day in high season and this has to be distributed quickly before it sours. Before refrigeration, and other processing developments, only dairies near large population centers were able to sell fresh milk to the people in those centers, simply because it spoiled too rapidly and could not be kept for more than a day or so. Pasteurization was a principal still not discovered and while refrigeration with ice was well understood, there were no commercial sources of ice available until the late 19th century.

[113]   Henry Wheeler died 16 October, 1860 and his will was probated on the 20th of November with his wife Emma Sarah Wheeler receiving the bulk of his estate of £140,000. According to www. measuringworth.com, this amount would be equivalent to about $US 680,000 in 1860, or in 2011 currency about $US 19,000,000 (based on the change in the consumer price index).

difficult to do, or would it? A good butler was always in demand, but of course there was his age. But his present position was so convenient, and with the passing of the master of the house, was far less stressful, so he waited for a few months before seeking alternate employment.

He was still in the Wheeler's service when his first cousin George's circumstances began to change. George Barham, son of dairyman Robert Barham on the Strand, had started a separate dairy company of his own in 1858 (the Express Country Milk Supply), and the savvy businessman was having a hard time keeping up with the demand. It is likely that George needed help at just the time when Alfred was also at loose ends. While we will never know the details of the offer and the negotiations that took place between George Barham and Alfred James Gurr, in the summer of 1861 Alfred James would set aside his career as a butler and become a milkman. Our best guess is that George Barham approached Alfred with a proposal, not only because his own dairy business was booming, but also because he saw the opportunity of expanding his own operations. By setting his cousin Alfred up with a milk route in Paddington, he could act as his supplier while Alfred learned the trade. This would certainly have pleased George's Aunt Mary, Alfred's mother, and if Alfred proved successful, perhaps a Paddington dairy might be a possibility, which would help George realize a profit, and at the same time help out Alfred at a time when his cousin's future was uncertain.

In the years before 1861, the Gurr and Barham families probably had only limited contact with one another. This is not surprising when you consider the difficulties involved in travelling from place to place in London in the 1850s and 1860s. The one person who would tie the two families together was Alfred's mother and George's aunt, Mary Barham Gurr. But Mary lived in Lambeth, her son Alfred James in Paddington, her brother Robert on The Strand, and her nephew George Barham in Bloomsbury, and although they were only a few miles apart, visiting would probably have been limited to family gatherings at Christmas or other very special occasions.

As fortune would have it, in the early 1860s there was an outbreak of hoof and mouth disease in the city of London and immediate vicinity. By 1864, the disease ridden London herds were being destroyed and George Barham found himself in the enviable position of being one of the few London dairymen capable of supplying the demand the loss of the city herds had created. He was scrambling to find reliable suppliers, distributors and all types of personnel to work in and to manage his booming company.

In the years after 1864 the Gurr family maintained a reasonably close relationship with the Barham family. However, George Barham's closest kin in the Gurr family were his Aunt Mary Barham Gurr and her son Alfred James. Mary Barham Gurr died in 1872 and Alfred James in 1874 and in the years following their passing George Barham must have been fully occupied in expanding his thriving business. George elevated himself and his family to the upper-middle class of the class-conscious society of 19th century London, and he became a very busy man, promoting his companies at the highest social levels. His company would become the sole supplier to Queen Victoria under a Royal Warrant that has continued through the Reign of Elizabeth. George Barham was not averse to what today might be called nepotism. His sons would help him run his dairy empire and would take over the reins from him when he retired. Though we can assume that the two families grew apart, there is also evidence that George

Barham remained a patron to several of Alfred James children, and to their children as well. George Barham was the executor of the will of at least one of Alfred James's daughters, and he stayed in contact with Edwin's and Ellen's children. He may also have had a financial interest in Gurr and Son, but proof of this has not yet been found.

Alfred Gurr may have been fortunate in being given the opportunity to participate on the distribution side of the rapidly growing milk supply business, but it also took courage on his part to make such a dramatic change in his life style. Whatever drove him to the decision to change careers at the age of forty, that decision would change the futures of his sons and daughters who survived childhood. His youngest daughter was not yet three and his namesake and eldest son was only fourteen. Including Mary Anne and Alfred himself there were eight mouths to feed and board, and those six surviving children needed to be clothed and educated.

Alfred had to learn the dairy business from the ground up. Although it would be impossible for him to earn enough to support his large family as a simple roundsman, it is quite possible that he pulled a milk cart more than once in his life. An educated, trustworthy, fastidious man, Alfred appears to have been exactly the type of person who would appeal to George Barham as a business associate. By 1871, Alfred would head up his own company (Gurr and Son, the Son being twenty year old Alfred Richard), which would include a dairy below their residence at 38 Southwick, selling a variety of dairy products. Gurr and Son were in all probability under contract to Express Country Milk Supply as a kind of middleman to handle the distribution of milk to vendors in the Paddington district. Apparently Alfred's career change resulted in early prosperity for, in the early 1860s, the couple had their portraits painted, a luxury they would have been unaffordable a few years earlier. **Photo 6.3a** and **Photo 6.3b** of the portraits of Alfred James and Mary Ann were taken and may be found on the following page. The whereabouts of the original paintings is unknown. When Alfred James died suddenly in 1874, his wife Mary Ann inherited and became the sole proprietor of the family business. She continued to be the owner and head of the firm until her death in 1884. At the time of Alfred James's death most of the immediate family was involved in the dairy business, with twenty-three-year-old Alfred Richard, the son in Gurr and Son, and probably the designated heir in Mary Ann's will.

With the death of their father, the two sons Henry Jonathan at 21 years and Edwin Robert at 19 years of age were dependent on their mother and elder brother, Alfred Richard. Within the next few months Henry would immigrate to America. In the early 1870's Edwin was employed as a wine merchant's clerk, but eventually he too would participate in the operations of the family company Gurr and Son, and eventually become a milk wholesaler and contractor.

Only 49 years old at the time of his death, Alfred James did not live to see how prominent and prosperous his cousin George Barham became, nor how well the family business Alfred established provided for his wife and children. He would have been very satisfied to learn that by seizing the moment of opportunity in support of his dairyman cousin, his family through their own hard work would be elevated to the middle class and would enjoy the many social benefits that came with that status in Victorian England.

Photo 6.3a
Alfred James Gurr
From 1860's Portrait
Ted Robert Gurr Family Collection

Photo 6.3b
Mary Ann Gurr
From 1860's Portrait
Ted Robert Gurr Family Collection

6.4   George Barham, Dairyman

Throughout the early 19th century, on what was then the outskirts of London there were agricultural lands, market gardeners and small dairy farms, while more distant from the city were many large dairy farms. [114] The greater the distance the dairy farm was from London, the less likely its milk would be sold there. As had been the custom for centuries, the milk that could not be sold by these more distant dairies had to be preserved in the safe dairy product forms of butter and cheese. The advent of the railway to London in the 1830s would bring many changes to the dairy industry, and opportunities for entrepreneurs like George Barham.

George Barham (b. 1836) and an elder brother (Robert, b. 1830) were born in London and raised at their father's dairy farm at 272 The Strand, where even as children they assisted their father in his dairy's operations. George's father and mother, Robert and Altezeera Barham, apprenticed him to a London cabinet maker at one time, but he continued to deliver milk for them in the evenings. In 1858 he opened his own dairy on Dean Street, in what was then the Parish of St. Andrew, in the Municipal Ward of Farringdon Without. He employed others to do the deliveries and began to import milk by rail from outside London.

Following George's 1859 marriage to Margaret Rainey (of Spilsby, Lincolnshire), the couple took up residence at 25 Dean Street, and operated their dairy, which as the census of 1861 indicates, employed one man and two women. The census also shows that George's father continued to maintain the dairy at The Strand, and he also employed two women.

Where George obtained his milk, at least in his early business days, is uncertain. He was not a cow-keeper like his father, and it is likely that, at least initially, his milk was sourced from his father's herd, as the Dean Street Dairy appears to have been only an outlet for milk. Beyond this, he could have ensured a milk supply by either buying milk from a wholesaler at the rail station, or establishing himself as a wholesaler. As a wholesaler, he would have needed to have made contact with a producing dairy and signed a contract with them. The milk would then be shipped to him from the suburban or rural dairy by rail. The likelihood is that he used a wholesaler at first, and eventually became one himself.

Robert Barham, George's father, was raised on a Sussex farm and it is quite possible that he had prior experience with farm animals and the dairy trade. On moving to London he took up employment as an Innkeeper before becoming a dairyman and cow-keeper. George Barham was raised in a dairy environment from the age of about six, and it is evident that he worked in the dairy trade through most of his childhood. This meant that George knew the milk business from cow to customer, that is from production to the sale. His knowledge of the milk trade, his insight and exceptional ability as dairyman would be demonstrated again and again.

---

[114]   The term dairy farm is correctly used here. Dairy farming implied the keeping of cattle for their production of milk, part of which was sold 'fresh' and part of which was converted to butter and cheese. Some 'dairy farms' became 'creameries' at the beginning of the twentieth century because they processed the raw milk into cream, butter, cheese and other dairy products, and also bottled their milk with automatic bottling equipment. Creameries also had some means of refrigerating their products, and were usually situated at or near major train stations, so that their products could be more easily shipped.

George Barham eventually renamed his firm Express Dairies. Such was the quantity he brought in that it became necessary to organise transport to and from the trains, and to design special equipment for handling milk in bulk. The increase in business generated for the railway companies was so great that they had to extend their facilities, building additional sheds and sidings exclusively for Express Dairies.

George Barham's transition from that of being a dairyman's helper (assisting his father), to being a milk tradesman running his own dairy in South Islington (as well as continuing to assist his father), to becoming an entrepreneur with his own company, took place over a mere five years. George Barham was an astute businessman, and under his supervision the Dean Street dairy prospered. The demand for his milk outgrew his original suppliers' capability and he began buying milk from many sources. We know he was one of the first, if not the first, to buy milk from dairies outside the city and transport it to the city by rail. By 1865 he was launched on what would be an outstanding career, and in the final analysis one in which he would demonstrate his ingenuity and entrepreneurial genius.

How George accomplished this transition in such a short time is a question for which we may never have an answer. Although he had the backing of his dairyman father, he apparently had no partners, except for a supportive wife. How he managed to finance his early operations, and incorporate and launch his first company is unknown. The first dairy of which he was sole owner was established in 1858, four miles from the Great Northern Railway Depot, where the new Paddington Station would eventually be built. The neighborhood he chose was upscale, putting him close to those middle and upper class customers who could afford to buy fresh milk. He also was astute enough to have predicted the impact the railway would have on the London dairy business. He positioned his first dairy just south of High Holborn street which connected to Oxford Street running directly to the rail terminal, a choice that suited his future plans.

In 1864, George Barham, formed the Express Country Milk Supply Company with its depot located at 28 Museum Street, near Kings Cross Station, and sometime later opened a larger depot on Wakefield Street, Bloomsbury, north-east of the original depot. The quality-conscious entrepreneur promised that only top quality fresh milk would be sold, and he brought his product in from the country by rail each morning, and immediately distributed it around the West End of the city. A publicity campaign was undertaken to promote the fresh milk concept and word spread of the new company's dedication to quality. In a community where people were not unaccustomed to being supplied with milk that was often watered down with water from the River Thames, this unique company, promising fresh country milk, and sporting the trademark of an express locomotive, was an immediate success. Quality and cleanliness became synonymous with the company's name.

It is indeed "an ill wind that doesn't blow somebody some good", and a singular event the following year was to change the dairy industry dramatically and provide the Express Country Milk Supply Company with phenomenal success and George Barham with great wealth. The event was the breakout of hoof and mouth disease mentioned above. London area dairy herds were literally wiped out overnight, and even in the surrounding suburbs many herds had to be destroyed in order to prevent the disease from spreading to dairy herds throughout the country.

George Barham found himself in the enviable position of being one of only a few dairymen in a position to supply milk to the city of London. He quickly widened his lists of suppliers and distributors, and used the new rail system to bring milk to London from as far away as 150 miles.

A remarkable entrepreneur and inventor, George Barham spent the next few years improving the quality of milk and milk distribution methods. He is credited with the invention of the milk churn and with the development of chilling methods to keep milk fresh, as well as other milk related equipment. Such was the demand for this improved equipment that he saw a new opportunity and founded a new Company The Dairy Supply Company. In 1888 he built a new building for its headquarters **(Photo 6.4b)** and began building dairy equipment and selling it to others. [115] His son Arthur would eventually become the head of Dairy Supply and by 1900 that company was reputedly the largest supplier of dairy equipment in England.

Photo 6.4b   The Dairy Supply Co. Ltd. Building
Erected 1888, Photo c. 2011, by Ian Mansfield (www.ianvisits.co.uk)

---

[115] The building stands to this day, a historic building with the company name Dairy Supply Company Limited etched in stone and a plaque bearing the name of George Barham and others. It is located on Coptic Street in the Borough of Holborn and the lower floor is occupied by a pizzeria.

It was in 1882 that George renamed his Express Country Milk Supply Company *the Express Dairy Co. Ltd,* and by 1885 he was bringing 30,000 gallons of milk into London every night. [116] His company was also the first British dairy to use milk bottles. Although Louis Pasteur published his findings on the process of pasteurization in 1865 and George Barham was quick to recognize the advantages of pasteurization, he continued to offer raw milk to his customers into the 20th century, because the heating process needed to pasteurize required tight control to prevent over or under treating and it took many years and much experimentation for the process to be simplified and universally applied. Pasteurization would eventually transform the milk industry, by putting an end to deadly milk-borne epidemics among children. Still, it wasn't until early in the 20th century that authorities began to regulate milk processing.

George also bought a 97 acre dairy farm in London, and in 1883 thoroughly modernized it and gave it the name College Farm. An advertisement for both College Farm Milk and the Express Dairy Co. Ltd is shown in **Sketch 6.4a.**

Until recently College Farm was the only place in London where you could see cattle in a field. College Farm is in Regent's Park Road near Henly's Corner in Finchley in the London Borough of Barnet. George apparently leased Sheephouse Farm, a property of about 97 acres (390,000 m^2) as early as 1868 but in 1882/83 he had it rebuilt by Fredrick Chancellor as a model dairy farm, renaming it College Farm after the nearby Christ's College. It became a visitor attraction in 1909, but only a few of the adjacent fields from the original estate were

Sketch 6.4a
Ad for College Farm Milk
& Express Dairy Co. Ltd.

retained. By the 1930s the residue of the farm was surrounded by houses, but was open to the public, with tea rooms and an exhibition of objects related to the dairy industry. In 1973 Express Dairies left the site, and the dairy museum was broken up. A College Farm Trust has since been set up to reopen the farm as a family attraction. [117]

In 1895 George bought Sudbury Manor (the 14th century main residence for the Archbishops of Canterbury), located just west of Wembley, and renamed it Barham House.

---

[116] E.H. Whetham in his treatise 'The London Milk Trade, 1860-1900' cites the Local Government Board estimate for the year 1880 of 20,000,000 gallons of milk being brought into London by rail annually (almost 55,000 gallons per day). Granted that, because of the population growth of London, as well as the increasing desire by Londoners for fresh milk, the total annual rail quantity may have increased by 1885, the 30,000 gallons brought in daily by Barham's Express Dairies was still a substantial percentage of the whole.

[117] The preceeding paragraph includes data retrieved from http://www.wikipedia.org.

Barham Park in that area is the site of today's London Fair. For his contribution to the milk industry George Barham was knighted by Edward VII in 1904, the first dairyman to be so honored.

Sir George Barham died in 1913, and his business interests were divided between two of his sons, both of whom where integrally involved in their father's businesses at an early age. George Titus Barham ran Express Dairies, while Arthur Saxby Barham ran the Dairy Supply Company. There were three other dairy competitors when the First World War broke out, but financial considerations led the companies to discuss ways of cooperating, and because of a growing feeling that competition was unacceptable during a time of national emergency, they merged into United Dairies Ltd in 1917, under the leadership of George Titus Barham.

6.5   Transformation of the Milk Industry

With contributions from quality minded dairymen like Sir George Barham, milk gradually came to be considered an essential part of children's diets in England, as well as Europe and North America. Thanks to the work of Louis Pasteur, pasteurized milk would eventually be mass produced and sold in pint and half-pint bottles, but curiously and despite increasingly comprehensive regulation of the industry, even in the late 1930s a lot of milk was sold "raw" and had to be boiled to make it safe to drink. The dairy industry gradually became cleaner, more mechanized, and more profitable.

It is interesting to observe how the railway transformed the dairy industry, and this is nowhere more apparent than in London. In the 1850s there was a relatively small market in London, which was by then the largest city in the world, because milk was much less widely used than would be the case by the turn of the century. This limited use was partially due to the cost and the highly perishable nature of the commodity, but was also related to the difficulty in transporting the bulky product in a timely manner. Milk was more commonly used by the middle and upper classes at tea time, but the cost and the lack of any economical means of storing the product put it beyond the means of the lower and working classes.

During the last half of the 19th century it was the railroad that brought fundamental changed to the dairy industry. Railways made it possible to bring fresh milk hundreds of miles in hours, from the farm to the milk distributor, solving most of the perishability problem. Railways also made it possible to ship the heavy equipment required by the dairy farms for bottling, and eventually for pasteurizing and chilling the product. By the early 1900s, creameries were being built on or near farms (always beside a main rail line) allowing the farmers to make larger quantities of butter and cheese, while in 1903 a fully automatic bottling system became available providing a further stimulus to market expansion. [118]   Significantly, the new fully automated creameries were now able to provide bottled milk and other dairy products directly to retailers.

So it is that, during the roughly forty years after George Barham incorporated the Express Country Milk Supply Company, the milk industry went from being a "cow to customer" to a

---

[118]   Michael Owen, an Irishman, is credited with developing this equipment.

"creamery to customer" relationship. But it is at the beginning of this forty year period that opportunity was presented to Alfred James Gurr and his family.

6.6   Milk Contracting and Wholesaling

Between the dairy farmers, the London retailers and ultimate consumers of dairy products was the rail transportation system. As the railroad system extended outward from London, it sent spur lines off to more remotes areas, thus opening up access to new milk suppliers. Meanwhile the perception that the quality of milk was improved because it was "fresh from the farm", rather than from the "foul" urban dairies, helped increase the demand for fresh milk and other dairy products. With the introduction of cooling depots in the 1870s, (and later cooling rail cars) the quality of milk arriving in London was further improved, while milk storage in London was also becoming practical, extending the shelf life of the product and reducing waste. Those involved in the milk industry found new opportunities for specialization, such as contracting and wholesaling in a rapidly expanding market.

Milk contracting and wholesaling opportunities grew out of the increasing complexity of the supply and delivery system. At one end of the supply chain was the dairy farmer, whose inherent problem was variation in milk supply, not only unforeseeable from week to week, but also seasonally, being larger in the spring and lower in the fall and winter months. At the other end of the supply chain was the retailer who required a level supply of milk and other dairy products in order to supply a steady demand from the consumer. Before the arrival of the railways remote dairy farmers sold what milk they could locally and converted the excess to cheese. The railway offered individual dairy farmers the opportunity to sell large volumes directly to any number of retailers in cities such as London, but the distance between supplier and retailer presented logistical problems related to shipping and receiving, while any variation in supply was something that the retailer could not live with. These problems were overcome by the wholesaler, who offered to purchase all of the dairy farmers output and assumed the responsibility for transporting and selling that output to the retailer.

Wholesalers required personnel who would be their contact with the dairy farmers and secure contracts for farm output. This type of contracting was complex, for the contractor had to consider the logistics peculiar to the locale of the nearest rail station. Wholesalers preferred their contracts to read "delivered to London", so that the dairy farmer was responsible for the cost of rail carriage, and the wholesaler did not need to account for the differences in distance carried. But, the churns were the property of the wholesaler, and if the farmer was to ship daily, several sets of churns were required, the overall number depending on the daily maximum the farm could supply. Since the wholesaler owned the churns, it was he who had to deal with the railroad over lost or damaged churns, or any delays that resulted in the souring of the milk. It was the wholesaler who, as the consignee and thus not responsible for shipping costs, was responsible for the product once delivered to the railhead, until it reached London and landed in the hands of the retailer. Pricing was usually fixed for the year, so if a contract was to be profitable, the contractor's cost estimate had to be precise, or the wholesaler's profit line would be affected.

6.7   Gurr and Son and the Milk Industry

Throughout the 1870s, the 1880s and even the 1890s Gurr and Son and members of the Alfred Gurr family are listed in directories in various years as dairymen, wholesalers and milk contractors and this is evidence that the company and its family members had a complete farm-to-consumer approach to their market. As dairy operators they retailed directly to the consumer. As wholesalers they supplied their own dairy, their rounds-men and other small milk-sellers in Paddington. As contractors they were making direct contact with dairy farms and were responsible for their own overall profitability. The offices of Gurr and Son were located within walking distance of the Paddington Station, as was the dairy housed in the same building where they lived. As will become evident in later chapters, during the 1880s, the two brothers Richard and Edwin became more and more involved in wholesaling and contracting operations while their mother and sisters took more responsibility for operating the home-based dairy.

Once the brothers had committed Gurr and Son to whatever contracts they could establish, much hard work was required. Seven days a week, either Richard or Edwin or another reliable "platform agent" from their small company had to attend the receiving platform at Paddington Station to accept delivery of incoming milk. The platform manager had the responsibility of checking the milk for souring and the churns for damage, and for submitting claims to cover any perceived damage or loss. Once he accepted the shipment, the platform manager had to arrange for delivery of the product in a timely fashion to his dairy, the company's rounds-men and any other retailers who depended on him.

But the wholesaler's responsibility did not end here. The question of who was responsible for milk souring en-route to the London station, and for churn loss or damage was a continuous battle that had to be fought with the railroads. By the 1880s souring was becoming less of a problem, since a cooling depot was available in Paddington for temporary storage, and cooling depots were also being established at many outlying stations. The cost to the wholesaler of using the cooling depots was more than offset by the savings from avoiding souring. Because the day to day volume of incoming milk varied, the brothers often found themselves with either more milk than they could possibly use, or less than they needed to satisfy their retailers. Excess milk was sold to other wholesalers, while shortages were offset by purchasing from other wholesalers. As well as receiving and brokering milk at the platform, the wholesaler was responsible for transporting the milk safely, and without adulteration, to the retailers with whom it had negotiated contracts, and for handling any complaints from those customers.

Chapter 7
Life in London, 1861 to 1884,
A Gurr Family Perspective

7.1 England's Social and Political Environment, The Peaceful Revolution

Alfred James Gurr fathered eight children with his wife Mary Ann following their marriage in 1846. The eldest child was a daughter, Sarah Sophia, after whom three sons were born consecutively, Alfred Richard, Henry Jonathan and Edwin Robert Gurr, followed by three more daughters, Mary Ann, Emily Ann and Ellen, and finally a fourth son George James. Mary Ann passed away in December of 1862, at the age of five and George in 1864 shortly after his birth. The surviving six Gurr children were brought up in Victorian England, in a time when Brittania "ruled the waves" and English-speaking peoples were spreading their influence into the farthest corners of the globe.

The English was once derided by Napoleon as "a nation of shopkeepers", and it would seem to be true that middle-class Englishmen thought of the empire as their marketplace. The three Gurr brothers came of age in the middle of the reign of Victoria, Queen of the British Empire. She was the constitutional monarch of the United Kingdom of Great Britain, but she became Queen of each of a growing number of Commonwealth Nations. Midway through her reign she became Empress of India. The Gurr children would witness the growth of the British Empire, and watch many of their fellow "Brits" migrate to the new frontiers, as they capitalized on the British people's deep-seated confidence in their superiority in matters of trade, government, industry, science and morality.

If you ask someone of today's generation what they imagine the London of the Victorian era was like, you will probably find their responses describing an environment something akin to the fictional worlds of Jane Austen or Charles Dickens. They might envisage a world of carriages and great estates, of open fields and fox hunts, refined men and women with polite manners and good breeding, or on the other hand, of humble lodgings and slums, crowded streets and poverty, of thieves and orphans, of debtors prisons and social injustice. They will respond with their interpretation of what they have read, heard or seen in their lifetime with a bias imposed by the impression conveyed by the latest dramatic presentation they were exposed to by film makers. The writings of Austen, Dickens and others, and the movies based on their works have provided us with a welcome link to 19th century England, but they are only thumbnails linking us to an age that was a complex of dynamic industrial change, unprecedented scientific achievement, and social awakening.

A peaceful revolution was taking place, not only in England, but throughout the British Empire and the entire world. This revolution brought major advancements in transportation (the introduction and expansion of systems of canals, railways and public transportation), in communications (the introduction of telegraphy and the telephone), in health (the germ concept, pasteurization, inoculation), in welfare (control of water quality and sewerage), in technology (gas lamp lighting, steam generation, electricity) and in almost every field of human endeavor.

Just as England was the hub of the sprawling British Empire "upon which the sun never set", London was the epicenter of England and the English speaking world and arguably the leading nation in the world. Londoners considered themselves a chosen people, for London was the financial and political capitol of the British Empire. But London was changing as never before. The population of England increased from an estimated 2,500,000 at the time of the Magna Carta (1215) to about 10,000,000 in 1801, tripling to 30,000,000 by 1901, and Greater London accounted for 20 per cent of that population.

Although British subjects had begun to question aspects of their own social structure, they seldom applied this thinking to peoples who they considered less enlightened or less civilized. British boarding school education taught young men to be independent, trained them to be competitive and make the most of every opportunity, and encouraged them to accept leadership and to dominate when and where they could.

The stability of the United Kingdom under Queen Victoria was an important factor in the lives of its people. When Victoria ascended the British throne in 1837, at 18 years of age, she was not particularly popular, mainly because of her German background, but she soon became a favorite of her people and, by the end of her reign, the Empress Queen was revered. Victoria married German-born Prince Albert of Saxe-Coburg in February, 1840 and the popular consensus is that the couple were very much in love with one another. When Albert died in 1861, Victoria went into mourning for the next forty years. Albert remained Victoria's Prince consort during his lifetime, never receiving the title of King. Although he was a trusted advisor to Victoria, he generally kept out of politics, or at least this was the perception. Prince Albert was well educated and loved science. He was instrumental in arranging for the Great Exhibition of London and was the   president of the organizing committee for that event which took place in Hyde Park in 1851. The Crystal Palace and the entire exhibit, which was intended to show off the scientific and technical achievements of Great Britain, were a great success and the popularity of the royal couple soared in the following years. Victoria and Albert had nine children in all. Their first child, also named Victoria, became Queen of Prussia and Empress of Germany, while their second ascended the British throne on the death of Victoria as King Edward VII.

While her real contribution to the dynamic changes that occurred during her reign may be arguable, it was during that reign that Britain became the most powerful and prosperous nation in the world and London, its capital, the largest city in the world. Victoria took on a motherly persona and her long and stable reign provided a degree of continuity in a time of unprecedented change. The children of Alfred James would toast their Queen and country on many occasions during her lifetime, and in remembrance of her for years after her passing.

London was the heart of the British Empire and the physical changes taking place in that city in the 1860s, brought about by empire building, industrialization and population explosion were mind-boggling. Like the rest of metropolitan London, the infrastructure of the area in which the Gurr children were born and raised was torn apart and rebuilt around them. New roads and parks, a new water and sewer system, and an underground railway were constructed across the entire city, with the first underground railway terminal in their immediate neighborhood in the parish of Paddington. The new underground railway was the first subway system in the world and was an engineering marvel at the time it was built. The London sewerage system has been upgraded several times since its construction, but it is still considered one of the seven engineering wonders of the modern world.

Like so many other Londoners, the three sons of Alfred James would eventually leave their homeland confident in their ability to survive and prosper under any circumstances. Stimulated by the success stories of others, including members of their immediate and extended family, the three brothers must have dreamed of getting their share of the world's wealth. Across the seas was land that was virtually free for the asking, streams awash with gold dust, great open spaces and uncharted lands, where by one's labors an individual might become a kind of king in his own right.

7.2   London, the Center of the World

Living in the 21st century, enjoying as we do the conveniences that space age technology has provided us, it is difficult to envision the London of the lower and lower-middle classes, into which the three Gurr brothers were born in the mid-19th century. Consider what it would be like to suddenly find yourself: without running water, and having to hand-carry potable water from the nearest pump; without flush toilets and having to use chamber pots and cesspits to dispose of your excrement; without electricity and having to carry candles or gas lamps to light your way in unlit hallways and cellars and everywhere after dark; without circulated heat in your home and having to keep rooms warm by burning wood or coal in pot bellied stoves and hearths; with little in the way of affordable public transportation and having either to stay home or walk to wherever you needed to go; without free education and without free public libraries; without trained doctors and dentists and living in a world where anyone who wished could claim those titles; without all those wonderful forms of information and entertainment we now take for granted, radio, television, movies, the internet . . . the list goes on and on.

During their lifetimes, the Gurr brothers would witness the introduction of: modern water and sewerage treatment, with water piped directly into their homes and flush toilets carrying body wastes directly out; gas lamps and later electricity to light and heat their homes and power newly invented appliances; railways and public transportation systems; free public libraries and free education; modern theories of health care, with doctors and dentists trained and board certified; the invention of telegraphy, the automobile, the airplane, radio, movies, television. [119] This list also goes on and on.

---

[119] The laying of the transatlantic telegraph cable between England and the Americas was completed in mid-1865, and this meant that information could be transmitted across the Atlantic Ocean in minutes rather than weeks. The telegraph cable made distant places seem much closer, and the world became a smaller place. Governments, businesses and families found themselves able to exchange information with one another as never before. In the first half of the 19th century, it had taken sailing ships about two months to cross the Atlantic, though by mid-century with the introduction of steamships that time was reduced to fifteen days. That means that until mid-1865, for a Londoner

During the early years of their father, Alfred James, the antiquated water and sewerage systems in London contributed to staggering losses of life from repeated epidemics, while the lack of adequate transportation facilities led to virtual gridlock in the streets. The reconstruction of London's infrastructure began in the mid 1850s, when the Gurr brothers were infants and continued into the mid 1870s, when they were young adults. The brothers witnessed the massive water, sewerage and underground transportation system excavations that took place in their immediate neighborhood (Paddington Station was a short walking distance from their residence and was the first underground station of the new system). They survived the last great cholera epidemic of 1866. They would see "germ theory", the concept of the germ as a cause of illness, finally accepted, thanks to the father of microbiology Louis Pasteur, and attention to public health concerns improve dramatically.

What an exciting age it was! It was a time when every aspect of life was being examined and questioned. Social change was everywhere. The works of Charles Dickens (1812-1870) had people thinking about the lot of the poorest Londoners and questioning social norms. The works of Charles Darwin (1809-1882) had everyone talking about evolution and religion. The works of Karl Marx (1818-1883) had people pondering the pros and cons of a classless society. The three brothers probably laughed together at the similarities, real or imagined, bordering on their own lives that they noted in Dickens novels. They might have had some hilarious moments together considering Darwin's *Origin of Species* and comparing themselves to the great apes. They lived in a society that was class conscious and very capitalistic, but slowly progressing towards a more social welfare state. In their wildest dreams they would not have foreseen the coming spread of communism and fascism.

The Gurr brothers witnessed an almost exponential expansion of the British Empire during the 19th century and India, to which young Henry sailed as a cabin boy in the late 1860s, was included in that expansion. [120] Although the British presence in India dated back to 1600, when Queen Elizabeth I granted a royal charter to a new trading company formed by London merchants, which became known as the East India Company, India did not become part of the British Empire until the middle of the 1800s. In the intervening years, the East India Company became a world power with political sovereignty over a vast region occupied by hundreds of millions of people who were without representation. From the beginning there was turmoil and rebellion in many of the Indian kingdoms until the Indian Rebellion of 1857 ended the domination of the trading company. The Raj [121] officially began in 1858 when control of the

---

to ask a question of someone in New York and get an answer back took at least a month, but thereafter, it was possible to get a response in a matter of minutes.

[120] Late in life the Reverend Gurr wrote his memoirs, 'A Red-Blooded Anglican,' and they probably included recollections of his youthful visits to Indian ports. The ship or ships on which he sailed would have been his among the first to transit the Suez Canal. But as explained in Chapter 11.26, the memoirs have been lost.

[121] The British Raj (Raj is hindi for "rule") was the term used for the period (1858 to 1947), as well as the region (India, Pakistan, Bangladesh, Aden, Burma, Singapore and other princely states, and for a time British Somaliland

entire region was transferred to the Crown in the person of Queen Victoria, who became Empress of India in 1877.

By the 1870s British explorers, whalers and merchants had been sailing the world for centuries and wonderful stories of discovery were told and retold. Yet, details of the world's geography remained unknown. Exploration of the Arctic had been underway for several years, but the fate of the Royal Navy Admiral Sir John Franklin in his search for the Northwest Passage was still being debated, and the search for that route continued. At the opposite end of the globe, Antarctica had been sighted in 1820, but that region was risky for wooden-hulled sailing ships and steam driven steel shipbuilding was in its infancy.

During the 1870s, South Africa became part of the British Empire and large sections of Africa were or would soon become British protectorates, including Nigeria, Tanganyika, Kenya, and parts of Egypt. The Suez Canal was built by French-Egyptian interests and opened in 1869, but the Egyptian share in the canal was bought by the British in the year 1875, and in 1882 the British seized control of the canal to protect their interests. Most of the rest of Africa was still the Dark Continent, with its interior almost totally unexplored by Europeans. Missionaries had penetrated the interior and the much publicized search by the American newsman Stanley for the Scottish missionary Livingstone culminated in his being discovered alive in 1871, and "Livingstone, I presume" was headlined around the world. The British enthusiasm for travel and adventure was captured in Jules Verne's *Around the World in 80 Days*, published in 1872

7.3 London's Suburbs:

Manors - Administrative Parishes - Boroughs

During the middle ages the principal unit of local administration and justice in the villages surrounding London had been the manor. With the manors and Roman Catholic parishes often sharing the same boundaries, it was the church that eventually replaced the manor court as the administrative authority, with entitlement to levy taxes. Eventually, all responsibilities of the Lord of the Manor passed to the church and were administered by the Roman Catholic monasteries. With England's reformation and the eventual dissolution of monasteries by Henry VIII, it was the Church of England parish authorities or "vestries" who assumed these responsibilities. Initially the vestries included all the inhabitants of a parish, but this became more and more difficult as populations grew. Gradually "selected vestries" took over administrative responsibilities. This Parish system relied on the monopoly of the Church of England but, as Methodists and other religious groups became more powerful, the legitimacy of one group to dictate to another came into question.

During the 19th century parish vestries gradually began to lose their powers to ad-hoc boards and other civil organizations. The split between civil and ecclesiastical parishes was completed by the Local Government Act of 1894 which abolished vestries and required elected parish councils in all civil parishes. In 1899, the London Government Act was passed by the

---

and Iraq), referring to the rule of the British on the Indian subcontinent and adjacent areas. Ceylon (Sri Lanka) was a British Crown Colony and the Maldive Islands were a Protectorate but neither were considered part of the Raj. Nepal and Bhutan were kingdoms within the region not considered part of the British Empire.

Parliament of the United Kingdom, dividing the County of London into 28 Municipal Boroughs (from 41 Parish Vestries and District Boards of Works which previously administered the area).

Relief of the poor is an example of one of the responsibilities that was transferred from the Lord of the Manor to the monasteries and then to the parish vestries. The 1601 Act for the Relief of the Poor allowed the parish vestries to levy a tax to fund relief of the poor. The Poor Law Amendment Act of 1834 permitted replacement "boards" to levy their own taxes in the parish, and as a result church taxes ceased to be levied in many parishes. Church taxes were abolished altogether in 1868, following the Poor Law Amendment Act of 1866 which required all areas that levied a separate rate to become *civil* parishes. Large towns originally split between multiple parishes were eventually consolidated into a single parish.

Education was another parish responsibility that underwent dramatic changes during the 19th century. As late as the beginning of the Victorian period (1837 - 1901) the majority of children in England received no formal education and the literacy rate was perhaps 50%, with girls generally excluded from receiving any formal education. Moreover, in this class conscious society, it is estimated that only one in seven lower class children knew how to read and write. The social awakening that took place during the middle of the 19th century led to the passing of an 1870 law requiring all children between the ages of six and twelve, inclusive, to attend school.

One of the new Boroughs created by the 1899 London Government Act was the Borough of Paddington, previously a unit of civil government called the Parish of Paddington. All civil parishes were formally abolished in London in 1965 when Greater London was created and ultimately, the Municipal Borough of Paddington became part of the City of Westminster in 1974. The growth of Paddington during the 19th century was remarkable. Paddington was a rural farming community at the beginning of the 19th century, but the rapid expansion of London westward resulted in a population growth of the settlement from less than 2000 individuals in 1801 to almost 150,000 by 1901.

7.4   Paddington in the 19th Century

The first reference to Paddington as an "established" community is from 1773, when a historian referred to it as one of 46 villages surrounding London. [122]   A map from 1755 is the first verifiable document we were able to find referring to Paddington as a settlement. [123]   That document concerned a proposed new road, extending from Islington to Paddington, ordered to be built by an Act of Parliament, though the details of the road had as yet not been finalized. The map shows open fields and farms with little, if any residential development. The road, as proposed in this document, would originate in Islington, run north of Oxford Street and pass through the small village of Marylebone to Paddington.

The importance of improving roadways became apparent by the middle of the 18th century. The Industrial Revolution resulted not only in an enormous increase in the demand for coal and other raw materials, but also ever-increasing volumes of finished goods that required a

---

[122]   Noorthouck J, (1773) *A New History of London.* (Book 2, Chapter. 1)

[123]   Plan of the intended road from Islington to Paddington, 1755 Benjamin Cole in *Gentleman's Magazine* vol.25

means of distribution. This demand was far greater than the capacity of England's few bumpy roads and the horse-drawn conveyances used to transport those goods. Moreover, the few roadways (and barges on the waterways) that were in use could not support the heavier and bulkier equipment required by industry at sites where suitable labor was available.

The first answer to the transportation problem was to expand the capabilities of water transport by building canals. Between the 1760s and 1830s canals were built in many parts of England, and narrow barges were employed to carry goods and materials back and forth along the equally narrow canals throughout the country. Canals ran from Birmingham to Northampton to Paddington with branches to other cities in the north and south of England. The Grand Junction Canal between Braunston and Paddington is part of the Grand Union Canal System which is operational today and still expanding, but is now used primarily by pleasure craft. The advantage of Paddington's geographical position soon became apparent.

The 1801 census shows Paddington with 1,881 inhabitants, but it developed into a major borough of London during the next century. It had a population of 46,305 in 1851, which more than tripled to 143,976 by the 1901 census, then held steady until WWII, before dropping steadily thereafter. [124] The population surge began in 1801 following the completion of construction of the Grand Junction Canal connecting Braunston in Northamptonshire with Uxbridge and then with Paddington Basin. Paddington Basin became the terminus of a canal system that brought barges from all over England to the outskirts of London, and Paddington became the gateway to London from the west. Unfortunately, when the Regent's Canal was completed in 1820, there was a more direct water communication with the Thames at Limehouse, and as a result Paddington Basin lost importance for a few years.

Then, in 1833, the London and Paddington Steam Carriage Company began running an omnibus service from Paddington to the City of London, making travel easier between these areas. In 1836 the Great Western Railway made Paddington its terminus, and the area became the rail gateway to the West and South West of England. By mid-century, the rural village of Paddington had become a thriving commercial community of over 50,000. Large stately homes were built in the region north of Hyde Park and Kensington Gardens and the borough continued to expand at the rate of about 2000 inhabitants per year. In 1853, the Bayswater, Paddington, and Holborn Bridge Railway Company proposed an underground railway. The world's first underground rail system - the Metropolitan Line running between Paddington and Farringdon by way of Kings Cross - opened in London on Saturday, January 10, 1863.

In 1850, Alfred James Gurr and his wife Mary Ann moved to Paddington with their first daughter Sarah Sophia, soon after she was born in Peckham. In Paddington they had seven more children over the next dozen years, three boys, then three girls and finally another son. The Gurr family was the beneficiary of the remarkable changes that had taken place in the decades prior to their arrival, changes which had raised Paddington from a rural farm community to a thriving municipal community.

---

[124] From Census Tables in *Metropolitan Borough of Paddington, Statistical Abstract for London*, 1901 (Vol IV).

The Gurr brothers grew up within a few hundred yards of the newly constructed western terminus of the Metropolitan line, Paddington Station. Their residence during the 1861 census is listed as 488 Stanley St., but soon after all Stanley St. homes and many other homes west of Stanley were demolished to make room for the Paddington Terminus. In the late spring of 1861 the family relocated to 4 Upper Southwick St and a few years late to 38 Southwick St. That location, less than a half mile from Paddington Station, became a family residence as well as the family business address until the middle of the 1890s. The construction of the Paddington terminus and the proximity of the new rail system to their home may well have influenced Alfred James's decision to become a dairyman, and there is no doubt that the expansion of the British rail system contributed to the success of his new business, allowing fresh milk and other dairy products to be brought into London daily. Emily Ann, the third daughter was the last known Gurr occupant of 38 Southwick during the 1891 census, wherein her occupation is recorded as dairy-keeper. She was the only one of the children of Alfred James Gurr family that was still involved in the family dairy business. Edwin was still listed in that census as a milk wholesaler, though we do not know whether he was an independent or in the employ of his cousin George Barham or another dairy company.

It is not unlikely that the three brothers and other members of the Gurr family were among the 38,000 people who rode the new Metropolitan underground railway on its first day of operation. It is certain that the advent of the railway and the expansion of rail systems in England and in other parts of the world altered the course of their lives.

The Gurr brothers travelled many thousands of miles by rail. In 1869 a transcontinental railway was completed across the American continent. During the following twenty years each of the three brothers, accompanied by their families, would ride that railway from sea to sea, and two of them (Henry and Edwin) made that journey several times. Eventually all three brothers would leave England behind them. It was the railways that carried them across the North American continent to their new homes near the Pacific Ocean.

7.5   Paddington Churches

The parish that would become Paddington actually dates back to the middle ages, at which time there was a chapel on Paddington Green, a chapel of ease to the Parish of St. Margaret's, Westminster with that rectory held by the Abbey of St. Peter at Westminster. The Paddington chapel was moved or rebuilt from time to time and may have been known as St. James or St. Mary's before 1788-1791. In 1791, a new church was built just to the south of the original chapel and dedicated as St. Mary's. A second church, St. James was built as the population increased, but with the population explosion centered south of Paddington Green during the 19th century the old Parish of Paddington was gradually divided into several smaller ecclesiastical parishes. St. James was moved south to a site between Sussex Gardens and Gloucester Terrace in the early 1840s, and became the Administrative Parish Church of the District of Paddington in 1845. The growth of the congregation at St. James was such that in 1882 a new church was built, enclosing the old so that services would not be interrupted.

St. James was the Parish Church of Paddington during the time the Gurr family resided there, but there were a half dozen other churches near their 38 Southwick home, including St. John's in Southwick Crescent which was erected in 1831. St. John's the Evangelist was the church nearest to the residence of the Gurr family, at a walking distance of no more than five minutes, but there is no evidence that the family ever attended there. St. Michael's and All Angels on Market Street was another parish within a reasonable walking distance, as was All Saints, Norfolk Square, and even St. James, Westbourne Terrace was less than a mile away. There were 21 Parish Churches in Paddington in 1903, as shown in **Table 7.5a**, and most of these were open while Alfred Gurr family members were resident there from the 1860s until the late 1890s.

Table 7.5a		**List of Ecclesiastic Parishes, Paddington from 1903 Map** [125]
1	St. John	Kensal Green
2	St. John	Harrow Road, Kensal Green
3	St. Jude	Lancefield St., Kensal Green
4	St. Luke	Fernhead Road, Kilburn
5	St. Simon	Saltram Crescent
6	St. Saviour	Warwick Road
7	St. Augustine	Kilburn
8	Emmanuel	Harrow Road
9	St. Peter	Chippenham Road
10	St. Paul	Marlborough Place, Harrow Road Also Known as Christ Church
11	St. Mary Magdelen	Delamere Terrace
12	St. Luke	Tavistock Road
13	St. Stephen	Westbourne Park
14	Holy Trinity	Bishops Road
15	St. Mary	Paddington Green
16	St. Matthew	Moscow Road, Bayswater
17	Christ Church	Lancaster Gate
18	St. James	Westbourne Terrace Civil Administrative Parish (Hyde
19	All Saints	Norfolk Square
20	St. Michael, All Angels	Market Street
21	St. John the Evangelist	Southwick Crescent

---

[125] Parish boundaries traced from "*A map of the Ecclesiastical Divisions within the County of London, 1903*" published by Edward Stanford of London, reprinted as a facsimile by the London Topographical Society. List from that map is of parishes within the rural deanery of Paddington in 1903; they were all sub-divisions of the historic parish of Paddington.

Which church did the family attend? **Map 7.5b** shows all the Parishes of Paddington as well as the locations of the Alfred James Gurr home and the churches the family frequented. We know that Sarah Sophia was baptized at St. Giles, Camberwell, before the family moved to Paddington. All three sons, Alfred Richard, Henry Jonathan and Edwin Robert were baptized at St. James, the Parish Church of Paddington on Westbourne Terrace. Mary Ann, Emily Ann and Ellen were baptized at All Saints, Norfolk Square. When Ellen married Hugh Stott in 1881 they were married at St. Michael and All Angels, Market Street. These three churches, St. James, All Saints and St. Michael All Angels were ecclesiastical parishes within the Administrative Parish of St. James. Only St. John the Evangelist and St. James are still open today.

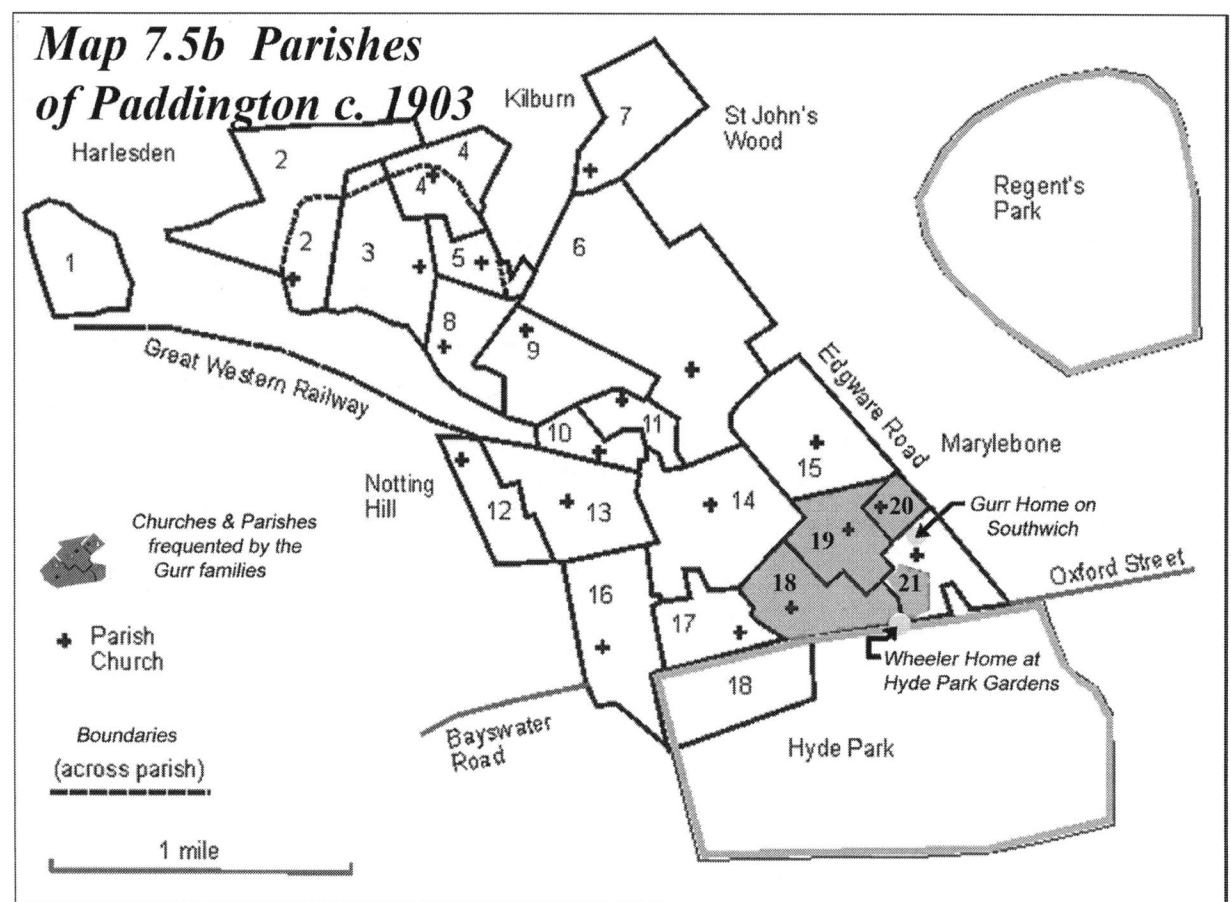

7.6   Housing in London and Suburbs

During the first half of the 19th century the migration of workers from rural to urban areas in search of work led to overcrowding and pollution on an unprecedented scale. This was especially true in London which by the 1840s had become the largest, most densely populated city in the world. The wealthier upper and middle class residents of London soon found themselves surrounded and pressed upon by ever-increasing numbers of lower class workers. Rather than rub shoulders with the multitudes, or suffer through the increasing stench from the growing number of cesspits and the increased volume of garbage, the wealthy escaped the developing slums and exposure to the miasma of the poor by moving into the surrounding countryside. Suburban London became a reality as villages such as Paddington, Kensington, Ealing and Chelsea began to develop.

Nowhere was it truer than in England: "A man's home is his castle." The desire to improve one's station in life, to rise from a lower to a higher class, to ultimately become one of the upper class, permeated English society. One's success in attaining this objective became linked to his dwelling. When moving to the suburbs, the upper classes and the wealthier members of the upper middle class continued to build their homes to suit their needs and, since money was no problem, the homes they built were usually unique and isolated. But the middle class was growing in numbers as never before and, by the middle of the 19th century, developers were building thousands of homes in the expanding suburbs, with surprisingly similar layouts, to satisfy the middle class trend to follow the upper classes out of the city.

Judith Flanders, in her book *The Victorian House*, provides us with a surprising statistic. Of more than six million terraced houses built in Britain during the reign of Victoria and the years preceding World War I, the majority are still in use in the twenty-first century. They are unique in that, while most other developing countries in the world were solving the housing problem inherent in the mushrooming growth of the middle class by building communal housing (multi-storied horizontal apartments with a common entrance, hallways, stairways, etc), British housing was single family housing, multi-storied with each house having a private entrance, its own hallways and layouts suited to the occupying family.

This was the case in suburban London, where side by side dwellings and multi-dwelling tenements were very popular with the middle classes, and were built multi-storied or vertical for each family. Most were built with a basement or half basement, a ground floor (raised for those with a half basement) and one or two stories above ground. The number of levels depended upon the number of bedrooms the family desired. Bedrooms were on the upper floors in all homes, the larger homes having studies and dressing rooms adjacent to the bedrooms.

The ground floor of larger dwellings might have a parlor, drawing room and dining room, and since this floor was usually the only area that visitors would be allowed to see, it was furnished and decorated with the best the family could afford without being ostentatious. Middle class Victorian drawing rooms were maintained in a fashion that reflected the status of the home owner. In the drawing room family members sat amongst their finest possessions, wore their finest clothes, and displayed their best manners to their family and their guests. In a class-based society such as Victorian England one strove to improve one's position and the benchmarks of success were set by the ruling and upper classes. Not only were these classes wealthy enough to afford the finest possessions, but they were also expected to have fine manners and in keeping with "noblesse oblige" to treat others with kindness and respect. London's middle class drawing rooms reflected these values. The idea that one's moral worth was represented by his possessions was pervasive. Perhaps it was a fundamental belief that one could not maintain success in any station of life without a high level of morality.

The ground floor of smaller dwellings had no drawing room and probably no dining room, but had a parlor with a kitchen and scullery behind it. The kitchen and scullery were in the basement alongside pantries, larders and other storage areas in larger homes. Although most middle class Victorians would have agreed that the purpose of the kitchen was for cooking only, the reality in the less affluent homes was that the kitchen also served as a bedroom for the domestic servant and frequently for one or more members of the family. Even in the larger or wealthier homes, which tended to have more servants, the kitchen and scullery were used as sleeping quarters for the domestics and occasionally for members of the family.

Kitchen ranges fired with coke were introduced in the early 1800s, but did not become common until the 1850s, so in the first half of the 19th century most of the cooking was done on an open hearth. The new kitchen ranges supplied the hot water for the house, and for this reason it usually ran most of the day and all year round. Fumes and soot accumulated in the kitchen and drifted upward into the family quarters. Since basement kitchens were common and were often without windows or other means of ventilation, the accumulation of fumes from the range and from cooking food could prove dangerous to the occupants. Indoor pollution was spread not only from the kitchen range, but also by back-drafts from hearths and from the burning of oil and gas lamps and candles. Soot from the coke, used as fuel for heating and for cooking in virtually every dwelling in London, vented from millions of chimneys, mixed with the damp air and drifted into every nook and cranny, blanketing the entire city.

Until the mid 1850s most London basements were waste storage areas, not only for ashes and other household refuse, but also for the storage of human waste in cesspits under the house, while most homes had outdoor privies in back. There was no routine municipal collection of garbage until the mid 1870s, and it was a common practice for London home owners to pay dustmen to pick up the ashes and even to sell the accumulated human waste as fertilizer.

Bathrooms began to appear in newly-built larger homes in the 1850s, but many of these still had lavatories at the back of the house. The Gurr family would have been quite familiar with the stench that then plagued London year round, and which became almost unbearable during the summer months, generated by the thousands of cesspools throughout the city, as well as by the polluted River Thames into which most human waste was dumped. As late as the 1870s smaller dwellings had no bathrooms and the lavatory was reached from the outside rear of the house, with a cesspit behind and below the scullery. But, by the 1870s the British were becoming health conscious, and because they associated the smell of human waste with disease, they were demanding improved bathrooms and modern flush toilets, and these started to become common in home construction. [126] This increased volume of waste material from flush toilets put a strain on the Thames, as the following passage suggests.

---

[126] Flush toilets were a wondrous novelty at the Great Exhibition in London in 1851. The Crystal Palace had the first major installment of public toilets, called the Retiring Rooms, in which sanitary engineer George Jennings installed his "Monkey Closet" flushing lavatories. Initially they were just for men, but such was the interest in them, that they began to cater to women as well. During the exhibition, 827,280 visitors paid one penny each to use them. This is often given as the origin of the British euphemism "to spend a penny."

On 3 September 1878 the paddle steamer *Princess Alice* was taking a "moonlight trip" down the lower Thames.

> Struck by a collier…she sank within minutes, taking 650 passengers down with her. Those who weren't trapped inside did not so much drown as succumb to sewage, millions of gallons of which had just been released from newly completed outflows for London's waste. There isn't much romance in an ordinary boat being rammed, sinking like a stone….and leaving survivors bobbing for a few minutes in shit. [127]

A massive effort began in the 1860s to correct these very serious water and sewerage problems. London went through an infrastructural revolution as a new sewerage system was constructed. One can only image how stressful a time this must have been for the city's population with most of the city's already congested streets closed or partially blocked at one time or another during the burial of thousands of miles of sewer pipe. [128] But, by the end of the 19th century the Thames through London began to recover, for the new sewerage system was completed and the effluent was diverted downstream.

7.7   Water Supply

Improvements in water supply through the first half of the 19th century had been slow, but gradually there was conversion from wooden to iron piping and sand filtering of the water by some suppliers. However, there were a number of water supply companies in metropolitan London by the 1850s, all taking water from the Thames, and the farther downstream (east) a water supplier's intake was, the more contaminated was the water. The 1872 Metropolis Water Act created a Metropolitan Commission of Sewers, and within a few years it became illegal to draw water from the Thames anywhere near the city of London, and water supply companies were forced to source their water well upstream. It also became mandatory to filter all water used for human consumption. New cast iron water lines were being installed throughout the city to comply with the new regulations and to provide cold water directly to the kitchens of homes in new housing developments. Even by 1870 few homes had water piped to their upper floors, where water pitchers and wash basins were kept in bedrooms to allow family members to wash up in the morning. In homes without servants, baths were usually taken in kitchens to avoid carrying water to higher elevations

---

[127]   From a review of new books on the sinking of the Titanic by Thomas Laqueur, (January 2013). 'Why name a ship after a defeated race?' *London Review of Books*, vol. 35, no. 2, p. 6.

[128]   Following the Great Stink of 1858, the urgent need for immediate construction of a metropolitan sewerage system became obvious to all. Sewerage ran along city streets in open culverts which emptied into the Thames River from one end of the city to the other. The plan was monumental, requiring diversion of all of the cities sewerage into the Thames Estuary, well downstream from the city. Over 100 miles of large intercepting sewers were built first, then 450 miles of main sewers connecting to the intercepting sewers, while the main sewers were fed by 13,000 miles of smaller local sewers. At first the system depended on gravity for its flow, but eventually pumping stations were introduced and later sewerage treatment plants were installed to partially neutralize the waste's effect on the Thames.

From the mid 1850s most new homes were built with cold water piped directly into the scullery, but cold water piping to upper levels (and to areas converted into bathrooms) was rare until the 1870s. In newer areas it was expensive, but practical to have cold water piping installed from the local water company's mains to older dwellings, and these conversions became common by the 1870s. Hot water piping (with water heated at the kitchen range) became available to the wealthy as early as the 1840s, but it was not until the 1870s that middle-class houses were routinely built with this feature. Until 1902, water supply was sporadic rather continuous and since water might be available to any district for only an hour or two a day, and not every day of the week, many middle class dwellings were built with cisterns to ensure a constant water supply. In some older areas of London standpipes for communal use by the poor were still in use till the end of the 19th century.

Although water was being pumped to many parts of London in the early 1860s, and the larger and wealthier homes had cold water piped into them, a substantial majority of homes did not. When the Gurr family moved to Southwick Street in 1861 they moved into an upscale neighborhood where cold water piping and sewerage systems were gradually being introduced into most of the newer homes and some of the older ones. Without both a cold water supply and a suitable sewer system few homes were able to accommodate the new flush toilets, which became commercially available during the early 1860s.

Since the Gurr children lived with their parents in an older structure on Stanley Street until 1861, it is almost certain that their lodgings had neither running water, nor a sewer system during their early years. The Gurr brothers probably carried water from a local pump when they were very young, and they would certainly have become accustomed to homes having an outhouse near, or a cesspool beneath them, as was normal in many districts as late as the 1870s. Emigrating to the American West in their later years, they would return to more primitive but familiar surroundings, where outhouses were common and fresh water had to be carried from its source.

Chapter 8
The Sons of Alfred James Gurr,
An Introduction

8.1   General Introduction

In keeping with the prevailing attitude towards women in England during the male-dominated mid-19th century this chapter focuses on the males in the Gurr family, not least because all three brothers eventually migrated to North America, leaving their sisters behind. Chapter 9 summarizes what we know of their sisters' less eventful lives.

It is difficult to assess the social status of the Gurr family in the early 1860s. At the beginning of that decade, the children were the offspring of a butler, and by the end of that decade they were the sons and daughters of a dairyman. Although butlers were the elite of the domestic servant class, they would at best be considered lower middle class, while a dairyman was at best lower middle class. Alfred Richard, the eldest son and therefore according to custom the natural heir, was sent off to boarding school at an early age. We do not know how or where Henry and Edwin were educated, but family tradition makes it almost certain that they also experienced boarding school at some stage of their childhood.

During the 1870s the Gurr family had aspirations of bettering its situation and was in a stage of transition. Before his death in 1874, the one-time butler, one-time dairyman Alfred James had founded a milk contracting firm, Gurr and Son, taking advantage of the convergence of new economic and transportation opportunities. Initially, we believe that the Gurrs bought milk from dairy farms outside London and sold it to dairymen for distribution in London. Gradually, the whole Gurr family, with the exception of the adventurous Henry Jonathan, became involved in the enterprise, and by the end of the 1870s the family had worked its way into middle class status. By the end of the 1880s the fruits of the father's ambition were realized and under the management of Alfred and Edwin, with support from their mother and sisters, the family became financially comfortable. Of some social significance is the fact that, thanks to the family business, coupled with technological and social changes, the three surviving sisters were employed with their brothers at some time during their lives.

It is safe to say that being very close to one another in age the three brothers had similar childhood learning experiences. They had one older sister, Sarah, who was seven when Edwin the youngest son was born (at which time Alfred Richard was four and Henry was two). Sarah would probably have been responsible for baby-sitting her brothers on occasion, but they must have been a handful for a seven year old, and too dominant for her to control as they grew older.

The brothers were inseparable when they were very young, and as they grew older they exhibited a lifelong tendency to stay in touch with one another. They sought one another's company whenever the opportunity arose, following one after another to America, albeit over a thirty year span. Their characters, and reasoned decisions for leaving London for America, are detailed in Part II.

8.2.1 Education of the Gurr Children

Until 1870, it was a child's parents' responsibility to arrange and pay for whatever education they wanted for that child. At the start of the 19th century the majority of girls and boys in England grew up without even the most elementary education. The ruling classes thought it would be dangerous to educate the poor, while employers were afraid that educating the lower classes would rob them of their work force. Subsequently, until 1870, education in England was largely a private affair with wealthier parents sending their children to fee-paying schools and the less fortunate using whatever local teaching was available. It is also worth noting that, although it was common practice in the late 1850s (when the first Gurr children began their schooling) for middle and upper class children to begin their formal education at the age of five or earlier, rarely did this apply to women of the lower classes, who were generally schooled at home. Moreover, lower class children were generally excluded from any formal education, unless they received it through some church or other charitable association. One literacy study shows that only 1 child in 8.36 of the population was attending school in 1851 and that this improved to only 1 child in 7.7 in 1861 (Newcastle Commission, 1861, p. 87). Another alarming statistic is that in 1841 England, 33% of men and 44% of women signed marriage certificates with their mark, unable to write their names.

Unlike Scotland, which had established regulations for education and for funding education of all children by act of the Parliament of Scotland in 1633, England and Wales avoided any responsibility for education until 1833, when for the first time limited funding was provided in support of schoolhouse construction for the Anglican National Society and the nonconformist British and Foreign School Society, whose charters addressed education of the poor. [129] Social pressure was such that by 1870, the British Government felt compelled to respond and finally passed the Elementary Education Act. In response, London initiated steps to set up a school board, and in 1871 the newly assembled London School Board instituted, for the first time, a policy of compulsory education, compelling parents to enroll all children between the ages of 5 and 13 in school. Attendance was not immediately enforced, except for children between 5 and 10 years of age (even this was not true for the rest of Britain until 1880).

The new regulations probably had little effect upon the Gurr family. By 1871, Edwin was sixteen and employed full time outside the Gurr and Son family business, while Emily was thirteen and Ellen nine. It seems unlikely that Edwin received any education beyond his 13th birthday but his two younger sisters may have somehow benefitted from the education reforms that gradually took place during the 1860s and 1870s, while the eldest sister (born in 1849) probably received little in the way of a formal education. Since there were National and other charitable schools in the district of Paddington during the 1860s and 1870s it is very likely that some of the Gurr children, including the younger daughters, attended these schools. It wasn't until the early 1890s that the school leaving age was raised from 10 to 13 throughout Britain, and

---

[129] For over two centuries, Scotland led all European nations in literacy. While never free, the cost of education was kept exceptionally low, with funding for the very poor provided by taxes and charity, in an atmosphere of recognition of the importance of literacy for all God's people.

the state began paying for all children attending state run schools. In 1902 the religious schools also became state funded.

Family tradition suggests specifically that the Gurr children attended Bayswater schools. Included amongst those that carried the name Bayswater by the year 1870 were Bayswater National (founded 1832), Bayswater Ragged (1850), Bayswater R.C. (1857) and Bayswater Jewish (1867). Historically, there was only one school in the Paddington in 1795, and that a Sunday school. Gradually Church, Public and Private schools were added. There were 16 private schools in Paddington in 1828 (five of them with Bayswater in the name). There were 69 private schools listed by 1863 (50 ladies and 19 gentlemen's) almost all with Bayswater addresses.

With one exception, that of the eldest son Alfred Richard, the fact is that we have little evidence as to how and where the children of Alfred James were educated, nor of the level of education each child attained. Based on the education level his children achieved, it is probable that Alfred James paid most of the expenses involved in their education, with the notable exception of the very well educated elder son. Alfred Richard was fortunate enough to attend Christ's Hospital and became a "Blue Coat." The significance of that may be deduced from the following details on that institution.

8.2.2 Christ's Hospital

Christ's Hospital was opened in 1552 and granted a Royal Charter by Edward VI in 1553. The fifteen year old King Edward, moved by a sermon by Nicholas Ridley, Bishop of London encouraging mercy for the poor, wrote to the Lord Mayor of London asking him to take action to correct the problem, and the mayor set up a committee of Protestant merchants to oversee the venture. The dissolution of the monasteries and the seizure of church properties by Henry VIII had thrown the poor and destitute out onto the street. Henry had granted the use of Greyfriars to the city before he died. Edward granted the Palace of Bridewell, his lands at the Savoy, and other rents and chattels to create three Hospitals, including Christ's at Newgate, exclusively for the education of the poor. [130] As early as the 1560s, graduates of Christ's Hospital went on to both Oxford and Cambridge. **Sketch 8.2.2a** on the following page depicts the Great Hall of Christ's Hospital, probably in the early 19th century. [131]

The school was known for the Tudor uniform: long blue coat, knee-breeches, yellow socks, and bands at the neck. The nickname "Blue-coat School" came from the blue coats worn by the students and its graduates were called Blues (**Photo 8.2.2b,** following page).

---

[130] Newgate on Newgate Street, was one of the historic seven gates of London Wall round the City of London and one of the six which date back to Roman times. Christ's Hospital used some of the monastery buildings on Newgate Street to house its students, while the students attended Christ Church, Greyfriars near the monastery. The gate itself was used as Newgate Prison, but was demolished in 1767.

[131] From Wikipedia Christ's Hospital site.

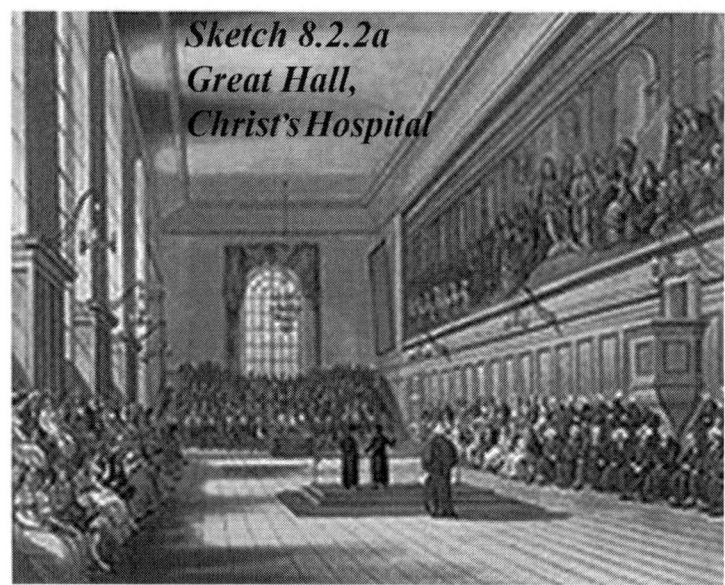

Sketch 8.2.2a
Great Hall,
Christ's Hospital

Photo 8.2.2b A Blue Coat

The history of this statue at
Christ's Hospital Hertford
dates back to 1721
www.hertford.net/history/bluecoats.asp

Although Christ's Hospital occupied Newgate for almost 350 years, the children attending were often housed elsewhere from time to time, especially during the Great Plague of 1665 and the Great Fire of London in 1666, when most of the buildings were destroyed (there were no casualties among the children). It took more than thirty years to rebuild the school and Christ Church, which was also destroyed in the 1666 fire. [132] Most of the girls attending Christ's Hospital in 1707 were sent to Hertford in that year. In 1761 some 200 boys were also relocated to Hertford, on a site about 30 miles due north of the City of London. During the 1790s the Hertford school was rebuilt, in order to accommodate the growing number of students. [133] Much later, land outside Horsham, Sussex was purchased and a new site completed in 1902. The Horsham school became the boy's school and Hertford the girl's school. The schools became co-educational once again in 1985 when the Hertford School was sold and the Hersham School took all students.

8.3   Alfred Richard Gurr

Alfred Richard was born March 13, 1851 while his parents were living on Conduit Street in Paddington, Middlesex and his father Alfred James was a butler at the Henry James Wheeler residence at Hyde Park. He was baptized on April 20, 1851 at St. James Paddington.

During the 1861 census the younger Alfred was in boarding school at Christ's Hospital Hertford, and was there enumerated. The ten-year-old Alfred Richard was one of 348 students

---

[132]   Christopher Wren designed the new church and Nicholas Hawksmoor designed the school.

[133]   Christ's Hospital graduates from this period include James Leigh Hunt, Charles Lamb, and Samuel Taylor Coleridge.

admitted that year, 37 of them girls. The boys were between 7 and 11, while the girls were 9 to 14 years of age. Records of admission show that Alfred Richard was admitted "clothed" on April 28, 1859 and discharged to the care of his father on March 10, 1866, age 15. That Alfred Richard was fortunate enough to have attended Christ's Hospital charity school is a benefit of his father Alfred James' employment by the proctor Henry James Wheeler. The recommendation by Wheeler forms part of the presentation papers submitted to the school, which undoubtedly ensured Alfred Richard's admission. This should in no way diminish the boy's contribution to his cause, for he must have shown some academic excellence to have been considered by the school.

The primary curriculum for the poor boys and girls admitted into the Christ's Hospital included reading, writing and arithmetic, but they were also exposed to science and the arts and were given an education that came close to that received by the upper classes. The original founders intended the school for poorer class children, but over time respect for the school's customs and high character attracted many middle class students as well, and it became one of the most prestigious educational establishments in Great Britain.

Alfred Richard was discharged from Christ's Hospital into his father, Alfred James's care in 1866, but the discharge documents show him officially apprenticed to a London stationer, for which his father paid an immediate £30 apprenticeship fee. We do not know how long Alfred Richard remained as an apprentice, but during the 1871 census, he is recorded as a dairyman's assistant working for this father in the family business Gurr and Son.

Alfred Richard married Emily Hunter on Dec 11, 1872 in Christ Church in Camberwell, Southwark and the couple had twelve children by early 1889. **Photo 8.3a** on the following page shows the family in a London garden c. 1887. During the 1881 census Alfred Richard is recorded as a Milk Contractor and jointly, with his brother Edwin, as heads of Gurr and Son at 38 Southwick in Paddington. At this time the census record indicates that they employed seven men and three women.

Alfred James, the father of the two Milk Contractors who headed up Gurr and Son passed away in 1874 and under normal inheritance law his estate would have passed to his eldest son, but Alfred James bequeathed his entire estate to his wife, Mary Ann Gurr. It would appear that Mary Ann became the sole owner of Gurr and Son as well as of the 38 Southwick property where Alfred Richard lived with his growing family and where the family dairy business was centered.

Mary Ann Gurr is enumerated in the 1881 census living with her three daughters and her sister Sophia Ann Bennett in separate accommodations in Shepherd's Bush, Hammersmith, Chelsea, with one servant. Shepherd's Bush Station was a stop along the underground west of Hyde Park, and an easy commute for Mary Ann and her daughters to work at the Southwick Street dairy. A visitor at the Shepherd's Bush residence at the time of the census is Hugh Stott, MD. Ellen Gurr and Dr. Hugh Stott married on April 19th, 1881. [134]

---

[134] Hugh Stott's name was erroneously transcribed in Ancestry.com as Hugh Holt, MD.

Photo 8.3a   The Alfred Richard Gurr Family
London Garden c. 1887
The six youngest with Alfred, Wife Emily and Emily's Mother?
Paul Magel Collection

8.4   Henry Jonathan Gurr

Henry Jonathan Gurr was born January 22, 1853, while his parents were living at Stanley Street in Paddington, Middlesex and while his father was a butler at the Wheeler Residence in Hyde Park. He was baptized on November 23, 1853 with his cousin George Benjamin, the son of his Uncle George Gurr, at Saint George the Martyr in Southwark (the baptismal record indicates that his father Alfred James was a servant and his uncle a gentleman). During the 1861 census, Henry was living with his mother and siblings on Stanley Street in Paddington, but the record does not indicate he was a student. During the 1871 census Henry was living with his parents at 38 Southwick, his occupation listed as dairyman's assistant.

It is probable that all three Gurr brothers received an above average education and they may even have been exposed to the classics by the time they were thirteen. Second son Henry Jonathan, went to sea as a cabin boy at about thirteen years of age. His entry in a 1929 clerical directory says that he attended Bayswater College in London. [135] While this may be the case, we can find no historical record of such a school, though it may well be that the directory was referring to one of the religious schools that were in operation on Bayswater Road in Paddington when Henry was a child.

Christ's Hospital Hertford was noted for preparing young men for merchant and naval careers. Since Alfred Richard was a student at Christ's Hospital it is possible that Henry also

---

[135] *Stowe's Clerical Directory*, 1929, Page 145. The information for this directory would have been provided by the Henry Gurr.

obtained admission there to prepare him for his years at sea. [136] In any case, Henry Jonathan had academic credentials that allowed him admission to the Seabury Divinity School in Minnesota when he was about 23 years old. There we know that he took classes in Latin, Greek and Hebrew in his three years of study before ordination, so it is almost certain that at least two of Alfred James' sons received a classical education customary for upper class gentlemen. Following the death of his father in 1874, Henry found passage to America (whether he worked his way across or paid for passage is unknown) and by 1876 enrolled in Seabury Divinity School, as detailed in Chapter 11.

8.5   Edwin Robert Gurr

Born in Paddington on January 15th, 1855, Edwin was baptized on April 15th of that year at St. James Church in Paddington, London.   He is enumerated in the 1861 census without any indication as to whether he was at school (usually this was indicated by the use of "scholar" under occupation). During the 1871 census Edwin was living at home with his parents and his occupation is recorded as "wine merchant's clerk." [137] It is almost certain that Edwin assisted his father and brother in the family business during his early teens, as Gurr and Sons developed from a milk route to a dairy operation during this period. We do not know where or how long Edwin was employed by the wine merchant, but it is likely that it was short lived, and seen as an opportunity to earn and learn something new at the same time.   Of the three Gurr brothers, we know the least about Edwin's early years, and nothing definite regarding how and where he was schooled. We can conclude from his later occupations that Edwin must have received a formal education, and family tradition suggests that he was probably educated at a church grammar school along Bayswater Road, just north of Hyde Park, less than a mile from his Southwick Street home. During the 1881 census Edwin was enumerated while at a dairy farm (Arthur's Bridge Farm in Somerset) with his occupation recorded as Milk Contractor, probably working for Gurr and Son.

8.6   Life After the Death of Alfred James Gurr

When Alfred James died in September of 1874, none of the three brothers received an inheritance, since his will left his entire estate to his wife Mary Ann. This was a bit unusual for it was still traditional in England that the eldest brother receive the bulk of his father's estate. Alfred obviously trusted his wife to manage the family business and to care for their children. It may also be that that the business was linked to, perhaps even financed by, George Barham for we know that George remained in contact with the Gurr family for decades to come. In any event, in the 3rd of April, 1881 census, the eldest son Alfred Richard is the head of the family

---

[136]   Christ's Hospital was given its second Royal Charter by Charles II in 1673. This charter specifically created the Royal Mathematical School whose original purpose was to train mathematicians and navigators who would serve as naval officers or merchant seafarers.

[137]   Wine houses (establishments selling only wine), were being licensed and growing in number during the 1870s, while wine merchants with contacts abroad were prospering from the new interest in their products. Wine houses appealed to the middle and upper classes, and the Borough of Paddington, the heartland of London's West Side, was where many of the growing middle class of the day resided.

home at 38 Southwick, where he resides with his wife and children, a nurse for the children, and a servant, but Mary Ann is living elsewhere.

Photo 8.6a was taken of Mary Ann Bennett Gurr a year or two before her death in 1884, while those of her three sons - **Photos 8.6b** of Alfred Richard, **Photo 8.6c** of Reverend Jonathan and **Photo 8.6d** of Edwin Robert Gurr - were all taken a few years later.

In their early lives the three brothers witnessed remarkable changes in their family's social status and in the fabric of the society surrounding them. They lived through an era that saw the reconstruction of London and the unprecedented expansion of the British Empire of which their London was the hub.

Photo 8.6a Mary Ann Bennett Gurr
In her later years
Ted Robert Gurr Family Collection

Photo 8.6b Alfred Richard Gurr
Extracted from Photo 12.4a

Photo 8.6c Henry Jonathan Gurr
Henry J. Gurr Album

Photo 8.6d Edwin Robert Gurr
Paul Magel Collection

Chapter 9
Sisters in London, Daughters of Alfred James Gurr

While all three sons of Alfred James and Mary Ann Gurr adventured off to America, all three daughters stayed home. While their brothers explored the new frontier of the American West, where a new culture was being born and social change was relatively unrestrained, the three sisters remained in the highly structured society of London which demanded that all its citizens conform to what was socially acceptable. Although we know fewer details of the lives of Sarah Sophia, Emily and Ellen Gurr than of those of their three brothers, what we do know suggests their lives were remarkable for their time, for all three were educated, at least two of them played a significant role in the family business, and each accumulated substantial wealth before an early death. Only the youngest married, and her marriage to a young surgeon would have been regarded as a marriage up the social ladder for the daughter of a butler turned milkman, the granddaughter of a publican. Following is what we know of the three set in the context of their time.

9.1   The Place of Women in 19th Century England

Pre-Victorian England was a male dominated society. Women were treated with the utmost respect but there was a sharp division of responsibilities between men and women. Men were the heads of the households and were responsible for providing for their families and for making all the important decisions, financial and otherwise. Women were homemakers and the governesses of their children. Women of the lower classes were employed as domestics, but in general most women were excluded from the workplace.

Sometimes women needed to find work, for traditionally all wealth passed from a father to the eldest son. Although it would have been considered callous, it was within the rights of an inheriting son to ignore the needs of his mother or his siblings, and as a result, mothers or daughters could find themselves on the street and penniless if no specific provision had been made for them in a father's will. There was some recognition that these rules of inheritance were unfair to women (Jane Austen's writings were popular among women throughout the 19th century) but, until early in the 20th century, women had no voice in making or changing laws.

Although it was traditionally accepted throughout the British Isles that women did not have a right to vote, it was not until the Reform Act of 1832 was passed that women were actually prohibited from voting. With the passing of this Act, advocates of a woman's right to vote began to voice their opinions, but it was not until 1872 that a distinct Suffragette Movement emerged in the U.K. By the early 1900s suffragettes were becoming militant, with some committing acts of vandalism and assault so that even MPs who had once supported the suffragettes began to disavow them. [138]

---

[138]   The struggle went on until 1918 when, in recognition of the contribution made by women working side by side with men during the Great War, women over 30 were given the vote. It was not until 1928 that women were enfranchised under the same conditions as men.

9.2   Education of Women

Nowhere was the gulf between the rights of men and women more pronounced than in education. For centuries gentlemen of the English upper and middle classes attended public schools (we call them private schools today) while the wealthiest were privately tutored. On the other hand, it was felt that a classical education would be wasted on a woman, and so even women of the aristocracy were rarely well educated. The notable exception (as mentioned earlier) was Queen Elizabeth I. [139] The leading woman of the 19th century, Queen Victoria was much less fortunate. As a child, Victoria received little in the way of a classical education such as men of the ruling class were entitled to, for as sixth in line to the throne it seemed inconceivable that she would one day be the Queen. Her early education prepared her to be a wife, not a monarch, and so the emphasis by her tutors was to teach her dancing, music, drawing and English. Her first language was German but, like Elizabeth I, she showed a talent for learning different languages and in this she was encouraged. Victoria's lack of a formal education, when she ascended the throne in 1837 at eighteen, must have been a source of vexation to her from time to time, and it is significant that early in her reign she promoted the education of all children, rich or poor, and her government began public funding of education. [140]

The English middle and lower classes emulated the upper classes, at least as far as their monetary worth permitted, and subsequently for most of the 19th century, educating young women to read and write was considered unnecessary. Women only needed to be prepared for marriage and they were expected to be demure, submissive and retiring. Moreover, since once married there would be no need for them to seek work of any kind, their education ordinarily was restricted to that which would attract a husband. Thus the emphasis for girls from middle-class homes was the study of music, singing and dancing, but even for girls of the lower classes, education in these feminine accomplishments was considered an advantage in those hoping to make a good match. Those who failed to find a husband were dependent upon their parents and spent their lives in virtual service to those parents or had no choice but to find work serving others as domestics.

Fortunately for Alfred James Gurr's children, both of their parents had received some formal education (Alfred at the Licensed Victuallers' School) and, as is typical for educated adults, they were committed to seeing that each of their children received proper schooling. Evidence of this is the effort of Alfred to have his eldest son, Alfred Richard, attend Christ's Hospital (his son attended from the age of eight until he was released to his father's care in 1866 at the age of fifteen). Thus, Alfred Richard received an education equivalent to that of an upper

---

[139]   Henry VIII respected Elizabeth's quick mind and allowed her to be tutored with her brother and sister who were first and second in line for his throne. Elizabeth, the daughter of Anne Boleyn, who was executed when Elizabeth was two, was a brilliant student. She was able to read, write and speak several languages including French, Italian and Spanish, but she could also converse in Welsh, Cornish, Scottish and Irish dialects, and throughout her reign she impressed her court and the many foreign envoys who visited that court with her intelligence and learning.

[140]   In 1839 Queen Victoria set up the first government education committee (the Committee of Council) to have limited control over education, charged with supervising the administration of government funding.

middle class gentleman, which undoubtedly encouraged Alfred Richard's siblings. The six who survived childhood were notably able to read and write, and there is evidence that the three daughters were very well educated relative to the norm of their time.

9.3   Marriage [141]

In Victorian England, the principal event in a woman's life was marriage. However, there were far fewer opportunities for women to meet and get to know potential husbands than there are today. Well-bred men would never speak to a woman to whom they had not been introduced. Men raised their hats to ladies they passed on the street, but offered no greeting, nor would a respectable lady respond to a greeting from someone to whom she had not been formally introduced. Men rose when a lady entered or left a room, but no lady would enter a room occupied by a man without being chaperoned. Formal dances and parties were held from time to time, at which young women might be introduced to young gentlemen, and might even indulge in a little discreet flirtation, but there were always chaperones in attendance and no respectable young lady would behave in an unseemly manner under their watchful eyes.

So, meeting unmarried men was a complicated process for young ladies in the middle and lower classes. A respectable woman had to be properly introduced to a man, and if the man and woman were attracted to one another, other meetings could be arranged, but only within the family circle. These meetings provided the opportunity for each to assess the other in terms of compatibility. If an interested male found a women to his liking, the next step was to obtain permission from her parents to speak to her, or if she was parentless the parental obligation could be taken up by a friend of substance. At this stage the prospective suitor needed to convince the parents of his affection and to demonstrate his ability to support the prospective bride in the manner to which she was accustomed. Permission received, the next step was the proposal and, if accepted by both the woman and her parents, the banns were usually read within a few weeks. A woman was discouraged from marrying below her station in life, and although marrying above one's station was acceptable, such opportunities necessarily meant that the prospective husband must be marrying below his station, for which there might be an unsavory explanation.

Love was considered secondary to a good match, but many 19th century women made devastating choices in order to secure a viable future, and loveless marriages were far too common. Because women were not allowed by society and convention to secure a livelihood through their own efforts, many felt compelled to find and marry someone who could provide for

---

[141]   Until the Divorce Act of 1857 an Act of Parliament was required for a couple to receive a divorce. Thereafter a woman could divorce on grounds of adultery, bigamy, incest or cruelty, while a man needed only to prove adultery. Initially, under the 1857 Act, separated or divorced women had few rights and as far as property rights they could only retain that which was legally their own and they had no parental rights. Although the law was gradually altered and became more favorable to women, equal rights to property and visitation of children were not achieved until after WWI.

them no matter what their initial misgivings. Moreover, women's rights were such that they remained in such unions no matter how odious they became. [142]

Only one of Alfred and Mary Ann's four daughters married, and that was the youngest, Ellen. The eldest, Sarah Sophia and their third daughter Emily Ann died spinsters, while the second daughter Mary Ann passed away at the age of five. We do not know the reasons why Ellen's two older sisters did not marry, but Ellen would be the only one of four daughters to have a husband and children. Following is the little we know of the Gurr sisters.

9.4 Sarah Sophia Gurr

Sarah Sophia was born on May 13th, 1849, three years after Alfred and Mary Ann were married at St. George Church in Hanover Square. At the time of Sarah's birth her parents were

Sketch 9.4a
Child in Stroller, c. 1847

living on Pitt Street in Peckham, not far from the Licensed Victuallers' Asylum off Kent Road where Alfred's mother resided with her eldest son, George, and her two teen-age sons Jonathan and Robert. Sarah was baptized on June 10th, 1849. By the time of the UK census of March 30, 1851, Sarah's father was already a butler at the Hyde Park home of Proctor Henry James Wheeler. Not yet two-year-old Sarah lived separately with her mother and two-week-old brother, Alfred Richard, at 488 Conduit Street in Paddington, within walking distance of the Wheeler residence.

May 1st of 1851 was the opening of the Great Exhibition at the Crystal Palace in Hyde Park which featured some thirteen thousand exhibits from around the world, but predominately industrial achievements and curiosities from the rapidly expanding British Commonwealth. The price of admission varied from the opening day till the closing day, but in the last weeks the price was only a shilling. Over 4 million visitors entered at this price before the Exhibition closed on October 15th, and it is probable that Sarah and her mother and father were among them, with Sarah and infant Alfred Richard in a stroller (example in **Sketch 9.4a**). [143]

---

[142] Edith Granger in Dicken's *Dombey and Son* is just one dramatic example of a woman enduring marriage in which there is neither love nor respect for her husband. The work's of both Charles Dickens and Jane Austen contain many characters that illustrate the attitude towards women and marriage during the 19th century.

[143] Sketch was taken from Wikipedia and is annotated as Public Domain. William Kent, an English garden architect is credited with inventing the first baby pram for the children of the Duke of Devonshire about 1733. By the 1830s baby strollers were popular in both Great Britain and America.

Also during the year 1851, the first submarine telegraph cable was laid across the English Channel and the first messages linking the European continent to the British Isles were sent between Paris and London. During the next two decades telegraph lines were extended to the Americas and throughout Europe and Asia. We mention this here because, during the 1871 census, Sarah at the age of 22, was employed as a telegraph clerk. Although we do not know whether she was a telegraph operator or an office worker, the fact that she was employed in a business involved in data transfer indicates that she received a substantial education for a girl born in the mid-19th century into a family of limited means. **Sketch 9.4b** is a period sketch of female workers in what was known as the Instrument Gallery at the Electric Telegraph Company general offices in London.[144]

The attitude towards women in the workplace and the lives of women like Sarah were altered by the technical and social changes of the 19th century, and the telegraph companies are an excellent example of this trend. The electric telegraph began in the 1840s as a railroading device that became the world's first instant messaging system. By 1865 there were a half dozen telegraph companies in London, each with a few to dozens of stations scattered throughout the city. [145] There were far more by February 1870, when all telegraph companies in the United Kingdom became national property, managed by the General Post Office, with its head office in London.

---

[144] From the late Stephen Roberts website www.distantwritings.co.uk

[145] Cruchley's *London in 1865 : A Handbook for Strangers*, 1865.

Initially employed as a cost-saving measure, women were successful as office clerks and telegraphers, and the goodwill that employing women created, led all telegraph companies to hire women by the 1860s. As the use of the telegraph spread around the globe, telegraph companies became substantial employers of women and the competition for positions was extraordinary. One company, the London District Telegraph Company, employed only women as clerk-operators from its inception. Although paid less than male telegraph clerks, women's working conditions were far more attractive than those of factory, domestic or other common female employments. However, there were strict age limits on their hiring; only women between 16 to 23 years were taken on, for it was assumed that women's main objective in life was to marry and inevitably female clerks would "retire" from their position upon marriage. [146]

During the 1881 census, Sarah Sophia was living with her mother in the Borough of Chelsea in Hammersmith along with her sisters Emily and Ellen (Nellie). Three of the four women gave their occupation as employees of Gurr and Son, Milk Contractors, Paddington, with Ellen the exception. Their residence in Hammersmith is of interest for we know that during the 1891 census Emily was still running the dairy and resident at 38 Southwick in Paddington.

Sarah Sophia died on 26 October 1890 at 38 Southwick Street, unmarried, but leaving a personal estate of almost £1800 to be administered by her brother Edwin of 16 Hamilton Road, Ealing. [147] We do not know the cause of her death at the age of 41 but her Aunt Sophia died one week before her. The fact that there was a worldwide pandemic of Asiatic influenza that year is one possible cause of their deaths.

9.5 Mary Ann Gurr

Mary Ann Gurr was born in Paddington on January 27th, 1857 and baptized on February 22nd of that year at All Saints in Paddington while the family was residing at 7 Stanley Street. She died at the age of five years, in the last quarter of 1862, cause of death unknown.

Both adults and children with illnesses were almost universally treated at home in mid-19th century England. Those who could afford it called a doctor to their home, for the voluntary hospitals that did exist were charitable establishments or workhouse infirmaries and were noted for being over-crowded and miasmic and more likely to decrease one's chances of recovery than improve them. Surgeries were conducted without anaesthesia, bloodletting was still practised, and, unfortunately, those who wished to work at these locations could claim that they were qualified nurses or physicians without disclosing references.

At the time of little Mary Ann's passing changes were underway to improve public health conditions and over the next few decades advances would be made that would eliminate diseases such as cholera and typhoid and dramatically reduce the incidence of death from childhood diseases. By the early 1860s corrective action had already begun to take control of sewage

---

[146] This paragraph contains excerpts from *Distant Writing, A History of the Telegraph Companies in Britain between 1838 and 1868,* by the late Steven Roberts.

[147] Her estate was £162,000 in 2013 purchasing power based on the retail price index. This was a goodly sum for a young lady living with her parents and employed by a family owned company, and shows that she benefited from a prosperous family business.

problems and ensure a clean water supply. Germ theory and the concepts of antisepsis and inoculation were gradually gaining acceptance among health practitioners. Specialty and Cottage Hospitals, intended for the treatment of patients with specific problems such as lunacy or contagious diseases, began to appear in the late 1850s. The Medical Act of 1858 established a General Medical Council to regulate doctors, and for the first time to examine and register qualified, as distinct from unqualified, practitioners and to make those registrations available to the public. One clause of the Medical Act even forbade Poor Law establishments from employing doctors who were not registered and approved by the Council. The Act also specifically recognized doctors with foreign degrees. Elizabeth Blackwell, who had received her medical degree in the United States, became the first woman doctor to be registered in England. Florence Nightingales wrote her *Notes on Nursing* in 1859 and established the first nursing school in England (the Nightingale Training School) at St. Thomas's Hospital on July 9, 1860.

How tragic it is to lose an infant or toddler or any child because of an ailment that might have been preventable, if only …! 19th century cemeteries in England are full of graves with headstones of a father flanked by those of a young wife and their children. The names and dates etched on those stones tell the stories. Many of the wives died in childbirth, for the dates of their death match those of their children. Many children had headstones with epitaphs that reflect how much they were loved and missed, and five year old Mary Ann was one of these. Dramatic changes were taking place in medical practice and regulation and these would greatly reduce childhood mortality during the following decades.

9.6 Emily Ann Gurr

Emily Ann Gurr was born in Paddington on the 25th of June, 1859, the third daughter of Alfred James and Mary Ann Gurr. She was not baptized until two years later on August 4,1861 at All Saints, Paddington at the same time as her newborn sister Ellen.

During the 1871 census eleven year old Emily Ann was listed as a scholar living with her parents at 38 Southwick so we can assume she was enrolled in one of the Bayswater schools within walking distance of home. In the 1881 census she was listed as a clerk for the family business Gurr and Son, although then resident in the Borough of Chelsea in Hammersmith. In the 1891 census, she was listed as Head of the house and as the dairy operator at the Gurrs' 38 Southwick home. One clerk who worked for the company was also resident with her. This confirms again that for over two decades the family operated a dairy outlet of some kind at 38 Southwick, while at the same time the family was milk contracting and wholesaling to others in London using the same business address.

Emily Ann never married. She died of breast cancer in the summer of 1898, only 39 years of age, probably while convalescing on the beaches of St. Leonards-on-Sea along the East Sussex coast, only a few miles from where her grandparents had met and married. The building at 5 Warrior Square in St. Leonard's, where she died, was still standing in June of 2011, when visited by her great-grand nephew, co-author Paul Magel, although it was under renovation. By coincidence, the author was residing at Hastings House, 9 Warrior Square on that visit, when he discovered the location of her death. Emily's home address at the time of her death is given as Danehurst Hampstead Middlesex in the England & Wales National Probate Calendar (Index of

Wills and Administrations) which was part of the Barham estate and this confirms George Barham's continued involvement with his Aunt Mary Barham Gurr's children. It should be noted that the Hampsteads is an affluent area of London four miles north-west of Charing Cross where the wealthy and many intellectuals and artists make their home, Sir George among them.

Probate was granted 10th Oct. 1898 to George Barham, Esq. with effects valued at £1760 4s. 8d (about £160,000 in 2013 currency). The fact that George Barham was granted probate may indicate that Emily's three brothers were still in North America (Alfred Richard and Henry definitely were, but of Edwin's whereabouts we are less certain). Moreover, since Emily Ann was the last operator of the Gurr dairy at 38 Southwick it is probable that the operation was closed down before her passing. The last trade listing for Gurr and Son was 1895, but it may be that George Barham kept the operation open under one of his other company names.

9.7 Ellen (Gurr) Stott

The youngest daughter of Alfred and Mary Ann, Ellen was born on the 4th of July and baptized a month later alongside her sister Emily Ann on August 4th 1861. During the 1871 census Ellen was a student and during the 1881 census she was living with her mother in Chelsea. Notably, she was never listed as employed in the family business, but only as a daughter of the family. A month after the 1881 census was taken, Ellen married Hugh Stott, Surgeon (B.M.)[148] born at Sandwell Place, Lewisham on 27 July 1858. [149] Dr. Stott became a member of the Royal College of Surgeons in 1884, was licensed by the Royal College of Physicians, London in 1887 and received a Diploma in Public Health from the Royal College of Physicians and Surgeons in 1892. Hugh Stott's father (also a Dr. Hugh Stott) was born in Boroughbridge, Yorkshire. [150]

Ellen Gurr and Hugh Stott were married in St. Michaels All Angels in Paddington on the 19th of April 1881. The couple had three children: Sophia Henrietta, Hugh and Mary all born in Friern Barnet, St. James London during the 1880s. The family moved to Patterdale, Chailey near Lewes, Sussex during the 1890s, where Ellen died of typhoid in 1902 at the age of 40. She had significant resources for, in her will, she asked that her husband's debts of 200 pounds be paid from her estate, which included a lodge that was leased out. She had also, at an earlier date, contributed the costs of building a new residence for the family.

Her son Hugh Stott, Jr. (he became Major General Stott), recalled his mother with great affection. In his memoirs he wrote:

---

[148] The B.M. indicates a United Kingdom degree in medicine. Later entries in UK Medical Registers list Dr. Hugh Stott as having, among other qualifications, the title of LSA (Licentiate of the Society of Apothecaries) dated July 28th 1881 (England). That license to practice was created under the 1815 Medical Act, and was maintained by further Acts of Parliament until the LSA became a medical qualification that could be registered when the General Medical Council was established by the Medical Act of 1858.

[149] The 1881 census record enumerates a Hugh Holt, Surgeon (B.M.) born in Yorkshire as a visitor with the Gurr family at the time of the census. This appears to be a simple transcription error of the surname. Another document gives Dr. Stott's birthplace as Lewisham, Kent

[150] The elder Dr. Hugh Stott received his LSA in 1840, and was a member of the Royal College of Surgeons in 1841.

Our mother loved horses and liked riding and driving. Her favourite was "Cliffie" a famous high stepper. Our mother was the greatest of persons, with a gentle affectionate quiet smile, and an unfailing love for her family. Of somewhat slight build, she was not physically strong. Sir George Barham, the executor of her parents and of her own Will, always spoke of her as an "angel person." Apart from her family, she loved the welfare of her home, her horses and the dogs. She was sincerely religious, with a true abhorrence of such indulgencies as alcohol and smoking. [In another reference her son mentions that she was active in the temperance movement.] She offered us such ideals in a simple kindly manner, tenderly guiding our footsteps to the true values in life. My sisters and I were deeply attached to her. I never remember from her a cross word but always ones of courage, kindness, help and appreciation. [151]

There is another clue in Hugh's memoirs about his mother's continued connection with George Barham:

In 1897 Queen Victoria's Diamond Jubilee was celebrated, and our family saw Her Majesty's magnificent procession with its colourful splendour of Imperial pomp as Sir George Barham's guests from a first floor window of the Express Dairy Company's premises opposite Marble Arch.

The fact that Ellen and her sisters each had significant estates, much more than was common for women at the time, suggests that Gurr and Son may have been sold to George Barham's Express Dairies for a significant sum that the family members shared.

Hugh Stott, Ellen's husband, practiced medicine in the Lewes area for many years, most of that time serving as Medical Health Officer for East Sussex as well as maintaining a medical practice. By his family's accounts he was very hard working and committed to improving public health throughout the region. Dr. Stott also served as Mayor of Lewes from 1911 to 1913 and **Photo 9.7a** shows him ceremonially robed in 1911. During the 1911 census he was listed as widower, living at 23 School Hill in Lewes with his two daughters Sophia and Mary, as well as a cook and a domestic. He died August 31, 1932 leaving an estate of over £10,000. [152]

Photo 9.7a Dr. Hugh Stott
Mayor of Lewes, Sussex 1911
Photo thanks to Col. Hugh Stott,
Great-Grandson of Dr. Stott

---

[151] From an unpublished ms.,"*A Biography of Mr. Hugh Stott* (1858 – 1932 aged 74)," provided by his grandson, Col. Hugh Stott. Col. Stott provided us documents on four generations of Hugh Stotts spanning more than 150 years. All but Col. Stott himself were physicians with distinguished careers, and much of the information here is from these documents.

[152] Equivalent to £550,000 in 2013 based on relative price index.

Ellen and Hugh Stott's son Hugh Stott Jr., born in 1885, became a registered physician on April 4th 1908 and served in WWI receiving the OBE and CIE during his years of service in the Indian Medical Corps of the Indian Army. He spent most of his career in India in the Madras region and the stories of his life and service there and the contributions he made to his profession are remarkable. He was surgeon to the Governor Generals of Madras and enjoyed the friendship of the Maharaja of Surguja whom he treated for a medical condition. He eventually became Professor of Pathology at King George's Medical College in Lucknow, India (which became Ghandi Memorial and Associated Hospitals in 1951, but has since reverted back to King George's Medical College). He was particularly concerned that women and children have medical care of the same quality as did men. During the 1920s he worked long and hard to secure the establishment of a 52-bed women's hospital at King George's. He helped train many Indian medical students who carried out his tradition elsewhere in India, before and after independence. He also published more than 30 medical research papers, mostly in the *Indian Medical Gazette*.

He returned to England from India in January of 1945, a retired Major General. Arriving aboard the *SS Strathmore* in Liverpool from Bombay, he gave his regional address (probably that of his daughter, Heather) as Heatherdown, Fair Oak Lane, Oxshot, Surrey. General Stott and his wife Ethel were married for over 50 years. They retired to Eastbourne, Sussex where Ethel died in 1963. Three years later Major General Stott died at his daughter's house Skye, The Avenue, Chobham, near Woking Surrey on May 23, 1966.

Ellen's grandson, another Hugh Stott, was born to Ethel in India in 1913. He was known throughout his life as Bill, and became a physician in 1938. He served as a regional medical officer in Kenya, then transferred to the colony's Labour Department. He was a specialist on occupational diseases of African workers and on tuberculosis. In 1953-54 he was tasked with evaluating the health care provided to some 30,000 Mau Mau detainees held in 30 camps throughout the country and became acquainted with Jomo Kenyatta and other imprisoned members of the Mau Mau leadership. Then for six years he served as WHO senior medical officer in Madras, directing a project on TB, and later returned to Kenya as director of the WHO/UNICEF Tuberculosis Project there. He shared his father's interest in medical research, publishing over 50 research papers, often in collaboration with East Indian and African physicians.

Bill Stott's first wife was Mary Lothian, the sister of a fellow Cambridge student. They had two sons, both born in Kenya (Hugh b. 1940, who pursued a career as an Army officer, and Robin b. 1942, who followed the family tradition by becoming a physician). Mary left him in 1944, distressed by his intensive work schedule, constant movement, and isolation. His second wife was Helen Campbell whom he married Dec 7, 1946 in Nakuru, Kenya, where they lived for the next eight years. She had three children from an earlier marriage and they had two daughters of their own, Elizabeth and Amelia, born in 1950 and 1952. From 1966 to 1978 Bill was back in England working as an epidemiologist with a TB research program in London. Helen had left him by then and his partner for the remainder of his life, including his retirement years in East Sussex, was Mary Newington, a nurse with whom he had worked on the Kenya Tuberculosis

Project. In retirement he became concerned with protecting wild badgers against claims that they spread tuberculosis to cattle, and spent much time observing them at his six-acre badger wood. He died in 1996 at the age of 83.

9.8   Sophia Ann Bennett

Mary Ann's younger sister Sophia Ann Bennett who was born on the 23rd of September 1821 and baptized alongside two of her siblings on 31 January 1825, deserves mention with her nieces in the Gurr family, for she lived with Alfred and Mary Ann and their children from the late 1860s until her death in 1890. Sophia never married and was listed as an invalid sister-in-law living with Alfred and Mary Ann during the 1871 census, and in the 1881 census as a retired teacher.

Checking earlier records we found Sophia in the 1851 census, lodging with a family where the husband was an auctioneer's cashier. His twenty-two-year old son was a Professor of Music. During the 1861 census Sophia is in lodging at the home of a pianoforte teacher with her occupation listed as a ladies (unreadable) professor of music. Though she spent her early years involved in music we have no information on where or by whom she was educated. Aunt Sophia died the week before her niece Sarah Sophia, on 19th October, 1890, at 38 Southwick Street. She left a personal estate valued at only £26, the estate to be administered by her nephew Edwin. In this respect Sophia was probably like most spinsters of her era, with a very modest estate by comparison with the substantial sums accumulated by her nieces.

9.9   Observations

The eldest of Alfred James's sons was sent to Christ's Hospital, a renowned boarding school, from the time he was eight until he was fifteen. We have good reason to believe that Alfred's two younger boys also spent time at boarding schools. British boarding schools taught young men to be independent, trained them to be competitive and make the most of every opportunity, and encouraged them to accept leadership when and where they could. Educated young men from London, the epicenter of England and the English speaking world, the hub of a great empire "on which the sun never set" were especially self-confident, and believed they could succeed anywhere as had those Englishmen who had gone abroad before them.

Contrast this sense of "can-do" superiority in the male population with how Victorian London women must have seen themselves. They were kept subservient by social custom and by government decree. Middle and upper class women were given an education only in those arts which would allow them to please a husband and care for their children, for it was expected that they would never need to support and feed themselves. Lower class women were given no education at all, but they might aspire to become a servant to the middle class, and failing that they could marry within their class and hope their husbands could earn enough to keep them and their children out of the poor houses.

In the last thirty years of the 19th century, as the Gurr daughters were coming of age, social change was taking place that would elevate the status of women, but that change was very gradual and the Gurr daughters benefited little from it, for cultural change takes time. There is little doubt that Sarah Sophia, Emily and Ellen had never been instilled with the self confidence that would allow them to venture off to America – at least not without the essential husband –

and Sarah and Emily never married. The two older daughters remained in London, where they felt reasonably secure, and succeeded modestly because of the opportunity and wealth provided by the family milk business, founded by their father Alfred. Ellen married well, as the saying goes, to a young physician. He was a physician's son and their descendants carried on the Stott family tradition for four more generations. In Part II we will trace in greater detail the lives of Ellen's three brothers and in Part III the lives of their descendents in North America.

Part II
America

Chapter 10
Discovery and Early Settlement

Chapter 10.1 The First Americans

When and how the first human beings arrived in the Americas is a fascinating study, and our knowledge of the subject seems to be constantly changing, as new discoveries are made and new theories are postulated. There is clear evidence of human habitation in North America from at least 18,000 years ago, and some authorities claim evidence dating to the limit of radiocarbon dating, or over 50,000 years ago. [153]

Arguably, the first people to arrive and the many that were to follow have some claim to the land, but none left any written record, and only traces of their presence, including artifacts such as stone tools. As for the native peoples who occupied the land when the first Europeans arrived, they kept no written records and had no concept of private ownership. They were tribal and while a few lived in permanent settlements, many were nomadic. They believed that the land they lived on belonged to their tribe, and when the tribe left it, it belonged to whoever came after them. They themselves were a part of the universe and they spoke of "Mother Earth" and "Father Sky." These were not just words to them, but were spiritual expressions, for they believed "the people" were "of the earth" and "of the sky", and their cultures and religions were enmeshed with nature. Individual land ownership simply did not exist, since all "the people" were entitled to the fruits of nature. However, at the tribal level, most resented intruders and all defended the hunting grounds on which they depended.

Several centuries before Columbus re-discovered the Americas, there were Europeans who were early arrivals in what is now the continental United States, evidence of this having been found from Newfoundland to the Carolinas, and disputed evidence of ventures far inland. A few explorers landed and some even did surveying with the hope of establishing settlements. The Europeans who first discovered unoccupied land (and to them this meant no European occupation) almost invariably laid claim to that land in the name of their sovereign and country. Once such a claim was made, other European sovereigns might accept or dispute that claim, though disputing a claim or occupying claimed land meant risking war. However, no claim was completely validated until the land was actually occupied by the claimant.

After the discovery of the new world, there were several attempts at settlement in North America by both the French and Spanish. They fought over the rights to that region we now know as Florida and other Gulf territories during the mid 1500s. The French had made several attempts to establish settlements in North America during the 1500s, but none were successful. They almost succeeded with the founding of Acadia in 1604, but this also ended in failure, and the first permanent French settlement (Quebec City) was not founded until 1608. New Orleans was not settled by the French until 1718. It was then ceded to the Spanish in the Treaty of Paris

---

[153] Radiocarbon testing of carbonized plants found with human artifacts along the Savannah river in South Carolina suggests human activity at the 'Topper' site at least 50,000 years ago, Science Daily (Nov. 18, 2004)

(1763), and reverted back to the French in 1801. The Spanish established St. Augustine in Florida in 1565, and it is arguably the oldest continuously occupied European city in what we now know as the continental United States. During the last third of the 16th century, St. Augustine was attacked repeatedly by both French and English forces, but although driven from the city on several occasions, the Spanish settlers always returned. [154]

10.2.1 The English – First Settlements

In 1584, Queen Elizabeth I granted Sir Walter Raleigh permission to establish a colony in the territory north of Spanish Florida. That same year Raleigh sent an expedition to explore the region which he is credited with naming Virginia in honor of the Virgin Queen. [155] Raleigh backed an early attempt to establish a settlement at Roanoke in Virginia in 1587, but the undeclared war between England and Spain (ending with the defeat of the Spanish Armada in 1588) distracted the English supporters from supplying the colony. It had disappeared without a trace (the lost colony of Roanoke) by the time a resupply ship reached the settlement some three years later.

In 1607, the London Company (later renamed the Virginia Company), under a charter granted by King James I, established a settlement on Jamestown Island in the James River. The Jamestown settlement was soon moved from its first island location to the mainland and then a few miles farther inland, where it eventually became Williamsburg, the first capital of Virginia. It is Jamestown that lays claim to being the first permanent English settlement in the Americas, and it is in Jamestown that the history of English America really begins.

Ignoring the existence and the resistance of the aboriginals, and despite the massive influx of continental Europeans in the last decades of the 19th century, it is English speaking peoples who have dominated North America, from the days of the settlement of Jamestown and the voyage of the Mayflower onward, with French and Spanish influence waxing and waning in specific regions at different periods from the time of Columbus.

With the discovery of the New World, it was the monarchs of Europe who stood first to benefit from colonization of the lands claimed in their names. Colonization meant extension of a monarch's power by validating territorial claims, the potential exploitation of new resources and the expansion of taxable trade. The Kings and Queens of England made their vassals agents of colonization, and in return some of the earliest settlements (Virginia, Jamestown, Carolina) were named to honor their monarch. But having received a royal charter, the agent was faced with the extremely difficult question of how to populate, nurture and protect the fledgling colonies until they became productive.

---

[154] In 1586 the city of St. Augustine was attacked and destroyed by Sir Francis Drake and the settlers there were driven out. They gradually returned after Drake made a strategic retreat, knowing he did not have the resources to defend the city he had hoped to make an English colony.

[155] This is a popular belief, but with no documentation of it as factual, it may well be that the region was named by the queen herself for the virgin territory which it was. Another suggestion is that it was named for a native leader whose name was Wingina. There is currently a town by that name in Virginia on the banks of the James River.

The earliest English colonies in America were in Virginia (1608), in New England (1620) and in the Carolina Territory (1653). The colony of Virginia was founded on a for-profit basis by the joint-stock owned Virginia Company of London. [156] The first New England colonists were actually heading for the mouth of the Hudson River which was the northern boundary of the colony of Virginia, but after a grueling ocean crossing they landed at Plymouth and could go no further. The first mention of the Carolinas was for a charter issued in 1629, but it was revoked for inactivity. In 1653 a rogue settlement was established at Albemarle Sound (just south of what was Virginia, in what is now North Carolina) by squatters from Virginia and New England.

In 1663 Charles II rewarded eight men for their support in regaining his British crown by granting them the land called Carolina, everything south of Virginia (including the Spanish settlement at St. Augustine) and from the Atlantic to the Pacific Oceans. They became known as the Lords Proprietors. Early during their control, settlements were established at Clarendon at Cape Fear (1665) and at Charles-Town in 1670. Charleston, with its natural harbor, developed more rapidly than Albermarle (1653) or Clarendon at Cape Fear (1665), becoming the center for trade with the other colonies and the West Indies.

Some of the early English settlers, such as the Puritans, came to America in order to avoid religious persecution at home, and a few were attracted by their sense of adventure. However, the early agents of colonization needed to attract families in large numbers if they were to settle the vast lands that they controlled. All kinds of schemes were devised to this end. One example was the "headright system", whereby land was granted to anyone who brought over a specified number of colonists. But settlers were also promised freedom of religion, free passage, free land, free provisions, freedom from taxation, start-up loans and many other incentives in an effort to attract them. The few that came were not enough and powerful people with vested interests in the new world sought more covert means of colonizing their properties.

10.2.2 The English - British Convicts

Most of us are aware that Britons convicted of crimes ranging from petty theft to murder were transported to Australia in the late 18th and early 19th century. Less well known is the fact that convicts were also transported to America during the 17th and 18th centuries. The sentence of "transportation" was a common punishment handed out for both major and petty crimes in Britain from the 17th century until well into the 19th century. It was seen as an alternative to local imprisonment as a means of keeping down costs, and for the more serious offenses, as a more humane alternative to execution.

Although the habit of transporting convicted felons to the colonies was a well established punishment by the middle of the 17th century, the Piracy Act of 1717, which became popularly known as the Transportation Act made the practice a matter of law. The Piracy Act established a seven year penal transportation to North America as one punishment for those convicted of lesser felonies, as well as murder or other capital crimes. The punishment could be commuted, if royal

---

[156] A joint stock company is a business owned by investors through control of stock. They organized and supported the colonies under royal charter. Although they officially worked for the crown, they made private profits.

pardon was granted. Transportation of criminals to North America was continuous between 1718 and 1776, after which the American Revolution made that impossible. From 1776 to 1778, those sentenced to transportation received hard labor or imprisonment, but starting in 1787 and right up until 1868, criminals were transported to the British Colonies in Australia.

Estimates vary, but at least 50,000 convicts (and perhaps as many as 120,000) were transported to the British colonies in North America in the 17th and 18th centuries. When the American Revolution brought an end to this means of disposing of the convict problem, the British Government began to look elsewhere. Following Captain Cook's voyage to the South Pacific, where he visited and claimed Australia in the name of the British Empire, the British Government saw a new opportunity; The courts in Britain began transporting convicts to Australia in 1788, and by 1840 as many as 150,000 had been relocated by transportation.

Some estimates suggest that as many as one quarter of those men and women who came from the British Isles to the North American colonies prior to the American Revolution were convicts. They were most often transported, especially during the early 18th century following the passing of the Piracy Act, under a system of indentured servitude. [157] Convicts were transported to the penal colonies by private merchants and once there, they were at the mercy of those merchants. Some were brought on the same ships as settlers and contracts were written up, with the new master compensating the merchant for the servant's passage. Some were auctioned off to plantation owners on their arrival, and became virtual slaves.

10.2.3 The English - Indentured Servants [158]

Not only convicted felons were transported to the colonies. Children, the elderly, many of the poor and hungry, drunks and the homeless, and in fact any individuals who could be lured by the promise of being fed and clothed were enticed to sign a document that indentured them. Some were seized by force, put aboard a vessel, and were at sea before they were given the alternative of signing the indenture document or being otherwise disposed of. The ocean journey to America under sail (sometimes in ships arguably seaworthy) took eight to twelve weeks, and though some passengers were treated humanely, this was not always the case. Stories of being packed into a ships hold without fresh air, of being constantly seasick, of starvation and deprivation at sea were common among those who survived the crossing. The lucky survivors who landed in the colonies had contracts of service worked out with the waiting colonists, usually four to seven years. The less fortunate were bought and sold like slaves.

Indentured servants had few rights. They could not vote, marry, travel, own property and seldom had any legal recourse. The master of the indentured could do as he pleased, and while some were treated justly, many indentured females were raped, while both males and females were whipped and beaten, and with no more rights than a slave, few dared to complain about

---

[157] 'British Convicts Shipped to American Colonies', American Historical Review 2, Smithsonian Institution, National Museum of Natural History. October 1896. http://www.dinsdoc.com/butler-1.htm. Retrieved 2007-06-21.

[158] Excerpted from: *Multicultural Activities for the American History Classroom.*

their treatment. Contracts between master and indentured were usually honored and after four to seven years the servant was free to leave, and the master was usually required to provide his former servant with the wherewithal to start his new life. For those who had no contract and for those who had an unscrupulous master, freedom was often difficult or impossible to obtain.

10.3   Slaves - White and Black

Slavery, once called serfdom, is a form of forced labor in which people are considered to be the property of others, and are held against their will from the time of their capture, purchase, or birth, and deprived of the right to leave, to refuse to work, or to demand wages. In some societies the slave-owner even had the legal right to kill a slave at his discretion.

It was extremely difficult to find individuals willing to emigrate from civilized Europe to what was seen as the savage wilderness of America, no matter what was promised. But, as the colonies in America gradually became more successful, the demand for cheap labor increased and forced labor was gradually accepted as a necessary option. Over half of all European immigrants to colonial America during the 17th and 18th centuries arrived as indentured servants, many of whom were treated as virtual slaves. [159]

An estimated 12 million Africans were shipped to the New World between the 16th and the 19th centuries. [160]   The first slaves from Africa arrived in Jamestown in 1619, and initially the white citizens of Virginia treated them as indentured servants. The attitude towards the Africans changed with time and the estimated 645,000 Africans brought to what is now the United States were treated as slaves, with little or no hope of ever being free. Although the first slaves in the Americas were brought there by Spaniards, most of the slaves in the United States were brought by English slave traders (including Sir Francis Drake on at least one occasion). The first legally recognized slave in what is now the United States was John Casor in 1655. [161] According to the 1860 U.S. census, 393,975 individuals owned 3,950,528 slaves.

10.4   Immigration

During the 17th century, approximately 175,000 Englishmen migrated to Colonial America. [162]   Estimates for the 18th century vary, but probably less than one million European immigrants crossed the Atlantic before 1800. Over half of all European immigrants to Colonial America during the 17th and 18th centuries arrived as indentured servants. [163]

---

[159]   Deanna Barker, *Indentured Servitude in Colonial America*. Frontier Resources.

[160]   Ronald Segal, (1995). *The Black Diaspora: Five Centuries of the Black Experience Outside Africa*. New York: Farrar, Straus and Giroux. p. 4. ISBN 0-374-11396-3. "It is now estimated that 11,863,000 slaves were shipped across the Atlantic. [Note in original: Paul E. Lovejoy, 'The Impact of the Atlantic Slave Trade on Africa: A Review of the Literature,' in *Journal of African History* (1989), p. 368.] ... "It is widely conceded that further revisions are more likely to be upward than downward"

[161]   Philip Burnham, 'Selling Poor Steven' *American Heritage Magazine*.

[162]   *Leaving England: The Social Background of Indentured Servants in the Seventeenth Century*. The Colonial Williamsburg Foundation.

[163]   Deanna Barker, *Indentured Servitude in Colonial America*. Frontier Resources.

The right to become a citizen of the United States was stated in The Naturalization Act of 1790 as being restricted to "free white persons" of "good moral character" who had resided in the country for two years and had kept their current state of residence for a year. In 1795 this was increased to five years residence and three years after notice of intent to apply for citizenship, and again to 14 years residence and five years notice of intent in 1798.

The 1790 Naturalization Act was not altered until 1870 at which time it was broadened to allow African Americans to be naturalized. However, this 14th Amendment to the Constitution included a clause that made all persons born in the United States citizens of the United States and of the State in which they were born. Perhaps as many as eight million immigrants arrived in the United States between 1790 and 1870, and in the following twenty years, another eight million, mostly European. But the peak of immigration occurred during the 1890s and up until the beginning of WW1, when perhaps fifteen million foreign born, again mostly European, entered the country.

United States census figures from 1790 indicate a total population of nearly 4 million people, and by 1870 that number had risen to almost 40 million. There were some states pushing for state control of immigration in the 1870s, (California among them) but in 1875, the US Supreme Court ruled that the Federal Government had jurisdiction, and so the "open borders" policy prevailed. By 1890 the population was almost 63 million and the 1920 census counted over 106 million.

The bias in the 1790 Naturalization Act allowing whites to immigrate freely, obviously excluded other racial groups from entry into the United States, and explains why so many Europeans landed in America during the 19th century. There were some non-whites who entered, primarily from Mexico, China and Japan, but their numbers were relatively small. The United States population also grew as a result of the annexation of Texas and admission of the south-western states to the union. Also, as many as 250,000 Asians immigrants arrived in the United States between 1850 and 1880, most of them from China. They came to the western United States because of unsettled conditions in China, attracted by job opportunities on the railways as they expanded westward. The Chinese Exclusion Act of 1882 was passed specifically targeting Chinese immigrants and actually prohibiting their further naturalization. The Act was not repealed until 1943.

10.5   Gurrs in America in 1880

If you conduct a search for all individuals, ***male and female***, with the ***exact*** surname ***Gurr*** that are recorded in the 1880 United States Federal Census, you will find 213 matches in all. [164] However, these records include 45 individuals with the surname Mc Gurr (or Mc Guire), and removing these one is left with 168 individuals. It should be noted that some of the 168 Gurrs were initially interpreted and recorded as either Gun, Graan, Guir, Gure, or Furr. However, members have written in to Ancestry to correct these to Gurr, and we have accepted these member corrections as valid. While we do not believe that this count is completely accurate, and

---

[164]   Retrieved from http://www. Ancestry.com.

we have observed many inconsistencies in birth dates and spelling, the data are still an excellent guideline for family research. There are errors and omissions in all of the original census data, and to complicate matters, many of the records are barely readable. However, Ancestry.com should be congratulated for a job well done in constructing their database and transcribing the data from those originals.

Having isolated the names of 168 Gurrs from the 1880 United States Federal Census, we identified a total of 36 "families" of two or more individuals, plus 18 individuals living alone. Seven of the families (a total of 36 individuals, plus one single) were living in Utah Territory (descendants of one Enoch Eldredge Gurr , born 1813 in Sussex, England, but arriving in America after a sojourn in Australia). Eight of the families (a total of 38 individuals, plus two singles) were living in Georgia (all believed to be descendants of one Daniel Gurr, born about 1750, almost certainly from England). These results are tabulated in **Table 10.5a.**

Table 10.5a	Gurr Families and Singles By State, U.S. Census 1880					
Region	**State**	**Total No.**	**# Families**	**(Family Size)**	**# Singles**	**Region Totals**
South	Alabama	2	1	(2)		47 of 168 10 House- holds
	Georgia	40	8	(3)(2)(2)(5)(7)(6)(9)(4)	2	
	Mississippi	4	1	(4)		
	N. Carolina	1	0		1	
Midwest	Illinois	9	2	(5)(3)	1	54 of 168 13 House- holds
	Indiana	11	2	(8)(3)		
	Michigan	14	4	(4)(3) (4)(2)	1	
	Minnesota	4	1	(3)	1	
	Ohio	10	3	(3)(4)(2)	1	
	Wisconsin	6	1	(5)	1	
East	New Jersey	1	0		1	29 of 168 6 House- holds
	New York	22	5	(2)(3)(3)(7)(4)	3	
	Pennsylvania	6	1	(2)	4	
West	Oregon	1	0		1	38 of 168 7 House- holds
	Utah Territory	37	7	(2)(7)(9)(6)(6)(3)(3)	1	
	Totals	**168**	**36**	**150**	**18**	**168**

Table 10.5b: A state by state summary of the US Federal Census Records of Gurrs 1600 - 1880.

Table 10.5b	US Federal Census Records, Gurrs - 1600-1880									
State	Joins Union	To 1800	1810	1820	1830	1840	1850	1860	1870	1880
Alabama	1819							6		2
Alaska	1959									
Arizona	1912									
Arkansas	1836									
California	1850						1			
Colorado	1876									
Connecticut	1788	12						1		
Delaware	1787									
Florida	1845									
Georgia	1788					11	26	39	21	40
Hawaii	1959									
Idaho	1890									
Illinois	1818				16	4	9	13	13	9
Indiana	1816							10	7	11
Iowa	1846								2	
Kansas	1861								6	
Kentucky	1792				16		15			
Louisiana	1812								1	
Maine	1820									
Maryland	1788									
Massachusetts	1788							3		
Michigan	1837						9			14
Minnesota	1858							5	5	4
Mississippi	1817									4
Missouri	1821						3			
Montana	1889									
Nebraska	1867									
Nevada	1864									
New Hampshire	1788				3					
New Jersey	1787								3	1
New Mexico	1912									

Table 10.5b Continued	US Federal Census Records, Gurrs - 1600-1880									
State	**Joins Union**	**To 1800**	**1810**	**1820**	**1830**	**1840**	**1850**	**1860**	**1870**	**1880**
New York	1788					5	15	17	12	22
North Carolina	1789			2	2					1
North Dakota	1889									
Ohio	1803				8				6	10
Oklahoma	1907									
Oregon	1859									1
Pennsylvania	1787	23				17	4		11	6
Rhode Island	1790								9	
South Carolina	1788	7	10	9	9				3	
South Dakota	1889									
Tennessee	1796			5					6	
Texas	1845									
Utah	1896							12	24	37
Vermont	1791						3			
Virginia	1788	1					6			
Washington	1889									
West Virginia	1863				9					
Wisconsin	1848								1	6
Wyoming	1890									
DecadeTotals		43	10	16	63	37	88	109	130	168

Summary of Table 10.5b Gurr Records by Region:

Southern States: Alabama, Georgia, Louisiana, Mississippi, North Carolina and South Carolina had a Total of 47 Gurrs in 1880 Census.

New England States: New Jersey, New York and Pennsylvania had a Total of 29 Gurrs in 1880 census.

Mid West States: Illinois, Indiana, Michigan, Minnesota, Ohio and Wisconsin had a Total of 54 Gurrs in 1880 census.

Western States: Oregon and Utah had a Total of 38 Gurrs in 1880 census.
Of the Total Gurrs in the 1880 census 34 of the 168 were born outside the United States: 23 England, 5 Europe, 5 Australia, 1 Phillipines, & 2 had an unknown birthplace.

10.6   The First Gurr in America - George Gurr

Jamestown was the first successful English settlement in America, established by the Virginia Company of London in May of 1607. During the early "starving years" from 1607 to 1610 only 61 of about 500 settlers survived, partly because the early settlement was on mosquito infested marshy land that was of marginal agricultural value. The Virginia Indians, the Powhatan Confederacy, were initially friendly and attempted to cooperate with the new arrivals, probably in the hope that they could bring them into their confederacy and so benefit from the settlers' knowledge of making iron, glass and creating other marvels. Gradually, the natives became openly hostile.

John Rolfe introduced tobacco to the region from the second Virginia Company colony of Bermuda, the first crops being harvested in 1614. Other plantations were gradually introduced and the colony began to prosper.   Prosperity and Rolfe's marriage to the Indian princess Pocahontas brought peace to the region for almost a decade. However, the Powhatans finally had enough of the encroaching settlers and in 1622 they attacked the outlying plantations hoping to drive the intruders from their lands. By the time King James revoked the Virginia Company's charter in 1624, making Virginia a Crown Colony, only 3400 of about 6000 landed settlers had survived. George Gurr was one of the casualties.

George Gurr probably arrived in North America in the year 1621. [165] He was probably from Lamberhurst, Kent, a village that was situated along the border between the counties of East Sussex and Kent on the most direct route between the cities of London and Hastings. [166] We know that a George Gurr married Francis Eastland in Lamberhurst in April of 1618. It is likely that he is the same George Gurr listed in the muster roll (census) taken of the "Living and the Dead" on February 16, 1623 in the English settlement at *"Plantation over against James Cittie"*, Jamestown, Virginia. He may have been an indentured servant recruited after the death of his wife Frances. In 1624 the muster roll of the "Dead at the Plantations, over the Water" lists George Gurr as one of two settlers "slain by the Indians."

Jamestown gradually ceased to exist after the capital of the new Commonwealth of Virginia was relocated to Williamsburg in 1699. Although services continued to be held at the Jamestown Church until the 1750s, the area fell into ruin and became an agricultural rather than an urban area. But Virginia flourished. The European demand for tobacco fueled the arrival of more settlers and servants, while the head-right system helped to solve a persistent labor shortage by providing colonists with land for each indentured servant they transported to Virginia. The labor problem was also resolved by the purchase of African workers. Although they were first

---

[165]   McCartney, Martha W,(2007). *Virginia Immigrants and Adventurers 1607-1635: A Biographical Dictionary.* Baltimore: Genealogical Publishing Co., Page: 351.

[166]   Today, the A21 is the main arterial route between London (Lewisham) and Hastings, a distance of about 60 miles. Hastings (although it has no natural harbor) was one of the major ports along the southern coast of England and Lamberhurst was one of the Roman centers for iron working, so it is probable that a roadway linked the port with London in Roman times, although it was definitely not a major Roman route and no signs of such a road exist today.

imported in 1619, slavery was not codified until about 1660. In 1788, Virginia would become the first state admitted to the Union.

10.7   First Gurr Family in America - Daniel Gurr [167]

The first Gurr family that we can identify in America is that of Daniel Gurr who was born in the colony of Virginia almost 125 years after George Gurr's death. We know nothing of his parents. His wife was probably also born in the 1750s. The couple had 5 children (3 male, 2 female) between 1770 and 1790. They moved from Virginia to the Camden District of the county of Richland, South Carolina between 1785 and 1790.

South Carolina was part of the original province of Carolina, which was established by Royal Charter and named for Charles I, (Carolus is latin for Charles). South Carolina was separated from North Carolina in 1729, joined the rebellion in 1776 and was the 8th state to enter the Union.

The town of Camden was established around 1730 and was located within Richland at the time South Carolina joined the union. As the population of the state grew, boundaries changed and the city of Camden is now in the county of Kershaw. Richland County was probably named for its "rich land." The county was formed in 1785 as part of the Camden District, the geographical center of the state of South Carolina. The capital of the state had been in Charleston, but a new site was chosen in Richland in 1786 and by 1790 the legislature was meeting there. That site became the village of Columbia in 1805 and a city in 1854. Columbia was then both the county seat for Richland and the state capital.

By the census of 1790, Richland had 18 families (30 males over 16, 19 males under 16 and 40 females, and there were also 167 slaves). They farmed cotton and tobacco. The region was prosperous and when the Santee Canal was built between 1786 and 1800, joining Columbia to Charleston, growth and trade were greatly stimulated.

Federal Census Results from 1750 to 1850 provide the following information for the Daniel Gurr family with the years highlighted:

1750 - Daniel Gurr born in Virginia moved from Virginia to Camden, Richland SC around 1788.
1790 - Daniel Gurr of Camden, Richland SC - family of 7 (4 male, 3 female)
1820 - Daniel Gurr of Camden, Richland SC - family of 3 (1 male, 2 female)
1784 - John Gurr (son of Daniel) born in Virginia in 1784
1810 - John Gurr (son of Daniel) of Richland SC - family of 4 (2 male, 2 female)
1820 - John Gurr (son of Daniel) of Richland SC - family of 6 (5 male, 1 female)
1830 - John Gurr (son of Daniel) of Richland SC - family of 9 (6 male, 3 female)
1810 - William Gurr (son of Daniel?) resident in Richland - family of 2 (1 male, 1 female).

---

[167]   Heads of Families at the first U.S. census. SC. By U.S. Bureau of the Census. Washington, 1908. (150p.):26

John Gurr of South Carolina moved to Georgia between 1830 and 1839. Georgia (named after King George II) was the last of the 13 trustee colonies named and claimed by England in 1732. Georgia became a crown colony in 1752, its governor appointed by the King. It joined the rebellion in 1776 and was the fourth state admitted to the Union in 1788. Continuing:

1840 - John Gurr of Houston GA (formerly of Richland SC) - family of 7 (5 male, 2 female)
1850 - John Gurr of Houston GA (formerly of Richland SC) - family of 6

During the 1850 census there were a total of 5 Gurr families living in Georgia and it appears that they were all descendants of Daniel Gurr.

10.8   Emigration from Britain Following the American Revolution

With the loss of the 13 colonies in America following the American Revolution of 1776, the British practice of exiling convicted criminals to the North American colonies was no longer possible. So common and accepted was this practice that a fleet of eleven ships was dispatched in 1777 to establish an alternate penal colony at Botany Bay in the area of New South Wales that Captain Cook had claimed for Britain in 1770. When the fleet arrived with its load of a few hundred settlers and 778 convicts (192 women and 586 men) in late 1777, it became apparent that Botany Bay was totally unsuitable for a settlement. In early 1778, exploration of the area led to the discovery of an excellent harbor only a few miles north of Botany Bay. This harbor was given the name Sydney Cove, and a settlement was established there January 26, 1778, with this date eventually becoming the official Australia Day.

Settlement during the first 50 years of the new colony was limited. Settlers included convicts and a trickle of free men and women as well as some soldiers and marines who were stationed there to police and protect the community. So critical was the need for mores settlers, and especially young women (there were more than three times as many men in the colony as there were women) that the colonial government attempted to attract settlers with schemes that offered passage and the promise of land and support from the community for both families and individuals. The colonial government offered bounties to ship owners for each individual brought to the new colony. The ship owners made offerings such as the following, which is a composite of typical excerpts taken from the Norwich Mercury: [168]

---

[168]   Conventional use of emigrate/immigrate is that you "emigrate from" and "immigrate to." The Emigration Committee was dealing with individuals in England who wished to emigrate from the British Isles, so their use of the term is correct. Following their arrival in the Australian Colonies the passengers on the Amelia Thompson became immigrants to those colonies.

EMIGRATION TO THE AUSTRALIAN COLONIES

The splendid first class ship AMELIA THOMPSON of 477 tons, fitted up under the direction of the EMIGRATION COMMITTEE sails from the Thames for Sydney in March 1838.

Married Agricultural Labourers, Gardeners and Shepherds, of good character are now assisted by the Colonial Government to the extent of £20 each family towards paying their passage. A limited number of such families will, when they have obtained the sanction of the Committee, be allowed to proceed, on liberal terms, by this conveyance. An experienced surgeon and a respectable Superintendent and his wife will accompany the Emigrants, to watch over the health, comfort and welfare of all on board.

For single women, the cost of the passage, if paid here, is only £5 each, which includes all charges for food and bedding, and when those who cannot pay this sum, will, when approved by the Sailing Committee as fit persons to proceed by the conveyance, be allowed to give their note of hand for £6 payable in the colony in a reasonable time. No females will be admitted to proceed by this opportunity but those of good moral character and industrious habits.

What led British citizens to leave the relative safety of their familiar homeland to travel half way around the globe to an uncertain future in Australia and New Zealand? They knew that the long voyage was uncomfortable and dangerous if not perilous. Yet over the period from 1835 to 1840 some estimates suggest that more than 100,000 individuals each year made the journey from Great Britain to Australia and New Zealand. From there many immigrated to other islands in the South Pacific and to America.

The American war of independence 1776 to 1783, the war with France between 1793 to 1815 and the war of 1812 between the British and the new American Republic drained the financial and human resources of the British Empire. The industrial revolution was leading to the creation of factories in major population centers in the British Isles Workers were migrating from rural villages to the cities to take advantage of job opportunities that promised a more prosperous future. Poor harvests and government interference (the Corn Laws) led to rising food prices and in rural areas lower wages put a strain on family resources.

Relief for the poor became an urgent concern and led to the passing of the Poor Law of 1834 which led to a rise in the number and population of Workhouses. The condition of village laborers continued to deteriorate until many reached such a state of despair that they were ready to revolt. In Enoch Gurr's county of Sussex and in Kent a decline in the demand for Southdown wool caused distress amongst agricultural workers. Parishes began encouraging emigration to colonies such as New Zealand and New South Wales. With these pressures at home a growing number of Brits opted to attempt a new beginning in a new land.

At about the same time, in order to attract new settlers, the colonial government in Australia came up with the Bounty System. Till 1835 money for passage was given directly to emigrants by the colonial government as a loan to be paid back when the new arrival had earned enough to do so. However, most new arrivals managed to avoid paying off these loans, so the government converted the loan scheme to a bounty scheme. Under the Bounty System settlers in New South Wales could recruit workers from Britain themselves. It was these settlers who paid the emigrants' passages. When the emigrants arrived they were examined by an examining board appointed by the Governor. If the board was satisfied that an emigrant was under thirty, baptized, sound of mind and body, and of good moral character (references were required) that emigrant was approved. The settler who had advanced the passage money for the new arrival was issued a certificate entitling him to claim the Bounty money for the emigrant. The settlers usually used agents in Britain to negotiate with potential emigrants and these agents set up Emigration Committees.

Emigration Committees were also established by ship owners, anxious to profit from the colonial government's bounty scheme. The bounty ships' voyages from England to Australia around the Cape of Good Hope, usually with stopovers in Capetown, Calcutta, Indonesia and other ports took three to four months. The loss of life on these ships' passages from England to Australia ranged between less than 1% to as high as 24%. The average loss of life in the years 1837-1838 for 24 ships carrying 6,824 passengers was about 7.08% (483 deaths, mostly women and children). It was usually the younger children who passed away. One of the worst voyages was that of the *Layton* in 1837. Of 300 passengers who embarked in England, only 228 eventually arrived in Australia, with an alarming 72 (24%) dying while at sea.

10.9   Enoch Gurr, American Pioneer

Perhaps typical of those who responded to the opportunity for a new life abroad was Enoch Gurr of East Sussex. At the beginning of the 19th century James Gurr and his wife, Sarah Eldredge lived in a farming area in East Sussex, somewhere between the villages of Northiam and Peasmarsh. They raised ten children: John, William, Sarah, Enoch Eldredge, Ann, Edward, Thomas, Harriett, Mary and James. The elder James' father was also born in Peasmarsh three miles northwest of the port city of Rye, and three miles southeast of Northiam.

The couples third son, Enoch Eldridge Gurr was recorded as being born in Northiam, Sussex England in 1813. Little is known of Enoch's early life, although it is known that he was raised in a Church of England parish, that he was certified of good character by the rector of the Northiam parish church and that he had been taught to read and write.

The details of Enoch's first marriage to Sarah Higgins are uncertain, but the marriage probably took place in December of 1832, soon after Enoch turned 19 years of age. Since Enoch had not reached the age of consent at that date, it would have been necessary that his parents approve the marriage. Whatever the circumstances, Sarah gave birth to a child, Mary, either out of wedlock in 1832 as some family trees suggest, or possibly during 1833. The couple's second child, William, was born in 1834 and they were blessed with a third child, Jane, in 1837.

Sketch 10.10   The Amelia Thompson

10.10   Aboard the *Amelia Thompson*

Enoch, Sarah and their three children sailed for Australia in March of 1838 on board the *Amelia Thompson*. On the same ship was a friend of Enoch by the name of John Buckman, his wife and his sister Ruth Buckman (a practical nurse) as well as other Buckman family members. The *Amelia Thompson,* seen in **Sketch 10.10** [169] above, was constructed in 1833 and advertised as one of the new "fast" ships with first class cabins built to transport emigrants to America and to the new colonies in the Pacific.   On the Gurr family's passage from Plymouth to Sydney in 1838, Enoch lost two children and his wife, all three being buried at sea.

Apparently the *Amelia Thompson* was hard hit by typhus, and according to some reports, smallpox. The total loss of life on the ship is not known, but the *Sydney Herald* carried the following on Monday July 9th, 1838:

> **QUARANTINE** - A proclamation was issued on Saturday (July 7th) declaring, that several cases of typhus fever having occurred on board the ship *Amelia Thompson*, His Excellency the Governor, with the advice of the Executive Council, has directed the crew and passengers of that vessel to be placed in quarantine.

The Quarantine was lifted July 23, 1838. Enoch and William survived the voyage as did Ruth Buckman and her brother John, whose wife was one of the dead. Enoch married Ruth after they were settled in Australia, probably in early 1839.

Ruth bore Enoch five children in Australia: James, Susannah, Peter, Sarah and Reuben. Ruth was well educated and taught her children to read and write. In 1853, the couple was

---

[169] Sketch reproduced here as Public Domain and available from several on-line sites.

visited by two Mormon missionaries, who taught them about the new prophet in America, and on 23 December 1853 they were baptized as members of the Church of Jesus Christ of Latter Day Saints. In1856, Enoch's son William, now 22 years of age, married Sarah E. Barker.

Their new faith would eventually bring Enoch, his wife and their children to America and as previously documented their descendants account for 38 of 168 Gurrs recorded in the 1880 Federal Census of the United Stated and 7 of 36 families. By the 1920 census descendants of Enoch Gurr would be scattered throughout the American West.

10.11 Enoch Gurr to America

Because of the activities of Johnston's Army [170] and trouble with local Indians, Brigham Young called Elders in America and around the world to migrate to Utah. For the Elders and Saints from Australia and the surrounding islands, Brigham Young made arrangements for passage on an old sailing vessel bound for America. Enoch and Ruth decided to immigrate to Utah Territory with their family and they sailed to America aboard the "Lucas" arriving in San Pedro, California in 1857. They passed through Parowan in southwest Utah, where Enoch's eldest son, William, and his wife decided to remain. Enoch and Ruth went on to Provo with their five children and initially settled their, but eventually moved a few miles south of Provo to Benjamin.

The three sons of Enoch and Ruth married in Utah and their daughters Susannah and Sarah entered into a polygamous marriage with William M. Wall, who died in Provo in September, 1869, leaving Susannah a widow with three children and Sarah a widow with two children and expecting another child in a few months. Enoch and Ruth moved from place to place in Utah, eventually returning to Benjamin to live with their granddaughter Ruth and her husband William Stewart. However, Enoch only lived about six weeks after coming back to Benjamin, dying on March 12th, 1887. He was buried in the Benjamin Cemetery. Two years later Ruth died and was buried by his side.

---

[170] In Utah Territory, during the winter of 1857-1858 there was open conflict between Mormon settlers and the U.S. government which is often referred to as the Utah War. In the spring of 1857, President James Buchanan appointed a non-Mormon, Alfred Cumming, governor of the Utah Territory, thus replacing the local leader, Brigham Young. In early September of that year U.S. troops, under the leadership of a Texan by the name of Johnston who had fought in the Mexican War, were dispatched to enforce the order. The Mormons prepared to defend themselves and their property; Young declared martial law and issued an order on Sept. 15, 1857, forbidding the entry of U.S. troops into Utah. The order was disregarded, with the U.S. army arriving on Sept. 28th. Throughout the winter sporadic raids were conducted by the Mormon militia (the Nauvoo Legion) against Johnston's encamped and strictly defensive army. On one occasion the Mormon militia attacked and destroyed 52 wagons of army supplies. In April of 1858, President Buchanan, under heavy criticism for his actions, dispatched mediators who eventually worked out a settlement with the Mormon community. On June 26 Johnston's army entered Salt Lake City unopposed, Cumming was installed as governor, and peace was restored.

Chapter 11
The Reverend Henry Jonathan Gurr
"A Restless and Not Very Practical Man"

11.1 Young Henry

Henry Jonathan Gurr was the most adventuresome of the three brothers and provided the inspiration that eventually led his two brothers to immigrate to the United States. He was born in Paddington, London on January 22, 1853, the third of eight children of Alfred James and Mary Ann Gurr, nee Bennett, as we summarized in Part I. His father, then 29, was a live-in butler for a wealthy family in Hyde Park Gardens, headed by Proctor Henry James Wheeler, while his mother, then 33, lived in a separate dwelling about a half mile from the Wheeler home. Though Mary Ann may also have been in service at the time of their marriage in 1846, like most mid-19th century lower class mothers, she spent her days caring for her children, and almost certainly without any domestic help.

As a boy Henry was sent to private schools but we do not know for how long or what he studied. [171] We do know that he was bright and well-enough prepared that in the late 1860s, when he was about 14, he was apprenticed to the captain of a ship in the East India trade. [172] Whether or not he passed an exam for ship's mate, as the family recalled, he acquired skills in navigation, seamanship, and boat-building that he often used in later life. By 1871 he was back in London where, according to that year's census, he and his older brother Alfred Richard worked as assistants in Gurr and Son. In 1875, likely after additional voyages to India, Henry immigrated to the United States, probably working for his passage on a ship in the iron ore and timber trade that sailed the Great Lakes to Duluth. For the next year he earned money by working on Great Lakes steamers and spent the winter of 1875-76 stoking fires on barges to keep them from being crushed by ice in the Duluth winter. Illness contracted in India supposedly led him to emigrate on the advice of a physician who recommended that he live in cool, high-altitude regions. Whatever truth there is to this, he lived and worked most of his ministerial career in northern climates. [173]

---

[171] Co-author Paul Magel speculates in Part I that Henry may have followed his older brother Alfred Richard to Christ's Hospital, Hertford (the Bluecoat School), which housed the Royal Mathematical School where promising boys of 10 or 11 were given basic education in such subjects as navigation and mathematics. If Henry studied there, it would have been a natural entry to his career at sea. Unfortunately, records of students at the school in the 1860s have been lost.

[172] The Gurr family sent their children to work when in their teens. The 1871 census shows that their oldest child, daughter Sarah, was working as a telegraph clerk, while Edwin, their fifteen-year-old youngest son, was employed as a wine merchant's clerk. Alfred James died in 1874, at the age of 50, and his sons Alfred Richard and Edwin took over the family business. The 1881 census lists them as Milk Contractors of the firm Gurr and Sons, employing seven men and three women. Two of the three women working as clerks were sisters Sarah and Emily.

[173] His obituary, ' Gurr Enjoyed Life of Many Experiences,' *Chelan Valley Leader*, June 24, 1931, says he sailed to India at age 15 and that he worked on Great Lakes steamboats after arriving in the US. An earlier article in the *Chelan Leader*, December 18, 1903, says that he returned to England "for a year" before he immigrated to the US, which he did in his 23rd year. The 1871 census has him in London, perhaps between voyages. All else in this

11.2   Divinity School

In the fall of 1876, at age 23, Henry enrolled as a student at the Episcopal Church's Seabury Divinity School in Faribault, Minnesota. Years later, from the pulpit, he told parishioners that he had once joined a posse to hunt down the James boys. Faribault is a few miles south of Northfield, where on September 7, 1876 the James gang of eight men staged a bloody but unsuccessful raid on a local bank. A citizens' pursuit followed leading to the capture of most of the survivors, and Henry Gurr was in on the chase. He told family members his posse was close enough to find smoldering campfires, but they never caught up to the gang. [174]

Although we have no record of Henry returning to London for a visit with his family, it is possible that he did so. However, we do know that Edwin crossed the Atlantic to New York in 1878, and presumably to visit his brother. Henry graduated with his class of five in the spring of 1879 and was ordained first as deacon and then, on June 13, as priest by Bishop Henry B. Whipple in the Episcopal cathedral in Faribault. [175]

11.3   Early Ministry

During seminary training and for the next three years Henry Gurr served in Minnesota churches in the towns of Redwood Falls, Marshall, Brownsville, Caledonia, and others. In 1880 he married Celia Frost, the sister of Edward Frost, physician and William Frost, druggist, all residents of Willmar, Minnesota. [176] Celia, a graduate of the Boston Conservatory of Music was unmarried and teaching music in Willmar during the June 1880 census. The Reverend Henry was usually responsible for several churches and in winter traveled among them by carriage or sleigh. "Harry poor fellow has such long cold drives to take between his stations that I hate to have him go and longingly watch for his return," Celia wrote her sister in the winter of 1880-81. [177]

Minnesota winters along the upper Mississippi were not only cold, but dangerous as well. In the same letter Harry added this note to his sister-in-law: [178]

---

paragraph is based on family recollections. Records at the National Maritime Museum in London cannot be used to confirm his merchant marine service without information on the ship(s) on which he served and dates of voyages.

[174] "From Warsaw," *Quincy (Illinois) Daily Journal*, dateline Sept. 30, 1894; http://en.wikipedia.org/wiki/Jesse_James_Northfield_Raid.

[175]   The principal events of Reverend Henry J. Gurr's life are summarized in his obituary, " Gurr Enjoyed a Life of Many Experiences." This was very likely written by his wife Mabel, who had access to his manuscript memoirs, "A Red-Blooded Anglican," a manuscript that has since been lost. His studies at Seabury Divinity School are confirmed by the Calendar of Seabury Divinity School, Faribault, Minnesota. 1878-9, in the archives of Seabury-Western Theological Seminary in Evanston, Ill. Bishop Whipple's letter of ordination has been preserved among the Reverend Gurr's papers.

[176]   Our research found evidence of Frost families living near St. John New Brunswick, Canada in the Canadian Censuses of 1860, 1870 and 1880. Celia's brother, Dr. Edward Frost apparently moved to Minnesota in 1869, but we do not know whether he was educated as a physician in the United States or Canada. His wife Marian's father was born in Maine, her mother in New Brunswick. The 1880 census was taken in June and Celia (a music teacher and still single) was living with another brother James H. who is a carpenter (the brothers live in neighbouring houses).

[177]   Henry was Harry to Celia, but we do not know whether this nickname was used by others in the family.

[178]   Letter from Celia Gurr "To Nellie, Xmastide" (days before Christmas 1880), transcribed by Ted Robert Gurr.

Last Monday two men went up to LaCrosse with a team of horses....They arrived in LaCrosse, sold their hoop poles, and got tipsy on the money. They did not leave LaCrosse [until] about 4:30 when it was getting dark. This morning, Friday, they found the hay rack floating in a large air hole with a mitten on top two miles outside of LaCrosse.... It is supposed the horses, men, and the wheel part of the wagon are under the ice.

Records of burials at Episcopal churches south of LaCrosse show that the Reverend Henry Gurr officiated at eight of them in 1880-81, including one H. J. Alexander of Brownsville, who "drowned in Mississippi through air hole, probably through drink," probably one of the teamsters described in his added note. Henry also presided over the burial of Dr. O'Conner of Caledonia who died of an "overdose of morphine." The other six were infants or children under 6, victims of diphtheria, cholera, or "general debility." [179]

11.4   To California

Harry and Celia's first child, son Alfred E., was born in 1881 in Minnesota and two years later his brother William was born in Wahpeton, South Dakota, where the Reverend Gurr served Trinity Church for two years. The boys were healthy but Celia became ill. According to Richland County's *Wahpeton Gazette*, "Mrs. Gurr's health had been poor before they took up their residence in this city. Since then her lungs have troubled her quite seriously until by the advice of physicians they decided to leave for California hoping a warmer climate would enable her to gain again her health."

In March 1884, the family left for the West Coast, travelling on the Northern Pacific en route to Portland. The trip was marred by a week's delay waiting to cross the ice-clogged, two and a half miles wide Missouri river at Mandan, North Dakota. Half of the track on either side of the bridge at Mandan was submerged and the passengers had to be ferried across by boat. [180] Celia wrote that:

Harry took a state-room or drawing-room for fifty dollars and it is really worth a hundred to us. We are entirely to ourselves with plenty of room to eat and rest....I am feeling much better and this seems such a pleasant rest. We get our meals as it costs seventy-five cents to buy them! Harry bought a spirit lamp...and we make our own coffee, boil eggs, etc. and have canned tongue and boiled ham. [181]

---

[179]   La Crosse Area Genealogical Society, *Episcopal Churches Burials, Houston County, MN*. Retrieved from www.rootsweb.com/~wilacgs/HoustonCoEpisBur.htm

[180]   The Northern Pacific Railway was approved by Congress in 1864 and granted 40,000,000 acres of land extending through Wisconsin, Minnesota, North Dakota, Montana, Idaho, Washington and Oregon, with branches to the city of Winnipeg and to southern British Columbia, Canada. Construction began in 1870 and the last spike was driven in September of 1883 near Gold Creek in Western Montana. The Missouri River at Mandan was finally bridged by a million-dollar span on October 21, 1882. Till then the river crossing had been handled by a ferry service most of the year, although during winters, when ice was thick enough, rails were laid across the river itself. When the Missouri flooded in the spring of 1884, the track leading to and from the bridge was submerged and the ferry had to be put back in service.

[181]   Ted Robert Gurr's transcription of letter from Celia Gurr to her mother, "Pyramid Park Sleeper, Bismarck, Sunday, March 30th/84."

The source of the $50 – a very substantial amount for a country clergyman – is suggested by a testimonial from the members of the Wahpeton Lodge of Odd Fellows. At the end of a reception for Harry and Celia, immediately before their departure, Judge Buxton spoke at length of the Reverend Gurr's services to the town and said, "I have the pleasure of presenting you this cheque for $71.50 as a token of the respect and affection in which we hold you as a man, an Odd Fellow, and a Christian clergyman." [182] It also was a customary practice for parishioners at the time to give clergymen a donation, called a "purse." His papers include several records of such purses from parishes where he served in later years.

11.5 Celia Dies

The Reverend Henry Jonathan Gurr served the next three years at churches in the San Francisco Bay area, mostly at St. James in Centerville, Alameda County, SE of Oakland. Celia died in Centerville on October 18, 1887 and was buried in Fremont (gravestone **Photo 11.5a**). [183]

Photo 11.5b Will and Alf c. 1887
Motherless
Henry J. Gurr Album

Photo 11.5b shows Will and Alf together and was taken at about the time of their mother's passing. Their expressions are rather unhappy and pensive and we might speculate that they are two motherless boys in mourning. Celia's death left her sons aged 4 and 6 with a grieving husband who habitually treated the two boys as young adults. Will remembers that he sometimes cried for his mother but seems to have received little comfort from his father, who never spoke to the boys about her. [184]

Photo 11.5a
Celia's Gravestone
Paul Magel Collection

---

[182]   Reverend Gurr's papers include a number of testimonials such as this from congregations he served. Most are in his own hand, transcribed from news accounts (as in this instance) or, more commonly, from handwritten originals that have not survived.

[183]   Note that the gravestone for Celia is in Irvington Memorial Cemetery, Fremont, Alameda County CA and indicates a death in 1888, but the 1887 date is correct. Henry left in 1888.

[184]   This and the following references to Will Gurr's recollections are from his edited memoirs, *Coming of Age in the West 1883-1906: From the Mississippi to California and Gold Rush Alaska with my Minister Father*, A Memoir by Will E. Gurr, Edited and Annotated by Ted Robert Gurr (CreateSpace, 2011, distributed by Amazon.com).

11.6 Itinerant Years - A Second Marriage

In the years after Celia's death the Reverend Gurr traveled widely and often, with his two sons in tow. In 1888-89 he took Alf and Will to Minnesota to visit Celia's family, then to England where he lived for a year visiting with his brothers Alfred and Edwin at their Southwark home. While there he met and married Alice McTaggart Gardner, the 20-year old daughter of Scottish parents. Their August marriage certificate lists Henry's address as Folkestone, which was a coastal village in Kent, and that of Alice as Regent's Park Road in London. We know from Will's memoirs that he and Alf spent time with family members during this period. Will had no contemporary memory of the marriage but did recall a visit to Scotland with his father – perhaps to meet her parents? The boys also recalled that their father had taken a trip to France, which might have been his honeymoon.

From London Henry and the boys took steamship passage back to New York City – a rough passage, according to Will - and then traveled by train through the southern United States to San Diego. Will recalls that when they got off the train in San Diego his father gave the porter a $1 tip and said to the boys, "There goes my last dollar." Asked why, he said "He was so good to us." It probably was during their stay in San Diego that the Reverend Gurr took a temporary teaching position. His 1931 obituary says that he was "professor of Greek in the San Diego College" while his son Will mentioned that he taught Hebrew in San Diego. [185] (His curriculum at Seabury Seminary included several years of instruction in both languages.)

11.7 "Dad went broke"

By the end of 1889 the Reverend Gurr was on the move again, this time to Merced in the California's Central Valley. He had by now persuaded his older brother Alfred Richard to immigrate to the US with his wife and 12 children. One compelling attraction, according to Alfred Gurr's descendants, was that public education in the US was free whereas in London they had to pay school fees. Alfred settled and took up farming north of Merced on what would become known as Gurr Road. Henry and his sons lived nearby for a while, until, according to Will's memoirs, his father "went broke." The boys were put in a residential school for boys near San Mateo for about two years. Henry was soon joined by his new wife, accompanied by her mother, and we can speculate that one reason he left the boys so long in the boarding school was to get settled into his new marriage.

When the boys eventually rejoined their father near Merced, Will Gurr remembered meeting his stepmother for the first time. She was "A beautiful woman, tho to say the least, she had no business being a minister's wife." She tried to teach Will to read but gave it up as a bad job. "Those were some days, we were living in a dilapidated, unpainted house, with a makeshift porch on two sides of it. My brother and I slept on the floor and the furniture was very much on the absent list." The marriage ended in separation and eventual divorce because of their stepmother's alleged infidelity, or as Will implied, because she was not accustomed to the privations of being the wife of a country preacher.

---

[185] Ted Robert Gurr's interview with Will Gurr, July 1971.

11.8 Medical Training?

Several sources say that Henry Gurr had medical training, but the extent of that training is not known. During Henry's youth the title of "Doctor" was used by anyone who considered himself a healer. It was not until the early 1870s that the Medical Act of 1858, which required that a Medical Board register qualified physicians and forbade hiring of the unqualified, was understood by the populace. A 1903 article [186] in the *Chelan Leader*, based on Reverend Gurr's conversation with the editor, says he explained his desire to do so because of family illness (we assume the illness of Celia) and referred to himself as doctor. Could he have received medical training during the years he was in the Oakland area? Years later, a son from his third marriage, Robert, was told that his father got medical training in the 1890s so he could deal with gunshot wounds. [187] Could this be during his years in Alaska? Perhaps, but Henry and his wife Mabel and Henry's two sons had lived in Buena Vista, Colorado in 1898, and Will Gurr once said his father gave up medical practice after being called to the Colorado Rockies, as an intern, and having to deal with the human carnage after a railroad snow plow ran into a work crew. [188]

Whatever the level of his medical training, there is no evidence that he practiced medicine in Chelan, though he may have ministered to members of his own household. However, during his years of service in remote areas he was undoubtedly an option for help in emergencies, and as an educated man and a servant of God, his opinion would have been sought by parishioners for any acute illness. Many religious people also accept the concept that healing can be achieved through prayer and the intervention of a religious healer. One of the authors has a faith healer as a neighbour and his church frequently sends its members to his home for the prayerful laying on of hands to invoke the intercession of the Holy Spirit.

11.9 Scandal in Warsaw, Illinois

In June 1893 Reverend Gurr was at St. James Church, Alameda, but ready to move on again, for the Church wardens gave him this document on his departure: "This is to certify that the Reverend H. J. Gurr has been in charge of St. James for five years, during which time he has conducted himself as a Christian gentleman, and devoted priest of the church; and has left many warm friends in this community." Reverend Gurr notes on the document that the congregation gave him a $100 purse when he left.

Father and sons moved back to the Midwest settling in Warsaw, Illinois, south of Keokuk on the Mississippi River, where the Reverend Gurr served St. Paul's Church. After about a year he became the target of anonymous accusations of improper behavior involving young women of his congregation. He was a handsome and well-spoken man of about forty and some women of

---

[186] *The Chelan Leader*, December 18, 1903

[187] David Gurr's notes of conversations with Robert L. Gurr in 1970-71.

[188] Author's interview with Will Gurr, July 1971.

the parish evidently were enamored of him, prompting jealously among their husbands and hostile rumors. A local correspondent wrote this dispatch to the *St. Louis Republic:*

> Warsaw, Ill, Aug 24. As announced by the Reverend Hy J. Gurr, in charge of St. Paul's Episcopal Church of this city, last Sunday morning, that gentlemen met his congregation last night and asked for specific and direct charges against his moral character, but received none.
>
> He then made a clean breast of his domestic relations: admitted that he had made a bad bargain in selecting a step-mother for his two little boys and was now trying to get a legal separation from her through a divorce court. He declared that he had tasted heaven in his first matrimonial venture and had received a good dose of hell itself in his second. He demanded the passage of a resolution by the congregation denouncing or commending his action. He had no trouble in getting a complimentary resolution and favorable response from the congregation. Reverend Gurr read scores of letters from clergymen, lawyers and doctors from different cities where he has had charge, all highly commending his ability, piety and morality. [189]

The scandal persisted, however, and by Sept. 23, according to the *Quincy Daily Journal,*

> The Reverend Gurr of the Episcopal church startled his congregation by distributing blank certificates which he requested them to fill in with any accusations they might have or hear against him, or any young lady member of his church. They were also asked to "set their hand and seal" to the same. The blanks were headed, "A Slander Choker." To say his congregation were paralyzed is expressing it mildly. Warsaw people have frequently heard of "chokers" and in a few rare instances have heard of slanders, but the combination, "slander choker" is something unique in this locality.

[The meaning of the phrase is clear enough, even if not common usage: the Reverend Gurr wanted signed documents that would choke off the malicious rumors.]

No parishioner at St. Paul's came forward with accusations but, in response to the ruckus, Bishop Burgess arrived a few days later and conducted what a journalist referred to as a "star chamber court" in which the Reverend Gurr had no opportunity to hear or rebut those who continued to censure him. The upshot was that the Bishop removed him from office. [190]

11.10 Chicago and a Third Marriage

During the winter of 1894 and for the next two years the Reverend Henry Gurr was on the road again, serving parishes in Minnesota, Wisconsin and Illinois. He visited the Frosts in Willmar, for Will so states in his memoirs. He was back in Illinois at Grand Crossing in 1896

---

[189] The Reverend Gurr collected a dozen news articles on the episode and pasted them into a notebook ironically labeled "Advertisements." The testimonial from the wardens of St. James in Centreville, California, quoted above, probably was one of the encomiums he gathered and read to his Warsaw congregation. According to the Michael Link (personal communication), the contemporary Episcopal Church would require a full hearing in such a case and the priest given the opportunity to respond to the charges.

[190] "From Warsaw," *The Quincy Daily Journal*, September 30, 1894. The interpretation of the circumstances that led to the accusations comes from his daughter-in-law Anne Gurr, wife of Robert Gurr.

and was minister at St. George's Church in Southside, Chicago where he met and, on January 1, 1897, married Mabel Ethel Lucas. Mabel was the youngest daughter of John and Mary Lucas, who were probably parishioners at St. George's. She was a plain young woman, judging from photos, but a good-tempered and patient mother to the five children born to them during the next ten years. Alf and Will were by now self-sufficient teen-agers and she had little in the way of responsibility for them. **Photo 11.10a** shows Will, Reverend Gurr and Alf c.1893.

Photo 11.10a   Will, Henry and Alf
Warsaw, 1893
Henry J. Gurr Album

Mabel's father was Captain John Lucas who edited a mining trade publication in Chicago. He was English-born and claimed to be a veteran of the Crimean War. [191] What he thought of his youngest daughter marrying a man 20 years older than her is not known, but Will Gurr recalled that Captain Lucas thought enough to give his new son-in-law a cane and a tall plug hat, badly out of fashion, which he wore a few times before discarding it.

---

[191]   See Chapter 15.2

Shortly after his third marriage Henry left Chicago for Colorado. His papers include this note, dated January 18, 1898, and signed by six women:

> We, the Teachers of St. Georges' Sunday School learn with sincere regret of your resolve to leave us; and do hereby tender you our heartfelt appreciation of your labors among us; and of your kindly bearing at all times and under all circumstances. In your departure, you carry with you the kindly wishes of each and all of; and the desire that God's Blessing, Happiness and Peace may ever abundantly be yours.

11.11 Colorado

Henry and Mabel Gurr's destination in early spring of 1898 was Buena Vista, a silver mining town high in the Colorado Rockies. The Reverend Henry served briefly at Grace Episcopal church, evidently with little success. In March he received this note from Bishop J. B. Spaulding of Colorado:

> I desire that you leave Buena Vista so soon as you can, and go to Silver Cliff. This is a much better Parish, with much better opportunities. This is a real promotion and a self-supporting Parish. You are very capable and win every heart. When can you be ready? Affectionately yours…. .

Rather than leaving Buena Vista, where he had bought a house on wooded land with a creek (**Photo 11.11a**), and accepting the Bishop's highly recommended move to Silver Cliff, the Reverend Gurr applied to be sent to Alaska, where the Yukon gold rush was in full swing.

Apparently the Bishop agreed. Henry decided that a burro he had bought in Buena Vista should go with him to San Francisco and on to Alaska. Household goods along with the burro

Photo 11.11a The Gurr Home at Buena Vista Colorado, 1897
Henry J. Gurr Album

were shipped by train, first to Denver, then to Salt Lake City, with a short stay at each stopover, before going on to San Francisco. The trip started in late April for Will recalled that when in Denver he heard of the onset of the Spanish-American War (which began on April 25, 1898). On the last leg of the rail trip the boys, now 14 and 17 years old, were placed in charge and commissioned to rent quarters in San Francisco. Alf had to travel with the burro because, as Will recalls, "You cannot ship livestock without having an attendant to go along. I think when my brother reached Frisco he was capable of out-braying a burro and at least he had all the burro he ever wanted." There's no further reference to the burro – no doubt it was sold in San Francisco.

11.12 Sailing the *Angelus* to Alaska

Once in San Francisco the Reverend Gurr decided to use his resources – evidently including an advance from the Bishop of Northern California – to buy a schooner and sail to Alaska. No doubt his youthful experiences at sea gave him the confidence to make the attempt, and he probably thought that the schooner would be of use along the southern Alaska coast. Henry, the boys, and several workmen spent the summer and fall of 1898 outfitting the 38' schooner. Henry named the craft the *Angelus,* and repeatedly attempted to sail it up the Pacific Coast. The crew consisted of his nephew Ted from Merced and his two teen-age sons and, initially, Mabel. On four separate occasions they set sail only to be battered by storms and forced to return to San Francisco. On their final attempt in September, the *Angelus* came close to being wrecked on the Faralon Islands, west of the entrance to San Francisco Bay. Mabel – now pregnant with their first child – returned temporarily to Chicago, Ted went back to Merced, and Reverend Gurr placed the boat into the custody of the Irish dock master of the Spreckles Sugar Company wharf at the foot of 3d Street in San Francisco. He went to the Bishop's office for more money – the *Angelus* had cost him all he had – and the Bishop instructed his secretary to accompany Reverend Gurr to the steamship office to be sure the funds were spent on steamship passage. [192]

11.13 Skagway

According to Will's memoirs, Henry and his two sons, Will and Alfred arrived in Skagway in early October at Pacific Coast Steamship Dock aboard the steamship Cottage City under a Captain Wallace (mentioned in Will Gurr's memoirs as a "gruff old sea dog, but a wonderful navigator") who reportedly treated his Gurr passengers kindly. On the following page **Photo 11.13a** shows the docked Cottage City Steamship, **Photo 11.13b** shows a Captain David Wallace and **Photo 11.13c** the Port of Skagway, Alaska.

---

[192] This is a summary of a much more detailed account by Will Gurr in *Coming of Age in the West*, pp. 59-65. The anecdote about the Bishop's secretary is from Ted Robert Gurr's conversations with Will Gurr.

Photo 11.13a Cottage City Steamship

**Photo 11.13b
Captain David Wallace**

Photo 11.13c Port of Skagway c. 1899
Photo by Case and Draper

We found a lot of contradictions in the on-line information regarding the Cottage City and David Wallace. One record says that the Cottage City began service in Alaska in1899, while another says the ship was sold to the Pacific Coast Steamship Company around 1897. Another site claims Captain David Wallace worked for the Pacific Coast Steamship Co. from 1888 until his death in Seattle c. 1908. However, the Cottage City was lost in a storm in 1911, and while all passengers and crew were rescued, news reports name Captain David Wallace as the ship's master.

147

Skagway was founded in December 1897, but it was a lawless frontier town which acted as one of the starting points for the thousands of men afflicted with gold rush fever, who were flocking to the Klondike in the Northwest Territory of Canada (the region became the Yukon Territory in 1898). The jump off point to the gold fields was Lake Bennett, and the trails that miners took through the mountains from Skagway to Lake Bennett were known as the Chilkoot and White Passes. **Map 11.13d** shows these routes.

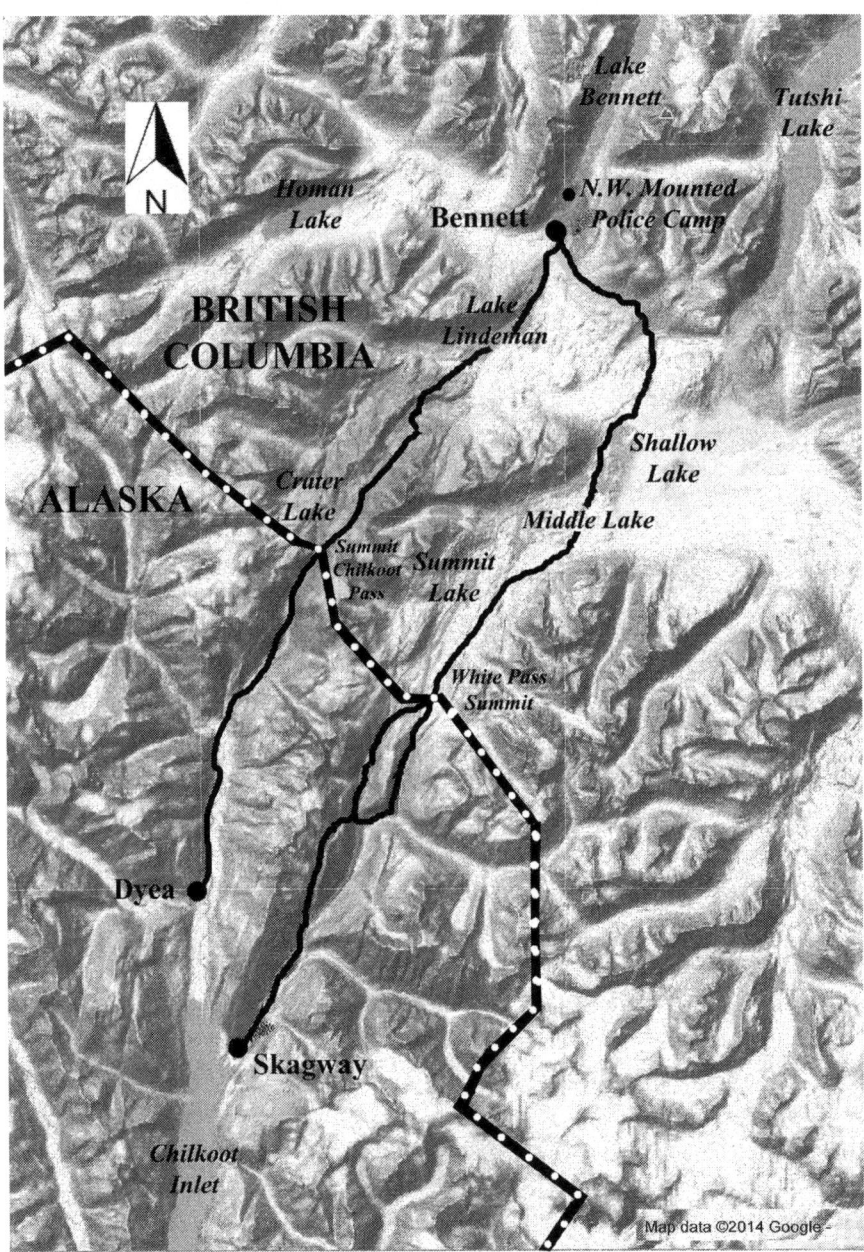

Photo 11.13d *The Trails to Lake Bennett*
Left: Chilkoot Pass from Dyea,   Right: White Pass from Skagway
Terrain Background: Map data copyright 2014 Google
Place details by Paul Magel

Among the founders of the town of Skagway were opportunists: outfitters, merchants, the hoteliers, the madams and their prostitutes and others with even less scruples, whose goal was to profit from the rush. Men like "Soapy Smith" and his band of thieves and swindlers terrorized the community. It is claimed that the only law in Skagway, the US Deputy Marshall, was on the take from Soapy, and for the first six months of 1898 the lawlessness of Soapy's gang was so flagrant that the honest locals set up a vigilance committee called the Committee of 101. Soapy and his gang responded with threats of mayhem against the vigilantes and for a time prevailed. In July Soapy was shot to death and two vigilante groups were formed (the Merchant's Committee and the Citizen's Committee) and began to dominate, but there was still little in the way of law and order. Throughout the region men took the law into their own hands and meted out justice according to the majority opinion of the group. In the last six months of 1898 that began to change, for the objective of the gold seekers was the Klondike and the Yukon Territories in Canada. Canada was responding to the reports of lawlessness in the region and re-enforcing the North West Mounted Police detachments. Men like Sam Steele of the Mounties became famous for enforcing Canadian law in the Yukon.

As early as 1896 gold miners were driving a population increase that justified the establishment of a NWMP (North West Mounted Police) post in the region. The increased population coming with the gold rush led to the separation of the Yukon district from the Northwest Territories (a vast region which had been governed and controlled by the Hudson's Bay Company but which joined the Canadian Confederation in 1870). From these Northwest Territories sprang today's provinces of Manitoba, Saskatchewan, Alberta, most of modern British Columbia, the Yukon and the 520,000 square miles that is the Northwest Territories of today.

The newly established Yukon Territory of Canada joined Confederation in June of 1898. Canadian Alien law was then applied and additional NWMP were dispatched to the region. US citizens were not required to leave, but were required to follow Canadian law. Incidentally, there is some evidence that the Canadian government had hopes of gaining access to the Chilkoot Inlet and possibly of annexing the Skagway area.

The NWMP ejected undesirables, collected duties, established the one ton rule (goods to prevent starvation) and enforced Canadian criminal law in what had been a lawless region. The one ton rule produced a list that became known as a Yukon Outfit and **Table 11.13e** on the following page is a copy of one such list.[193]

On July 21, 1898, an excursion train hauled passengers for 4 miles (6.4 km) out of Skagway, the first train to operate in Alaska. On July 30, 1898, the charter rights and concessions

---

[193] The miners (often referred to as stampeders) had to transport their outfit across the Canadian border between Skagway and Bennett. From Lake Bennett they found water transportation to Atlin or along the Yukon River to the distant Klondike gold fields. For those without horses this meant many trips carrying 50 to 80 lbs over the roughly 33 mile Dyea trail or 40 mile White Trail to Bennett. Some miners claimed to have walked over 1000 miles acting as packhorses.

A YUKON OUTFIT

8	Sacks Flour	1	Hand Saw
150	Lbs Bacon	1	Jack Plane
150	Lbs Split Peas	1	Brace
100	Lbs Beans	4	Bits, Assorted 3/16' to 1"
25	Lbs Evaporated Apples	1	8 inch Mill File
25	Lbs Evaporated Peaches	1	6 inch Mill File
25	Lbs Apricots	1	Broad Hatchet
25	Lbs Butter	1	2 Qt Galvanized Coffee Pot
100	Lbs Granulated Sugar	1	Fry Pan
1 1/2	Doz. Condensed Milk	1	Package Rivets
15	Lbs Coffee	1	Draw Knife
10	Lbs Tea	3	Cov'd Pails, 4, 6, 8 qt Granite
1	Lb Pepper	1	Pie Plate
10	Lbs Salt	1	Knife and Fork
8	Lbs Baking Powder	1	Granite Cup
40	Lbs Rolled Oats (or Oatmeal)	1	Tea Spoon
2	Doz. Yeast Cakes	1	Table Spoon
1/2	Doz. 4 Oz. Beef Extract	1	14 inch Granite Spoon
5	Bars Castile Soap	1	Tape Measure
6	Bars Tar Soap	1	1 ½ inch Chisel
1	Tin Matches	10	Lbs Oakum
1	Gal. Vinegar	10	Lbs Pitch
1	Box Candles	5	Lbs 20d Nails
25	Lbs Evaporated Potatoes	5	Lbs 10d Nails
25	Lbs Rice	6	Lbs 6d Nails
25	Canvas Sacks	200	Feet 3/8 inch Rope
1	Wash Basin	1	Single Block
1	Medicine Chest	1	Solder Outfit
1	Rubber Sheet	1	Pair Kowlocks
1	Set Pack Straps	1	14 Qt Galvanized Pail
1	Pick	1	Granite Saucepan
1	Handle	3	Lbs Candle Wick
1	Drift Pick	1	Compass
1	Handle	1	Candle Stick
1	Shovel	6	Towels
1	Gold Pan	1	Emery Stone
1	Axe	1	Axe Handle
1	Whip Saw		

Some of the foregoing articles are omitted by some miners.
Dealers will advise in all cases.

Table 11.13e   A Yukon Outfit – The One Ton Rule

Transcribed from a Skagway dealer's list by Paul Magel

of three rail companies co-operating in the region since 1897 to link Skagway with the Yukon were acquired by the White Pass & Yukon Railway Company Ltd, a new company organized in London, England by British investors. Construction reached the 2,885-foot (879.3 m) summit of White Pass, 20 miles (32 km) away from Skagway, by mid-February 1899. The railway reached Bennett, British Columbia, on July 6, 1899. In the summer of 1899, construction started north from Carcross to Whitehorse, 110 miles (177 km) north of Skagway. The construction crews working from Bennett along a difficult lakeshore reached Carcross the next year, and the last spike was driven on July 29, 1900. Service started on August 1, 1900, but by then much of the Gold Rush fever had died down.

11.14 Over the Dead Horse Trail

Winter was approaching when Henry, Alf and Will arrived in Skagway. Will who was born 16 Oct 1883, celebrated his 15th birthday there in 1898. Around that time Skagway Episcopal minister Reverend Campbell was replaced by Woodin both under Bishop Rowe. Because Henry was late arriving (delayed by his failed attempts to sail the Angelus from San Francisco to Skagway in September) Bishop Rowe had already left on his regular trip to the interior. The Bishop was a dedicated, no nonsense Canadian, who had been appointed First Missionary Bishop of Alaska in 1895. Rowe was not expected back from his annual dog-sled mission into the interior until January.

In August there had been a new gold strike in the mining town of Atlin, on Lake Atlin in British Columbia, less than fifty miles, as the crow flies, from Skagway. What was the as yet unassigned Henry to do until Bishop Rowe returned? Rather than attending immediately to church business, the adventurous Henry conceived the idea of going to Aitlin. In 1898, Atlin could be reached by taking either the Chilkoot Pass or the White Pass to Lake Bennett or Lindemann Lake, jumping off points for those headed for Atlin or the more distant Klondike.

There was a 65 mile overland route to Atlin, but this could be traversed only after freeze up. There was also a 105 mile water route following a twisting chain of lakes from Lake Bennett, and of course this was navigable only before winter set in. Henry decided to set out for Lake Bennett. Those attempting this passage had to get a winter's worth of supplies up the White Pass over what became known as the Dead Horse Trail because of the estimated 3,000 pack horses that died along it during the rush (the nickname is attributed to novelist Jack London, a witness to the rush in 1897). **Photo 11.14b** shows prospectors along the White Pass in March of 1899. [194]

Mounties at the head of the pass would eventually enforce Canadian regulations that denied entrance to any travelers – virtually all of them gold-seekers – who did not have enough supplies. We do not know what supplies Henry and his sons carried with them that late October, but indications are that they could not have had the one ton outfit, so how Henry managed to convince the Mounties that he and the boys should be allowed entry will remain a mystery. During the winter of 1898-1899 there were estimated to be over 10,000 camped at Bennett on the lake of the same name, and another 10,000 camped on Lindemann Lake a few miles south of

---

[194] Prospectors along the White Pass trail to Lake Bennett, March 1899. Public Domain. Source University Library, Washington. Author Eric A. Hegg.

Bennett. Most of the 20,000 were preparing to go to the Klondike via the Yukon River. After reaching what was then Bennett (the town has since been abandoned, though listed as a historic site) via the Dead Horse Trail, Henry, the seaman turned priest, opted to take himself and his

sons along the water route to Atlin. Henry's route is shown in **Map 11.14a**. [195] In the face of the first winter snowstorms, father and sons had to transit Lake Bennett and then Lake Atlin – which they did sailing and rowing a clumsy double-ended dory that Henry bought for $15. In Aitlin they built a log cabin prepared to stay the winter, but a message came from Bishop Rowe, ordering the Reverend Gurr to meet him back in Skagway.

Photo 11.14b Prospectors on the White Pass, 1899
Taken by Eric A. Hegg, from University of Washington Digital Collections

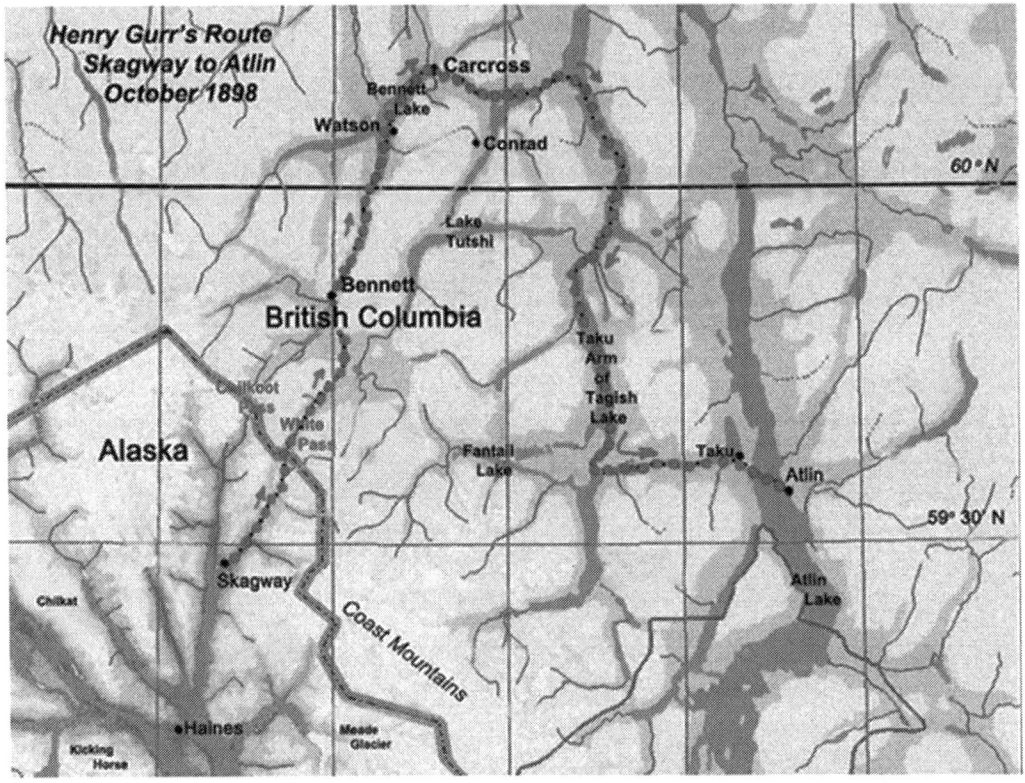

Map 11.14a Reverend Henry Gurr's Route to Atlin, 1898
Background Map from Encarta, Detailed by Paul Magel

---

[195] Map by Paul Magel with Encarta Atlas map used for background.

Henry and Alf returned to Skagway and eventually went on to Juneau. Fifteen year old Will Gurr decided he had had enough of adventuring and stayed over in Aitlin with the supplies they had packed in. [196]

11.15   From Alaska to Chelan

From January 1899 until mid 1902 the Reverend Gurr served various parishes at Skagway, at Douglas across from Juneau, and at Holy Trinity Church in Juneau. [197]   His albums include multiple photos of Holy Trinity and its rectory, exterior and interior, though the contemporary (2005) list of rectors there does not name him, perhaps because he was a supply priest during this period. Other album photos show he traveled by steamer along the Alaskan coast, to Nome and Dutch Harbor.[198]   Mabel joined him in Juneau after the birth of their daughter Eileen.

While in Alaska Henry continued to indulge his passion for sailing. The episode of the *Angelus* is proof that Henry considered himself a competent sailor. Not only did he feel capable of the passage to Alaska, he must have thought that having such a craft in Alaska would be a benefit to him and his Bishop when he got it there. One contemporary photo shows him on the Sound (off Juneau?), in clerical garb, sailing a skiff. Once in Juneau Henry bought a larger gasoline-powered boat called the "FJ" – it appears to have been about 40 feet long - and had a cabin built the length of its main deck. This was probably the main means of transport for the family and parishioners on picnics and other excursions along the rugged coast near Juneau that appear in his photos. But the bad winters and, perhaps, a desire for a more settled life led him to accept a call from St. Andrews Church in Chelan, where he took over as priest on the last Sunday of July 1902. The "FJ" was left to his son Will who used it to earn his living transporting supplies and hunters along the coast.[199]   **Photos 11.15a and 11.15b** illustrate Skagway in 1899, while **Photo 11.15c** shows the Episcopal Church Rectory in Juneau where the Reverend Henry J. Gurr resided during some of his stay in Alaska.

---

[196]   *Coming of Age in the West*, pp. 71-82.

[197]   Holy Trinity in Juneau was built in 1896 and burned to the ground in 2006. Its rectors are listed in *Church of the Holy Trinity*. Retrieved from www.trinityjuneau.org/photos.cfm.

[198]   We know that Reverend Gurr was taking photographs as early as 1884 because Celia Gurr, in the letter cited above, says she will ask Harry to photograph their rail car stateroom for her mother. Note that most of the photos in the photo section attributed to Reverend Henry J. Gurr where taken, developed and printed by him. The albums have been dispersed; the oldest in the family's possession includes photos taken in Buena Vista in 1898. An album of Alaskan photos includes his notation, 'Taken with the Blair Camera and Films by the Reverend H. J. Gurr.'

[199]   The boat is mentioned in the biographical article in *The Chelan Leader*, December 18, 1903, which says – inaccurately – that it was operated on Lake Bennett. The name "FJ" – perhaps an abbreviation – appears in Henry Gurr's handwriting beneath a photo in one of his albums. Will Gurr describes his adventures with the boat in *Coming of Age in the West*, pp. 105ff.

Photo 11.15a Camp Skagway #1
Arctic Brotherhood Hall, built 1899
Henry J. Gurr Album

University of Washington Libraries

Photo 11.15b Downtown Skagway
Clancy's Saloon centre right

Photo 11.15c   Rectory
Episcopal Church, Juneau
Henry J. Gurr Album

11.16   A Well Respected Man

The Reverend Gurr was 49 years old when he arrived in Chelan. He was a short black-haired man with a full beard and long sideburns. [200] He was well-liked and respected, as is evident from the many testimonials he collected over the years. A 1903 article in the *Chelan Leader* characterizes him as "mechanic, engineer, machinist and master of all trades." [201] According to Will Gurr his father was well-spoken and insisted on proper usage and never swore. Co-author Paul Magel believes this was true of Henry's younger brother Edwin as well, for Edwin's eldest son, Paul's grandfather George Herbert Gurr, who was very well educated, also had the bearing of a gentleman, never swore and had impeccable manners.

---

[200] His stature is evident from contemporary photos and is confirmed by Marcia O'Leary, *A History of Holy Trinity Episcopal Church.* (1996 ms.) of Spokane, where Reverend Henry Gurr served after his retirement from Chelan. He was described as "short but taller than Father Palmer, well-liked and respected." Beards were very common at the beginning of the 20th century but, as son Will mentions, his father wore sideburns long after they went out of fashion.

[201] *The Chelan Leader*, December 18, 1903.

In the 23 years before arriving in Chelan the Reverend Gurr had served at least two dozen churches in eight different states and territories. [202] In his lifetime, he had traveled an extraordinary number of miles, with multiple sea voyages to India, across the Atlantic, to Alaska and back, criss-crossing the United States by train, and traveling by horse, carriage, and sleigh among multiple parishes. Seldom had he served any congregation for more than two years, but Chelan was to be an enduring exception. In his third marriage he seems to have found some of the happiness and stability lost with Celia's death in 1887.

11.17 Gurrland

On November 28, 1902, a few months after his arrival in Chelan, Henry Gurr filed a homestead application for 160 acres on the north slope of Bear Mountain. The site was and is spectacular, a saddle at 3000 feet elevation with views down the lake to the town, across to Wapato Point, and up the lake to the Cascades. A recent book argues persuasively that Lake Chelan is "the greatest lake in the world" and by family accounts Henry chose this site because of the views it afforded, rather than practicalities. [203]

Henry began to develop the site almost immediately. What would become known as "Gurrland" was a combination of the original property and additional acreage purchased by Henry along with another package purchased by his brother Edwin when he arrived in Chelan from London by way of Winnipeg, Canada in 1906. The two brothers would homestead together atop Bear Mountain and the expansion of Gurrland is described in more detail in Chapter 14.

11.18 The Gurr Clan Grows

By 1910 more than a dozen members of the extended Gurr family lived in or near Chelan. In 1903 Captain John and Mary Lucas, Mabel's parents, moved from Chicago to Chelan with several of their grown sons. They acquired a cottage in town and a ranch to the east, but Mary spent considerable time at Gurrland visiting her daughter and a growing brood of grandchildren. Robert Lucas was born in 1906, John in 1907, Harriet in 1908, and Helen in 1910. On New Year's Eve, 1904, Will Gurr returned to the lower United States from Alaska and decided to settle in Chelan, where he lived the rest of his life, making his living as jeweler and later serving as fire chief, mayor, and justice of the peace (Chapter 17). Henry's brother Edwin settled in the valley in 1906 and was joined by his second wife Ada the following year. The couple homesteaded next to Henry and his family at Gurrland but Edwin would eventually work for orchardists along the Columbia River. [204]

---

[202] Minnesota, South Dakota, California, Illinois, Wisconsin, Colorado, and Alaska, as well as serving as supply priest at St. Mark's in Seattle for several months at some time just before his years in Alaska, according to St. Mark's *Rubric*, undated Episcopal publication of Seattle, quoted in *The Chelan Leader*, December 18, 1903.

[203] John Fahey, *Lake Chelan: The Greatest Lake in the World* (Spokane: Gray Dog Press, 2012).

[204] See entries for Reverend H. J. Gurr and Edwin Gurr in Elizabeth Watson Perry, *"We Left Because the Creek Went Dry": The People of the First Creek District Lake Chelan, Washington 1888 – 1932* (Manson, WA: Point Publishing, 1999).

11.19 "Little Financial Inducement"

Looking back in 1921, the Reverend Gurr wrote that when he arrived in Chelan, Bishop Wells of the Spokane diocese "could give but little financial inducement to stay in the field," i.e. to serve the St. Andrews congregation. A brochure from 1899 or 1900, when the Willard H. Roots was rector at St. Andrews, summarized the finances of the church: Offerings for the clergyman, $73.47; current expenses, $26.90; missionary offerings, $6.20; Sunday school, $41.31; improvements, $60; total $207.88. [205] In 1915 the Diocese's budget request to the General Board of Missions included $400 for the missionary in charge at Chelan, the Reverend Claude Black, and $150 for the associate missionary, the Reverend Henry J. Gurr.

From records of the District of Spokane **Table 11.19a** was produced covering the annual receipts for St. Andrews from 1902, the year before the Reverend Gurr arrived, through the year 1914. [206] The income from a congregation that varied between 20 (1905) and 48 (1912) members, had to pay for Sunday school and the maintenance and heating of the church as well as supplement the minister's Diocesan salary.

Table 11.19a Receipts for St. Andrews Between 1902 -1914			
Year	**Receipts**	**Year**	**Receipts**
1902	$352.42	1909	$259.99
1903	$376.76	1910	$168.00
1904	$349.08	1911	$211.30
1905	$319.19	1912	$80.70
1906	$307.00	1913	$499.84
1907	No Data	1914	$410.66
1908	$535.99		

Captain Lucas complained in his 1911 diary of the lack of funds to buy wood for the church stove or to hire a reliable person to start the fires before services. When a new organ was bought in 1912 it cost $350 paid from funds collected by the Vesper Choral Society and St. Andrew's Guild. [207] Son Robert recalled that his father received $20 a month, though this may refer to a pension he received after retiring in 1921.

---

[205] Partial pages from an undated promotional brochure in the Chelan Valley Museum, *The Organization and Official....of Chelan County.*

[206] The "little inducement" quote is from "Historic Notes", previously cited. The receipts are from a ledger page from the archives of the Episcopal Diocese of Spokane that includes 1894 through 1914 and also enumerates baptisms, confirmations, and communicants.

[207] Numbers of communicants are listed in the ledger cited in the previous note. The organ purchase is described in the *Chelan Valley Leader* for April 25, 1912.

The receipts from the congregation in the years 1910 to 1912 could not even have provided this token amount, except if one includes any gifts Henry might receive for baptisms, marriages, and funerals. There also was competition with the Methodists who had the biggest congregation in Chelan. Robert L. Gurr recalls his father saying that banker Van Slyke (whether the father John or his son Howard is unknown) "took his business over to the other church because Dad wouldn't go along with a deal to buy his way to heaven." [208] Whatever incident lay behind this recollection, it suggests a rivalry in which the St. Andrews congregation came out second-best.

The church records do not provide a full account of a country clergyman's income. In December 1908 twenty parishioners gave the Reverend Henry Gurr a purse of $54 with a note headed, "Not grudgingly, or of necessity, the members of this congregation, desiring to make you some small recompense for the time and trouble you have spent in their behalf, have taken advantage of the season and subscribed the enclosed amount, and we beg your acceptance of the same with our best wishes." There were other purses of a similar nature. Moreover, churchgoers often gave gifts of food, baked goods, fruits in season – that were part of a substantial network of food exchanges in Chelan and surrounding communities.[209]

11.20 Eking out a Living

The ranch at Gurrland was one of the ventures by which the Gurr family sought to make a living. Over the years Mabel sold cream (strained by hand), eggs, and put up as many as 100 quarts of prunes and apples from the orchard each year. Her son Robert remembers that the children's clothing came mostly from mission barrels, i.e. barrels of second-hand clothing sent from more prosperous congregations back East. Breakfast consisted of cornmeal mush with the leftovers fried and served with syrup for lunch. Mabel and her mother baked much or all their bread. Peanut butter was bought by mail-order in 25 lb. buckets from Sears and home-made jam and peanut butter sandwiches were a staple. A cow had to be sold to send daughter Eileen off to Episcopal boarding school in Spokane.

Henry Gurr may not have been very practical, as parishioner Myrtle Whaley recalled many years later, but necessity prompted him to try his hand at commerce. By 1906 he ran a business in the old post office on Woodin Street, advertising his services in the *Chelan Valley Leader* as optician, jeweler, and purveyor of watches, clocks, cameras and supplies at "Department Store Prices." In September 1907 he sold a four-fifths interest in the business to son Will for $400 with another $220 due in 1910. In about 1912 Henry and his brother Edwin bought a portable steam-powered sawmill from a neighbor, Luke Jackley, whose health was failing, planning to mill their own logs, to save transporting them down the mountain, and to charge

---

[208] Notes by David Gurr on a conversation with Robert L. Gurr in late 1970 or early 1971.

[209] From a typescript, perhaps a transcription by Reverend Gurr, found in his papers. The individual contributions ranged from $1 to $10; three of the smallest came from women. Food gifts and exchanges are frequently noted in John B. Lucas' 1911 diary; see Gurr and Perry, *Daily Life in Chelan, 1911*, details in Chapter 15.

neighbors for sawing their timber.[210] The entire family served as the crew. Robert L. Gurr recalled that "I was engineer, dad sawyer, mom was foreman, Eileen hauled water, trailed the saw, and greased the steam engine."

Running a sawmill was a dangerous occupation. Henry Gurr's use of children – Robert was 8 or 10 at most – suggests a lack of concern for their well-being that, a century later, is hard to comprehend. Yet the family sawmill operation parallels the ways in which Alf and Will were treated in the years after their mother's death. They were placed in a home, given responsibility for transporting family goods, taught ship-building, asked to sail toward Alaska in bad weather, and taken into the interior of British Columbia in harsh early-winter conditions. By the late Victorian era the concept of childhood, and of children as a special category of people in need of protection and nurture, was well established. But Henry Gurr seems to have lived and raised his children by an earlier standard according to which children were "little grownups," expected to take on adult responsibilities at an early age, as he had himself when going to sea in his teens. His lack of open affection toward his children – according to Will's memoirs and Robert's recollections – may be a corollary attitude.

11.21 Supply Priest

"During his incumbency," the Reverend Gurr continued, in the *Church and Clergyman's Record Book* (note 23), "services were held at Chelan, Chelan Falls, First Creek, Falls View, Marysvale, Union Valley, Waterville, Wenatchee, Cashmere, Brewster, Okanogan, Omak, Oroville, Winthrop." These were the circumstances in which Myrtle Whaley reported seeing him often, valise in hand, waiting at the Chelan docks for the "Lady of the Lake" to take him uplake, or to Chelan Falls for the Columbia River ferries. He was en route to Sunday services, baptisms, weddings, and funerals at more than a dozen churches up and down the Columbia valley. Wenatchee was 40 miles south, Oroville was 90 miles north near the Canadian border.

The Reverend Gurr's services as a visiting priest, also known as a supply or missionary priest, no doubt contributed to his income as well as satisfied his restlessness. The outlying congregations likely helped pay his steamship fares. It was customary to provide visiting clergy with food and lodging, and to give them parcels of food for their onward journey. And each congregation was expected to provide an agreed sum of dollars to his purse.

11.22 Travels in Methow Valley

The Reverend Gurr's service as a missionary priest brought him in contact with a wide set of people. One of his friends was Guy Waring, a rancher and businessman in the Methow valley some 20 miles north of Chelan. Waring, born in 1859, was an adventurous Harvard graduate from a prosperous Eastern family who in 1897 built a large log cabin overlooking the village of Winthrop that was called "Waring's Castle," and the Reverend Gurr probably was his guest there. Waring also was a college friend of Owen Wister, who honeymooned in the Methow valley in

---

[210] Perry, "*We Left Because the Creek Went Dry*," pp. 51, 90.

1898 and a few years later wrote the classic western novel *The Virginian*, thought to have been inspired in part by his friend Waring's life and environment. [211]

The Reverend Henry's services in Winthrop were first held in the old "Duck Brand Saloon." He recalled that "The first bar made in Okanogan county became a lectern, while the old mirror took the place of a reredos….but the surroundings were not as conducive to sacred thoughts as one would desire." So services moved to a building put up by Guy Waring for Owen Wister's use when writing *The Virginian*. According to the Reverend Gurr the building later became Saint James' Church, Winthrop, "built ideally on a bluff with charming views in every direction." [212]

11.23 Stranded in a Blizzard

Not all the churches the Reverend Gurr served were on the river. Others lay overland and could be reached only with difficulty. The *Chelan Leader* reported in this front-page article in January 1914:

> In attempting to go to Waterville last Sunday to hold services at the Episcopal church there, Reverend H. J. Gurr had the most desperate experience with snow and storm that he had had in all his life services as minister, notwithstanding he spent a number of years in Minnesota and the Dakotas. Snow fell just as heavily on the Douglas side of the Columbia [Waterville is some 15 miles SE of Chelan on the east side of the river] as it did here, but unlike the gentle, quiet fall in this valley, over there the snow was driven by a fierce wind and the storm amounted almost to an eastern blizzard. Before Reverend Gurr reached the top of the grade through Brown's canyon the roads had become so badly drifted that he found it impossible to proceed farther. He turned back but found the return almost as difficult as the advance. It was about noon when he gave up the attempt to reach Waterville and turned back to the river and he did not reach the Rason ranch, which afforded the first chance of shelter and which is about four miles from the Winesap ferry, until nine o'clock at night. He remained there all night, and about noon the following day, after have rested from the ordeal of the previous day, he again set out for home. He encountered almost as difficult a trip on this side of the river as on the other side. He was forced to abandon his sleigh at the river, and it was only with the greatest difficulty, after breaking trail for his horses in many places in snow waist deep, that he reached home at nine o'clock Monday night. [213]

---

[211] Will Gurr talked about his father's friendship with Guy Waring in an interview with Ted Robert Gurr in July 1971, and recalled that the Reverend Gurr officiated at Waring's marriage to a local woman (presumably a second marriage). On Waring's life and connection with Owen Wister see www.ghosttownsusa.com/bttales24.htm.

[212] From a one-page note by The Reverend H. J. Gurr, *'The Old 'Duck Brand' Saloon*, published in a compendium of Episcopal Church documents sometime in the mid-1920s and found in the Spokane Diocese archives. The note includes at least one factual error: the Reverend Gurr says that they had recently laid Owen Wister to rest, but in fact Wister died in 1938 in Rhode Island, long after the Reverend Gurr's death in 1931.

[213] *Chelan Leader*, January 29, 1914.

11.24 Between Ranch and Town

During the years of hardscrabble living at Gurrland the Reverend Gurr was often away, staying at the rectory next to St. Andrews for several days most weeks. This is evidently where he prepared most of his sermons and also took care of fraternal lodge business. He had been a member of the Lodge of Odd Fellows in Whapeton in the early 1880s and was an active member of this and other fraternal orders for much of his adult life. Mabel also came down to the rectory to give birth to Robert and probably the other children as well. When family members at Gurrland were ill, treatment was either prescribed by telephone or required a trip down the mountain to town. [214] Periods of drought made it necessary to bring laundry down from Gurrland for washing at the rectory. The rectory was also the setting for some family meals, especially during holiday seasons, when members of the extended family would join Reverend Gurr and others who came down from the ranch. [215]

By 1911 Mabel suffered badly from rheumatism. This, along with other difficulties of living on the mountain, may have prompted the Reverend Gurr to temporarily relocate the family to the lakeshore in summer 1911. They returned to the ranch again, though, and it was not given up until 1916 or 1917, when the family moved to a rental house in Chelan. Being in town made it easier for the children to attend school – before that Eileen and Robert had walked four or five miles from Gurrland to the one-room First Creek schoolhouse.

From 1912 to 1917 the Reverend J. C. Black was placed in charge of St. Andrews, which freed Reverend Gurr to pursue other activities. He served as curate for St. Andrews when needed and, as documented above, traveled to a growing number of more distant parishes. When Reverend Black left in 1917, Reverend Gurr resumed his duties at St. Andrews and continued, sometimes sharing with other priests, until he retired on August 28, 1921, and prepared to move his family to Spokane. By his own account, during his years in Chelan Reverend Gurr had baptized 98 church members, buried 63, confirmed 56, and married 50. [216]

11.25 The Reverend Henry Gurr in Spokane

In Spokane the Reverend Henry Gurr was listed in diocesan records as a general missionary and may have received a stipend for that work. He and his family lived in a house at 2407 West Dean, not far from Holy Trinity Episcopal church. **Photos 11.25a and 11.25b** show the house on West Dean c. 1920 and in 2006. The family included Mabel, the younger four of their five children – now in their teens and early 20s – and Mabel's mother, Mary, whose

---

[214] The US Forest Service put in a telephone line across Bear Mountain to fire lookouts uplake and Gurrland was hooked up to the line by 1911, which soon became what Elizabeth Perry calls "a large party line." Perry, Elizabeth Watson, (1999). *We Left Because the Creek Went Dry.* P. 105., Manson, WA: Point Publishing.. On illnesses at Gurrland and the use of the telephone to communicate between town and the ranch see *Daily Life in Chelan 1911*, Chapter 15.

[215] Gurr and Perry, *Daily Life in Chelan 1911.* Chapter 15.

[216] *Historic Notes*, cited elsewhere. Whether this includes ceremonies at other churches, for example uplake, or only St. Andrews is not clear. Henry's total of 98 baptisms over 18 years compares with 43 enumerated in the Diocesan records for 1903 to 1912, above.

Photo 11.25a The House at 2407 W. Dean, Spokane early 1920s
Rev. Henry J. Gurr seated left, Behind him son John, facing him wife Mabel,
On the railing, son Robert Lucas. On the steps, daughters Helen (left) and Harriet.
From Anne Cook Gurr Album

Photo 11.25b The House at W. Dean, 2006
Photo by David Eyre

husband Captain Lucas had died in 1912. Robert's wife Anne, who often visited the family, recalled that she and Robert would take a walk with Henry after Sunday dinner. At home "he could not get a word in edgewise because his wife and mother-in-law talked incessantly." This observation suggests another reason why, in the Chelan years, the Reverend Gurr did his work at the rectory in town, and traveled so frequently and widely.

The Reverend Henry Gurr also served as unpaid Associate Rector to the J. A. Palmer of Holy Trinity, who was chronically ill. Parishioners quoted in a recent history of Holy Trinity church characterized the Reverend Gurr as "elderly, patriarchal and sprightly." [217] He also continued to travel widely as a supply priest, "holding services in practically every Episcopal church in the Inland Empire. He was well known and revered not only in Spokane, but all over the district." [218] The author found records of his service as supply priest as far afield as Republic, in northeast Washington. To reach Republic from Chelan he would have had to travel some 75 miles up the Columbia by steamship, then 40 miles east over mountainous roads. If coming from Spokane the distance was 120 miles, a trip he could have made by Model T Ford – which son Robert says he acquired late in his Chelan ministry.

11.26 The Lost Memoirs

It was not easy to piece together this sketch of Reverend Henry J. Gurr's life from multiple, fragmentary sources. All the more frustrating, then, to learn several years ago that he had written a memoir of at least 150 typewritten pages, "A Red-Blooded Anglican," and sought to have it published. A letter from a Boston publisher, Richard G. Badger, dated December 7, 1928, was found in the Reverend Gurr's papers, saying that a reader's report recommended publication on terms that almost certainly chilled the author. Badger required an advance of $1125 and said, in later correspondence, that they would publish at least 1000 copies and market them for $2.00, on which Reverend Gurr would receive 20% royalties. Follow up correspondence suggests that the Reverend Gurr would not give up on the idea, even though the subsidy was almost surely far beyond his reach. The correspondence of Richard G. Badger is held in the Houghton Library at Harvard, but includes no book manuscripts, nor can we find any trace of the manuscript or any family recollection of it. [219] We know several things from his surviving correspondence. He gave two reasons for writing the book and for its title.

First, the instances where I had been so evidently protected in danger and hazard [are] an encouragement to those who semi-doubt that God *IS* over all his works.

---

[217] Marcia O'Leary, *A History of Holy Trinity Episcopal Church.*

[218] *Death Takes Reverend Gurr*, photocopy of obituary in a Spokane newspapers, not dated, probably June 19, 1931.

[219] The Houghton Library, bMS AM 2067 (19), *Badger, Richard G., Information from: Correspondence with prospective authors, 1926-1929.* Go – Gw. Folder 16 of 17. The Boston publisher Richard G. Badger's records were turned over to the Houghton Library at Harvard following his passing.

Secondly, the fact that several times recently…articles have been written making out that clergymen were weaklings. [220]

The correspondence also gives clues to "incidents that have occurred in my life," for example "a miraculous escape from being drowned in Minnesota, i.e. Lake Warsaw" (p. 90 in the ms.), "breaking through the ice on the Mississippi" (pp. 102-03 in the ms.), and "wonderful evidence of guidance" (presumably divine guidance; p. 147). He added that:

I have tried to tell things without any undue laudation….The whole of these incidents are absolute facts just as they have actually occurred. The only variation I have made has been possibly to transfer the occasion from one particular time to agree with another, and to write two occasions that happened at different times as though they were one. [221]

---

[220] Reverend Henry J. Gurr correspondence dated December 18, 1928.

[221] Reverend Henry J. Gurr correspondence dated November 25, 1928.

Chapter 12
Alfred Richard Gurr

12.1 Second Brother to America

Alfred Richard Gurr was the second of the three Gurr brothers to migrate to America. He boarded the Etruria in Liverpool with his family in October and landed in New York on November 4th, 1889. The Etruria, illustrated in **Sketch 12.1a** was a modern ship for its time, capable of steam or sail with a passenger capability of about 1350. Its maiden voyage was in April of 1885. It was the last single-screw ship to set the speed record for passages between Liverpool and New York, just over six days each way, in August, 1885. Initially it had cabins for up to 550 and third class accommodation for another 800, but later was outfitted for Cabin, Intermediate and Steerage classes. On Alfred's crossing there were 276 passengers in Cabin, 117 in Intermediate and 296 in Steerage Class. Alfred had his wife and family in Intermediate Class. The Etruria carried passengers from Liverpool, England and Queenstown, Ireland on this voyage.

Sketch 12.1a The Steamship Etruria c. 1889

The family's departure took place within a year from the day that Alfred's brother Henry returned to America in late 1888 following a lengthy visit in London, accompanied by his two sons William (five) and Alfred (seven). Henry had spent almost fifteen years in America since he had left England in September 1875, apparently with no plan to ever return to his native country. During those fifteen years, Henry had become familiar with the mid-western states, where he had lived, married and worked for most of those years. However, more recently he had lived in California, and his stories of his years there with his beloved wife Celia and of the temperate weather, the availability of land, work, education and of opportunity in that far away state must have been inspirational.

12.2 Rise and Fall of Gurr and Son

When and how Alfred became convinced that the best future for his wife and twelve children lay in America will never be known, but he left behind what appears to have been a profitable although declining dairy business. How successful the operation was we can only speculate, but it is quite apparent that the family moved from the lower to the middle class by the mid 1880s, and it is indisputable that the wealth of the family increased due to the profitability of the family business. In their home on Southwick in Paddington the women ran the dairy, probably selling not only milk, but butter, cheese and other dairy products, while Alfred Richard and Edwin Robert worked as milk contractors using the same business address. The dairy was apparently in the lower level of what was then a new three level building, while the offices and living quarters were located on the ground and second floor above. [222]

Alfred James started into the dairy business as a milkman in the late spring of 1861, for his occupation is so recorded on the August 4th baptismal certificate of his daughter Ellen that summer. In the 1861 census taken on the last day of March just four months earlier he was still a butler at the Wheeler residence. The occupation "milkman" suggests that Alfred James was involved in the distribution of milk, and this is what one might expect for someone learning a new profession. Alfred Richard was not released from his studies at Christ's Hospital until 1865, and even then had to serve as an apprentice with a London stationer, under an agreement negotiated by Christ's Hospital. We do not know how long Alfred remained as a stationer's apprentice, though the normal apprenticeship was five years. However, we do know that the two Alfreds were incorporated as Gurr and Son by the time of the April 2, 1871 census. The company also employed Alfred Richard's mother Mary Ann, son Henry Jonathan and at least one other female as dairyman's assistants. There may also have been other workers who lived off the premises. **Photo 12.2a**, taken in 2008, shows the building as it appears a century and a half later, now a four story

Photo 12.2a Gurr Home in London
Ground level of 3rd door from corner was the Gurr & Son Dairy
Now an upscale restaurant (2008)
Photo by Paul Magel

---

[222] The building today has four levels. The fourth level was added to these homes after WWII due to considerable bomb damage in this district, although it was not as frequently hit as the more eastern districts.

structure. Note the lower three-story building behind and to the left of the central four-story structure in the photo, which we believe was how the building occupied by the Gurr family was originally built. [223]

It is evident that Gurr and Son continued to grow throughout the 1870s, despite the passing of Alfred James in 1874. The 1881 census shows that Alfred Richard, now the head of the household at 38 Southwick, and occupying the living quarters with his growing family, employed seven men and three women in the family's dairy operation. Meanwhile, his mother, Mary Ann has moved to a residential area in Chelsea, and is listed as employed by Gurr and Son, milk contractors, along with her daughters Sarah Sophia, Emily Ann and Ellen (recorded as Nellie). Alfred's brother Edwin is not shown as residing at either family residence, but he was enumerated out of town on business, apparently arranging a contract with a dairy farm in Somerset. By 1881, Edwin was undoubtedly a Milk Contractor, or one who contracts for and is responsible for the wholesale transferring of milk between the dairy farmer and the retailer.

So by the 1880s Gurr and Son has entered a new phase of business development, with both Edwin and Alfred Richard doing contract work, while their mother Mary Ann is listed in the 1882 London directory as a milk wholesaler. Alfred Richard is probably still running the distribution end of the business from 38 Southwick, including the dairy and probably some milk routes the company had established. The family business appears to have expanded to include all facets of the milk industry excluding farm production, but including contracting for milk and other dairy products from the farm source, dealing with rail transport and warehousing, then wholesaling, and finally distribution by way of milk carts and a dairy store. Until 1884, it is Alfred Richard, Edwin Robert and their mother Mary Ann who hold the key positions in Gurr and Son. When Mary Ann dies, in 1884, a major director of the company is lost, and probably some of the company's momentum.

There were other events that changed the milk business during the 1880s, primarily related to hygiene and new regulations. Selling adulterated milk (additives to dilute, color or otherwise alter milk) became an offence in 1860 with the passing of the Adulteration of Food or Drink Act, although local authorities largely ignored its enforcement. However, the law was given some teeth with the passing of the Adulteration of Food, Drink and Drugs Act in 1872. In 1875 the Public Health Act and the Sale of Food and Drugs Act made cowsheds, dairy plants and milk-shops subject to medical inspection, while the Contagious Diseases (Animals) Act of 1878 required basic cleanliness in anyone selling food. Further regulations were added to these Acts in 1885. When such laws were finally enforced, many London dairies and other small milk traders were eliminated, which left room for expansion for the better operations, but also made conducting business more expensive for those who survived.

---

[223] Today, the lower level of 38 Southwick is an upper scale restaurant specializing in Indian food. There was little WWII bomb damage to this area which is adjacent to Hyde Park so the lower levels of the building are probably almost identical to the original, and possibly at the level of those in this photo's left background. The area is mostly residential, but the corner house next door has a coffee house on the lower level.

Other changes taking place that had a negative effect on the smaller milk businesses resulted from the continuous expansion of the milk corporations, and the technical changes that gradually put the improved equipment now required out of reach of the budgets of even some of the larger milk companies. Improved equipment included coolers to allow farmers to cool their milk from the cow; cooling depots to ensure that the milk was stored under proper conditions while waiting for transport as well as after transport to the wholesaler's station; continuous refrigeration plants, which allowed cooling during transport; centrifugal separators; and condensing plants which made condensed milk in containers that were storable. The advantage of the cooling, cooling depots and refrigeration plants was that the old 24-36 hour delivery schedule farm-to-user once needed to prevent souring, gradually increased to several days.

Other forms of milk also became available c. 1890, including canned condensed milk, sterilized milk (glass bottled, capped and then boiled), and pasteurized milk. Bottled milk was introduced in the 1880s, and although the bottling process was not fully automated until 1903, this and other such developments were changing the face of the milk industry, and reducing profits for small dairies. The milk industry was gradually falling under control of the larger milk companies and government regulation, and small dairy companies, such as Gurr and Son, found it increasingly difficult to compete in the marketplace.

As the new regulations of 1885 were gradually enforced, the Gurr and Son Dairy business came under new pressures that made it gradually less and less profitable. By 1887 the business was in obvious decline. It is very likely that these conditions encouraged Alfred to emigrate in 1889, leaving the management of what remained of the dairy to sister Emily and perhaps sister Sarah Sophia. Edwin married and moved to Ealing in 1887. He would continue working as a milk contractor, possibly on a contract basis for other firms, until as late as 1905, but only Emily is resident at 38 Southwick during the 1891 census and occupied in operating a dairy at that site. Phone and other directories show her there through 1894.

12.3   Merced, 1889

The County of Merced was formed in April 19, 1855, deriving its name from El Rio de Nuestra Senora de la Merced (River of Our Lady of Mercy). The name was given to the river by a Spanish army officer, Gabriel Moraga, who led an expedition through the region between 1806 and 1808, and after a long hot day was thankful to find refuge along its banks. The watershed of the Merced River includes many lakes, creeks and rivers in Yosemite Valley, from which the river flows down the foothills of the Sierra Nevada, and across the plains north of the present day city of Merced. Its waters empty into the San Joaquin River, eventually reaching the Pacific Ocean. Moraga was one of the first Europeans to explore central California, and became one of the most famous Indian fighters in California history. Garrisoned in Monterey and San Francisco, he is credited with naming many rivers, lakes and valleys between the Pacific and the lower elevations of the Sierra Nevada.

In 1890 Merced County's total population was 8,085 while the city of Merced, incorporated the year before, counted for 2,009. There were 5,413 males and 2,657 females in the county, a ratio of over two to one, with 5,658 native-born and 2,427 foreign-born. Alfred Richard and his family accounted for 14 of the latter. Whites numbered 7,262; Negroes, 47;

Indians, 30. This accounts for 7,339 out of the 8,085. Most of the remainder were probably Chinese, who were not entitled to most of the rights of others in the population, because of the Exclusion Act of 1882.

By 1900 the county had a total population of 9,215, an increase of only about 14 per cent over 1890. Of this total 5,644 were males and 3,571 females (notice the improved ratio). There were 7,020 native-born and 2,195 foreign-born, or now just about one third foreign-born. There were 8,780 whites, 31 negroes, 4 Indians, 357 Chinese and 43 Japanese. Of the native-born there were 3,941 males and 3,079 females; and of the foreign-born, 1,703 males and 492 females. Under pioneering conditions, there is usually a preponderance of males over females.

12.4   The Newcomers

Alfred Richard Gurr arrived in the County of Merced in mid-winter of 1889-90 having travelled some 3,000 miles by sea, and a further 3,000 land miles across the American continent. He travelled one-quarter of the way around the world with his wife Emily and their twelve children, with each member of the family undoubtedly uncertain as to what exactly lay before them.   His brother Henry, who was familiar with the region, must have made some prior arrangements for their lodging, and it is almost certain that Henry was there to meet the family on its arrival.   Still, Alfred, his wife and children must have wondered what they'd gotten themselves into during those first few days and weeks, while they attempted to settle themselves and their children into their new environment.

The family would have been impressed with the region's natural beauty.   The Sierra Nevada dominates Merced's skyline to the East and the fertile San Joaquin valley would have had a skyline that was almost unbroken with no signs of human habitation for as far as the eye could see in 1890.   The climate is moderate and during the month of December when the family arrived, the temperature ranges between an average high of 55° F and an average low of 36° F, with an all time record low of 13° F.   The town of Merced would have been a relatively primitive settlement compared to anything they had known in England.   In 1890, the streets were un-surfaced and most of the buildings were wooden frame structures, many unpainted and weather beaten from the sun and rain.

Although the family was certainly not wealthy, they had sufficient funds to maintain themselves for the first year and enough to bargain for a piece of land.   In any case we know that Alfred purchased a strip of farmland in Township 2, just over four miles northwest of the fledgling City of Merced, making a deposit on the property and taking out a mortgage for the balance. He developed a family business there, which he named the Fountain City Hatchery.

The following excerpts from a biographical sketch of Alfred Richard written in 1905 illustrate how successful and well respected he became. [224]   The sketch confirms that Alfred was

---

[224] Guinn, Prof. James M., A.M., (1905). *History of the State of California and biographical record of the San Joaquin Valley, California. An historical story of the state's marvelous growth from its earliest settlement to the present time*. Chicago: The Chapman Publishing Co. Notes: Missing Pages: 865-866,983-984,1175-1176. Transcribed by Peggy Hooper for California Genealogy & History Archives, www.rootsweb.ancestry.com/~cagha/index.htm.

one of the first settlers from Britain in that area and also the fact that during Alfred's first few years there his brothers Henry and Edwin also became residents, apparently planning to permanently settle in California.

Biographical Sketch of Alfred Richard Gurr, 1905

An active, brainy and progressive man, noted as a promoter, and an early settler, of the British Colony, Merced county, Alfred Richard Gurr is a prominent exponent of its agricultural, manufacturing and business interests. By occupation he is a general farmer, raising grain, cultivating fruit, manufacturing olive oil and keeping a large apiary, in every branch of his industries meeting with eminent success.

After his graduation, in 1866, from Christ's Hospital, better known as the Blue Coat School of London, England, Alfred Richard Gurr entered into business in London with his father, remaining in that metropolis until 1889. Emigrating then to the United States, he came directly to California, and bought his present farm, which lies four and one-fourth miles west of Merced. About twenty acres of his ranch he has sowed to alfalfa, and in addition to general farming he has a fine dairy, keeping Jersey cows, and also raises many hogs each year. He is an expert horticulturist, and has made great success in caring for his vineyard of four acres, at the mid-winter fair in San Francisco winning the bronze medal for his exhibit of three and four crown raisins. A man of great enterprise and keen foresight, Mr. Gurr manufactures a fine quality of olive oil, having established a plant on his farm, and buying his olives from the growers of that fruit. He leases land on the San Joaquin river, and on this land are his apiary, which contains three hundred stands of bees, and yields him large quantities of honey each year.

The area became known as the British Colony, and the road to their farmlands the British Colony Road (now Gurr Road). His brother Henry left the area with his two sons following his 1893 separation from his second wife. Edwin also left the area with his two sons sometime after his wife Alice died in Merced in early 1894. The latter two brothers would reunite in 1906, homesteading together in the Chelan Valley of Washington. Alfred Richard lived on that farm in Merced County with his wife for over 30 years, before selling it and buying another poultry farm on Bay Road, Township 3, near Redwood City in neighboring San Mateo County. [225]

Alfred and Emily arrived in Merced with their 12 children in late December of 1889. On their arrival the children ranged in age from one to sixteen years. How much they appreciated their new environment, and how quickly they adjusted to farm life after living in the largest most densely populated city in the world is not known. [226] Doubtless it must have been a difficult time for the older children, leaving friends and familiar 203surroundings far behind them. **Photo 12.4a** on the following page is the only group picture of the entire family taken c. 1897.

---

[225] From the *Memoirs of Will Gurr*, second son of Alfred's brother Reverend Henry Jonathan Gurr and his first wife Celia Frost.

[226] Chapter 18 expands on the lives of Alfred Richards children and Table A3 in Appendix A provides a summary of the verifiable information we have about family members and their movements up to 1940.

Photo 12.4a Alfred Richard Gurr and Family, c.1897 Merced

Top Row: David, Ethel, Alfred James, Ellen, William, Mary Maude, Henry Robert

Bottom Row: Beatrice, Edwin, Emily, Gordon, mother Emily, Ernest, Alfred Richard

Beatrice and Edwin stayed in Merced all their lives.

Photo by Silver of Merced, a copy provided to Ted Robert Gurr by one of the descendants.

During the 1900 Census Alfred and Emily still had nine of their children living with them in Merced, with only Alfred James, Edwin and Mary Maude having left home. By 1910 all of the children were off the farm, with the exception of Harry and Bea, while James had returned (James had been working on the railroad in Madera County). Harry appears to have remained single and continued to assist his father on Alfred Richard's farms in Merced and San Manteo well into the 1930s. Gordon and Ernest are shown in the table, but while they were traced in the same manner as the others, some date discrepancies do exist and the information as outlined is still unconfirmed.

12.5   Education of Alfred Richard's Children

Descendants of Alfred Richard recalled that a primary reason their grandfather chose California as the place to settle his family was the free and liberal education system that the citizens of the state enjoyed. Most of the family members were naturalized by 1896, and from that time forward (if not earlier) the Gurr children were entitled to free education. "Free education for all children" had been one of the promises that California's political leaders, including Robert Semple had made when they brought the state into the Union in 1850. [227] It was finally implemented by John Swett, in his term as Superintendant of Public Instruction. [228]

In Chapter 18 we take a closer look at the lives of the children of Alfred Richard from the time they arrive in America until their passing. Although we do not know what level of education each of the twelve Gurr children received, we can make a fairly accurate guess, and from the 1900 census we know that the youngest five children were all students and at least three of those were in high school.

Up until 1890, there were only three traditional programs offered at senior high schools throughout most of the United States: college entry for those proceeding to a higher education; English literature for those intending to be civil servants, journalist or businessmen; and normal school for those planning on teaching. Education of children was not compulsory in all states until 1918, but as of 1900 thirty states had such a statute on their books. By the early 1900s the standard education program in many states was six years of elementary, three years of secondary, or junior high school, and three years of senior high school. By the 1920s this program was almost universal throughout the United States, and since California was arguably the most

---

[227] In Robert Semple's speech at the Constitutional Convention of California in Monterey in 1849, he said: "If the people are to govern themselves, they should be qualified to do it. They must be educated; they must educate their children; they must provide means for the diffusion of knowledge and the progress of enlightened principles."

[228] Wood, Will C. Early vision of Semple, Swett realized in broad, firm educational system. *The Bulletin*, Diamond Jubilee Edition (September, 1925). Note: During his term (1863-1867) Swett secured the passage of laws creating a state board of education, providing for teachers' institutes where poorly equipped teachers might get help, organizing the schools into grades, establishing school libraries, providing for the certification of teachers and laying a splendid financial basis for the support of public education. He secured the abolition of rate bills under which parents were charged tuition and made the schools absolutely free in all districts for at least five months each year. He succeeded in having school boards build better school houses, secured necessary increases in teachers' salaries and lengthened the school year. Retrieved from http://www.sfmuseum.net/hist3/schools.html.

progressive state, it is probable that this was what was available to California children during the 1890s. [229]

When the family arrived in California, the eldest of Alfred Richard's children was 16 year old Alfred James, the second eldest Henry age 14, and the third eldest Edwin age 13, while the other nine were between 12 years and 1 year old. It is possible, even probable, that one or more of the eldest three children attended high school, but certainly the younger nine went through one or all of the various levels of the California school system. The Gurr farmland lay between the town of Atwater and the city of Merced, along what is now Gurr Road North (there is also a Gurr Road South). Both authors have visited the area in the past few years and driven along Gurr road trying to pinpoint the location of the Gurr farms. **Photo 12.5a** shows one abandoned farmhouse on Gurr Road, and it may well be though it is not certain, that this was one of several Gurr properties.

Photo 12.5a Abandoned Farmhouse
on Gurr Road in Merced c. 2000
A Gurr Farm ? Photo by Ted Gurr

There may have been an elementary school in Atwater, but there was no senior high school there in 1890 (the earliest reference to one is in 1925), so it is likely that the younger as well as the older children were taken about four miles into the city of Merced for schooling. We do not know whether any of the Gurr children excelled at school, but we do know that three of

---

[229] Details in this paragraph from: Ballantyne, Paul F., Chapter 3: American Schooling, Administrative Reform, and Individual Ability Testing: Assimilation and sorting before World War I. *Psychology, Society, and Ability Testing (1859-2002): Transformative alternatives to Mental Darwinism and Interactionism.* York University..

the girls furthered their education beyond the high school level. Ellen graduated from the nursing school at St. Luke's Hospital in San Francisco in 1906, at the age of 27 (probably a three year course) while Ethel and Emily May (Queenie) graduated from the same school in 1909 at the ages of 25 and 32, respectively. [230]   Of the boys in the family, only David appears to have furthered his education, and it is certain that he became a trained electrician, but it is also possible that he attended a college while in San Francisco, for the newspaper report of his early death states that he was a well-respected electrical engineer.

12.6   Marriage, Separation, Divorce - Alfred Richard's Children

Of the twelve children of Alfred and Emily, only Harry and Queenie remained single. The other four girls, Mary Maude, Ellen, Ethel Elizabeth and Beatrice married and had children. The other six boys, James, Ted, William, David, Gordon and Ernest married but only three had children, the exceptions being James, David and Ernest.

Six of the seven male children of Alfred and Emily (Ted was the exception) moved out of Merced, four across central California, one into Nevada and one south to San Diego looking for work and a future. Five of those six would find work as general or poultry farmers, two of them in farm related industries. Of these, David is the exception, for in the 1910 census he was listed as an electrician with a telephone company, and in later directories as an electrician. In Nevada he was designated as an electrical engineer (in Yerington, Lyon County, Nevada, southeast of Reno and North of Yosemite) where he was manager of a Light and Water Utility until his early and tragic death in 1925.

Of the four girls who married; Mary Maude was divorced after having 6 children with her husband; Ellen and her husband seemed to live separate lives while their son Frederick was often living with other family members; Ethel and her husband eventually separated, with their only daughter living with the husband.

Alfred Richard and Emily would survive into the 1940s with Queenie attending them until the end of their days. Alfred Richard would outlive his two younger brothers, Reverend Henry Jonathan and Edwin Robert, by almost fifteen years. This loving couple who had brought twelve children into the world would outlive two of them and be grandparents to at least 17 grandchildren. We do not know how many great-grandchildren owe Alfred and Emily their thanks for their futures in America.

---

[230]   Retrieved from http://www.sfgenealogy.com/sf/. San Francisco Genealogy site. Type in surname Gurr, and check St. Luke's Hospital 1914-15 list of nursing graduates.

Chapter 13
Edwin Robert Gurr

13.1 Introduction

Edwin Robert Gurr, the youngest son of Alfred James would, like his brothers, immigrate to the United States, but whereas his older brothers came to America and stayed there, Edwin made several trips back and forth as his circumstances changed. [231] He was actually the second member of his family to visit the United States, for he landed in New York in June of 1878, almost certainly to renew his relationship with his brother Henry, who was in the middle of a course of studies at Seabury Divinity School in Minnesota. This is one of the first indications of the close relationship the two brothers had with one another, and the fact that they ended up homesteading together on the same mountain top in Washington almost thirty years later provides further evidence of this.

Because of his coming and going between two continents, the details we present of Edwin's life necessarily cover periods in England as well as periods in America. For Alfred Richard and Henry Jonathan from the time they first set foot in America they and all members of their families were thereafter American.

13.2 Edwin, Milk Contractor

On Edwin's first trip to America in 1878, it is probable that Edwin was between jobs, for he is listed on the ships manifest as a "gentleman" (usually this meant an unemployed man of independent means in the 1800s). We know that sometime during the 1870s he changed his occupation from wine merchant's clerk to milk contractor, although the exact date is uncertain. From the 1881 census onward, Edwin always states his occupation as milk contractor. We know that he worked in this capacity for Gurr and Son throughout the 1880s, and during the early 1890s. However there is reason to believe that he worked for other employers and probably for George Barham after his return from America in the mid 1890s. We cannot be certain what Edwin's exact duties were as clerk to a wine merchant, but we can make some assumptions. English wine merchants contracted with vineyards in Europe for large quantities of bottled and casked wine. Edwin would certainly have learned from his wine-importing employer the details of how such contracting was done, as well as how the contracted wine was shipped, landed and distributed to the London wine houses. [232] Undoubtedly, young Edwin brought concepts he had learned during his apprenticeship to the wine merchant to Gurr and Son.

---

[231] Alfred Richard never went back to England. Reverend Henry Jonathan returned once for about a year following the death of his first wife Celia.

[232] Portuguese wines were very popular in Britain for centuries. In the 1700s the fortified wine known as Port became extremely popular in England. The lucrative trade in Port prompted the Portuguese authorities to establish one of the world's first protected designation of origin establishing boundaries and regulations for the production of authentic Port from the Douro region of Portugal.

With their father gone, the family business would have needed all the support it could get, and it is probable that Edwin spent some, if not most of his time between 1874 and 1881 contributing to Gurr and Son in some capacity. By 1881, however, Edwin is clearly involved with Gurr and Son as a milk contractor, and he would continue to use this designation for his occupation until his final journey to America via Canada in 1905. Both Alfred Richard and his mother Mary Ann also refer to Gurr and Son as a milk contracting firm in their census declarations of 1881. Mary Ann continues to be listed in trade directories as the operator of the Gurr and Son dairy at 38 Southwick until her passing in the summer of 1884.

In 1881, Edwin is recorded as a visitor in the home of Lot Shepherd, a dairy farmer of 16 acres employing three people. Edwin's occupation is listed as that of milk contractor, and he is staying at Arthur's Bridge Farm, in Lamyatt in Somerset about 120 miles west of London and 35 miles south of Bristol. Lamyatt is in the center of rich farmland with rolling hills and many streams, and its name listed in the Domesday Book, means lamb's gate. There were many dairy farms in that area in the late 19th century, as well as apple orchards, but historically the region is mostly under grass and is historically noted for raising sheep, cattle, horses and hogs. Arthur's Bridge may take its name from the mythical King Arthur, for there is some that believe that Camelot actually once existed in that part of England that is now Somerset. This record of Edwin being temporarily resident on a farm 120 miles from London and apparently conducting business as a milk contractor is significant, for it is certain that he is there negotiating a contract for that dairy farms output.

13.3 Hard Times

When Mary Ann died in 1884, the firm of Gurr and Son was reduced to four active family members, namely Richard, Edwin, Sarah Sophia and Emily Ann, although there were probably additional non-family staff employed. It is almost certain that, during the 1980s the family business was experiencing a downturn in profitability, due to the imposition of new regulations and the economic recession of the last quarter of the 19th century, which impacted both Europe and the United States. The so called "long depression", was a worldwide economic downturn that

began c. 1873 and lasted until the mid 1890s. It's intensity in Europe and the United Kingdom is one of the reasons that emigration to the United States peaked in the 1890s, and that the influx helped lift that nation into a period of relative prosperity early in the 20th century.

Significantly, the United Kingdom's share of world trade dropped from one-quarter in 1880 to one-sixth by the beginning of WWI, while the United States total exports would surpass those of the UK's for the first time in 1913. In England, the depression resulted in falling prices and wages during the 1880s, and this put a financial squeeze on many smaller firms such as Gurr and Son. Working a seven day week, 365 days of the year was not an easy life, and the declining profitability must have put a financial strain on those family members still depending on the Gurr family business.

Edwin Robert's involvement in his brother Alfred Richard's decision to emigrate from England to America in 1889 is unknown, although the three brothers were so close that it is almost certain that the decision was made with unanimous approval. How Alfred Richard disposed of his interest in Gurr and Son is not known, but it is probable that he sold off the wholesaling portion of the company and any milk routes that he controlled to third parties. We do not know whether Edwin took over control of Gurr and Son, but this is not probable in light of later events. Edwin was an experienced milk contractor and would have had no problem in finding employment with one of the established wholesalers. It is interesting that the dairy at 38 Southwick continued to operate until the middle of the 1890s, with Emily Ann running that operation perhaps with support and input from her brother Edwin who maintained a primary residence in London, off and on, until at least 1905. The dairy at 38 Southwick seems to have ceased operations by 1896 and the unmarried Emily Ann died of cancer in St. Leonards on Sea in August of 1898.

13.4   Marriage to Alice Santer

Thirty-two year old Edwin Robert Gurr married twenty-two year old Alice Santer on September 15th, 1887 at St. Luke Holloway in Islington. **Photo 13.4a** shows the pair in a London garden c. 1887. The couple moved into spacious accommodations at 16 Hamilton Road in Ealing in West London. They had three children over the next five years, two of which survived childhood. They lost their third son within a few months of his birth in 1891, and Alice, who had been unwell during her final pregnancy, appears to have been seriously ill during the following few months, for the census lists a live-in nurse, hired by Edwin to assist his wife Alice in caring for their children.

Photo 13.4a Edwin & Alice Gurr
in a London garden, c. 1887
Henry J. Gurr Album

13.5   Emigration to America - Initial Attempt

In September of 1892, Edwin and Alice took their two surviving children George and Harold and sailed for America, accompanied by their live-in nurse (Emily Card) who had been with them in Ealing during the 1891 census. They travelled saloon class on the Richmond Hill, a small cargo ship, capable of carrying 38 passengers landing in New York on September 21st. This journey may have been an attempt by Edwin to move his wife to a healthier climate, for the ship's manifest shows that they were California bound. Russian influenza may have influenced the family's decision, for it was pandemic in 1889-1891, originating in Russia and spreading throughout Europe and into the UK in the late 1890s. Edwin's eldest sister, Sarah Sophia and his maternal Aunt Sophia Bennett both died within days of one another in the fall of 1890, probably from the flu or flu-related complications.

How Alice fared crossing the Atlantic, as ill as she appears to have been, is worth consideration, for tragedy was soon to follow their arrival in America. The Richmond Hill was a small vessel capable of only 13 knots and it took two weeks for it to make the crossing. After the ocean crossing there still remained a further week or so of travel from New York to California by rail, without stopovers.

Although completion of the transcontinental railroad in 1869 allowed passenger travel from New York to San Francisco in about two weeks, rather than the several weeks by mixed modes or months by wagon, these early travelers were transported on trains that had no sleeping accommodations and no food service. For the first decade and a half, trains made stops which allowed passengers the opportunity to dine and sleep. During the late 1880s, passenger cars were being introduced, and these were gradually becoming more luxurious, with closed off vestibules, individual car heating, sleeping quarters, dining areas and lounges.

The first named route "the Overland Flyer" (later the Overland Limited) began service in 1887, offering uninterrupted carriage between Chicago and Oakland in about four days. This is the route that Edwin and Alice probably took in 1892, for the famous Atchison, Topeka & Santa Fe's "California Limited" with sleeping cars, and a dining car with a lounge (making the run from Chicago to San Francisco in less than three days), did not begin service until November of 1892, at least five weeks after the couple arrived in New York.

We have not been able to determine exactly how Alice fared following the family's arrival in New York, nor along the journey west, but we know that she never recovered from whatever she was suffering from. The Edwin Gurr family reached Merced in early October 1892. Edwin left his wife and two children in Alfred Richard's care and returned to London in early November, but why he returned to London so abruptly is speculative, although it is almost certainly business realted. He then re-crossed the Atlantic on the Aurania out of Liverpool arriving back in New York on December 5, 1892, with a large number of checked bags. The landing documents on this crossing show that he intended a protracted stay, and we now know that he was planning to become a landed immigrant at this time. His later statements to authorities when he applied for a homestead and eventually became a citizen in 1905-1906 designate 1893 as his "landed" arrival in the United States.

13.6   Wandering

As fortune would have it, Alice died in Merced on January 4th of 1894, and whatever long-term plans Edwin had where set aside. He took his two sons home to London for a short visit landing at the port of Southampton on the 7th of February, 1894 aboard the *City of Paris*. This voyage was probably made to return the body of Alice to her family, although we have no way of being certain that this was done. It may have been that Edwin simply wanted to extend condolences to Santer family members and to settle his wife's affairs. The authors have been in contact with descendants of Alice's family in England, but none have any knowledge of what became of her. After a five week visit, Edwin once more sailed for New York, this time in a first class cabin aboard the Majestic out of Liverpool, arriving on the 15th of March, 1894, with his two sons in tow, and again planning a protracted stay according to the manifest.

We know little about Edwin's movements between 1894 and 1901. Family tradition suggests that he may have been entrepreneurial during this time, and in some way involved in a jam making enterprise. We also believe that he had purchased land in Merced, but eventually disposed of it with no intention of ever returning there. During the 1901 census, we find him resident in Tonbridge, Kent with his two sons, and one domestic servant. His occupation is recorded as milk contractor and he is listed as a widower. There is little doubt that he remained in the Merced area for most, if not all of 1894, but since oral tradition has his eldest son George Herbert Gurr receiving his elementary education at schools in London, and we know that George and his brother were in a London boarding school in 1901, it is probable that Edwin returned to London in late 1894 or early 1895. By 1894 enrollment and attendance was compulsory for British children 5 to 13, and state run schools were fully funded, so the return could have been as early as the fall of 1894, when the British school year officially began.

13.7   Marriage to Ada Alice Hall

Edwin re-married in Portsmouth, Hampshire during the summer of 1903. His new wife was forty-seven year old Ada Alice Hall, the daughter of Joseph and Frances Hall of Lambeth. Joseph was a bricklayer and later a Superintendent of Building Trades and the couple had four daughters and a son. One report suggests that Ada had been previously married and had two children from that marriage [233], but we have been unable to find proof of that claim in British Records.

13.8   Edwin's Final Crossing to North America

Edwin entered the United States through New York on each of his voyages from Britain to America until his last in 1905, at which time Edwin, Ada, and Edwin's sons George and Harold entered Canada enroute to Chelan, Washington. They appear to have entered at different times, for we have obtained a record confirming Edwin and George arriving at Halifax (and a day later at St. John, New Brunswick) from Liverpool aboard the *Bavarian* in April of 1905. The passenger list legibility is so poor that it is impossible to tell whether or not Ada and Harold were

---

[233]   Suggested in Perry, Elizabeth Watson, (1999). *We Left Because the Creek Went Dry.* P51. Manson, WA: Point Publishing.

aboard. But, as late as the June 1906 Manitoba Census, Ada (Alice), George and Harold are boarders in Winnipeg, recorded as having entered Canada in 1905. Edwin is not listed as resident during that census, for he was, in fact, already in Washington applying for a homestead alongside his brother Henry's property.

Three questions come to mind. Why did Edwin choose to enter the United States through Canada when there is almost no doubt that he and his family were en-route to Washington? Why did it take over a year for Ada to join him? Why did Edwin's two sons never join their father and Ada in Washington?

Addressing the first question, we note the following. Wait times for entry through Ellis Island and other major entry ports became longer and longer as the number of immigrants increased along with increased efforts to ensure exclusion of undesirables. The first decade of the 20th century saw over nine million new arrivals entering the United States through legal ports of entry, about three times the number that arrived in the previous decade. The majority of these came from Europe, and for reasons ranging from economic hardship to religious and political persecution. During 1905 and 1906 the arrivals at Ellis Island numbered several thousand per day with a one day peak of over 11,000 in April of 1907.

Subsequently, not only did wait times increase but new arrivals in New York were detained on Ellis Island until cleared by immigration officials, no matter how long that took, or until they were marked for deportation. [234] Accommodations were crowded and families were often separated during examinations. Travelling through Canada, as members of the British Commonwealth, British citizens expected a much more comfortable experience than travelling through New York.

In answer to the second question, Edwin was already registered as a landed immigrant (from 1893) and although Ada may have been legally eligible for admission as his wife, Edwin's two sons required permission to enter as immigrants. While Edwin continued on to Washington in late 1905 or early 1906, Ada, George and Harold apparently waited in Winnipeg for permission (visas) allowing them to cross the border as permanent residents. Ada finally arrived in Washington in late 1906. Either Edwin's two sons never received that permission, or they developed other interests as they waited.

The third question may never be answered. One possibility is that one or the other of Edwin's two sons was ineligible for admission. Family tradition has it that then 16 year old George Herbert Gurr had been expelled from a college of higher learning in England (for reasons

---

[234] Following the shooting death of President William McKinley by a Polish anarchist in 1901 the Congress of the United States became concerned about the effects of immigration on the nation. The 1903 Anarchist Exclusion Act tightened up admission standards in an attempt to prevent radicals and criminals from gaining entry. The Naturalization Act of 1906 further standardized new naturalization procedures developed in this effort to raise immigration standards. The Act established the Bureau of Immigration and Naturalization in the Commerce Department to oversee national immigration policy. In 1907 the Dillingham commission was established to further study immigration effects and the commission eventually warned that immigration threatened to subvert American Society and recommended a quota system that came into full force following WW1.

unknown) and that Edwin had to return to England to resolve the issue. This would be consistent with the fact that Edwin and George Herbert are recorded as crossing the Atlantic together (without Ada and Harold) on the Bavarian in 1905. Might Geroge's expulsion have some bearing on the matter?

By 1907 both Edwin and Alice had landed in the United States and taken up residence in Chelan, where Edwin's brother Henry had finally settled down five years earlier. Chapter 14 is devoted to the two brothers who homesteaded together in Washington in 1907.

Edwin's youngest son, Harold returned to England and served in WWI before marrying Ida Muriel Stanton in 1919.

Edwin's elder son George remained in Winnipeg, where he married Ellen Mabel Wilton in 1909, with whom he had three children (George Edgar, Dorothy, and Constance). George would not see his father for almost fifteen years after his arrival in Canada, when he visited Edwin in Chelan Washington in 1919.

Edwin never saw England again, but Ada did. She applied for a passport for the purpose of returning to England in the fall of 1917. The trip must have had great importance, and as detailed in a later chapter was family related. [235]

---

[235] This was during WWI, after the USA had entered the global conflict in April.

Chapter 14
Two Brothers Homestead in Chelan

14.1   Chelan, Washington [236]

In the beautiful Cascade Mountain Range of north central Washington State lays the Chelan valley. Through the center of the valley a deep, long, narrow fjord-like lake extends from the settlement of Stehekin at its northern tip to Chelan some fifty miles southeast. Lake Chelan, fed by the Stehekin River and other smaller rivers and streams flowing from the mountain glaciers of the Northern Cascades, empties into the Columbia River at Chelan Falls.

The aboriginal peoples inhabiting the region are known as the Wenatchi and they had numerous villages along the shores of Lake Chelan as well as along the Wenatchee and Columbia Rivers. The first contact between whites and the Wenatchi was made by fur traders travelling along the Columbia beginning around 1811. Conflict between the natives and anyone trying to trap, to settle or even travel through the area continued until a treaty was successfully negotiated in 1855. A ban by the U.S. Army on white settlement in the area was lifted in 1859, following ratification by Congress of the 1855 treaty. Although some trappers, prospectors and mountain men may have penetrated the area earlier, the first permanent settlers, mainly gold prospectors, cattlemen and missionaries did not begin to arrive in the valley until 1860.

Although they were considered unfriendly, in the mid 1820s several Wenatchi were transported to missionary schools at the Red River Settlement of Winnipeg to be educated in the ways of the white men. In later negotiations with the United States, the Wenatchi turned out to be savvy traders. Unlike many of the plains Indians tribes, they refused to be resettled or accept cash for their lands and they negotiated a treaty which gave them permanent ownership of some of the choicest properties in the valley.

Settlement in the area was very limited until the Great Northern Railway completed track into the Wenatchee Valley in 1892/1893 (The Wenatchee Valley is about 40 miles south of the Chelan Valley). The addition of spur lines stimulated trade from surrounding areas to the rail terminals. At about this time it was discovered that the Chelan Valley was ideal for growing certain kinds of fruit, including apples and pears. This led to an orchard planting boom and land development and population growth in Chelan County from 3,931 in 1900 to 15,104 in 1910. During this decade new arrivals were active in building irrigation facilities, organizing fruit growers and expanding fruit marketing. Four of these new arrivals were Edwin, Reverend Henry and their respective wives Ada and Mabel.

---

[236]   Data source: Wenatchee Valley Convention and Visitors Bureau, Historical Summary, Retrieved from wenatcheevalley.org

14.2   Homesteading in America

By the early 1900s, Land Runs were becoming a thing of the past, and the Wenatchee Valley became one of the last regions in the continental US where homesteading was officially sanctioned.

Homesteading began in the United States in 1862, when Congress passed new provisions for the settlement of public land under the Homestead Act. Under the terms of this act, by paying modest fees (up front, a $10 filing fee and a $4 application commission) US citizens (or those who were intending to become citizens) who were either the head of a family, or single and over twenty-one years old, could claim up to 160 acres of available public land. If married, a couple could double the claim up to 320 acres. Once a claim had been made to the local General Land Office, the entrant was required to live on the land for five years, and carry out certain "improvements." Improvements were: provide evidence of residence; build living quarters of a certain size; and cultivate a certain percentage of the land for agricultural crops. A claimant had seven years to fulfill these terms as long as they didn't abandon the homestead at any time during that period. If after paying an additional $4 final proof fee the claimant had "proved up" in the judgment of the Land Office agents, a land patent or title to the land was granted. [237] One other alternative was that the homesteader could, having worked the land for a minimum of six months, purchase the property outright for $1.25 per acre. The Homestead Act of 1912 reduced the time required to live on the land to three years, but with the exception of the Territory of Alaska almost all of the available arable land had already been claimed.

Henry must have been familiar with homesteading from his extensive travels in North America. The attractions of free land on which one could live, raise crops and herd livestock must have been very appealing to his adventuresome character. Within four months of his arrival in the Chelan Valley in the summer of 1902, Henry filed homestead papers on 140 acres on Bear Mountain, as mentioned in Chapter 13. Edwin arrived in Chelan by early 1906 and in the summer of that year acquired land adjoining Henry's property. The brothers were fifty-four and fifty two at the time, but both knew how to handle a life with few amenities, and they saw many opportunities in the rapidly growing southern Chelan valley.

In 1902, when Henry filed papers on the Bear Mountain tract, homesteading was hardly as difficult and dangerous as it had been when he first arrived in America in 1875. During the thirty-two years that had passed since then, the central plains had been settled, thanks largely to the U.S. Army. Custer's Last Stand, the Battle of the Big Horn in 1876, demonstrated that the native tribes were serious in their desire to unite and resist the encroachment of the white man, but it also brought the powers in Washington to the conclusion that they must drive the natives off the best lands by whatever means possible if they were to satisfy their people and populate the West. The brutality of Washington's approach, morally justified to the American people by the reported massacre at the Big Horn, has no place in our considerations, except to point out that

---

[237] Excerpts from *Northwest Homesteader*. Center for the Study of the Pacific Northwest, University of Washington. Retrieved from: http://content.lib.washington.edu/curriculumpackets/homesteaders/intro.html

even the most rebellious populations had been completely pacified by the turn of the 20th century. However, it must be said that the policy was essentially to exterminate any natives who dared take up arms against the Republic, and to starve out, or isolate on marginal treaty lands, those who did not resist. Gradually, control of the central and southern plains (which the United States claimed from the Louisiana Purchase and the Mexican Wars) was seized from the native tribes and became Federal property.

Newly opened lands were sold first-come, sold by bid, or won by lottery or by a land run. The settlers, no matter how they acquired occupancy, purchased the land from the United States Land Office. For former Indian lands, the Land Office distributed the funds to the various tribal entities according to previously negotiated terms. The American land runs were events where a previously-restricted land, or land seized from the natives by the United States, was opened for homesteading on a first arrival basis. The Oklahoma Land Run of 1889 was the most prominent of the land runs, when over 50,000 "Runners" entered the lands on the first day, among them several thousand former slaves and descendants of slaves. Some who illegally entered Oklahoma before the official start of the race were labeled "Sooners." When the race began at noon, thousands of horses, wagons, buggies, carts, and others rushed across the boundary into Oklahoma. The law-abiding "Runners" fought with the law-breaking "Sooners" on several instances. When the race was over, thousands of disappointed runners were forced to leave the area without filing any claim. There were four other land runs in the Oklahoma Territories in 1891, 1892, 1893, 1895, but the Cherokee Strip Land Run of 1893 was typical. It opened up 7,000,000 acres to settlement, land bought from the Cherokees for $7,000,000.

14.3   Washington State

Explorers [238], traders [239] and many prospectors visited the Chelan Valley after the Lewis and Clark Expedition travelled the Columbia River in 1805. The region was originally known as the Columbia District, but the name was changed to Washington Territory to prevent confusion with the nation's capitol, the District of Columbia. Washington Territory was granted statehood on Nov 11th, 1889 and became known thereafter as Washington State (the 42nd state in the Union).

The first legal white settlers on that part of the Washington Territory known as the Columbia Reservation, which included Lake Chelan, began arriving in 1887 following the 1886 revoking of the Moses Columbia Reservation Treaty of 1879. In that Treaty the United States government had established a reservation for the Sinkiuse-Columbia people of Chief Moses, after the tribe ceded their Columbia Basin homeland to the United States, and white settlement. The Reservation was well north of the tribes traditional range which was south of the Columbia River, and it included land north of the Columbia River, east of the Cascades, west of the Okanogan

---

[238]   Shortly after Lewis and Clark's expedition, David Thompson of the North West Company began exploring the Columbia Basin, and between 1806 and 1814 mapped the entire reach of the Columbia River.

[239]   Alexander Ross's 1814 expedition to establish a North West Company overland route through the Rocky Mountains to the Pacific Coast led to the establishment of Fort Vancouver, near what is now Portland, Oregon.

River and South of the Canadian border. The Columbia Reservation overlapped areas that had already been allocated to Wenatchee and Chelan tribes by earlier treaties. The 1886 revoking allowed white homesteading, but forbade the establishments of town-sites. However, within a few years, there were several hundred buildings standing at the point where the Chelan River leaves Lake Chelan and in 1892, when it was first mapped, Congress had little choice but to permit the expansion of the settlement. It was incorporated as the Town of Chelan in 1902. The County of Chelan was formed with Wenatchee as the county seat in 1899.

14.4   Homesteading Alone

As detailed in Chapter 11, the Reverend Henry Gurr arrived in the Chelan Valley in 1902. Chelan was a small town with perhaps five hundred inhabitants, and St. Andrew's Episcopalian Church where Henry was to be Vicar, had only about fifty members. With so small a congregation it is not surprising that Henry soon filed a homestead application, as mentioned above. He must have been concerned about providing for his growing family and the homestead could be expected to provide land for a house and agriculture. [240]

In the early days there was no easy access from town to the homestead. Henry Gurr began to improve the land by planting an orchard, but later wrote of himself, in the second person, that "at first - having no horse – he walked to Chelan for service the distance being eight miles." [241] Sometimes he was able to hitch a ride on a wagon for part of the distance, but even then the trip typically took three and a half hours. [242] A horse and a new road eased the trip. Local settlers turned out to build the first direct road to Chelan in July 1904, when the *Leader* reported that "a road has just been opened from Bear Creek….It starts at Gurr's place and runs over the hill to the county road and gives the First Creek, Bear Creek and New Oklahoma settlements an outlet to town without going to the Columbia River." [243]

Henry Gurr had great plans for the homestead on Bear Mountain, which he would later name Gurrland. In September 1904 the *Leader* reported that:

> Reverend H. J. Gurr is having a swell log residence built on his homestead west of Lakeside. When completed the structure will be two stories high. A 10-foot fireplace will be build at one end of the house and so constructed that large and heavy logs can be rolled on the fire from the outside. The down stairs will contain one large living and dining rooms and have long French windows. There will be three rooms upstairs, with dormer windows. A kitchen will be built adjoining the main building. [244]

---

[240]   The purchase of a local jewelry store in Chelan is one further indication of his concern for additional income. Henry sold the Gurr's Photo, Optician and Jewelry business to his son Will in 1906 when the 23 year old returned from Minneapolis after taking classes in watch making.

[241]   Entry in *St. Andrews' Historic Notes*. Church and Clergyman's Record Book. "written by the Reverend H. J. Gurr during Lent 1921."

[242]   Perry, Elizabeth Watson, (1999). *We Left Because the Creek Went Dry*. P. 49. Manson, WA: Point Publishing.

[243]   *Chelan Valley Leader*, July 28, 1904.

[244]   *Chelan Valley Leader*, September 2, 1904.

No definitive photos of Gurrland from the homesteading days can be found, but it is unlikely that it had most of the features Henry Gurr hoped to include. As a practical liability there was no reliable source of water and his son Robert, born in 1905, remembers that they tied barrels on the family's two-wheeled gig to haul up water from lower down the mountain. The cliffs to the north and east are precipitous and Robert recalled that a cow and horse died when they went over a 1600-foot drop-off.

In July of 2004, development of the residence was already underway, but the new road was steep and hazardous – as it remains today. That month Henry enlisted his older son Alf, who was visiting from Alaska, to move materials to the site, but near disaster struck:

> Alfred E. Gurr met with an accident Monday afternoon that he'll probably remember for some time. While hauling a load of wood out at the ranch, the whole outfit, including himself, went over the steep grade above [sic; probably below] his father's place. After the atmosphere had cleared away enough to take an inventory, it was found that the wagon was more or less demolished, the harness broken and the horses cut and bruised. While the young man got a thorough shaking up fortunately he received no injuries. [245]

Chelan had electric lighting and water service by 1903, and telephones soon after, although a line to Bear Mountain was not put into service until 1909. Henry and Mabel lived at St. Andrew's Rectory in Chelan with their growing family. Mabel's parents, John and Mary Lucas joined them in the Valley in April of 1903, and in 1905 Henry's son, Will, also settled there after visiting from Alaska in 1904 and being impressed with the valley.

Further evidence of Reverend Henry Gurr's intentions to stay in Chelan came in March 1906 when his petition for US citizenship was granted. Later that spring, on May 18, he proved (obtained final rights to) the Gurrland homestead and a few days later purchased another 160 acres on Bear Mountain for $200.

14.5   Homesteading Together

Edwin arrived in the Chelan Valley in 1906, followed by his second wife Ada a few months later. The two brothers appear to have had a very close relationship all their lives, so it is quite possible that they had, at some earlier date, made plans for Edwin to join his brother in Chelan, and join him he did. In any case, when Edwin arrived he immediately filed for a 40 acre homestead on Section 10, Township 27 Range 21E.W.M, a site adjacent to Henry's property. By 1907 the two brothers were living on the mountain and set about developing their properties together.

Both brothers had "proved up" the original homesteads by 1912 (that year the proof time was reduced from five to three years). Henry acquired additional adjacent holdings by purchase from other homesteaders who abandoned their properties. **Map 14.5a** shows the roads of the

---

[245] *Chelan Valley Leader*, December 16, 1904.

First Creek District, including Bear Mountain, as of 1931. Elizabeth Perry states that as of 1908 the Gurr brothers owned parts of sections 10, 11, 14, and 15. [246]

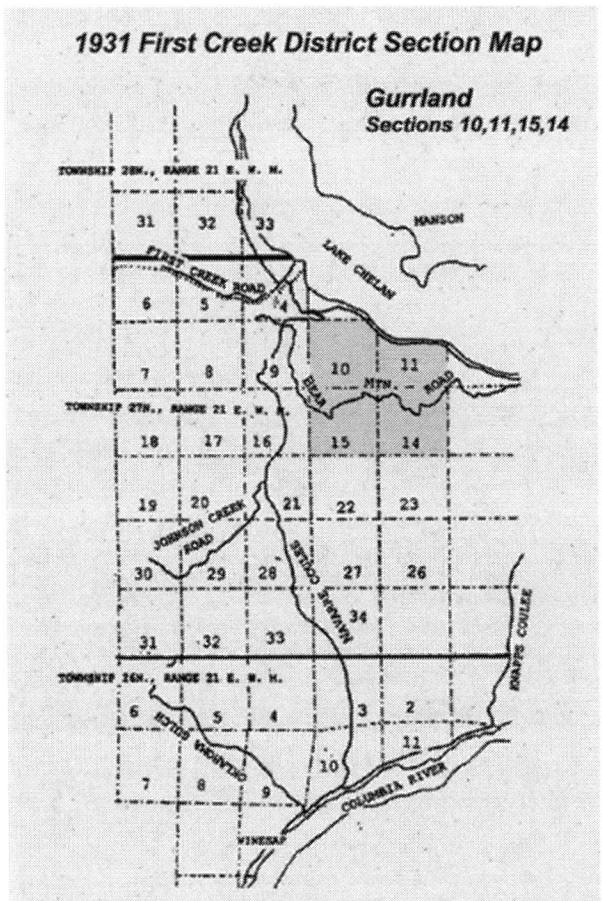

Map 14.5a   First Creek Section Map
Showing Gurrland

In 1912, landholders adjacent to what was now known as Gurrland were J.F. Johnson, F.W. Vollmer, W.V. Cook, J. Theis, D. Fleming, L.C. Meier and G.C. Weirser.

The Bear Mountain wagon road ran from the town of Chelan along the mountainside, bisecting the Gurr properties and on up to First Creek. In 1909 the Forest Service established telephone service over Bear Mountain to First Creek. **Photo 14.5b** on the following page is a north-northwesterly snapshot of Lake Chelan Valley taken from atop Bear Mountain in 2006, just a few hundred yards to the northeast of Gurrland (probably from what was once either Vollmer's or Cook's homestead). Across the lake is the Wapato Indian Reservation with Dry Lake, Roses Lake and Wapato Lake visible, and Manson on the right. Some two thousand feet below and to the left at lake level is Lake Chelan State Park, which can be reached directly from Chelan by East Woodin Ave and South Lakeshore Road.

---

[246] From Perry, P 21

Photo 14.5b Lake Chelan Valley, 2006
Looking northwest from Gurrland atop Bear Mountain
Photo by Paul Magel

14.6   The Road to Gurrland

The wagon road to the Gurr homesteads was probably part of what is now known as Bear Mountain Ranch Road, and it was an eight mile commute from Chelan to Gurrland. This is a trip that the Reverend Gurr must have made back and forth at least once and probably several times a week to fulfill his obligations to his congregation at St. Andrew's Church, as well as to serve other communities along the Valley as a supply priest. Edwin, on the other hand, probably avoided the trip unless it became a necessity.

The Chelan Valley Leader weekly issue of November 30, 1911 includes a front page item ***Team Runs, Horse Killed***, describing a runaway accident involving two horses and a wagon owned by E.R. Gurr of the Bear Creek Settlement. Edwin lost the wagon as well as one of the horses when the startled team broke away from its hitching in Lakeside. With the wagon attached the team bolted for several miles before the wagon was wrecked on a large boulder. The team, detached from the wagon, plunged over a high bank killing one of the pair. **Photo 14.6a** shows Mabel in the Gurr carriage on the road to Gurrland in 1910. **Photo 14.6b** was taken along the same stretch of that road in 2006.

Photo 14.6a   Road to Gurrland
with Gurr Carriage c. 1910
Henry J. Gurr Album

Photo 14.6b   Road to Gurrland, 2006
Photo by Paul Magel

14.7   Gurrland

The homesteads were on marginal land at an elevation of about 3000 feet. [247]   Years of hard work went into proving them.   The brothers built sound, but modest, frame houses with sharply gabled roof lines and gabled dormers capable of withstanding buildup of the heavy winter snows common to the Rocky Mountains.   A photo of what was probably Henry's homestead shows that the roofline had as much as a 15-12 pitch (15" vertical rise for each 12" horizontal

---

[247]   Lake Chelan is at 1079 ft elevation and the nearby high point of Bear Mountain is 3565 ft. The highest peak in the neighborhood is that of Stormy Mountain, about six miles west northwest at 7,219 ft elevation.

run) and at least two dormers with the same pitch, indicating expectation of very heavy snowfalls. The dormers provided light and ventilation for the second floor of the structure. The home also boasted a bay window, an unusual feature for the period.

The western slopes of the Washington Cascades experience some of the highest snowfalls ever recorded on the globe, with peaks near Mount Baker holding the seasonal world record of 1140 inches. Snowfall on the eastern slopes of the Cascades is substantially less, but above 2,000 feet elevation for six months of the year there is always the risk of heavy falls of several feet or more. For Gurrland at over 3,000 feet, deep snow was not an infrequent occurrence, and the brothers undoubtedly experienced the occasional Chinook. [248] Washington counties west of the High Cascades have average annual precipitation levels greater than eighty inches, while those counties east of the range progressively become semi-arid as one moves eastward, and average less than 10 inches beyond the eastern foothills. One example of the diminishing precipitation levels: the upper reaches of Lake Chelan average about 40 inches of precipitation, while Chelan at the lower end of the lake averages about 11 inches. The average low temperatures atop Bear Mountain during the winter months (from November to March) are in the twenties, with sub-zero temperatures common. Like most houses in the region the Gurr homes were heated with wood stoves, and any insulating of the walls or roof would have been accomplished using sawdust and wood chips.

Edwin and Henry built their houses close together and they cleared several acres of their mountaintop properties. They built a corral and a small barn for storage and to protect their livestock, and they put up fences and woodsheds. Like others atop Bear Mountain and the First Creek settlement, the two brothers tried their hand at orchard farming apples, and perhaps they raised some peaches, while lower in the valley homesteaders also experimented with cherries and grapes. The brothers also ran a small sawmill for a time, hoping to be able to supply their neighbors with lumber and firewood. For Edwin the homestead had to provide food and income, or he had to find outside work to support himself and his wife. For Henry, there was the small income from his activities as a priest to fall back on, and he could refuse or accept missions as a supply priest with its small remuneration depending upon his family's needs, or upon the demands that homesteading and orchard farming placed on him.

14.8 Income from Apples

The rich soils and peculiar climate of the lower Chelan Valley convinced many of the early settlers that fruit farming held commercial promise, and Edwin and Henry joined many others in an attempt to establish productive apple orchards. The brothers cleared land, planted new seedlings, and waited three to five years for the trees to fruit out. We do not know what, if any, previous experience they had at fruit farming, although both Edwin and Henry had spent time in Merced with their brother Alfred, and Alfred and his neighbors did raise some fruit.

---

[248] Chinooks are sudden changes in temperature caused by warm ocean winds that sweep in across the mountains and into the interior of the Pacific Northwest, often extending many hundreds of miles inland. The author has personally witnessed a change of temperature from -27F to +35F followed by a return to -39F in a period of 24 hours in Saskatoon, Saskatchewan, over 400 miles east of the foothills of the Rockies.

However, even if the brothers had previous experience, weather and climatic conditions in the Cascades are much different from those in the foothills of the Sierra Nevada and it is likely that the brothers made many errors in their early days as orchardists. While the lower Chelan Valley is ideal for apple growing with its sunny humid summers and cold winters, and the soil is rich with volcanic ash, proper pruning, fertilizing and pest management are key to obtaining a good crop. The lack of a constant source of water on the mountain top meant that during drought the trees were left dry, and even drinking water had to be brought up the mountain in five gallon containers.

The bounty from an orchard is seasonal, but care of the trees is a year round occupation, with a period of intense effort involving picking, packing and shipping to market. A healthy apple tree can produce eighty to two hundred pounds of fruit each year, so even a small orchard of three to five acres, with two or three hundred trees, can produce ten to thirty tons of apples annually. [249] We do not known how many acres the Gurr brothers put into apples during their homesteading years, but during the 1990s, the apple orchards of Washington State produced sixty percent of the apples consumed annually in the United States. [250] By the time the brothers had proved their homestead in 1912, the first apple trees they planted were bearing fruit.

14.9   The Fate of Gurrland

The ranch was not completely abandoned when the Reverend Henry Jonathan Gurr family moved off the land in early 1917 and moved back to the St. Andrew's rectory in Chelan, probably at the time when Reverend Black who had been the rector at St. Andrews between 1912 and 1917, left to join the war effort when the United States entered the conflict in April of 1917. Edwin and Ada remained there until at least 1920 and they continued to harvest the fruit from the orchards. The sawmill was also still in use, though operated by others. Gurrland was completely abandoned by 1921, for in August of that year, shortly before he left for Spokane, the Reverend Gurr published this notice in the *Chelan Valley Leader*:

> Will the parties that have taken drag saw, frame, gearing, belts, nuts off the engine and bolts off the steam pumps, my ¾ bed from cabin and other hardware, peavies and maul please send or return them at their earliest convenience to my house in town. [251]

Whether this elicited any response is unknown.

Edwin remained in the valley for some time after Henry left for Spokane for there is some evidence that he worked for others, perhaps as late as 1924, before he and Ada moved to the

---

[249]   Apple trees are spaced at about 25 ft from one another, or about 65 trees per acre, far enough apart to allow sufficient sunlight but close enough to permit proper cross-pollination.

[250]   Desmond, Andrew (1994). *The World Apple Market*. Haworth Press. pp. 144–149.

[251]   Chelan Valley Leader, (August 11, 1921) as quoted by Perry, Elizabeth Watson, (1999). *We Left Because the Creek Went Dry*. P51. Manson, WA: Point Publishing. A peavie is an implement having a wooden shaft with a sharp metal point and a hinged hook used to handle logs. A maul is a heavy hammer with a wedge-shaped head used for splitting logs.

western part of the state around Puyallup just east of Tacoma. According to Will Gurr the house and barn at Gurrland were still standing in the 1930s and were used for shelter by hunters. Sometime thereafter the buildings burned. Abandoned homesteads eventually revert to public ownership and most of Reverend Gurr's land, along with that of some of his neighbors, is now part of Wenatchee National Forest. The site of Gurrland is about 200 yards south of the radio relay tower on the north slope of Bear Mountain. There are no visible remains of the ranch buildings and second-growth forest now conceals the view up the lake.

Chapter 15

From the Diary of Captain John Lucas
Daily Life in Chelan, 1911 [252]

15.1   Preamble

During the second decade of the 20th century, sixteen members of the Gurr clan were residents in or near Chelan.   Reverend Henry Jonathan Gurr and his wife Mabel lived with their five children at Gurrland on Bear Mountain. Edwin "Teddy" Robert Gurr and his second wife Ada Alice, lived on an adjoining homestead. Mabel Gurr's parents, Captain John B. Lucas and his wife Mary Amanda, had a home in town and a ranch to the east, where their son Clifford sometimes lived with his wife Florence and their baby. Reverend Gurr's youngest son by his first wife, Will Gurr and his wife Maude lived in town and operated his jewelry store on Woodin Avenue. We have an invaluable source of information on how these families lived and interacted with one another and their fellow citizens thanks to a diary kept by Captain Lucas in 1911. This chapter recounts his life, as best we can reconstruct it, and uses his diary entries, supplemented by contemporary news accounts, to sketch the daily life of a small western town in the early 20th century.

Visitors to the valley added to the clan total from time to time. Alfred Edwin Gurr, the Reverend Gurr's eldest son by his first marriage, paid several extended visits to Chelan in the twenty years that his father resided there, as we know from news accounts. As late as 1919 Edwin's son George Herbert Gurr and his wife Ellen Mabel, along with their three children visited for a few months contemplating emigrating from Winnipeg, Canada to Chelan.[253]

15.2   Captain Lucas's Background

John Benedict Lucas was born December 6, 1836 in the British Midlands. When he retired to Chelan in 1903 he told a local journalist that he had earned the title Captain under the British flag in the Crimean War and at the siege of Lucknow, during the Sepoy Mutiny in India, while serving in "Campbell's Army." [254]   No British officer of that name is listed in contemporary military records. But several soldiers named John Lucas served in Scottish regiments commanded by General Sir Colin Campbell and two of those regiments, the 42nd Regiment of Foot and the 93d Highlanders, saw duty during the Crimean War (1853-56) and the

---

[252]   A previous version of this chapter was published with this title in the 2005 Lake Chelan History Notes, pp. 30-39, by Ted Robert Gurr and Elizabeth Watson Perry. The primary source is a diary sent to a Chelan resident in August 1992 by Virginia Robinette of Spokane. The diary was transcribed by Elizabeth Perry for the Lake Chelan Historical Society and is drawn on selectively for this account. The full transcript is available from the Society. The chapter also incorporates news items from The Chelan Valley Leader, other materials in the Society's archives, and documents on the Reverend Henry J. Gurr referred to in Chapter 11.

[253]   Some details regarding that visit are provided in Chapter 20.5

[254]   *The Chelan Valley Leader*, December 28, 1903.

Indian Mutiny (1857-58). Another John Lucas (no middle initial) was on the paybook of the 79th Regiment of Foot, which served during the Indian Mutiny, and spent three months in lockup in 1858 as punishment for desertion. Commissioned officers were entitled to leave to resolve private affairs, while enlisted men were not. As a result even good soldiers occasionally "deserted" to sort out personal problems. [255] In later life John Lucas was a stickler for honesty, judging by diary entries, so it is likely that he did serve in one of Campbell's regiments even if not as a commissioned officer.

Lucas is a Scottish clan name and also a fairly common family name in the English Midlands: British census records identify a half-dozen John Lucas's born in 1835-37. Captain Lucas consistently told US census takers that he was born in England and mentions, in his diary, that his mother's brother lived in Leek – a town at the edge of the Peaks district in the Midlands. He is possibly the John Lucas enumerated in the 1871 British census, born in Staffordshire and then residing in Derby, a town some 20 miles SE of Leek. Scottish regiments recruited mainly from population centers near their depots, so we can only guess how John Lucas joined such a regiment. Perhaps he was born into a family with Scottish connections and, in his late teens, ventured north to enlist in a Scottish regiment.

The U.K. 1871 census record shows that a 35-year-old John Lucas of Derby married to Elizabeth, age 28. It is a year later that our John Lucas immigrated to the United States, apparently alone. In January of 1873 he married 20-year-old Mary Amanda Wilson, nee Miller, in Kankakee, Illinois. She already had a son from a short-lived early marriage to William Wilson in November 1869, and she bore six more children by John Lucas, three of whom lived to adulthood.

John Lucas's occupational background was in coal mining. The only direct evidence is that he worked for trade publications in Chicago that served the iron and coal industries. From 1888 to 1896 he was listed in Chicago city directories as an editor for *The Industrial World and Iron Worker*, a journal that dealt with economic and technical issues. In 1896 he took over as editor of *The Black Diamond*, a weekly, "Published in the Interest of the Coal Industry" according to its masthead, and focused on trade and economic topics. He left in 1902 and took out incorporation papers for the Fuel Publishing Company, with his wife Mary and a Clarence McLaughlin as co-directors. [256]

Working backwards, we can infer that John was in coal mining before he left England. Derbyshire is the locale of the South Derbyshire colliery district where commercial mining was underway from the 18th century onward and is being revived today. It is likely that he worked there as a miner or as a mine boss or supervisor. Kankakee, Illinois, where he met and married Mary Amanda, was the locale of major coal mines in the 1870s and 1880s. He was still living

---

[255] Thanks to Len Barnett, a London researcher, for his search for records of John Lucas' military service, and for his observations about the circumstances of desertion in the mid-19th century.

[256] This and the following information on Captain Lucas's life and work in the Midwest is based on archival research by Peggy Tuck Sinko of Oak Park, Illinois.

Kankakee on April 3, 1883, when he became a naturalized citizen, and in later life he often corresponded with friends there. John and Mary's second child, Noel Lucas, was born in 1886 in Kansas. Southeast Kansas was the site of the Pittsburg-Weir Coalfields, which reached peak production in the 1890s. [257] We know that in the 1890s John was aligned with the operators, not the miners. In a *Chicago Tribune* news article in January 1899 he is listed among the mine operators attending a joint convention of miners and mine owners in Pittsburgh, Pennsylvania.. And this may be a clue to his sobriquet. It was common for supervisors of any group of workers to be given the courtesy title of Captain and we can suppose that an immigrant Englishman with wartime and mining experience would easily find employment in the American coalmines and given such responsibilities and title. We know too that he was addressed as Captain in correspondence to the journals on which he worked.

John's favorite son was Harry, born in Illinois in 1884. In 1907 Harry lost a leg in a railway accident at Pasco junction, on the rail line to Wenatchee, and by 1911 was living in Spokane, where he worked as county clerk. It was Harry who sent John Lucas a blank diary, writing, "father I want you to write something in it every day. It will be nice for me to have something of the kind – better than letters, when you are under the turf. Not that we should need any to keep you in our minds, but it will be pleasant to read what we know you have written for us" (diary entry, January 5). Father and son were in frequent correspondence – few of John's diary entries are so happy as those written after a letter arrives from "Harry Boy."

15.3 The Move to Chelan

The move to Chelan began with John and Mary's oldest daughter Mabel, who was born in Kankakee in 1875. By the late 1880s her family was living at 6518 Union Street on south-side Chicago. The Lucas family probably attended St. George's Episcopal Church, where in mid-1896 a new minister arrived, the Reverend Henry Gurr. The 43 year old Reverend Gurr was a short but handsome, full-bearded man, and temporarily single. He had two teen-age sons by his first wife Celia, who had died in California in 1887, and in 1894 had divorced his second wife, Alice because of her alleged infidelity. Within months Mabel Lucas became Henry's third wife (15 February, 1897). We do not know what John and Mary Lucas thought of Mabel marrying a man twice her age. The Reverend Henry was about 18 years younger than his new father-in-law, but the fact that he too was an immigrant from Britain may have forged a bond between the two men.

Early in 1898 Henry and Mabel Gurr moved from Chicago to a congregation in Buena Vista, a silver- and gold-mining town high in the Colorado Rockies. Their home is shown in Photo 11.11. After less than a year there Henry moved again, this time to Alaska, attracted as much by the Klondike Gold Rush as by pastoral duties (see Chapter 11). Rather than face the

---

[257] Pittsburg is in Crawford County, Kansas northwest of Joplin, Missouri. Coal was surface mined in the County for years before the Pittsburg and Midway Coal Company was formed in 1885. Thousands of workers flooded into the area in the late 1880s, and apparently John Lucas was among them. In Nov. 1888, 150 miners died in an explosion at Frontenac, a town a few miles north of Pittsburg, and it is possible that John Lucas was still in Kansas with his family at the time.

rigors of the journey north, Mabel returned to Chicago to give birth to Eileen, the first of their five children. She later joined her husband in Juneau but after several daunting winters there, in July 1902 Henry moved his family to Chelan to serve as vicar of St. Andrew's Episcopal Church.

Back in Chicago, John and Mary Amanda's publishing venture failed and in less than a year they too were on their way to Chelan. Captain Lucas was said to have retired early – retirement at age 68 would not be early, then or now – because of ill health. Mary Amanda's son by her first marriage lived in Helena, Montana – also mining country – and the Lucas's visited there, evidently thinking of living there. But encouragement from Henry and Mabel Gurr was decisive in persuading the Lucases to move to Chelan, where they arrived in April 1903.

15.4   The Lucas and Gurr Families in Chelan

By 1911, the year of Captain Lucas's diary, much had happened to both families. Henry and Mabel with four more children lived on the Gurrland homestead high on Bear Mountain. The rigors of life on the ranch, which lacked sufficient well-water, often brought them to town to stay at St. Andrew's Rectory, a frame building next to the church. In dry weather Mabel and several of the children would bring a wagon-load of dirty laundry down to the Rectory for washing. On July 28 John writes that "Mabel washed, the Mother helping, got no water to spare at ranch, barely sufficient for the cattle and domestic use other than washing." The costs of raising a large family prompted Reverend Gurr to supplement his meager income from St. Andrews by preaching at other Episcopal churches along the middle Columbia, by business ventures, and operating a sawmill on Bear Mountain. [258]

As small as parish stipends were in frontier towns, they were better than pension income – which for John Lucas was probably nonexistent. Soon after his arrival he set up business as a stationer and news agent, working out of a storefront on Woodin Avenue that he shared with the Post Office and the Gurrs' photo, optician and jewelry business. A photo in the Lake Chelan Historical Society's archives shows the interior of the store; the post office is at the rear of the store, Lucas' newspapers and stationary display at the right. But a town of less than 700 people provided little trade and after 1908 the news shop disappeared from the Chelan business directory. It is as though Captain Lucas himself vanished for no photos of him, either in Chelan or Chicago, have been found.

Nonetheless John and Mary Lucas had resources enough to be living in their own home. In spring 1906 they had purchased the building formerly occupied by Henry Gurr's photo studio, moved it to Johnson between Bradley and Navarre streets, and fitted it up as a dwelling.[259] This dwelling, invariably referred to in the diary as "the Cottage," was furnished well enough to have a piano. On June 28, when John was splitting wood for Mary at the Cottage, "in came Clif, Florence, baby, hired girl (Green), and Mrs. Duhamel. Clif and the girl got at the piano." In October John bought an adjacent lot for $200. (The Cottage was among the structures later demolished to make way for an elementary school playground).

---

[258]   See details in Chapter 11

[259]   *The Chelan Valley Leader*, May 1906.

By 1911 Lucas worked for Harry H. Walker (HHW in his diary), a painter and paperhanger, whose store on Emerson occupied the site of what is now the Chelan Transfer building. Walker's store stocked a wide range of supplies and filled orders for ranchers and homeowners throughout the Chelan valley. HHW himself spent most of his time on painting and papering jobs while John Lucas managed the stock, kept accounts, and – because most purchases were on credit –delivered bills and dunned [260] creditors in person at the beginning of each month. His diary often refers to business difficulties. On March 1, "I find collections very slow and money really scarce. Walked over to Lakeside but nothing was doing." A month later, "I was out all AM (2 hours) 'great cry and little wool.' Much the same in afternoon."

In late 1910 John and Mary separated after 37 years of marriage. The 1910 Census, taken in May, lists John, Mary, and their 18-year old son Clifford as a family unit, so the break with Mary probably occurred later that year. Afterwards Mary continued living in the Cottage until spring 1911 while John moved in with HHW about four blocks away. "Mater," as he usually refers to her, seems to have been a bad-tempered dominatrix.

Photo 15.4a Mary Amanda Lucas
From Anne Cook Gurr Album
Photo taken by Elite Studios, Spokane

---

[260] Dunning is the process of methodically communicating with customers to ensure the collection of accounts receivable. [Not easy in hard times.]

Photo 15.4a on the previous page shows Mary Amanda, a stern-visaged woman with thin, pursed lips staring directly at the photographer. On January 14, "The boss came to dinner and stayed to supper. The infernal nagging got me so hot under the collar that HHW noticed it....I'm just plum sick of it and the author of it." Many other entries refer with irritation to her incessant demands and criticisms. On October 6, when John was seriously ill with a cough and fever, "I vowed to myself that I'd go to the Rectory and get the Mother to nurse me today. THAT shows how VERY miserable I was feeling. Well, I didn't."

What Mary thought of John is not recorded, but they unquestionably remained codependent. She relied on him to chop wood and help with the laundry at the Cottage – "four hours straight washing and wringing" on February 27. On April 24, "The Mater washed all by her lonesome and what's more carried water from Calver's barn, half a block away. This I did not know until evening when I went up to Cottage for bread, which I got, as also a SCORING for not coming up at noon for pie." Mary often was at the paint store for meals. "The Mater surprised me by a timid little knock on the door at 7 AM just as we were eating breakfast....So I had to do a trifle more cooking both bacon and eggs. All of which she enjoyed apparently tho she didn't say so" (February 23). Just as often she invited John and HHW to the Cottage for dinner and supper, or brought stews and pies to the paint store for shared meals. On Sunday, March 5, "HHW and I had an invitation to dine at the Cottage as also Reverend Gurr. The mutton stew and etceteras were excellent and we ate and ate." There also are a number of cryptic initials in the diary margins – most common are G.P.B. and G.P.C. – which usually coincide with days and occasional nights that John and Mary spent together at the Cottage, Rectory, or ranch. They may refer to intimate relations – or perhaps only to comfortable conversations or a decent night's sleep.

15.5   Food on the Table

Most meals described in the diary are familiar today as plain country cooking. Stews were regular features as was "sausage and crunched spuds." Less common but much appreciated were roast beef and, in season, fresh halibut steak. Lamb chops, veal cutlets, and beef tongue also were worth a diary entry. A Sunday dinner for four at the Rectory in September featured "baked apple pie, mutton stew, creamed cabbage, mashed potatoes, etc. all very good." On Thanksgiving, which was celebrated at the Rectory with nine members of the extended family, "We had a turkey, very nicely cooked, Boston baked beans supplied by Mabel – very good. The [plum] pudding was grand, cake ditto, but somebody or some animal got away with the remainder. The vegetables – squash, carrots and spuds were excellent."

Fresh foods and baked goods rarely were store-bought. In spring and early summer local farmers sold asparagus, berries, green peas and new potatoes; later in the season cherries, peaches, and apples were available in abundance. Milk, butter, and eggs came from local producers. On March 31 John Lucas bought 3 dozen eggs from Gurrland for 60 cents. (Perhaps a family discount, because later in the year he reports that eggs cost 30 cents a dozen.)

Mary, along with other Chelan women, supplemented her income by baking. In May, after Mary had moved temporarily to the Lucas ranch east of town, John took out "rising or yeast stuff" from her friend, Mrs. Wells. At the ranch she baked pies and breads sent them, courtesy of neighbors going to town by wagon, for family and for sale. On a late May visit to town, "The Mater baked at Rectory and left a couple of 10 cent loaves for HHW." Supplies were cheap: in June "the Mother bought 200 lbs. (4 sacks) flour from Henry B., Lakeside, at $1.20 per sack – a saving of $1.00, here the price is $1.45." Fruits for her pies also were cheap. Early in July "Kleinsmith has lots of dew and loganberries, 40 cents per gal."

Barter and gifts were another major source of foodstuffs. In June John Lucas mentions putting up a 6-quart can of cherries, cherries "given to HHW by Tom Shollenburg." On July 21, he "got some cherries from Mrs. Baker's and proffered my services to pick some [more] for her." The next day "Mrs. Sinclair baked three pies, two large and one small one for HHW." Later in July John Lucas "received a small 10 pound sack of beets from ER which the Mater cooked, so I guess she earned her share." The same month neighbors encouraged them to help themselves to windfall apples for Mary's canning and baking.

Canned store-bought foodstuffs occasionally appeared on menus, for example oysters for stews and sardines. Peanut butter, ordered in 25-pound buckets from Sears, was a staple of the diet at Gurrland. But most preserved foods, like fresh produce, were local. Like other farm wives Robert's mother Mabel canned, putting up as much as 100 quarts of prunes and apples in a season. Local farmers raised and slaughtered the pigs that provided the pork chops and smoked bacon and sausages mentioned in the Lucas diary, their calves were the source of veal chops and roasts and stews. In May John Lucas mentions paying 55 cents for 1¾ pounds of bacon. In December a sirloin roast cost $1.40 for 8 pounds (probably bought from Dickson's, the town butcher). A Christmas turkey was bought from a farmer in Lakeside for $2.15.

Several restaurants operated in Chelan in 1911, catering to visitors, workers on the Wapato irrigation project, and ranchers in town on weekends. The Pruett House advertised rooms for $1.00 per day and single meals at 25 cents, but when John Lucas and HHW ate there on New Year's Day, 1912, they paid 40 cents a plate for "a passable dinner but nothing extra, and certainly not worth what it cost." Locals earned good money supplying food for weekend and holiday visitors: "Mrs. FS had a good Fourth of July weekend supplying the Pastime Parlor with pies, hams etc., $32 and upwards." Women's church groups provided food to raise money: in September the St. Andrew's Guild "decided to…serve lunch or supper in the Harris Batchelors' quarters to raise money for wood for church, cleared about $25."

The only beverages on the Lucas and Gurr tables evidently were milk, coffee, and occasionally cider. John mentions having a cold bottle of beer with Ted on a hot July day, but at the hardware store, not at mealtime.Wine and hard liquor never are mentioned, though they were readily available in town – perhaps too much so, as this notice from the April 13th *Leader* attests: "Notice: Anyone selling, giving or furnishing any liquor to Mr. Theodore Laguee will be liable to damages. – Mrs. Theodore Laguee." The Women's Christian Temperance Union was active in Chelan and probably contributed to the large number of registered women voters. Of the 283 voters registered for the November 1911 municipal election, 114 (40%) were women. John's diary makes no reference to the fact that Washington State granted suffrage to women that same year.

15.6.1 Weather and Travel in Chelan

Bad weather is today a topic for conversation; in early 20th century Chelan it was a source of damage and discomfort. On January 7, 1911, John Lucas wrote in his diary, "Very high wind (chinook) all night, windows blown in and quite a little damage done…The church, St. Andrew's here in Chelan, plainly showed the effects of the gale and the seats, books, etc. were covered with dust and debris…" A few days later the editor of the weekly *Leader* wrote that "It is fortunate that there was not a heavy coating of snow on the hillside…when the big chinook wind swept down the lake last Friday night, for in that event there would have been a repetition of last spring's washouts." A contemporary newspaper photo gives a panoramic view of Chelan after a snowfall.

By January 11th temperatures were down to zero with a biting wind from the SE, and Lucas noted that he awoke shortly after midnight "and lay chilling more or less until I got up at 6:45." On November 9, after the first winter snow, is a similar entry: "I dread the night because I know I shall be cold after my hot stoves lose their heat." Up at 6:00, his first task was to light the wood stoves and begin breakfast in the bachelor quarters he shared with Harry Walker. "It was 6:40 before the kitchen-dining room got at all warm and comfortable."

Whatever the season, few people had autos in 1911 so travel in the Chelan valley and up the nearby coulees and gulches was usually by farm wagon or surrey, while around town people almost invariably walked. The Gurrs travelled to and from Gurrland in a two-wheeled gig (see Photo 14.6a). John Lucas again, on November 10: "The trip across the bridge to Geo. D. Brown's for milk is a trying one as the wind sweeps up the stream between banks something fierce." Lucas also owned a ranch an hour and a half's walk east of town, occupied at various times by Mary and son Clif and family. On May 24, John carried a basket with milk and pie tins from the paint store out to the ranch at 7 pm, stayed 15 minutes, and walked back at 9 pm "somewhat tired." When lucky they could go on a rancher's wagon, not necessarily for free because Lucas mentions that Mary got a ride to the ranch with a Mr. Heller who "only charged 50 cents." But more typical was his entry of June 29: his grandson Robert, age 5, "accompanied his Grandma out to the ranch – shank's pony, not a team in from or toward that way."

15.6.2 Long Distance Travel

Long-distance travel also was rigorous. By 1911 Lake Chelan was a popular destination for summer tourists as well as friends and family visitors of its thousand-plus residents. If arriving from Spokane or the Pacific coast they would likely take the Great Northern passenger trains to Wenatchee and then a steamboat up the Columbia to Chelan Falls. Steamboats plied the middle reaches of the river from 1890 until sometime after the coming of the railroad in 1914.

From the steamboat landing to town it was a four mile walk or four-horse-team stagecoach ride up the wagon road on the south side of the treacherous Chelan River gorge, a road whose poor condition and steep grades prompted frequent complaints from *The Leader*'s editor. By spring 1911 the road had been improved enough that George D. Brown was able to motor to Wenatchee, 35 miles away on rutted and rock-strewn roads, in three hours (*The Leader*, May 11). Motorized service to the town did not begin until 1914, when an open-air six-passenger bus carried passengers from the Falls to Chelan town.

Once the tired and dusty visitors arrived in Chelan they had their choice of hotels such as Campbells or Pruetts, or Harris' bachelor quarters. In summer some took the mail boat "Lady of the Lake" to the resort lodges at Stehekin, 50 miles up lake. Like the "Lady of the Lake," locally-owned launches also provided transportation and supplies for ranches at landings serving outlying communities such as those at Manson, Minneapolis Beach, Hollywood Beach, and 25-Mile Creek. Will's launch was typical of those on the lake and the launch 'FJ' is shown as **Photo 15.6.2.**

Photo 15.6.2   Launch 'HJ'
Henry J. Gurr Album

15.7   Community Life in 1911

The 3-day 4th of July celebrations were the biggest social event of the year in Chelan. On July 6 *The Leader* reported that large crowds of visitors from upriver arrived by steamboat to celebrate the three-day national holiday along with the locals. They filled the City Park to hear patriotic music by the Chelan Band and Chorus of 30 voices and were subjected to speeches by the Honorable M. E. Field, Major C. C. Campbell, and Palmer Edmunds. Mary rented the Cottage to several families from Brewster and John Lucas' cot at the paint store was let to Clifford Sly of Entiat, "a very nice young fellow" who paid $1.50 for two nights. Lucas, who slept temporarily at the Rectory, was awakened on Tuesday, July 4th, at 3:45 am by a giant firecracker. Later he and Mary "took in the open air speaking in the Park, all of it good" and in the evening, joined by Clif, watched fireworks "let off from a barge in the lake."

The celebration included horse and harness races, swimming and rowing competitions, and dances on all three nights. The Chelan baseball team won three games from Brewster with Lucas' stepson Will (Bill) Gurr as pitcher and Louis Wapato, a Chelan Indian, as catcher. *The Leader* reported that "Long Jim, the stately, dignified hereditary chief of the Chelan Indians, attended the celebration this week and entered some of his horses in the races."

Before TV and cell phones people kept in touch through visits, social events, and entertainments that occurred with great frequency throughout the year. The OK Band gave Saturday evening concerts at the park during good weather. The Lakeside hall hosted all-night dances. The Chelan Auditorium on Johnson Avenue was the venue for plays like "The Old Homestead," whose March 11 performance was directed by Mrs. C. T. Black, winning *The Leader's* praise for "her well-known histrionic and elocutionary talent." The Etude Society sponsored concerts and lectures throughout the year. A sample concert program (from 1908) features more than two dozen local performers: piano solos and trios, Ed Richardson playing "The Spring Chicken" on his trombone, selections by the mixed quartet, and performance of a farce-tragedy, "Where Do You Go From Here?" In 1911 the Etude lecture series cost $1.50 for the season; a single ticket in November to hear Congressman George Washington Norris of Nebraska was 50 cents adults, 25 cents children.

The churches advertised and hosted musical events in the guise of church services: "Chelan is blessed with an unusual amount of musical talent for a community of so small a population. Our good fortune…was again manifested in the two large choruses which participated in the Easter Sunday services" at the Methodist church and St. Andrews (*The Leader*, April 20). The churches' Ladies Guilds organized social lawn parties as fund-raisers. One such event on July 14 featured "strawberries and cream and coffee and lemonade" but was too expensive for John Lucas, who hadn't the price to attend. **Table 15.7a** consists of a list of prices in 1911 Chelan taken from the Diary of Captain Lucas.

Table 15.7a Chelan Prices in 1911	
From the Diary of Captain John B. Lucas	
Dozen eggs from the family ranch	0.20
Dozen eggs in town	0.30
Pound of butter	0.40
Pound of bacon	0.30
Loganberries from the grower per gallon	0.40
50 pounds of flour	$1.20-1.45
Sirloin roast per pound	0.175
Christmas turkey	2.15
Everyday restaurant dinner	0.25
New Years' Day dinner	0.40
Mailing a package	0.23
Wagon ride from town to ranch	0.50
1 pair men's shoes	4.00
Lenses for eyeglasses	0.50
Part payment on new false teeth	$10.00
Rental of furnished cottage per month	$15.00-
Annual tax assessment on hardware store	$16.25

Meetings of Chelan's numerous fraternal lodges were another source of social interaction. John Lucas attended a Masonic meeting on April 1 that lasted until nearly midnight, and wrote that "the wild excitement of last night's lodge work upset my nervous system and I did not sleep a wink."

Late fall was the season for travelling shows. King Kennedy, whose ranch adjoined the Lucas's, was an accomplished ventriloquist who used three or more dummies and also performed magic tricks and gave lantern slide shows. He performed in school houses, churches, and meeting halls, beginning each season with several performances in Chelan before taking his show on the road – with footlockers in a horse-drawn rig – to towns in north central and eastern Washington.[261] Other travelling entertainers were less successful. In November 1911, according to a self-serving article in *The Leader*,

> A minstrel troupe drifted into town from the upper country Saturday and put on a show at the Auditorium....As they had not advertised in *The Leader* very few knew they were here, and they did a poor business. They showed again Monday night and on Wednesday night gave a dance in the hope of raising money enough to get out of town.

Complementing the public side of community life was a great deal of social visiting among households. Members of the Lucas and Gurr family were often invited to dinner and supper by friends and parishioners of St. Andrews. Just as often Mary called on lady friends, sometimes for a social visit and sometimes overnight. *The Leader* filled its columns with reports of visits, for example, "Mrs. H. J. Gurr is spending a few days in town with her parents, Capt. and Mrs. Lucas. She has been suffering from [a] severe attack of rheumatism and has not been able to leave her home on the ranch since early in the winter until now" (April 13). Out-of-towners were often noted: "Jay Farnham and Gage Shannon, of Oregon, are guests at the B. F. Smith home...Mr. Farnham is a nephew of Mr. Smith's and he and his friend came up there to spend an outing and vacation on Lake Chelan. They made the trip – nearly 500 miles – on horseback" (July 13).

15.8   Disease, Injury and Death

Members of the Lucas and Gurr families were frequently ill or injured. John Lucas reported physical ailments in nearly a third of his daily entries, from pain due to chopping wood to tooth extractions to flu. For a full month beginning late September he was sick with "la grippe," pleurisy, and headache. He tried to work throughout but often took to bed in pain and weakness. He saw Dr. Mitchell once during the siege but reports that the only relief came from a "celery nerve tonic." Mary was often ill as well, sometimes with la grippe, other times with unspecified illnesses that kept her in bed, and she occasionally stayed with lady friends who could nurse her. Henry H. Walker, though considerably younger, also was often sick – eating

---

[261]   A detailed account is found in the article: King Kennedy, Pioneer Showman. *Lake Chelan History Notes*, Spring 1978, pp. 5-9.

little and spending much time sleeping. In mid-November, according to *The Leader* and the diary, he suffered a life-threatening attack of indigestion that required 12 hours of near-constant attention from Dr. Harvey, mainly in the form of purgatives.

The younger Gurr children were born at the Rectory and all of them survived to adulthood, despite the difficulties of ranch life. On Bear Mountain the family suffered from periodic bouts of flu. Mabel Gurr's acute rheumatism, referred to above, "is from the waist line to the shoulders – back as well as front – and she suffers mostly at night, that is about midnight until 8 AM." Contrary to *The Leader*'s report (above), she came down to Chelan in early February to consult a doctor about the condition. The children on Bear Mountain suffered from accidents as well as infections. In May little Robert "inadvertently drank some lye water at Gurrland which severely burned his throat and stomach" but did no lasting damage. In late October 2-year-old Helen fell from her high chair and suffered a concussion from which she did not fully recover for a week. The diary makes one reference to a physician's house call to Bear Mountain because a child was too ill for the rough 8-mile ride to town. For the most part they survived by home care – with encouragement and advice by phone calls from family members in town. The U.S. Forest Service ran a telephone line to Bear Mountain in 1909 and the Gurr family was among the early subscribers. John Lucas refers often to phone conversations with family at Gurrland, calls that he usually made from the paint store or St. Andrew's Rectory.

Accidents were common and sometimes fatal. On a Saturday in March the Reverend H. J. Gurr "stepped on two nails protruding from a board….One of the sharp points penetrated his foot nearly 2 inches" (*The Leader*, March 16), but the injury did not keep him from the pulpit. In mid-July John Lucas recorded three other episodes. Deputy Sheriff J. M. Bennett went up lake on July 14 to make an arrest, but "in stooping over to get a drink at a spring in the rocks his revolver dropped from holster and was discharged, the ball going thro the heart, killing him instantly." Several days later, "young William Howser while handling his new rifle at slaughter house Lakeside accidentally shot a stranger – man named Torpey." The .22 caliber bullet entered Torpey's leg and exited his buttock, sending him to hospital. The next day "a young man (boy) McClure, a tourist from Seattle was killed – neck broken, by a fall from a horse. Body brought down lake by steamer, Lady of the Lake" (July 20).

Earlier in the year four Indians died of wood alcohol poisoning, which *The Leader* described as the "tragic results of a drunken orgy at the home of Sylvester Wapato…last Saturday night and Sunday" (March 16). In fact Deputy Sheriff Bennett was implicated in their deaths. Enforcing a prohibition on Indians drinking spirits, Bennett intercepted a shipment of 5 quarts of whiskey from Seattle that had ordered by the Wapatos for their weekend party for visitors "from the upper country." Lacking whiskey, one of the visitors, Billie Ambrose, brought wood alcohol. Ambrose, his wife, and Wapato's wife were among the fatalities.

15.9 The End of the Story

John Lucas's diary ends on January 1, 1912. His health continued to decline and in March, according to *The Leader* (March 28, 1912) he left for Spokane for "a surgical operation of bladder troubles. He was accompanied by Mrs. Lucas and Dr. Harvey who went as far as the Falls to see him comfortably placed on the river steamer. George D. Brown took the party down in his auto. Operation is necessary to save the Captain's life...." The condition proved "much more serious than was anticipated" but surgery on a Friday morning in early April was successful – until the evening, when a blood clot caused complete paralysis of his right side. Mary's care was now essential to John's convalescence. She closed up the Cottage, sold some of their effects, and took others to Spokane where she set up a new household for them. Captain John Lucas died in early September, 1912.

Mary Lucas was widowed at the age of 58. From then until her death in 1938, when she was 84, she lived in her daughter's household, first in Chelan and then at the rectory of Trinity Church in Spokane, where the Reverend Henry J. Gurr retired in 1921. Her son Harry, John's favorite, died early. His younger brother Clifford Lucas, who is frequently criticized for laxity in his father's diary, married and then divorced in Chelan and remarried in Spokane. He succeeded his brother Harry as Spokane county clerk. A son was killed in a firearms accident when he was about 12, the daughters married and we can guess that one of them was Virginia Robinette of Spokane, who sent a photocopy of the diary to a Chelan resident in August 1992. Later attempts to contact her failed.

Will (Bill) Gurr was a life-long resident of Chelan but no descendants of the Lucas or Gurr families remain in Chelan today with the exception of Will's adoptive granddaughter, Barbara Von Epps, whose recollections are incorporated in Chapter 17. Like so many people who settled on the western frontier, most of them stayed a while and then moved on.

Chapter 16
Three Gurr Brothers – Legacy

16.1   The Summing Up

The absence of a full time father, while Alfred James was a butler during the first five to ten years of the brothers' lives together, probably reinforced their dependence on one another. At the same time it instilled in them a confidence that they could survive independent of a male mentor. The Victorian attitude to child-rearing seems to have been that, not only should children be seen and not heard, but that they should start to behave like little adults as soon after they were weaned as possible. There is no evidence that Alfred Richard held this view and he kept his 12 children close at all times, but in later years both Henry and Edwin effectively abandoned their children without any signs of remorse when those children were no more than fifteen years of age. Although this cavalier attitude would probably lead to charges being laid in the present day, it was clearly condoned and considered acceptable in Victorian times.

As diverse as their characters and personalities were, there was a family bond among the three brothers that always brought them back together, and their common desire to better their lot and that of their families would eventually lead all three from England to America.

Alfred Richard, Henry Jonathan and Edwin Robert came of age in London, England in the early 1870s in the middle of an era of dynamic social and industrial change. The impact of this changing world in which they lived was profound, but being of different natures the responses of the brothers to it were different. Alfred Richard appears to have adjusted to change with ease, despite uncertainty and hardship, keeping his wife and family close, and remaining the most conservative of the three throughout his ninety-three years. Henry Jonathan was excited by change. While he appears to have been the most devout and introspective of the three brothers, he seems to have sought far and different places throughout his life, the opportunist and adventurer, always on the move. Edwin Robert relished change, but more grounded than Henry and less conservative than Alfred, he seemed satisfied living in the moment, and enjoying the company of family or friends.

Alfred Richard, the eldest son, seems to have been the most stable and practical of the three brothers. As was expected in their era, it is he, the eldest son, that became the Son in the family business, Gurr and Son, and it was he who would eventually inherit the family business following the death of the boys' father, Alfred James and their mother Mary Ann. A devoted father and family man, it is around Alfred Richard that the others would gather on special occasions, and whenever the two younger brothers returned to London from abroad, it was to Alfred Richard's home that they would make their way. When Alfred moved to California the two brothers would be frequent visitors.

Henry Jonathan, the second son, had a more intellectual nature than his two brothers, and yet he was also the most footloose. During the first fifty years of his life he was almost continually on the move; at sea to ports in the Far East, and on land across the American continent, north to Alaska and to the Aleutians. He kept a journal and wrote home frequently, but it is on his return to England with his two sons in the winter of 1888/1889 that the stories of his adventures in the remote and exotic places he visited provided the decisive stimulus. Within the year Alfred would leave England for America, with his wife and twelve children.

Edwin Robert, the third son was apparently the most outgoing of the three. As Major General Hugh Stott (the son of Edwin's sister Ellen) would much later describe Edwin: "Edwin (Ted), was a much loved uncle, of a jolly disposition." [262]
He sought the company of both men and women, and seemed capable of putting everyone at ease, which probably accounts for his success as the front man in the family business, for his easy going nature and sense of humor made it logical for the family to use him in dealing with the people in their business world. Although he did not distain hard work, he was usually the first to lay down his tools and the last to say goodnight at family gatherings. Like any younger brother, he looked up to his older siblings and delighted in their company. He did not lead, he followed and enjoyed. It was Edwin, who in 1878 at 23 years of age travelled to America to spend time with his brother Henry, who was studying for the ministry in Minnesota. It was to Edwin that Alfred would transfer control of the family company Gurr and Son in 1889, when he packed up and moved to California with his large family. It is Edwin who accepted the responsibility for the management of the family business and for the welfare of the remaining female family members. Edwin would cross the Atlantic at least three times during the next five years, en-route to California, to be with Alfred and his family. Edwin seems to have become accustomed to the "good life" and managed to travel first class on more than one occasion.

It is interesting to note that Edwin first made arrangements to follow his brothers to America as early as 1892. That year Edwin crossed the Atlantic with his wife Alice and their two children, apparently with the intention of taking up permanent residence in America. The death of Alice in Merced, California just over a year following their arrival brought Edwin back to England with his two sons only to return to America a few weeks later. He may have made yet another return crossing to England in the same year, leaving his sons in the care of his brother Alfred in Merced. Henry's son William, who lived close by at the time, suggests in his memoirs that his uncle returned to England to find another wife. Edwin would return to America at least once more, before finally migrating to Washington in 1906, never to see England again. As described earlier in Chapter 14, he and his brother Henry homesteaded on a mountainside overlooking the Chelan valley.

We have two pictures of Edwin Robert Gurr. One was taken in a London garden in 1887, the other in the Chelan Valley in 1919 when he was 64 years old. The relaxed smile on Edwin's face in the 1919 photo, **Photo 16.1a** on the following page, contrasts with his more contemplative expression in the earlier picture. The "jolly disposition" he was known for seems apparent in the latter. Perhaps it is the nature of some individuals to laugh at their mistakes and try again, even against the odds, enabling them to overcome more than their share of life's problems.

---

[262] From *A Biography of Dr. Hugh Stott (1884-1966),* as yet unpublished manuscript. from the Stott family history collection of Colonel Hugh Scott (1940-present), which includes biographical information on a continuous line of seven Stotts who practiced medicine dating from the mid-18th century to the present.

This appears to be true of both Edwin and his brother Henry who struggled to survive on their Bear Mountain homesteads, enduring what most of us would consider hardship, but they remained resilient and hopeful.

Photo 16.1a Edwin Robert Gurr
Chelan, 1919
Paul Magel Collection

Henry planted his roots in America in 1875 at the age of 22, Alfred in 1889 at the age of 38, and Edwin in 1906 at the age of 50. In contemplating the lives of Alfred, Henry and Edwin Gurr and their adventures in America, one is reminded that men are their most impulsive when they are young and feel they have an eternity of life before them. Therefore, it seems reasonable to most of us that a twenty-two year old like Henry would have a strong desire to see the new world and explore it. While we sometimes scoff at youthful impracticality, we still admire those who, cheerful and determined, go out into the world and struggle to achieve their goals. We respect those who are successful in our very competitive world, and we sometimes overlook the achievements of those who simply open new avenues for the rest of us, without ever seeming to prosper themselves. Whatever motivated Henry, his curiosity, his sense of adventure, wanderlust or something else in his nature, one cannot help but admire the fact that he endured much hardship and lived an exceptional life. His communications to his brothers about the new world he saw drew them like a magnet.

Hardship can also make one more and more conservative, and often the optimism of young people, and that wonderful willingness to sacrifice and to dare anything is lost. Where life's experiences are particularly harsh, men who have been gifted with an innate sense of humor seem to fair best, while those who don't see the irony of life's failures become increasingly pessimistic. It cannot be said that any one of the three brothers Gurr had an easy life, especially homesteading in America where they struggled to survive, and where many of the simple conveniences they had taken for granted in London, simply did not exist, but there is no evidence that any one of them regretted his decision to emigrate from England. Which of the three brothers faced down the greatest hardships? We will never know. But the important outcome is that the three helped one another and persevered, and their descendants in America have benefited greatly from their sacrifices. In the final analysis, this may be part of what each brother was seeking.

16.2   The Passing of Edwin Robert Gurr and Ada

Both Edwin and Henry were in their mid sixties when they abandoned Gurrland. We believe the hard life on the mountain, coupled with the perennial lack of water became too much for them. The 1920 census indicates that Edwin was still working for others at the First Creek Settlement, while Henry was at the rectory in Chelan. The Reverend Gurr retired as Vicar of St. Andrews Episcopal Church in 1921, and shortly after moved to Spokane. Edwin remained at First Creek until the summer of 1925, when he and Ada moved west and settled on a ranch between Sumner and Puyallup, a few miles outside of Tacoma, Washington. The reason for the move westward, rather than to join his brother and family in Spokane, is unknown.

The brothers' abandoned homesteads atop Bear Mountain were stripped to their foundations by neighbors, while the land remained unoccupied for the balance of the 20th century, and even to the present day. Almost one hundred years after the two brothers labored to receive their patent, there are few signs of previous habitation remaining, a few small clearings and overgrown roadways as the forest creeps back to reclaim the land.

Following a prolonged illness, Edwin Robert Gurr died at Pierce County Hospital in Tacoma on Feb. 7th, 1929. He was buried in Sumner Cemetery a few days later. His death certificate lists the cause of death as cirrhosis of the liver complicated by senility. Ada married a neighbour, William Rowley, following Edwin's death, but William left her a widow (for a third time . . .?). On what was probably a visit back to First Creek, Ada died in the County of Chelan on November 18th of 1934, following a stroke (cerebral hemorrhage) on October 27th. She was buried beside Edwin in Sumner Cemetery. Their gravesites are recorded in the cemetery registry, but there are no gravestones or other markers.

16.3   The Passing of the Reverend Henry Gurr and Mabel

Reverend Henry Jonathan Gurr died at the age of 78 on June 18, 1931, at his home on West Dean in Spokane. He had been ill for several months but the immediate cause of death was a pulmonary embolism. He was eulogized in a service at Holy Trinity and buried at Riverside Cemetery. The $149 bill [263] for his casket and burial was paid for by "Mrs. Gurr and Harry Lucas" – and since Mabel Gurr was impecunious, it is likely that the bill was actually paid by her older brother Harry, who was then Spokane City Clerk. **Photo 16.3a** shows the gravestone of the Reverend Gurr in Riverside Cemetery.

---

[263]   Riverside Cemetery record obtained by Paul Magel.

Photo 16.3a Henry's Gravestone
Riverside Cemetery, Spokane
Photo by Paul Magel

Photo 16.3b St. Andrews Church
Chelan, Washington, 2006
Photo by Paul Magel

Photo 16.3c   Reverend Henry Gurr
Juneau, Alaska c. 1900
Henry J. Gurr Album

One last echo of money problems for the Gurr family comes from 1940, when Mabel Gurr died. Several weeks after her cremation Lavina Mason, the wife of Holy Trinity's current priest, visited one of the daughters, still living at the West Dean house, and asked about a small box on a shelf. The daughter – no doubt Harriet, since the other daughters now lived elsewhere – explained the box contained her mother's ashes and she did not know what to do, since a cemetery inurnment cost $35 which she did not have. "Lavina went straight home to bring Father Mason back. In a simple devout procession, the small group returned to the church grounds to bury the ashes, accompanied by a brief religious ceremony." [264] Today that grave is among a handful of unmarked burials on the north side of Holy Trinity.

There is another marker from Henry's past that still stands today. St. Andrews, the 1897 log church in Chelan, where the Reverend Gurr spent twenty years of his life in service, was added to the National Register of Historic Places in 1992. **Photo 16.3b** is a photo of that Historic log church taken in 2006. Hanging in that church is the original of **Photo 16.3c** of Reverend Gurr taken in Juneau, Alaska c. 1900.

---

[264] Marcia O'Leary. *A History of Holy Trinity Episcopal Church.*

16.4   The Passing of Alfred Richard Gurr and Emily.

Alfred Richard Gurr died on April 5th, 1944 just three weeks after his 93rd birthday. Alfred and his beloved wife Emily had celebrated their sixty-seventh wedding anniversary together on December 11th of 1939. Emily passed away the following September. Each of them from a family not known for longevity, the couple were rarely parted and they and their twelve children remained a close knit family throughout their almost 68 years of marriage. In their final years it was their daughter Mary Maude who resided with and cared for them in their retirement home at 2261 Clarke Avenue in San Mateo.

Alfred Richard outlived his brothers Henry and Edwin by almost fifteen years. While all three were alive they maintained close contact with one another, although in their later years these occasions became notably less frequent. There is no evidence, for example, that Alfred ever visited his brothers in Chelan, nor that he in any way contributed to or supported their homesteading. It is also unlikely that Henry or Edwin were ever financially capable of visiting Alfred in San Mateo. Alfred, on the other hand appears to have been financially comfortable in his latter years and there is even some evidence that he dabbled in real estate during the late 1930s and early 1940s, for we have found several land transfer records in his name.

His occupation, listed in the several censuses in which he was enumerated, was either dairyman or poultry farmer but he was obviously entrepreneurial and his activities were multi-faceted. "Active, brainy and progressive" are used to describe Alfred Richard in the 1905 biographical sketch presented in Section 12.4. This description might be included in his epitaph to describe a rather remarkable individual.

16.5   Legacy

Of the twenty-two children born to the three brothers Alfred, Henry and Edwin, only one died in infancy and none as children, a significant improvement from their parents and grandparents days. Their parents, Alfred James and Mary Ann, lost two of eight and their Gurr grandparents, Jonathan and Mary, lost three of eight children in infancy or early childhood. Only Reverend Henry Jonathan's seven children were all born in America. Alfred's twelve children and Edwin's two surviving sons were all born in London.

The next four chapters of this book outline the little we know about the lives of the children of the three brothers in America, and there are a few details on several of their grandchildren. We have asked ourselves:

> ***What enticed the Gurr brothers to leave the relative security***
> ***of their middle class lives in familiar surroundings***
> ***for an uncertain future in the new world?***

There is no single answer. In Henry we think it was his taste for adventure, in Edwin a man who sought the company of the older brothers he obviously admired. But for Alfred Richard we believe his motivation was the legacy he would provide his children – the opportunity to live the American dream.

Part III

Living the American Dream, Children of the Brothers Gurr

Part III is a collection of information

concerning the descendants of

the three Gurr brother

Chapter 17

Will Gurr: A Special Story

17.1 The Life of a Minister's Son

William Edward Newton Gurr, the second son of the Reverend Henry J. Gurr, survived a difficult childhood and a danger-filled adolescence.[265] Those challenges helped give him the self-reliance to live and work on his own on the Alaskan frontier from 1899 to 1906. They also formed the strength of character and moral compass that made him a leading citizen of the town of Chelan from his arrival in 1906, at the age of 23, until his death in 1977. We know more about his remarkable life than any other of the three Gurr brothers' first-generation descendants, in part from his memoirs and letters, and in part from the recollections of family members. This chapter is taken from his edited memoirs, *Coming of Age in the West 1883-1906.* [266] It fills in many of the details of daily life and work in Chelan in the first half of the 20th century.

17.2 Early Years

Will was born in Wahpeton, Dakota Territory, on October 16, 1883, the second son of the Reverend Gurr and his beloved first wife, Celia Frost Gurr. Will was less than a year old when the family relocated to the San Francisco Bay area, because of his mother's failing health, and was only four when she died. **Photo 17.2a** shows mother Celia and **Photo 17.2b** Will and Alf taken c. 1886. Years later Will wrote:

> It was there we lost her and oh God, how I was to miss her later on. I can well remember one day when Mother was confined to her bed, she had my brother on her right and I was on her left when Father came into the room. I remember oh so well him saying, "Oh Celia you should not do that" and she replied "Oh I want to." It was just a few days after that that when I went into the room, and the bed was empty, but not made up. [267]

For years after Celia's death Will's father lived the life of an itinerant clergyman. First he took his sons to England and back, then to a dozen towns and parishes in California, the upper Midwest and the Mississippi, the Colorado Rockies, and Alaska during the Gold Rush. The two boys lived rough years between 1889 and 1892 in a boy's home in San Mateo, evidently while their father sought to establish his second marriage to a young Scots woman, Alice McTaggart Gardener. That marriage was doomed to failure - Will recalled her as "A beautiful woman, tho

---

[265]   As a boy William was often called Billy, in adulthood the family called him Will, but during his Chelan years he was usually called Will.

[266]   This and the following references to Will Gurr's recollections are from his edited memoirs, *Coming of Age in the West 1883-1906: From the Mississippi to California and Gold Rush Alaska with my Minister Father*, A Memoir by Will E. Gurr, Edited and Annotated by Ted Robert Gurr (CreateSpace, 2011, distributed by Amazon.com). Will's own title for his typescript memoirs was *Life of a Minister's Son*.

[267]   *Coming of Age in the West*, p. 18.

Photo 17.2a Celia Spur Frost Gurr
Henry J. Gurr Album

Photo 17.2b Alf and Will, c. 1886
Henry J. Gurr Album

to say the least, she had no business being a minister's wife from any angle." [268]

Will had little affection from his then 25 year old stepmother Alice. She tried to teach him to read but "gave it up as a bad job." On another occasion in 1892 or early 1893, when they were living in a dilapidated farmhouse near Merced,

> My stepmother was walking on my eyebrows for some reason or other. She had a butcher knife in her hands and was brandishing it pretty close to my head, in fact so close with the result that she nicked me in the right ear. I guess she figured she was going to scare me. [269]

His father's third marriage, after the second ended in separation and divorce in early 1893, provided no more mothering to Will and Alf. In February 1897, their new stepmother was Mabel Lucas, 22 years younger than her husband and only 8 years older than Will, now aged 14. Evidently she cared for the boys, when they shared households in Colorado and Alaska, but none of his recollections of her reflect any particular closeness. Instead he chronicled rivalries with one of her younger brothers who was on the losing end of confrontations with the Gurr boys.

---

[268] *Coming of Age in the West*, p. 33.

[269] *Coming of Age in the West*, p. 34.

17.3   Education

Will's schooling was episodic, ironically so for the son of a man who had several years of rigorous education at an English boarding school, and three years of divinity school that included instruction in Hebrew and classical Greek. Will's recollections of early schooling are sparse. In a country school near Merced he recounts only the severity with which the male teacher whipped students. He recalls starting school in Sonora, when he was nine or ten:

> This school had readers with stories of adventure, also some with a moral to them which I never forgot. I think they had a good effect on me later in life and chances are I needed the good that I obtained from them. I also remember the druggist's boy who sat across the aisle from me. One day he said to me, I hear that you are poor, I told him we were. [270]

In Montevideo, a railroad town in Minnesota, ten-year-old Will had fond memories of one teacher. One day his desk partner pushed him into the aisle and the teacher sought to punish him for the disruption by asking him to stay after school and write "I will behave" 200 times.

> Later she came down to my desk, asked me if I was going to write that, I told her no, finally she asked me why, and I told her I did not do anything to write it for. She said, "Why didn't you tell me?" and I said, "You did not ask me." She said, "You may go home." She was a red-headed teacher by the name of Miss Kennedy and I liked her. Not because she did not whip me but because she was very likeable and a good teacher....She was one of the sweetest teachers I ever had, even if she did make me sit with a girl one afternoon. [271]

In Juneau in the winter of 1901-02, when Will was 17 or 18, he challenged the authority of a teacher who punished him and a friend because they were throwing snowballs on the schoolyard. He thought she was unjust and the two went to a school official, who said that if they told her the whole story, she would change her decision, and if she didn't, "Tell her to go to hell." Miss Collison blew up at them, telling them to take their punishment or go – whereupon Will, his friend, and two other boys "gathered up our books and left" and he says no more about schooling, except for one later incident when he and a friend offered to take Miss Collison and another teacher on a bobsled run down Juneau's steep, snow-covered streets. "Miss Collison said, "Will you promise not to tip us over?" and I answered, "I have never tipped you over yet have I?" Because of a flaw in the bobsled's construction they did indeed tip over.

> When I looked around Miss Collison, who was a tall woman and wore a coat just about down to her shoe tops, occupied a good part of the road, and between the music teacher, Ki Winn, myself and the bobs, we took up the rest. They left me sitting there laughing, I would have laughed if I had been shot for it. [272]

---

[270]   *Coming of Age in the West*, p. 35.

[271]   *Coming of Age in the West*, p. 48.

[272]   *Coming of Age in the West*, pp. 99-100, 103

So much for schooling, except for a rare moment of self-reflection in his memoirs when Will writes,

> I very often wish some of my teachers were still alive and I could have the pleasure of meeting them again, and telling them how much I thought of them. I would not have a bright and shining career to hold up before them, however I would aim to convince them that tho I had kicked life away, yet how much I appreciated their efforts. [273]

17.4 Dangerous Travels in Alaska

Much of Will's education was of a practical sort, gained through travels with his father and living on his own in Alaska. When Will was 14 the Reverend Gurr decided to leave the Colorado mining country for a post in Alaska, booming with gold-seekers headed for the Canadian interior. Will was sent alone to San Francisco with instructions to find a rental for the family – his father, step-mother, and older brother – and with money enough for hamburgers.

Once the family arrived his father decided to buy and outfit a 40 foot schooner, the *Angelus,* on which to sail to Alaska. The boys spent the late summer caulking and overhauling the boat. This is Will's account of their failed, storm-battered voyages:

> We pulled out of the Golden Gate headed for Alaska about the first of September, when the equinox storms were due to start. On board were my dad, brother, stepmother, cousin Ted and myself. We ran into rough weather from the start and in about a week put back into Frisco. My stepmother had been sick from the time we sailed through the Golden Gate until we got back so she went back to Chicago, where later on she had her first baby.

> On the next try, one night about eight o'clock we were tacking in a brisk N.W. wind when a squall struck us, snapping the bobstay under the bow sprit, tearing the bow sprit loose and blowing away the flying jib. Again we put back thro the Golden Gate and had things repaired, also getting fresh water. As we were pulling out for the third time my cousin figured he had had all he wanted of that and I cannot blame him.

> I figured Dad would ask my brother and me if we were willing to try it again and told my brother so. We talked it over and figured there was so much invested in the expedition that we would tell him we would try it again. Sure enough he asked and we told him we would give it another try, tho to be honest about it I figured it would be only a matter of time before we would get drowned.

> On the third try we were tacking and making pretty good headway for a few days when a heavy storm came along with the result that we drifted south for about three days with a storm anchor. [274] One could see the big ocean liners shove their noses up into the

---

[273] *Coming of Age in the West*, p. 48.

[274] Authors Note: Probably south of the Farallons. The Farallon Islands are part of the County of San Francisco and can be seen from San Francisco on clear days. They lie about 30 miles west of the Golden Gate Bridge and, interspersed with sea stacks, banks and shoals, they extend for about five miles in a south to north line. They are not open to the public and, teeming with wildlife including seabirds, seals and whales, they have been designated a

sky then gradually start toppling over into the next trough while pivoting on the crest of those mountainous waves. With everything hanging in the air with the exception of the midship section, you could not help but wonder how they kept them from breaking in two. Then down they would go out of sight and it would seem like the longest time before you would see their bow show up again, pointed toward the heavens, before the ship toppled over into the next down-hill glide.

At last the wind and waves started to go down and when it had moderated a lot, whales and sharks from every degree of the compass came up to get fresh air. I used to like to swim in the ocean but lost all interest in it after that. As we neared the Farallon Islands again Dad left me on watch, showing me the compass point to keep the boat on. I had a wonderful breeze and was making good head way tacking when it was my time to go off duty, so called him. I remember waking up later and hearing the boom as it swung back and forth as each wave hit us and it was not long after when Dad called us to get up and help furl the sails. The ocean eventually became as calm and placid as was possible.

Later on the keeper of the lighthouse together with his helper and son rowed out from the islands, hooked onto us with a sixteen foot skiff and towed us into a harbor on the island where we stayed for a week, with not a breath of wind to disturb the surface of the ocean,. Then a slight breeze came along and a couple of Italians fishing smacks came out from Frisco, and did one of the men walk all over Dad. I can see and hear him to this day. He told Dad that he had absolutely no business taking us out on a voyage like that especially at that time of the year, that he was simply taking us out to drown. I will admit that I did not think we would ever pull through on it, but on the other hand it was a gamble, and so is life.

If you go to the San Francisco Examiner of the dates between about Sept 12 and the 15, 1898, you'll see the schooner Angelus reported missing. Well we finally headed back for the Golden Gate and Frisco and sailed the Angelus around to the Spreckles dock at the foot of Third Street. Dad left the boat in charge of the Irishman who looked after the dock, with all the provisions on her, and as far as I know it was a total loss. [275]

Henry, Alf and Will took steamship passage to Skagway, arriving in early October, and "procured the use of a lovely log cabin. I had my 15th birthday when we were staying at that cabin. Dad bought some wonderful venison chops and also made a suet pudding for my birthday." This is one of a handful of fond memories Will had of his father. He had nothing good to say of his father's next decision, to take the boys into the interior, over the White Pass

---

National Wildlife Refuge. There have been many shipwrecks along these rocky outcroppings but sailing these dangerous waters in summer you face two additional obstacles; first, the California Coastal Current is part of the clockwise flowing North-Pacific gyre: second the winds are generally north to south. Subsequently, sailing north from San Francisco towards Alaska means both wind and current are opposing you. During late fall, winter and early spring increased atmospheric storm activity results in rough seas and deep mixing of waters along the shallow continental shelf and the passage becomes even more difficult.

[275] *Coming of Age in the West*, pp. 63-64.

and Lake Bennett to Atlin, British Columbia, where gold had been discovered a few months earlier. Their hard trip to Atlin, in the face of winter storms, is described in Chapter 11.13.

In Atlin father and son where in a cabin the three had built and stocked with a winter's supply of goods they had packed in when they received a firm message from Episcopal Bishop Rowe for the Reverend Gurr to return to Skagway in early January to take up his responsibilities as a missionary priest. Will recalls,

> Henry asked my brother if he wanted to stay or come out and he said he wanted to come out and get a square meal. He asked me what I wanted to do and I said, stay there, so he and my brother went out to Skagway and I held down the cabin….Those were the great days. I lived on evaporated potatoes which had partly soured before they were dried, Lion coffee (none worse), flour, beans, salt pork, and baking powder biscuits, but had no sugar, milk, tea, or butter. Later I traded a .38 I had for an old 45-70 [276] and some rice. [277]

The lawlessness that characterized the rush to the gold fields resulted in political changes in Ottawa that gradually brought the North West Mounted Police (the Mounties) into the region in greater numbers and had them enforcing new laws to protect both Canadian citizens and aliens. [278] Many aliens left the Yukon, lacking the resources to comply with the new laws. Will and an old prospector piled a Yukon sled with their bedding and food and made a hard three-day trip through deep snow and barren wastes to the top of the pass and then back down to Skagway.

Once in Skagway Will shared a drafty, snow-blown shack with his brother Alfred, next to a cabin where several sporting girls lived. He had several observations about them, and other prostitutes he met at the Skagway hotel where he worked a while, but did not judge them: "I could not help but think that tho they were in a poor business, others should not condemn them." [279] The memoirs also show something about Will's attitudes toward the social mosaic of the Alaskan frontier. His shared his father's acceptance of Negroes and worked with Japanese contract laborers with no evident animus, as well as with "Slavs," presumably Russians, and often interacted with native Americans. Will's prejudices were not directed at minorities but at

---

[276] Based on a 45 caliber cartridge loaded with 70 grains of black powder, standardized by the U.S. government in 1873, all 19th century rifle manufacturers eventually made a 45-70 lever action hunting rifle before 1898, but Will's reference "old" probably means it's an early Springfield. The trade probably means that Will was more concerned with big game hunting than in protecting himself with the 38 handgun.

[277] *Coming of Age in the West*, pp. 79, 80.

[278] By 1896 gold miners were driving a population increase that justified the establishment of a NWMP (North West Mounted Police) post in the region. The increased population coming with the gold rush led to the separation of the Yukon district from the Northwest Territories, a vast region which had been governed and controlled by the Hudson's Bay Company but which joined the Canadian Confederation in 1870. From what was then the Northwest Territories came the Provinces of Manitoba, Saskatchewan, Alberta and most of modern British Columbia. The newly established Yukon Territory of Canada joined the Confederation in June of 1898. Canadian Alien law was then applied and additional NWMP were dispatched to the region. US citizens were not required to leave, but were required to follow Canadian law. The NWMP ejected undesirables, collected duties, established the one ton rule (goods to prevent starvation) and enforced Canadian criminal law in what had been a lawless region. Incidentally, there is some evidence that the Canadian government had hopes of gaining access to the Chilkoot Inlet and possibly of annexing the Skagway area

[279] *Coming of Age in the West*, pp. 68, 83-84, quote from p. 84.

fearful and incompetent men newly arrived in Alaska. He also had little liking for hop-heads, as he called them, and alcoholics.

Photo 17.4a Alf & Will, Alaska 1898
Henry J. Gurr Album

Photo 17.4a shows Will and Alf somewhere in Alaska c 1898. Beginning in 1899 Will collected bills for the Juneau newspaper, delivered goods for a merchant named Louie Levi, was deckhand on a cannery launch, and was a painter and scullery worker at a goldmine. Although he was briefly in school, more often he was off with a friend or two on overnight duck-hunting trips. After his father left Alaska in 1902 Will took over Henry's 32-foot gasoline launch, the "FJ," and used it for charter voyages for hunters and builders up and down the Inside Passage. He recounts many adventures with the launch, some of them dangerous. One voyage in particular nearly resulted in the sinking of the launch and the drowning of Will and his passengers. Will's account of this misadventure follows:

> The first part of December a fellow was sent to me who wanted to go up to Taku. [280] He wanted to take enough lumber along to put up a shack, also a fellow to build it. I told him I would take him for $25.00 for the trip and $10.00 a day for each day he kept me there. That was satisfactory so he loaded the lumber in the cabin, hired his man and we pulled out. It was only about a 21 mile run, however there are two dead glaciers at the head of Taku, and when a Taku wind blows, the ice comes down with the wind. We got to Point Bishop, by the Taku Indian village.

---

[280] Taku Inlet is the mouth of the Taku River, some 20 miles south of Juneau.

We went over to the Indian village which faced the south to cook our dinner. When we were about half through eating, the wind started to go down....We got over to the boat, hoisted anchor and headed out.   We were within about a mile and a half from where we wanted to go, when the wind came up again and ahead of it a snow flurry, which left about a half inch of snow on the deck and cabin.   I went out on the bow, putting on an overcoat, and watched for ice, however we were making practically no head way and it was also getting dark so that it was practically impossible to see any ice on account of the white caps. I suggested to the fellow that we had better head back for Point Bishop, which suggestion was heartily approved.   As we rounded Point Bishop I shut the engine off, went on deck and personally put the anchor over board, so as to be sure that the rope did not get caught on one of the flukes.

About midnight we rolled in, then some time during the night I noticed that the boat was pitching pretty heavy. Since I had a good strong anchor, also a new 1 and 1/2 inch anchor line so went to sleep again.   The wind had switched and was coming from the south, where the wind and waves had a long straight sweep at us.   All of a sudden I was awakened again with a heavy crash and thought the boat might have dragged anchor. There was a hatch over the engine which I climbed through and noticed a chunk of ice about 12 to 15 feet in diameter alongside the boat.   I piled on deck, hooked my arm around the mast, grabbed the pike pole and shoved the boat and ice apart, then went down the hatch to get my clothes on, when bang, it hit us again.   I told the man to pull up the anchor as we had to get out of there, however he could not as the wind and waves were too strong for him, so I told him to gather in the rope as I started the engine and ran up over the anchor.   I told the fellow who had hired me that we could head up to Taku, but he said we would drown like rats in a trap.   I told him we would have a stern wind however he did not want to head that way, so I told him it was either Juneau or Taku, and just then the engine quit.   I went to the engine and put my hand down near the fly wheel and there was water there.   I went aft, took up the floor boards and the water was just flush with the floor boards so I knew the ice had made us spring a leak.

I told his hired man to get the sail up as I wanted to see if I could reduce the water enough to take it away from around the engine. He stuck his head in the cabin and told me the lumber was tied on with the main sheet, I told him to hell with the lumber, get that sail up.   In the meantime his boss was cussing about the fact that this was his first time on a gasoline boat, they had always told him they were no good and now he knew it, this was his first time and it was going to be his last.   I could not convince him that the ice had punched a hole in the hull.   He wanted to head for the Indian village and beach her. I replied that the waves and the undertow from them would drown us, that we would never be able to get to shore, and told him to head her off a point that we had to clear before turning toward Juneau.   He told me we could never clear the point, but I said we were going to try.   I had a six-gun on board and he knew it, otherwise I am afraid I would have lost the boat.   We cleared the point by about fifty or sixty feet.   It kept one of us bailing a good part of the time to keep even with the water.   When we reached Juneau it was high tide and I sailed her up on the beach in front of the Auk Indian village, then we went ashore.   That morning when the tide had gone out I went and looked her over.   The hunk of ice … had cracked a plank between two of the oak ribs and pushed the plank in just far enough to let enough water in to keep us busy. [281]

In 1903 now twenty-year-old Will signed on to do maintenance work for a businessman in Sitka, the one-time capital of Russian Alaska, and stayed there for six months. He found Sitka a small and dull place by comparison with Juneau. Of his many encounters the most interesting were with two bitterly unhappy Russian exiles who were hosted by his employer, and whom Will later suspected were Vladimir Lenin and one of his associates. Perhaps he was mistaken about their identities and what he thought was their antipathy to him, but he missed a chance to interact more closely with men who likely were among the professional and intellectual opponents of absolute rule in Czarist Russia.

Back in Juneau in 1904-05, Will worked as a guard in the Federal jail but decided against making a career of it. In 1904, on a trip escorting federal prisoners from Juneau to Seattle, Will borrowed money from friends to visit his father in Chelan. **Photo 17.4b** taken c. 1906 shows a mature and well-dressed young man, in sharp contrast to the boy who had arrived in Skagway in 1898. Two years later he left Alaska for the last time and joined his father in Chelan.

17.5   A Life in Chelan 1906-1977 [282]

Chelan's natural beauty appealed to Will much as it did his father a few years earlier. John Fahey has recently celebrated the Lake and the town itself:

Photo 17.4b Will Gurr c. 1906
Lake Chelan History Museum
Portrait by Winter Pond, Juneau

> Within the Wapato glacier basin was a crystal blue warm-water lake that nestled into a mosaic of fruit-laden hillsides. It was a region that exemplified a Rockwellian vignette of American small town life…This was just the tail end of the lake. The mighty Lucerne Basin represented a more awesome depiction of nature's power. It was the incredible grandeur of the great outdoors…stretching through rugged untouched mountains with beauty rivaling any location in the world. [283]

This was the setting in which Will lived for 70 years, one that he recorded in many photos and postcards. He became one of the town's leading citizens: a businessman downtown for 40 years, pitcher for the local baseball team, founder and chief of the town's fire department, and at

---

[281] *Coming of Age in the West*, pp. 107-110.

[282] The remainder of this chapter is excerpted, with a few revisions, from *Coming of Age in the West*, pp. 141-171.

[283] John Fahey, (2012). *Lake Chelan: The Greatest Lake in the World.* Spokane: Grey Dog Press, p. 230.

various times served as mayor, council member, deputy sheriff, justice of the peace, and municipal judge before his death in 1977, at age 93. What follows is a reconstruction of his life in Chelan.

17.6 A Character Formed in Adversity

Will at 23 was self-confident and self-reliant. He also had a moral code instilled in him by his father and reinforced by some of his teachers. He was a skilled sailor, like his father, and adept at other trades from typesetting to cannery work. He also had considerable people skills, as they are called now – he made enduring friendships and impressed many employers. Or so he recalls in his memoirs. And it seems unlikely that he would have been entrusted with so many challenging jobs or to charter voyages in Alaska if the praise was exaggerated or undeserved. Rather, as he said in a 1969 letter to his half-brother Robert, he did not want to "look as though I were trying to lay it on, which I do not believe in."

Still, Will remembered and recounted praise from employers in his memoirs. For example the US Marshal in Juneau who said, after his 18 months service there, that Will was the best guard he ever had. And on Will's last voyage from Alaska the Reverend Roth, an Episcopal priest, told him that he was the only boy he knew of in Alaska that had not been led astray urging him to consider a career in the ministry. Will's love of the environment also animates many passages in his memoirs. He had a romantic's appreciation of Alaska's natural beauty and a great fondness for hunting trips in the wilderness, often alone, seldom with more than one companion.

The other side of Will's self-reliance and skills was a degree of self-certainty that bordered on cockiness, often convinced he was right and others wrong. He recounts several "I told you so" episodes in his memoirs, for example about people who sailed on his launch in perilous situations and friends who discounted his advice about hunting. In 1950, during his term as mayor of Chelan from 1949 to 1952, he arranged the resignation and replacement of all city council members over a disagreement on hiring and firing city employees, in an episode described later in this Chapter. And he probably instigated a 1927 episode when the 10 members of Chelan's new volunteer fire department, which he had founded, turned in their wrenches to Chief Gurr, saying they would all quit if the city council did not provide them with adequate fire-fighting equipment. [284]

In counterpoint, Will long harbored resentment about those who in his eyes criticized or punished him unjustly. In his memoirs he puts down Juneau employers for paying him too little or rejecting his job applications. In the most remarkable instance, at age nine he was punished for a spitting contest with a California girl, Helen Haley, though she started it, and nearly 40 years later on a visit to San Francisco planned to visit and confront Helen and her mother "in a nice sort of way." Or perhaps Will is spoofing himself here. In any case the plan fell flat because he learned that Helen had died giving birth.

Two Chelan episodes also suggest an unbending disposition. In 1911 his relative, Captain John Lucas, repeatedly asked if Will would write Clausins' jewelry supply in Spokane so John's

---

[284] *Chelan Valley Leader*, April 28, 1927, p. 1.

son could get a watch at wholesale. Will stalled and then refused, explaining that "I've had trouble with those Clausins, so don't care to write them." [285] David Hellyer, the executor of his will, told me that Will wanted to be buried in Wenatchee because he did not like the Chelan undertaker. [286]

In Chelan Will was often on the water in a launch that he hired out to carry visitors and supplies up-lake and used for his own camping and hunting trips. Barbara Van Epps remembers that "He did talk of Alaska and enjoyed well-crafted boats all his life. One of the attractions of Chelan was the water." He also loved to hunt and fish and did so until his failing sight made them too hazardous. The visual evidence of his naturalism are the many photos he took of the lake and environs. Most were lost or destroyed after his death but some remain on postcards. [287] **Photos 17.6a and 17.6b** show Lake Chelan from War Creek Trail and from a point near Goat Mountain (from postcards by Will Gurr).

Photo 17.6a Lake Chelan from War Creek Trail
By Will Gurr from Ted Robert Gurr Collection

---

[285] From the Diary of Captain John B. Lucas – 1911, entries of March 6, 16, and 21. This is an unpublished transcript from the Lake Chelan Historical Society.

[286] Personal communication, July 2004. In fact he was buried in Chelan.

[287] In 2011 Barbara Van Epps of Chelan wrote down her childhood memories of "Grandpa Bill," who had married her widowed grandmother in 1954. They offer invaluable details about his personality and his life in Chelan and are quoted below at length.

Photo 17.6b   Lake Chelan from a point near Goat Mountain
By Will Gurr, from Ted Robert Gurr Collection

He also kept hunting dogs, according to Barbara,

> but they stayed outside and were never pampered and always carefully trained. He did love them and they were a source of pride to him. Later in his life they came into his home more often and were, I believe, good companions. Mike, a Wiemariner, was his last dog and I think his favorite. Mike was the first of his kind I ever met, the breed being little known at the time. Grandpa was a very disciplined and responsible man and I feel Mike was never replaced because Grandpa thought it would be unfair to die and leave a dog behind.

The moral compass of Will's life probably was imbued from the Reverend Gurr, a strict and unemotional man who nonetheless was remembered for his small kindnesses to his boys. Will concludes his memoirs by saying that he almost never drank alcohol – because he disliked the taste – nor did he gamble. And while he recounts fond memories of a number of girls and women from his youth, he hints of no sexual adventures.

17.7   Will in Business:

When Will settled in Chelan in 1906 the town's population was about 600, some of them dry-land farmers and others in small businesses that served farm families throughout the region. Some residents worked elsewhere in the Columbia Valley as seasonal harvest hands, others at mines along the lake or, after 1911, at the Wapato Irrigation Project northeast of the lake, on land purchased from Indian allotment holders. The town also had a growing summer tourist trade, mostly vacationers from Pacific Coast cities who stayed at hotels in Chelan or went 55 miles up-lake to a lodge at Stehekin, gateway to the North Cascade wilderness area.

The Reverend Henry J. Gurr had supplemented the meager income provided by his congregation and the Episcopal bishop of Spokane by buying and operating the Chelan Jewelry Co. "which consists of jewelry, optical & stationery departments." Despite this ambitious description it was housed in a small wooden storefront on the north side of Woodin Avenue in downtown Chelan. In September 1907 he sold a four-fifths interest in the business to Will for $400 plus a promissory note for $220 for future repayment. The Reverend Gurr had been an amateur photographer before and during his years in Alaska and reserved "the privilege of taking the Kodak department out of said store" along with photo equipment at any time, with a compensating reduction in Will's indebtedness. [288] There is no evidence that he ever invoked this right – or that Will ever paid the $220. **Photo 17.7a** shows the interior of Will's Jewellery Store.

Photo 17.7a Will's Jewellery Store
Courtesy Lake Chelan History Museum

Will recalled that in his early years in business, during salmon season (before the Chelan Dam was built), the shop owners would take turns minding all the stores while the others went fishing. **Photo 17.7b** shows Will with a group of friends c 1918.

---

[288]   From a contemporary copy of the contract dated September 28, 1907.

Photo 17.7b Will and Friends, c 1918
Will Gurr's Album, Courtesy Barbara Von Epps of Chelan, WA

Will writes:

"Business was slow then and one guy would sit on Woodin Avenue with all the keys, and if a patron came along, he would open the store and get the fellow what he needed. The next day someone else would stay home and do the shop-keeping." [289]

Under Will's management the jewelry business survived and was moved from one building to another until 1919 when he built a concrete block building faced with brick in the first block of Woodin Avenue and expanded his photo business. Will tried other branches of merchandise as well: a 1927 ad in the local paper advertises "Leather Goods... buy a leather billfold, purse, or pocketbook at Gurr's Store." In May 1935 he applied successfully to be appointed the state's liquor vendor for Chelan, after the death of the previous vendor. He moved the $1000 stock of liquor into his jewelry store and announced plans to partition the store with separate entrances to each shop. The 1940 business directory for Chelan lists him as agent for the State Liquor Control Board as well as jeweler.

The Depression hit hard. Will told a newspaper reporter years later that "in three months during the Depression we took in $226 and I think 65 cents... No, it was rough! We were $10,000 in the hole." [290] In 1948, when Will was 65, he sold the business to Daryl Nutley, a long-time friend from their days on the fire department.

---

[289] From Barbara Van Epp's recollections, January 2011.

[290] Transcript of an interview by Daryl Curtis, January-February 1972, in the Lake Chelan Museum files, p. 6.

17.8   Will in Baseball

There's no evidence from Will's account of his California and Alaska years that he was interested or skilled in sports, other than hunting, yet he was and remained in good physical shape almost all his life. He got around Chelan on his bicycle, even after his eyesight failed. In the summer he swam in the lake almost daily. Barbara Van Epps remembers that in his 60s he would walk or ride to her father's Chelan Airways dock, put on a white bathing cap, swim to a point about a mile up lake, and then back. "He made quite a picture, but he was respected by everyone, and I never heard a negative comment."

As a young man baseball gave Will an entry into Chelan community life. Elizabeth Perry observes that "By the 1870s almost every town in the United States had its amateur team to give pride and unity" to the community. In Chelan, as elsewhere, players were local and there were no franchises or salaries or paid admissions. Chelan put together its first town team c. 1907 and the *Leader* recounts its victories and losses in contests with teams from other communities along the Columbia. Rosters compiled by Elizabeth Perry list Will on the team from 1910 through 1916 – the records are incomplete.

The competitive and community nature of town baseball must have appealed to him. He recalled playing in the nearby towns of Waterville, a farm town about 15 miles south on the east side of the Columbia, and Pateros, about 20 miles up the river. "I know I went up in the early days to play ball at Waterville and we had to get off the wagon for 50-60 feet and push it up there." The

Photo 17.8 Chelan's 1916 Pennant Winning Baseball Team
Will Gurr, Center Right
Courtesy Lake Chelan History Museum

Chelan team would play in Pateros on alternate Sundays and the Pateros team would come down to Chelan the following Sunday.[291]

In 1913 the Chelan town team took the name of the Giants and in 1914 finished at the bottom of the local league. However, by 1916 they won its pennant. **Photo 17.8** shows the 1916 pennant winning team. Will played a number of positions during these years but mainly as a

---

[291] Daryl Curtis interview, pp. 5, 6.

pitcher, being caught by Louie Wapato, an Indian from Wapato Point. [292] In a 1974 interview Will reminisced that he had been on the team when they went to play in Wenatchee. The team "stopped at Douglas County and loaded wheat sacks and played poker and won enough for round trip tickets." In Wenatchee they stayed in an old bedbug-infested hotel. "Next day I pitched. Joe Wilkinson was coach. Bob Harris couldn't catch the ball and we got beat 15-1. Duffy, the Wenatchee coach, gave us a bottle of beer." [293] (A bottle each, we hope.)

17.9   Will and the Fire Department

Western towns in the early 20th century were built almost entirely of wood. Fire safety inspections and the use of fire retardant materials were decades in the future. Fires were frequent and, when driven by wind, could devastate entire business districts. Chelan is on the dry eastern slope of the Cascades and gets relatively little rain – which increased the fire risks. Will recalled that when he arrived in town the public water supply was a 2" pipe running up the center of the street, probably Woodin Avenue.

A volunteer group of fire fighters had formed in Chelan in 1916 but there was no regular fire department until Will organized one in 1926. By the time the department was established there were regular water lines and some hydrants. **Photo 17.9**, dated 1926-28, shows Will and ten men in fire-fighting clothing standing next to a fire truck, evidence that the City Council had provided them some resources.

Photo 17.9   Chelan's 1st Volunteer Fire Dept. 1926-28
Chief Will Gurr at left   Courtesty Lake Chelan History Museum

---

[292] Elizabeth Perry, (2004). *Baseball – Chelan Town Team, History Notes*, Published by the Lake Chelan Historical Society, vol. 19, p. 21-30. Members of the Wapato family, who owned substantial allotments, were frequent participants in Chelan community events. *The Chelan Leader*, in its account of the July 4 celebrations of 1911, said that "Long Jim, the stately, dignified hereditary chief of the Chelan Indians, attended the celebration this week and entered some of his horses in the races."

[293] Excerpts from a taped interview dated 1974, provided by Elizabeth Perry.

In a 1972 interview Will recalled a serious fire in Chelan.

> The Auditorium was really the worst fire we had. We lost the City Hall, the Jail, and a house on the corner where I think Doctor Mitchell lived. Anyway, it wiped that out and it jumped across the street and set the Anthony building afire about four times. I was on the nozzle on the hose located between the Auditorium and Anthony's and I'd keep playing the hose back on the Anthony building and then throw it on the Auditorium again.[294]

Fire fighting in the early 20th century was at least as dangerous as it is now because fire fighters had little or no training and not much equipment. Will came close to losing his life when fighting a fire at a warehouse in Chelan Falls, a tall building between the river and the railroad tracks. This is an edited version of Will's recollections:

> We got a call from a fellow that worked for the Washington Water Power, he got up during the night to go to the bathroom, looked out the window, and happened to see the whole roof raise on the warehouse down at the Falls. He called the department and we went down there. Mike Harris had been on the Spokane Fire Department so I thought he might know something about handling a warehouse fire so I asked him how he would handle it and he says, "I'll be darned if I know.

> So I set out to walk around the building and said, "Mike, you or George put that smoke mask on, will you, put the rope around you, and go in there and see if you can open that door." The door was 30 feet along the side. After I walked around the building sizing it up, and just as I came around the corner, I heard Mike say to George, "I'll be damned if I've lost anything in there, have you?" George said no. So I told Mike to get the fire extinguisher and the smoke mask and I tied the rope around me and put the mask on.

> The smoke in there was awful thick but I went in and headed to where I thought the side door was. I got over to the wall and ran my hand along and couldn't feel any casing, but I hit a club 'bout that long that was hanging there on a leather thong. I started down then to the lower side of the warehouse, the downriver side, and floor started to give under me. I backed up then and knew where the fire was. I went outside and told the boys just rip the lower boards off the building, in that corner, and wash it out. And that's the way we got it.

> Then I went up to the roof and was walking along – I was on the land side, which was frozen, though the side toward the river didn't freeze at all - and my feet went out from under me. A man and a woman were standing on the track, watching me, and I suppose the fire boys below, and the woman saw me fall. We had placed a fire ladder on that side of the building and, as luck would have it, as I went over the edge I was just able

---

[294] Daryl Curtis interview, p. 12. No date is given for this fire or the Chelan Falls warehouse fire described in the following account.

to reach out and grab the top of it. She hollered at some of the firemen underneath, "Grab that ladder!" As I went over I caught one rung and when I swung over got ahold of another, and saved myself. But I pulled the ladder over about 5 feet and as luck would have it, two of the heaviest boys on the department happened to be holding it – Les Bumgarner and Harry Varney. If it hadn't been for them I'd have been cooked.

Later on I was on the river side checking. We had a little portable water pump and it started to miss, so I started down to it because I knew more about handling it than anybody. George Givens, who was down there, found out the gas tank was empty so he took the gasoline can, filled and overflowed the tank, and set the whole works on fire. I carried a two-and-a-half gallon fire extinguisher on the running board of my pickup so I grabbed that and when I used the last drop I had the fire killed in the gas tank. But the carburetor was still afire, so I grabbed the hat off my head and smothered it. That's how close we came to losing the building.

And we can count three times when Will 's life was at risk on that fire: when the burning floor began to buckle beneath him, when he fell from the roof, and when the pump caught fire. At the beginning of his narrative Will mentions that the warehouse was insured for $10,000 and cost $2,500 to repair. He also says the fire was set but never elaborates. [295]

17.10 Will in Public Office

We know almost nothing of Will's thoughts about events in the world outside Chelan. He lived through two world wars and the Great Depression, but, aside for the latter's effects on his business, there are no records of how he was affected, if at all. None of his correspondence between his arrival in Chelan and the 1960s has survived. In his later correspondence, though, he never refers to larger political or economic issues and he may not have done so in earlier years.

Will was active in local politics and government for most of his adult life. He was a member of the Chelan city council from 1914 to 1916, and probably later. For a decade from 1918 to 1928 he was deputy sheriff, with one surviving record of an arrest. In June 1923, he found 220 gallons of corn mash in the house of one Peter St. Luise. Peter was fined $250 for operating an illegal still and sentenced to 60 days in jail. [296] After organizing the Fire Department in 1926, Will remained as chief for eight years. He also was justice of the peace and municipal judge, though the records do not say when. And he was elected mayor in 1949 and served to 1952, when he was 69 years old.

It is not likely that Will's public service was motivated by political ambition. Rather, a man of his reputation and ability was expected to serve the community. And perhaps, given what we know of his character, he thought he was better able to do so than most of his peers. Aside from his recollections about firefighting the only story we have about his public life concerns his dispute with the city council about city employees. Will was dissatisfied with the performance of several employees, including the water superintendent and city clerk, and sought to replace them

---

[295] Daryl Curtis interview, pp. 8-10.

[296] *Chelan Valley Leader*, June 23, 1923.

with more responsive and efficient people. The five-man city council objected to the firings and the procedure used – they claimed they were not consulted, Will said they were - and some at least did not like the idea that he chose a woman as the new clerk. The council then resigned, one man at a time, and Will appointed an entirely new council. "What action I have taken has been because I thought it was just and for the best welfare of the taxpayers and the community," he wrote to the *Chelan Valley Mirror,* "and…I told the Council that I would do the same thing over if the occasion arrived." [297]

17.11 Two Marriages and Two Deaths

In May 1909 twenty-five year old Will married twenty one year old Maude Pruett at her home, with Judge C. C. Campbell officiating and only two friends as guests. Maude was the daughter of early settlers in the wheat country of southeast Washington, Robert and Mary Pruett. After Robert and Mary separated Mary and several of her five children moved to Chelan in 1902 where she operated a boarding house called the Home Restaurant and Lodging House on Woodin Avenue. She later changed the name to Hotel Pruett. Maude worked at her mother's hotel serving meals, which may be where she and Will met. Maude had been married before, in June 1906. That was a brief marriage to one William Green and probably annulled, as Maude resumed using her maiden name of Pruett. We know virtually nothing about her 43-year marriage to Will except that it ended in her death in 1952 after a long bout with cancer.

Contemporary census records list no occupation for Maude – no euphemisms like home-maker were in use at the time. In a letter written years later Will mentions that he and Maude often would go to the Chelan House, later known as the Campbell Hotel "with two other couples, clear away the tables in the dining room, and dance." [298] Aside from that reference there is no contemporary correspondence, newspaper items, or even family anecdotes. Like that of most other women of her time and place, her life is a blank page. **Photos 17.11a and 17.11b** show Will and Maude as a couple but the dates they were taken are undetermined.

In 1954, two years after Maude's death, Will married Gladys Waring Gibson. He was 71, she was about 62. We know from census records that she and her first husband, Arthur Gibson, had lived in Maryland, Missouri, and Aberdeen, Washington, before she was widowed and moved to Chelan. Will acquired two stepsons, one of them 36-year-old Ernest Gibson, a wartime flying instructor who in 1953 (or 1957 – sources differ) bought and operated Chelan Airways. The Airways' float planes provided passenger service from the Chelan waterfront to Stehekin and Lucerne, the lake-side landing of the Howe Sound Mine.

Ernie and his wife Edith had three children, of whom Barbara was the youngest. Will had no children of his own but after his marriage to Gladys he grew close to Barbara. She recalls

---

[297] From statements by Mayor Gurr and the City Council in a Supplement to the *Chelan Valley Mirror,* April 6, 1950. With thanks to Dwane Van Epps and Linda Liles, Chelan city officials, who tracked down the 1950 Council minutes and the news accounts of the controversy.

[298] Letter dated August 7, 1972, to his nephew the John Gurr, S.J. (known as Father Jack to the family).

Photo 17.11a Will and Maude
Courtesy Lake Chelan History Museum

Photo 17.11b Will & Maude
Courtesy Anne Cook Gurr

visiting her Grandma, learning to crochet, and "often Grandpa would come home for lunch and admire our needle work." He also taught her about fishing and gardening.

Barbara recalls:

I remember him taking me fishing a few times, teaching me to cast my line, reel the line in at just the right speed, patiently wait for the second gut on the line before I set the hook. I was always in a hurry and jerked the hook too soon, losing the fish more often than not. Grandpa remained patient. One day he took me and my Grandma out to Lake Perrigan….We rented a boat and were trolling for trout. I was hopeless with the gear, constantly tangling the long lines of lures and reeling in with no fish in sight. Fortunately Grandpa was able to catch enough fish to make the trip worthwhile, and was as happy as me when I managed to catch a surprisingly large fish.

He was also one of the first "organic gardeners." He had a small garden at the front of a tiny house one door down from us on Nixon Avenue. He kept a compost pile which sometimes smelled a bit rotten but he grew tasty tomatoes and other vegetables. He also grew mint, comfrey, chamomile and other herbs he used for tea and poultices. I once skinned one of my fingers and it took on the look of infection setting in. He made a poultice and wrapped my finger in what I think was a comfrey leaf and the very next day my finger was much improved.

He had planted and maintained beautiful roses for my Grandma at the home where my Dad and I lived [after Barbara's parents divorced]. He was unwilling to let them suffer the fate of forgottenness, and showed up at the house one morning with loppers, aphid-spray and a small saw. He sat me down on the couch with paper and pen and instructed me on the care and feeding of roses, and I did write down everything he said. He taught me the difference between the Tea Roses and the Floribundas and how each should be pruned, what to spray, and when. Then we went outside and together, on our hands and knees, we pruned a dozen rose bushes....His favorite rose was the Mirandy, a dark red rose with velvety petals, perfect from bud to full bloom, and the proper smell for a rose. [299]

Barbara also remembers that when she graduated from high school in 1970, "Grandpa Bill gave me the most beautiful white gold watch....He brought three of them to the house for me to choose from....All were beautiful, the one I chose was flower shaped and I have yet to see a prettier one." And he gave her a children's novel, *Captain January* (a children's book by Laura E. Richards, first published in 1891), inscribed "William Gurr – From Holy Trinity [Juneau] Sunday School Christmas 1900."

Gladys died in 1963 after nine years of their marriage, a victim of breast cancer. **Photo 17.11c** shows Will and Gladys in the late 1950's.

Photo 17.11c Will & Gladys
Will Gurr Album, Ted Robert Gurr Collection

Photo 17.12 Will on Bicycle, 1977
Courtesy Lake Chelan History Museum

---

[299] From Barbara Van Epp's recollections, January 2011.

Will lived alone for the last 15 years of his life, though he did take in a housemate in his declining years. For a while he remained close to other members of the Gibson family.

Barbara recalls:

When I was 15 [in 1957] my mom was in a car accident and suffered a broken neck. Grandpa rode with us on two occasions to visit her. When I entered the room I was stunned to see my mom with a weird contraption screwed onto her shaved head. I stood speechless for a very long moment, until Grandpa came behind me, put his hand on my shoulder and whispered, "Barbie, go kiss your mother." I did as he asked and felt better immediately. Later he said that he felt she was nervous and needed it. He was really very kind in thought and deed.

My mom did quite a bit of his correspondence for him before she left my Dad. Grandpa had intended to leave the house he lived in, next to ours, and the house next to it, to my Dad. Unfortunately, after they divorced when I was about 20, my mother ended up with all the houses. The house we lived in was originally my Grandma and Grandpa's; he split it into a duplex so my Dad and Mom had a place to live when they came to Chelan.

Later Will's relations with the Gibson family became strained, for what reason we do not know. In a letter dated September 27, 1971, his sister-in-law Anne Gurr wrote that "He seems to have no contact with the Gibsons - he mentioned that Mrs. Gibson [presumably the second wife of Ernie Gibson] used to do his washing but she got too busy. There seems to be some friction there – he mentioned that she had a photo album of his but when he asked for it she said she had lost it." This may be the album that Barbara found and shared with Ted Robert Gurr in 2011, the source of several of the photos used in this chapter.

17.12   Declining Years

In his late 90s Will's eyesight began to fail, though he continued to use his bicycle to get around town, apparent from **Photo 17.12** on the previous page. [300]

Anne Gurr described a visit to Will in September 1971.

"He seemed very glad to have us, and was a most generous host. While we took the trip up the lake he stayed home and prepared a lovely dinner of chicken and rice and blueberry pie….Will says his sight has deteriorated considerably this summer….He still rides his bicycle but says he cannot see a car head on, only by looking out of the side of his eye….he is finding it difficult to eat, his close vision is the worst. He keeps house after a fashion but only goes through the motions and really needs a person to come in once a week and clean, but he is so independent, I feel he will not admit to outsiders his helplessness." [301]

Will kept up correspondence with family members until shortly before his death in 1977, writing in an increasingly shaky longhand after 1970. His correspondence often incorporates

---

[300] This photo accompanied Will's obituary in the *Chelan Valley Leader*, May 18, 1977.

[301] Letter from Anne Gurr to Father Jack, September 27, 1971.

stories from his memoirs as well as more mundane accounts about Chelan's weather, articles he has read about Alaska, and work on his house at 127 E. Nixon Street. The last suggests that he was far from helpless. Despite age and infirmity he continued to do major maintenance, saying in a May 1975 letter to Father Jack:

> In the last year I spent about a thousand dollars insulating the building, putting in 220 for an electric heater and paying part on a Stainless Steel double sink, having the two carpets cleaned, and other incidentals. Right now am starting to paint the house … at least three walls need it. Scrape the paint today and plan to paint tomorrow.

17.13 Last Will and Testament

By early 1977 there was evidence that Will was failing. Barbara recalls that:

> There had been some incident which landed him in the nursing home. I am not sure, but experiences since have made me suspect a sundowners-like episode. My Dad [Ernie Gibson] truly loved and respected Bill and visited him every night after work. I went with him a few times, on the last visit I remember him sitting on his bed, very calm and dignified, stating that he could not understand why he had done what he did, he had not been feeling well, regardless he was sure it would not happen again, and he would like to return to his home. My Dad told him if that was what he wanted, it was his decision and we would make it happen.

It was not to happen.

> His condition deteriorated rapidly and my next and last visit with Grandpa Bill was at the hospital. He was in a coma. I could think of nothing to say, so I took his hand and said the Lord's Prayer, kissed his forehead and said goodbye.

Will died on May 12, 1977, in Chelan Community Hospital after four months of care. The immediate cause of death was pneumonia, the contributing factor – according to Dr. William Danke – chronic mild cerebral arteriosclerosis. His funeral, four days later, was held at St. Andrews. The church was filled with mourners, even sitting in the choir chairs and as many folding chairs as could be fitted in. He was buried in an embossed coffin at Riverview Cemetery next to the grave of Maude, his first wife – though the actual interment was delayed because the gravediggers struck rock. It seems a fitting resting place for Will, a grave that had to be blasted from rock even more resilient than he was. [302]

Will's will showed that he had property worth about $11,000 and a small bank account. He had already dispersed some of his possessions, for example two TVs that he gave away when he could no longer see them. To his half-brother Robert and half-sister Harriett he bequeathed $1.00 each "and my love and affection." To his half-sister Helen, living in the San Francisco Bay area, he bequeathed $200, not that he was close to her but more likely because she was living in

---

[302] From his death certificate; and a postcard from his sister-in-law Anne Gurr, who attended the funeral.

hard circumstances. Robert Nichols evidently shared Will's house on Nixon Avenue for a time because Will left him a $300 bond and most of the house's kitchen furnishings. His stepson Ernest Gibson inherited much of his residual estate as well as many odds and ends of household goods, a Colt .32 handgun, a filing cabinet, and "all pictures." In a 2004 visit to Chelan I was unable to learn what had happened to the pictures or the contents of the filing cabinet. So this account relies on family correspondence and items in the Lake Chelan Museum archives.[303]

Local people in Chelan remembered Will as a rather quiet man who enjoyed a joke and visiting with friends. Barbara says "he was a gentleman, always." He also had a strong sense of family. Even after his eyesight began to fail he kept up a voluminous correspondence with relatives, some of whom were regular visitors to Chelan. He fathered no children, despite two marriages, but treated the grandchildren he inherited from his second wife as though they were his own. Barbara recalls that he spent many hours telling her stories about his Alaskan adventures and not until she was 11 or 12 did she learn that he was not her real grandfather – "and knowing the truth changed nothing."

He had a long and good life and it is fortunate that there are enough records and memories that we can reconstruct it.

---

[303] With thanks to David Hellyer, attorney, who gave me a copy of the will and also shared his memories of Will Gurr's last years.

Chapter 18

Descendants of Alfred Richard Gurr

18.1   Pedigree, Marriage, Children of Alfred Richard

Alfred James Gurr b. Oct 1823 d. 29 Jun 1874	Mary Ann Bennett b. 06 Dec 1819 d. 1884	Robert Hunter b. 1819 d. Apr 1887	Emma Unknown b. 1824 d. 1889
Married 21 Mar 1846			Married c. 1847
2nd child of 8			5th child of 11
Alfred Richard Gurr b. 13 Mar 1851 d. 5 Apr 1944	> Married < 1872		Emily Hunter b. 8 May 1854 d. 12 Sep 1940

Children of Alfred Richard and Emily Gurr			
Alfred James Gurr	Henry Robert Gurr	Edwin Gurr	Emily Mae Gurr
b. 14 Jul 1873 d. 21 Dec 1961	b. 01 Feb 1875 d. 21 Aug 1948	b. 28 Jan 1876 d. 03 Jan 1960	b. 03 Mar 1877 d. Oct 1969
William Gurr	Mary Maude Gurr	Ellen Gurr	David Gurr
b. 24 Mar 1878 d. 1965	b. 03 Oct 1879 d. 17 Jul 1967	b. 15 Mar 1881 d. 12 Feb 1967	b. 30 Aug 1882 d. 01 Aug 1925
Ethel Elizabeth Gurr	Gordon Gurr	Beatrice Gurr	Ernest Gurr
b. 20 Mar 1884 d. 14 Oct 1965	b. 28 Nov 1885 d. Jan 1933	b. 01 Jul 1887 d. 11 Jan 1985	b. 11 Oct 1888 d. 19 Aug 1980

Alfred Richard Gurr landed in New York with his wife and twelve children aboard the steamship Etruria on November 4th, 1889. They boarded a train for California, where they were met by their uncle, Reverend Henry Jonathan Gurr. [304] We believe that Henry made their arrival less stressful by pre-arranging a place for the fourteen new arrivals to stay (probably Oakland) before they continued on to their ultimate destination, Merced.

All twelve children of Alfred Richard's were born in Paddington, Middlesex, England, and all twelve would become naturalized American citizens. The route to citizenship for the children differed because of their ages.   James and Harry applied for citizenship and were

---

[304] Henry knew California well from his four years there with his first wife Celia and during the first four years that Alfred Richard Gurr family members were establishing themselves, he actively assisted them in adjusting to their new surroundings. It was Henry, after all who had convinced his brother to come to America, as described in Chapter 12.

naturalized April 30, 1896, the same day as their father. [305] James and Harry were the only two family members who had reached the age of consent at the time their father was naturalized, so they were not automatically citizens at their father's naturalization, as were the rest of Alfred Richard's children, and his wife.

Chapter 12 describes Merced and the family's early days there and gives some details about the children's education and how they fared in the first few years they spent in America. Following is a slightly more detailed account of what became of these twelve new American children during the 20th century. Data were collected from U.S. Federal Censuses taken June 5 of 1900, April 15 of 1910, January 5 of 1920, April 1 of 1930 and April 1 of 1940 and these are the basis of much of what we know about the Gurr children. Other sources are the Draft Registration Cards submitted by the male children or their spouses before WWI and WWII, as well as Voters Lists, Phone and City Directories. Some of the birth, marriage and death dates were taken from a Gurr family bible and much of the birth data was verified by referring to censuses, birth and baptismal records from England and Wales.

18.2   Alfred James (James) Gurr

It is probable that James worked on the family farm in Merced, rather than attend school after they arrived in California, although the 1940 census shows him as having completed two years of high school (which may mean two years of Junior High). Mandatory attendance at British schools to the age of thirteen was not required until 1893 and James was already sixteen years of age in 1889, when the family arrived in California (a grown man by English standards). It is probable that he had been working at the Gurr and Son Dairy on 38 Southwick for some time before leaving London, so a willingness to return to school seems unlikely.

Census and Other Records:

Birth: July 14, 1873 (Family Bible).

Marriage: to Daisey (nee Unknown) c. 1917, she was born in Oregon in 1872.

1900 Census: Madera, James was boarding out, working as a railroad labourer in Madera County, and was still single. Census records: born July 18, 1872 in England, naturalized in 1896.

1910 Census: Merced, James recorded as Alfred Jr., single but working on his father's farm. Only brother Harry and sister Beatrice, both single, are residing at their parents home with Harry listed as a farm worker and Beatrice as unemployed.

1920 Census: Merced Robla, James recorded as a farmer, living with his wife, Daisey at a different address than his parents. Daisey's father was from Missouri and mother from Illinois.

1930 Census: No record found for Daisey or James (but they lived in Santa Clara).

1940 Census: Fremont, Santa Clara, Los Altos, widower, listed as caretaker.

Draft Registration: The Sept. 13, 1918 draft registration records James with the same birth date as the family bible, but he is now married to a Daisey Gurr, and at 45 year of age, working as a farm labourer for Gurr Co., with a postal box that is different from that of his father's farm.

---

[305] California State Library, California History Section; Great Registers, 1866-1898; Collection Number: 4 - 2A; CSL Roll No.: 26; FHL Roll No.: 976937

Voters Lists: Alfred and Daisey appear on the voter registration lists in Robla precinct up to the 1924 registration, then on the Santa Clara list, residing at 481 Pettis Ave, until 1928. On the 1938 and 1942 voter lists for Santa Clara, Alfred James is a gardener living alone in Mountain View.

Directories: 1918 Postal Directory Rte 1 Box 139. Alfred and Daisey are listed in the San Jose phone directory from 1926-1933, at 481 Pettis Ave, poultryman, gardener.

Death: Alfred died in Santa Clara on Dec 21, 1961. Daisey's death estimated 1934.

Children: no children

18.3   Henry Robert (Harry) Gurr

We do not know whether Harry attended school following his arrival in California. At fourteen, he would have completed any compulsory education in England, and it is likely that he would have preferred to help his father on the Merced farm, rather than go back to school. Harry never married. He lived with his parents until the mid 1930s, then for a time with his youngest brother Ernest and Ernest's wife Bertha (according to the 1938 voter registration they resided at Route 1, Box 64 Merced). In his later years he moved in with his younger sister Emily (Queenie), who had graduated nursing school in 1909, but who also never married.

Census and Other Records:

Birth: Feb 1, 1875.

Marriage: Unmarried.

1900 Census: Merced, living with parents on family farm, farm laborer.

1910 Census: Merced, living with parents on family farm, farm laborer.

1920 Census: Merced, living with parents on family farm, farm laborer.

1930 Census: San Mateo, living with parents on family farm, no occupation listed.

1940 Census: Merced, living with brother Ernest (farmer) and Ernest's wife Bertha. Harry is listed as a labourer and recorded as having a grade 8 education (2 years of Junior High?).

Draft Registration: September 1918, listing his father Alfred Richard as next of kin. In that record he also confirms his birth date of February 1, 1875, and that he was sound in mind and body, had blue eyes and brown hair (as was true of most of the family members). He is also recorded as being of medium height and medium build.

Voters Lists: 1928, 1932, 34, 35, 36 living with parents at 545 Clark Ave and Republican.

Directories: 1926 City Directory, living at 519 Clark Ave E., Palo Alto with Alfred Richard and Emily. Queenie is living with her parents also. William and Hattie (Hedwig) living at 518 Clark Ave.

Death: Harry died in an auto accident in East Palo Alto, California on August 21, 1948. The report of the accident appeared on the front page of the August 23 edition of the San Mateo Times (as one of a rash of Saturday traffic accidents). Following are excerpts from the report.

Aged Rancher Killed as Car Strikes Bicycle

Killed was Henry R. Gurr, a retired Merced rancher, 18 years resident of East Palo Alto. He was riding a bicycle and was smashed to the pavement when trying to make a U-turn in heavy Saturday Bayshore Avenue traffic. The elderly bicyclist met his death in the view of several horrified onlookers. James W. Martinelli of San Jose, one of the witnesses, said:

"I saw the man halt his bicycle at the stop sign at Capital avenue in East Palo Alto, then ride south about four feet from the west side of the highway. After looking around as if to see if the road was clear, he turned left to cross the Bayshore. He was about in the middle of the highway when the automobile hit him."

Stopped for Signal

The driver, Richard Mozza, a San Jose tavern owner, told highway patrolmen he had stopped at the University avenue signal and was just starting to pick up speed when Gurr turned into his path. Gurr, formerly a native of England, was unmarried and lived with a sister, Emily Gurr at 380 Fulton street, East Palo Alto.

18.4 Edwin Robert (Ted) Gurr

Ted, at 13 years of age, was probably still attending school when he left England, and it is uncertain whether or not he continued his education in California, although the progressive attitude towards education was one of the reasons his father came to California. We believe he probably did continue with his schooling in Merced, for in California in the 1890s children were encouraged to stay in school, and that decade a high school education was becoming more and more necessary for advancement and pursuit of the American Dream. **Photo 18.4a** shows Ted as a young man.

Census and Other Records:

Birth: January 28, 1876.

Sept 1898: On the *Angelus* with his uncle the Reverend Henry Gurr and his cousins Alf and Will, in their first two attempts to sail to Alaska.

Marriage: 1899 to Stata McKenzie, born Aug 1879 in Illinois.

1900 Census: San Joaquin County, Ted (farm laborer) and Stata are living in the town of Elliott. The town no longer exists, but at the turn of the 20th century it was near Stockton.

1910 Census: Merced, Ted and Stata have moved back to Merced with their two children (Edwin Donovan and Melvin L.), and are farming near Alfred Richard's farm, although it is not certain that they owned their own land at this time.

1920 Census: Merced, the couple have had a third child (Kenneth William); they are still farming.

1930 Census: Merced, Ted and son Edwin are now both farming, but Edwin Donovan has married and the couple (with one child) are living with Ted and Stata.

Photo 18.4a Ted Gurr
3rd Son of Alfred Richard Gurr

Ted sailed on the "Angelus"
with Henry J. Gurr and
Cousins Alfred and Will
Henry J. Gurr Album

1940 Census: Merced, with Stata and Melvin. Edwin is listed as an investigator for the government concerning the soil conservation industry. He is also recorded as having two years of high school (same as his two elder brothers). He owns his own home and is salaried at $3,000 per year.

Draft Registration: September 12, 1918 registration card shows Stata Gurr next of kin;confirms his January 28, 1876 birth date.

Voters Lists: Registered in Robla Precinct in 1898 and in many voter registers thereafter.

Phone Directory: No separate listing.

Death: January 3, 1960.

Children: Edwin Donovan b1903, Melvin L. b1907, Kenneth William b January 13, 1913. Edwin Donovan had two children: Marvin D. b1929 and John Edwin b 1940.

Obituary for Alfred Richard and Emily's Grandson, Kenneth Gurr:

Merced Sun-Star - (May/29/2004) W. Kenneth Gurr "Slim"

Kenneth Gurr was born on January 13, 1913 and passed away on May 25, 2004 at the age of 91 in Merced, California. Mr. Gurr was a Merced native self-employed rancher and farmer.

Slim enjoyed doing handwork in silver and engraving as a hobby. Kenneth especially enjoyed reading Louie LaMour books, good food, and especially his daughter's apple pie, he had a soft spot for under privileged kids. Mr. Gurr was always there to help a friend with work or personal projects, but most of all he liked to listen to his Irish music and snuggling with the grand kids.

Slim is survived by his daughter Karen D. Gurr Mous of Merced, 2 grandsons Dirk Shane Gurr Mous and Kenneth Preston Gurr Mous. Also surviving are nieces and nephews with their spouses: Dorothy and Les Van Someren, John and Margaret Gurr, Marvin and Joyce Gurr, Lee and Becky Wisdom, Robin and Tom Spensky, Richard and Sherry Wisdom, Pam and Keith Lunney, Peggy and Bobo Clendenin, Jeannie Daniels, Becky and John Maus, Mary and Jon Clark, Greg and Irene Gurr. Slim also leaves behind a multitude of great nieces and nephews.

Visitation for "Slim" will be held on Friday, May 28, 2004 from 4-8 p.m. in the Chapel of Evergreen Funeral Home. A graveside service will follow on Saturday, May 29, 2004 at 10:00 a.m. at Evergreen Memorial Park.

A Memorial Service will be held on Sunday, May 30, 2004 at 4:00 p.m. at the Central Presbyterian Church.

All funeral arrangements are under the direction of Evergreen Memorial Park and Funeral Home, Inc. at 1480 "B" Street in Merced, California 95340 at (209)383-4651.

18.5   Emily May (Queenie) [306] Gurr

Queenie was twelve when the Gurr Family arrived in California and it is certain she continued her education in Merced for she entered a school of nursing around 1906. Both Queenie and her younger sister Ethel followed their elder sister Ellen to San Francisco, where all

---

[306] She was nicknamed Queenie to differentiate her from her mother, Emily.

three attended St. Luke's Hospital School of Nursing, Ellen graduating in 1906 and the younger two in 1909.

Census and Other Records:

Birth: March 3, 1877.

Marriage: Unmarried.

1900 Census: Merced, Queenie is resident on the Gurr family farm along with her mother and father and nine of the Gurr children, five of whom are shown as attending school (Ernest was 11, Beatrice was 12, Gordon was 14, Ethel was 15, David was 17).

1910 Census: San Francisco, Queenie and her younger sister, Ethel are listed as lodgers in the home of the Evans family in San Francisco and are both nurses at a hospital. Another lodger in the Evans home is Cornelius D. DeLongh, a bookkeeper at a bank. Ethel and Cornelius will marry by 1920.

1920 Census: San Francisco, but not found in census.

1930 Census: San Mateo, Emily May is residing with her parents, elder brother Harry and her nephew Henry R. DeLongh, age 9.

1940 Census: San Mateo, nurse, living with parents Alfred Richard and Emily. Four years of high school is indicated in the record.

Voters Lists: From 1926 through to 1944 Emily May's address is usually that of other family members. 1922, 1928, 1938 San Mateo with parents, 1940 at 2261 Clarke Ave with parents.

Directories: 1926 City Directory, 519 Clark Ave E., Palo Alto with Alfred Richard, Emily, Henry, Queenie. Same group (except for Queenie) at 545 Clark Ave in 1928, 1931,1933. Note: William and Hattie (Hedwig) are at 518 Clark Ave.

Death: Contra Costa, California on 13 October, 1969.

Children: no children

18.6   William Gurr

William completed 4 years of high school education and we know he worked on the family farm in Merced for several years. He then became an Oakland transit conductor before 1910, but by 1930 had returned to poultry farming.

Census and Other Records:

Birth: March 24, 1878.

Marriage: to Hedwig Noschka around 1914. Hedwig (Hattie) was born in California Jan 7, 1885 of German Immigrants.

1900 Census: Merced, William is living on his father's farm in Merced County and his occupation is recorded as farm laborer. He is working for his father in the family business.

1910 Census: Known to be in Alameda, but not listed. He is not with his parents, so it is probable that he has already moved to Oakland and found employment with the city's transit company.

1920 Census: Alameda, William and his wife Hedwig are living on Clarke Ave in Menlo Park with their two children, Jack and William Jr., and William is a street-car conductor.

1930 Census: San Mateo, William has changed occupations and is once again a poultryman, where he lives (still on Clarke Ave) with Hedwig and their two children.

1940 Census: San Mateo where he owns his own home and operates a poultry farm. His son William Jr. is living with his parents and he is working as a painter at the University Paint Shop. No info on Jack's whereabouts.

Draft Registration: Sept 12, 1918 Draft Registration Card lists him as a conductor with the San Francisco-Oakland Transit Railway out of Oakland.

Voters Lists: In the 1916 Oakland Voter Registration, William is listed as a carman. His brother Ernest is listed in the same record, as living at the same address and is a conductor.

Directories: 1926, 1928, 1933 City Directory, at 518 Clark Ave, E. Palo Alto. Parents, Henry and Queenie at 519 Clark Ave in 1926, then 545 Clark Ave in 1928, 1931, 1933. San Mateo City directories also show William and Hedwig living together into the mid 1940s.

Death: William died in 1965, while his wife Hedwig passed away on Dec 29, 1971.

Children: Jack b 1916, and William A Jr. b1918.

The couple's youngest son, William A. Gurr, born 29 Sept. 1918 enlisted in the Army on 18 May 1942. He survived the war and retired to 4 Temelec Cir. in Sonoma where he is recorded as resident from 1993 until his death on 28 Feb, 2001. Records show that William A. completed 4 years of high school and was a pressman with a printing company before enlisting. No info on Jack's whereabouts..

18.7   Mary Maude Gurr (Crookshanks)

Mary Maude was ten when she came to America and it is almost certain she finished high school, then helped her parents on the family farm for a year or two. She was one of the first of the twelve children to marry but we have no information on her marriage date or when and how she met her husband.

Mary Maude's husband, Madison was a farmer who registered to vote in Fresno in 1898. The couple lived in Exeter, Tulare County during their first twenty years of marriage. In 1900, there were no paved highways in California but the main route for travelers moving north or south through the central California valley passed through Modesto, Merced, Fresno, Tulare, Delano, Bakersfield and Los Angeles, on a route that approximates Hwy 99 today. Since the couple had no possibility of meeting before 1898 (we believe that Madison arrived in the central valley that year), it is likely that farming and/or marketing had something to do with their first meeting.

Census and Other Records:

Birth: Oct 3, 1879.

Marriage: to Madison Parker Crookshanks around 1900. Madison was about 33 and Mary Maude about 21 when they married. Their first child was born in Dec. 1901.

1900 Census: Tulare probable, except no record found, but Mary was no longer living with her parents.

1910 Census: Tulare probable, except no record found.

1920 Census: Tulare, Mary Maude and Madison are recorded as living on a farm they own in Exeter, East of Tulare, with six children. But Madison (Martin P.) is also recorded as a lodger with Emma Hutchings and her three sons at 211 N Front St. Exeter City, Tulare County, although he is still listed as married.

1930 Census: Tulare, Mary Maude is listed as divorced, living with her two youngest children and one eight year old boarder. The boarder is Frederick C. Dewar, her nephew, the son of Nellie and Frederick C Dewar. This is the only reference we have to Nellie having any offspring. Meanwhile Madison (Martin P.) is a lodger with Emma Hutchings and her three sons at 211 N Front St. Exeter City, Tulare County and is there listed as married (but to whom).

1940 Census: San Mateo living with her parents at 2261 Clarke Ave.

Draft Registration: Not applicable .

Voters Lists: During the period 1900 to 1919 Mary Maude and Madison were ranching in Waukena, west of Tulare, and are so listed in the 1900-1914 voter registration lists They are listed as Socialist and Democrat, respectively.

Directories: In the 1937 San Jose City Directory, Mary Maude Crookshanks (wid) is living at 481 Pettis Ave (see eldest brother Alfred James, shown at same residence).

Death: Mary Maude 1866, Madison Crookshanks 1959 (so Mary Maude was not a widow in 1938 as listed in the San Jose Directory, but divorced).

Children: Alfred Robert b1901, M. Thelma b1903, Donald P. b1905, Mildred M. b1907, Evelyn E. b1913, Ivan C. b1916.

A note on Mary Maude's Grandson: The younger son of Mary Maude's eldest son Alfred Robert Crookshanks was Rex John Crookshanks (b 1926) who served in the Navy during World War II and then received a bachelor of engineering degree from the University of Southern California in June 1954. He obtained credentials in mechanical and electrical engineering. He was hired as an engineering consultant at Hughes Aircraft to create a detailed design solution for a challenging satellite-communications-system requirement — which no one else was able to accomplish. Later, he transitioned to the Hughes staff as a senior scientist. Accompanying his creative mind was his desire to help others become creative and more successful in various fields of endeavor. He was an avid inventor, credited with more than 200 patents across a broad range of engineering and mathematical areas while working at Hughes Aircraft. He was also an active real-estate investor, which included buying, developing and remodeling properties both within and outside of the United States, up until his death in 2007.

18.8.1 Ellen (Nellie) Gurr (Dewar)

Ellen completed her high school education in Merced and was living at home with her parents during the 1900 census. Her whereabouts for the first two or three years of the 20th century are uncertain, but she graduated in Nursing in 1906, having received her training at St. Luke's Hospital in San Francisco. There was at least a two year training requirement at that time. The Hospital was damaged in the 1906 quake and by the subsequent fire. The entire hospital staff was assigned to the Red Cross immediately following the earthquake.

Ellen was a lodger in a San Francisco boarding house during the 1910 census (her brother David was also lodging there and was working as an electrician for a telephone company). She was in China during the 1920 census. Ellen applied for her passport in 1919 and travelled to China in October, 1919 (probably answering a call for trained nurses during the worldwide influenza epidemic). She returned to San Francisco aboard the *SS Venezuela* (a cargo/passenger ship belonging to the Pacific Mail Steamship Co. on Dec 4, 1920.

Census and Other Records:

Birth: March 18, 1881

Marriage: To Frederick Craik Dewar in 1924. They had a son, Frederick Craik Jr. out of wedlock in 1922.

Ellen appears to have followed a nursing career for at least twenty-five years. The 1930 census shows Nellie as the wife of Frederick C. Dewar (he immigrated to America in 1920 and was manager of a health club in the 1927 directory). The census indicates that they married in 1924. (He had been previously married, but we know nothing more than that his first marriage took place c. 1904).

1900 Census: Merced, living with her parents.

1910 Census: San Francisco, living in a boarding house with brother David, occupation: nurse.

1920 Census: Not found, but Nellie was in China during the census.

1930 Census: San Francisco, Nell, age 49, a professional nurse, married to and living with husband Frederick, now a law student, although 59 years old. Their son, named Frederick Craik Dewar Jr. living with Ellen's sister Mary Maude in Exeter, Tulane during the 1930 census.

1940 Census: Palo Alto.

Voters Lists: none found.

Directories: Frederick C. Dewar Sr. passed the bar and was listed as an attorney living with Nell, graduate nurse in San Francisco directories (e.g. 1945/6) over the next thirty years.

Death: Nell died on 12 Feb, 1967, at 85 years of age.

Children: One son, Frederick Craik Dewar Jr., b1922.

18.8.2 Notes on Nell's Profession

Nell was one of the earliest graduate nurses in America, completing a 2-3 year training period to so qualify. Nursing became a profession in the late 19th century with the first nursing schools in America dating to the early 1870's.

Florence Nightingale (1820-1910) received worldwide recognition for her services to the wounded during the Crimean War (1853-1856). 'The lady with the lamp' founded the Nightingale Training School at St. Thomas' Hospital (1860) in London and wrote notes on her theories of nursing, which became the foundation for nursing practices in England and around the world. She is considered the founder of scientific nursing and credited with formalizing the education of nurses. The first school of nursing in America was opened in 1873 (the Bellevue Hospital Training School) and the John Hopkins School of Nursing opened in 1889 in direct consultation with Florence Nightingale.

The first training of nurses in California following Nightingale principles began around 1889 and one of the first hospitals to establish a training school was St. Luke's Hospital in San Francisco. In most training schools, a high school diploma was desirable (but not an absolute requirement in the early years) and the program involved two years of training. The first five months were probationary and endurance was a key requirement. The uniformed trainees worked seven days a week and were on duty at least twelve hours a day. They did not pay tuition, and of course were not paid, although they received free meals and lodging. They were occasionally allowed a half day off and might be given a two week vacation during the two years of training. Graduates received a diploma and were entitled to the title of 'Trained Nurse'. Eventually trained nurses received a nursing licence which regulated access to the nursing profession. The roles of trained (and registered) nurses as compared to licensed practical nurses was eventually defined.

Photo 18.8.2a Nell Gurr

Ellen Gurr, the sister of Ted, graduated nursing in 1906 and was a volunteer during the great San Francisco earthquake and fire. She answered the call for nurses again in 1920 serving in China during the worldwide flu pandemic.

Ted Robert Gurr Collection

Photo 18.8.2c The USS Breese
Credited with damaging Japanese aircraft during the attack on Pearl Harbor the Breese also served in the Central and Western Pacific throughout WWII, and was in action at Leyte Gulf, Iwo Jima and Okinawa.

Photo 18.8.2b Frederick Dewar
Nell's son, who served on the minesweeper USS Breese in the Pacific Theatre throughout WWII.

Photo 18.8.2a on the previous page shows Nell proudly wearing her nursing uniform, while **Photo 18.8.2b** is her son, Frederick Craik Dewar in 1952. He re-enlisted following his discharge after WWII. **Photo 18.8.2c** is the USS Breese, a mine-layer that Fred served on throughout WWII.

18.8.3 Notes on Frederick C. Dewar, Nellie's Son

Frederick C. Dewar Jr. enlisted in the Navy on 6th January, 1939 at about 17 years of age. He served almost exclusively on the *Oglala* (flagship of the Pacific Fleet Mine Force) until 4th Jan 1941, at which time he was re-assigned to the mine laying *USS Breese* (shown above) where he served throughout WWII.

The *USS Breese* arrived in Hawaii December 10th of 1940 and Frederick C. Dewar was assigned to the ship's crew on 4th January, 1941. On 7th December 1941, *USS Breese* was anchored at Pearl Harbor and by 0767 she opened fire with her machine guns at close range on the attacking Japanese planes. Although she received no material damage from the Japanese attack, she aided in the sinking of one midget submarine and damaged numerous enemy planes. The *Oglala* was not so lucky and was sunk in the harbor, although subsequently recovered.

The *USS Breese* operated in the Central Pacific from 7th December 1941 until 10th October 1944. She then extended her sphere of duty westward to include various islands in the Marianas-Philippine area and continued to serve as a mine layer and patrol ship until 7th November 1945.

During her wartime career she carried out minesweeping duties during the consolidation of the Solomon Islands (1–13 May 1943); New Georgia-Rendova Vangunu operation (29 June-25 August); occupation and defense of Cape Torokina (1 November-8 November); Leyte landings (12–24 October 1944); Lingayen Gulf landings (4–18 January 1945); Iwo Jima operation (7 February-7 March); Okinawa seizure (25 March-30 June); and 3rd Fleet operations against Japan (5 July-31 July). In August and September 1945 *Breese* swept mines in the East China Sea and Kyūshū-Korean area. On 7th November 1945, *Breese* steamed to the west coast arriving 26th November. She transited the Panama Canal and put into New York on the 13th of December. She was decommissioned 15 January 1946.

Frederick Craik Dewar continued his naval career after the war and served on the *USS Briareus*, a repair ship in 1952, after re-enlisting in 1950. He was released from service 31 July 1960. He Died in Lancaster PA in 1988.

18.9 David Gurr

David received a full high school education in Merced before heading off to San Francisco where he apparently apprenticed to an electrician or received some post graduate training at a trade school. He was boarding in the same lodging house as his sister Ellen (a graduate nurse) in 1910 and was working as an electrician for a phone company.

Census and Other Records:

Birth: August 30, 1882

Marriage: to Jessie Unknown born in Michigan in 1894, married about 1916

1900 Census: Merced, During the June 1900 census (at 18 years) he was listed as living with his father and attending (high) school.

1910 Census: San Francisco, lodging at the same boarding house as his sister Ellen (Nellie) and there his occupation is listed as electrician with a phone company.

1920 Census: Lyon County Nevada, David and wife Jessie are listed in the January 1920 census living in Mason. It records Jessie as being born in Michigan, the child of an England born father and Scotland born mother.

Draft Registration: David registered for the draft [307] in Sept of 1918 at the age of 36 while working for a company (Nat Lane ?) in Mason, Lyon County, Nevada as an electrician. In this document he gives his birth-date as Aug 30, 1884 (not the true date of Aug 30, 1882 - why?). He also declares that he is married to a Jessie Gurr, though we have not confirmed their marriage date.

Voters Lists: In a Voter Registration list for 1912-13, David is listed as an electrician (and a socialist) and living at 1220 Pine in San Francisco.

Directories: no listings found.

Children: None.

Death: David died on August 1, 1925, electrocuted while investigating a power failure at a railway company shop.

The Mason Valley News carried the following headline on August 2, 1925:

Mason Valley Man is Killed
David Gurr Meets Death From Electrical Shock at Railroad Shops
Special to The Journal

Mason, August 1. - David Gurr, manager of the Mason Townsite Company was electrocuted tonight while attempting to locate trouble which grounded a transformer at the shops of the Copper Belt railroad. During an electrical storm, the power system, controlled by the Townsite Company went out of order and Mr. Gurr had gone to the shops. It is believed that while at work he fell against the galvanized iron building and 2200 volts passed through his body. A transformer, in which the trouble was located, had grounded so that the electricity was sent surging through the walls of the shops. Physicians attempted to resuscitate the man but he was unable to survive the shock.

Mr. Gurr is well known throughout Nevada and especially in this section where he has resided for some time. He was classed as one of the best-informed electrical engineers in this part of the state.

He is survived by his widow who resides in Mason.

The *Nevada State Journal* dated Aug 2, 1925 covering his death mentions only an unnamed widow and no children. This does not prove that no child was born to the couple during

---

[307] The Selective Service Act of 1917 required registration of all males between the ages of 21 to 31 years of age, so David was exempt until 1918 when the draft age was extended to 45.

their wedded years (probably 1915 to 1925), though it makes a child less probable, since the reporter would probably have been certain to report the fact that any small children survived their father. But with no children listed at the time of the 1920 census and no mention of any children in the report, we may assume there were no other dependents than his wife Jessie.

Attending David's funeral was a couple, Lewis C. (b 1892) and Elsie DeArmond of Blairsden CA (Plumas County, west of Reno, west of Portola). There were DeArmond's living in Mason during the 1910 census. In the *Nevada State Journal* dated Aug. 24, 1924 Dave Gurr and Lewis DeArmond were entered into a tennis tournament in Yerington, NV. A Lewis C. (operator, General Store) and his wife Elsie (postmistress) can be found living in Cromberg CA in Plumas County during the 1930 census, but this Lewis's parents were Ohio born (not foreign born as were Jessie's). Lewis C. was a well-known Portola rancher (a mason). His wife Elsie died in Portola Dec 22, 1960. We list this information as it may be that Lewis C. was an older brother of Jessie, though it is also possible that Lewis was simply a good friend who travelled home to pay his respects on David's death.

The *San Mateo Times* (Friday, June 15, 1928) carried information regarding the transfer of title to lots in Ravenwood and of moneys belonging to the estate of David Gurr to M. Maloney and cash to the estate of Jessie Gurr. We know nothing about Jessie's life, but expect she remarried.

Another point of interest is the *Nevada State Journal*'s report on David's death which calls him and electrical engineer. It is possible that David followed a degree course in engineering after finishing high school, and if so he would have been the first college graduate in the Gurr family.

18.10 Ethel Elizabeth Gurr (DeJongh)

Ethel completed her high school education in Merced and lived with her parents until c. 1905. She attended St. Luke's School of Nursing in San Francisco, graduating in 1909. In 1910 she was living with the Evans family in Nob Hill, nursing at St. Mary's Hospital, about a mile west of her lodgings. Queenie, who graduated from St. Luke's at the same time as her sister is also nursing and probably at the same hospital. Another lodger with the Evans is Cornelius D. DeJongh, listed as a bookkeeper at a bank. Ethel and Cornelius are single in the 1910 census.

The 1920 census record shows that both husband and wife are naturalized, but it appears that the years of naturalization are reversed, suggesting Cornelius became a citizen in 1913. This is not so, according to his declaration on his 1918 draft registration. There are variations in the spelling of Cornelius's surname and this obviously makes the record search for the couple more difficult. Some records show DeGough or DeLongh, both common Dutch names, but DeJong (and variations of it) are the most common name in the Netherlands. In fact, it is the draft registration that records the name DeJongh, and his clearly legible signature confirms this spelling.

We assume that Ethel and Cornelius were separated or divorced before the 1930 census. We could find no evidence of them being together after the mid-1920s. We did find their children in the 1930 census: Henry R. DeJongh, age 9, living with his grandparents Alfred

Richard and Emily (on Bay Rd, San Mateo); Emily M. DeJongh, age 8 living with Beatrice and her husband Alvin Weaver in Merced. Beatrice's brother Ernest was also living with his sister at that time.

Census and Other Records:
Birth: March 20, 1884.
Marriage: To Cornelius D. DeJongh, date unknown. Cornelius was born in Spain of Dutch parents, and was an alien who immigrated to the USA in 1907.
1900 Census: Merced, Township 2 with parents, listed as student.
1910 Census: San Francisco, 1319 Octavia St. in the Nob Hill area, unmarried, nurse (St. Mary's Hospital).
1920 Census: San Francisco, 530 22nd Ave, married (Ethel De Jongh), unemployed and living with her husband Cornelius, bank cashier, both listed as naturalized by this time.
1930 Census: assumed San Francisco, but no entry found for Ethel or Cornelius.
1940 Census: San Francisco, probable.
Draft Registration: Cornelius registered for the draft on Sept 12, 1918 giving his and Ethel's address as 1501 8th Ave in San Francisco CA. Cornelius names his wife Ethel DeJongh as next of kin and his occupation as Assistant Cashier at the Sea Board National Bank, 101 Market St., San Francisco. He is recorded as an alien.
Voters Lists: none found.
Directories: In the 1912 and 1913 Crocker-Langley San Francisco City Directories, Ethel was listed as resident at 1319 Octavia St. and as Miss Ethel Gurr, nurse. In the 1936 San Francisco Polks Crocker-Langley directory Cornelius is listed at 333 Pine St.
Death: October 14, 1965.
Children: Henry R. DeJongh b1921, Emily M. DeJongh b1922.
Note: In the 1942 San Francisco phone directory, we found Emily M. *Delongh* living with her father and he is listed as bank book keeper.

18.11 Gordon Gurr

Gordon was not quite four when he arrived in America and would not have started school until the fall of 1892. At fourteen years of age during the 1900 census, he was still attending school along with David, Ethel, Beatrice and Ernest, and probably completed high school as did most of Alfred's and Emily's children.

Census and Other Records:
Birth: November 28, 1885.
Marriage: unknown first marriage before 1920, second marriage to Florence (nee unknown, born in New Jersey) date unknown, but probably 1924.
1910 Census: Imperial Valley.

1920 Census: San Diego, CA on 9th St., divorced, occupation drayman (with own wagon [308]).

1930 Census: San Diego (Chula Vista) at 2279 Ocean View Blvd, occupation is laborer in a cotton mill, living with wife Florence and their two children.

1940 Census: Chula Vista, Florence with the children only.

Draft Registration: Gordon registered for the draft on Sept 12, 1918 while he was working for the Hercules Powder Co. in San Diego (living at #19 Twelfth St.) Curiously, his birth year is given as November 28, 1886 and he signs an affirmation that the information he has provided is true (family bible states November, 1885, and must be correct for Beatrice was born July 1, 1887).

Voters Lists: Years 1900-1916 (no year specified) living in Imperial County and working as a farmer. In the 1916 Voter Registration for San Diego County, he is listed as a socialist living at the Hotel Phillips and working as a farmer. In 1922, he has become a Democrat and is working as a rancher in Hillsdale, El Cajon, San Diego County. In 1926, he is back to being a socialist, but is listed with Florence G. Gurr (Democrat) living at 3577 Dalbergia, occupation cattle feeder.

Directories: In the 1924 San Diego City Directory, Gordon is listed as a laborer, living at 3577 Dalbergia (no Florence). In the 1927 San Diego directory, Gordon is listed along with Florence living at 2892 Market Street, and his occupation is oil worker. In the 1929 directory he is still on Market Street, but his occupation is cattle feeder. In the 1931 directory, Gordon and Florence are still at 2279 Ocean View Blvd and he is listed as a laborer. In the 1932 directory, Florence is listed as the widow of Gordon.

Death: On or before January, 1933.

Children: Emily M. b 1925 and Richard P. b 1928 by his second wife Florence.

18.12   Beatrice (Bea) Gurr (Weaver)

Beatrice (known affectionately as Bea and Aunt Bea) lived with her parents in Merced County where she finished high school, then helped out in the family poultry business. Circa 1917, Beatrice married Alvin Ellsworth Weaver, who lived with his family on a farm adjacent to Alfred Richard's property. In the 1910 census, Alvin Weaver was working on his father's farm. Beatrice spent her entire life in Merced County.

Census and Other Records:

Birth: July 1, 1887.

Marriage: to Alvin Ellsworth Weaver in 1917. Weaver was born in California in 1891 of Pennsylvania born parents.

1900 Census: Merced, Township 2 with parents, student.

1910 Census: Merced, Township 2 with parents, no occupation.

---

[308] This probably refers to a truck with a flat-bed and removable sides for hauling heavy loads. Earlier, draymen used horses to pull drays which were intended for heavy loads. It is possible, though unlikely, that Gordon was using a horse in 1920 San Diego, and more unlikely that he would be manually pulling a wagon.

1920 Census: Merced, In the 1920 census we find Beatrice married, living with Alvin and their infant daughter Emily D. Weaver, born 1918 in Merced. Alvin is recorded as an electrician, working for an electric company.

1930 Census: Merced, Alvin, Beatrice and their two children living on family farm and occupation of Alvin is farmer. Living with them are Emily M. DeJongh, the daughter of Ethel Elizabeth DeJongh, Beatrice's sister, as well as Ernest Gurr, Beatrice's brother.

1940 Census: Merced.

Draft Registration: In his 1918 Draft Registration Alvin certifies that he is married, a farmer and supporting his wife and mother.

Voters Lists: None found.

Directories: None found.

Death: Jan 11, 1985.

Children: Emily D. b1918, Barbara b1921

18.13 Ernest Gurr

Ernest was barely a year old when his family arrived in Merced. He lived with his parents until early in the 1910s when he left for Oakland and worked as a conductor with the transit company, as did his brother William. During the 1900 census, Ernest was still at school in Merced where he finished eight years of school and during the 1910 census he was working on his father's farm in Merced. In the 1930 census he is listed as living with his sister Beatrice, but Bertha is no longer mentioned.

Note: A death registry was found for a Bertha C Gurr dated 1957-58.

Census and Other Records:

Birth: October 11, 1888.

Marriage: to Bertha C (nee unknown), date unknown. Second Wife Lempi Hakala (AKA Kohonen, age about 20 years younger than Ernest) in January 1961.

1900 Census: Merced, Township 2 with parents.

1910 Census: Merced, Township 2 with parents.

1920 Census: Merced probable, though no record found.

1930 Census: Merced, living with his sister Beatrice.

1940 Census: Merced, living with Bertha and brother Harry. Listed as a farmer, having 8 years of elementary school.

Draft Registration: June 5, 1917, he registered for the draft in Merced, and there he lists a wife, but does not name her. He also states that he works in Merced for a company called Mynex.

Voters Lists: None found.

Directories: 1917 Oakland City Directory listed as carman. Also listed in numerous directories throughout the 1920s, 1930s and 1940s with and without Bertha C. as his spouse.

Death: August 19, 1980.

Children: No Children.

Chapter 19

Descendants of Reverend Henry Jonathan Gurr

19.1   Pedigrees, Marriages and Children

First Wife

Alfred James Gurr b. Oct 1823 d. 29 Jun 1874	Mary Ann Bennett b. 06 Dec 1819 d. 1884	William Benedict Frost b. 27 Jul 1816 d. 23 Aug 1870	Emma Jane Spurr b. 1819 d. 1901
Married 21 Mar 1846		Married 22 Feb 1838	
3nd child of 8		5th child of 6	
Henry Jonathan Gurr b. 22 Jan 1853 d. 18 Jun 1931		Celia Spurr Frost b. 1851 d. 18 Oct 1887	
Married 1880			
Children of Henry Jonathan and Celia Frost Gurr			
Alfred Edwin Gurr b. 22 Jul 1881 d. 25 Sep 1961		William Edward Newton Gurr b. 16 Oct 1883 d. 12 May 1977	

Second Wife

Alfred James Gurr b. Oct 1823 d. 29 Jun 1874	Mary Ann Bennett b. 06 Dec 1819 d. 1884	Charles B. Gardner b. Unknown d. Unknown	Unknown b. Unknown d. Unknown
Married 21 Mar 1846		Marriage Unknown	
3nd child of 8		Unknown	
Henry Jonathan Gurr b. 22 Jan 1853 d. 18 Jun 1931		Alice Gardner b. 1868 d. Unknown	
Married Aug 1, 1888, Divorced 1893			
No Issue			

Third Wife

Alfred James Gurr b. Oct 1823 d. 29 Jun 1874	Mary Ann Bennett b. 06 Dec 1819 d. 1884	John Benedict Lucas b. 06 Dec 1836 d. Sept 1912	Mary Amanda Miller b. 1853 d. 1938
Married 21 Mar 1846		Married Jan 1873	
3nd child of 8		1st child of 4	
Henry Jonathan Gurr b. 22 Jan 1853 d. 18 Jun 1931		Mabel Ethel Lucas b. 1875 d. 18 Mar 1940	
Married Feb 15, 1897			
Children of Henry Jonathan and Mabel Lucas Gurr			

Eileen M. B. b. 13 Apr 1899 d. 01 Jan 1975	Robert Lucas b. 25 Sep 1905 d. 20 Jan 1980	John Bennett b. 04 Sep 1907 d. 30 Aug 1971	Henrietta b. 23 Dec 1908 d. 12 Feb 1985	Heline Florine b. 25 Aug 1910 d. 25 Jun 1989

The Reverend Henry Jonathan Gurr fathered seven children, two with his first wife Celia Frost Gurr, and five with his third wife, Mabel Lucas Gurr. He was 28 years old on July 22, 1881 when his first son, Alfred Edwin, was born in Wilmar Minnesota. He was 57 when his last child Helen was born in Chelan on August 25, 1910. We know much more about some of his descendants than others. Some led adventuresome lives like their father, especially his second son Will Gurr, who is the subject of Chapter 17, and his first daughter Eileen (see below). Others left behind a few public records, some old photos and correspondence, and family memories of ordinary lives sometimes afflicted by poverty and debility. All had children except Will, but like their parents most of them lived poorly documented lives. The exceptions include Alfred Gurr's son Jack, a Jesuit priest, and author Ted Robert Gurr. Following are sketches of the lives of each of his offspring and a few of their children.

19.2 Alfred Edwin Gurr

Alf, as he was known to the family, was almost three in March 1884 when his parents left Dakota Territory for the Pacific Coast. After his mother's death in California, three years later, he and his younger brother lived a whirligig life as their father took them to London and back, across North America, and to Gold Rush Alaska, all chronicled in Will Gurr's memoirs. The brothers briefly parted company in the winter of 1898-99 when Alf returned to Skagway from Atlin with his father while Will stayed behind in the British Columbia interior. They reunited a few months later in Skagway, sharing a draughty shack and working odd jobs there. Dancehall girls lived next door and Alf ran errands for them. Soon thereafter the brothers moved to Juneau where Alf lived for a time with his father and stepmother in the Episcopal Church rectory. After that we have only glimpses of Alf.

Unlike his father and younger brother, Alf remained in Alaska until 1930. In 1912 he married Mary Helena Santle, a devout Catholic who was born in Heartland, Michigan in 1880. They had two children, John (Jack) and Cecelia. Alf worked as a cashier and Notary Public for the First Territorial Bank of Alaska in Douglas [309] during the early years of his marriage, and during the 1930 census was enumerated in Wrangell, Alaska with his occupation recorded as bank manager. It is also possible that he was employed as a jeweler, as one source suggests, in Juneau, Douglas and Wrangell in southeast Alaska. He also lived for a time in Surf Inlet, near Prince Rupert, British Columbia, where he was joined by his wife in March of 1921, according to a Canadian Immigration Service document, which lists her as a settler joining her husband already in Canada. There is no mention of their two children in the document. It may be significant that an Alaskan-based mining company was active in Surf Inlet between the years 1918 and 1926 following the discovery of gold there. Whatever the circumstances that brought Alf and Helena to this remote but beautiful site on Princess Royal Island, the couple returned to Alaska and Alf to banking sometime during the mid-1920s.

Alf came down from Alaska to visit his father's family in Chelan on several occasions that were reported in *The Chelan Valley Leader*. However, in 1930 he and Helena left Alaska

---

[309] As recorded in Polk & Co.'s *Alaska Gazetteer and Directory (1915-16)*

for the last time, perhaps for family reasons, and eventually settled in Oregon. During the 1940 census Alf, Helena and daughter Cecelia are living together in North Vancouver, Multnomah County, Oregon, a suburb of Portland with Alf's occupation recorded as bookkeeper for a retail florist. In his 1942 WWII draft registration the 61 year old Alf lists his address as 2238 NE 13th in Portland, Multnomah, Oregon and his employer as the St. Vincent de Paul Salvage Dept. in Portland. We speculate that, with his banking background, it is probable that he also worked for this company in some accounting capacity. Author, Ted Robert Gurr remembers visiting Alf and Helena in the 1940s, when they lived in a small steam-heated apartment and of being very impressed by their Murphy bed that pulled down from the wall. Alf died on September 25, 1961 in Multnomah, Oregon at the age of 80, predeceased by Mary in 1957.

19.3   Alf's Children

Alf and Helena's son Jack was born in Yakima, Washington on the 12th of February 1913, most likely during one of the couple's extended visits to Chelan. Their daughter Cecelia was born in Douglas, Alaska, on July 24, 1914, evidence that her parents had returned to Alaska after her brother's birth. Cecelia attended public elementary school and began high school in Wrangell, Alaska. She completed high school in Portland, graduating in 1931 from Immaculata Academy in Portland. Jack also began his education in Alaskan public schools and continued it in Prince Rupert, but graduated in 1930 from the Catholic Church's Gonzaga High School in Spokane, probably as a boarding student. Influenced by their mother's faith and their schooling, both Jack and Cecelia joined religious orders.

19.3.1a   John Edwin Gurr, Father Jack

Father Jack told his cousin, Ted Robert Gurr, that as a youth he worked in the salmon fisheries along the Alaskan coast and said he always wanted to return to the North – which he did, but not until after an academic career as a Jesuit priest and theologian. He entered the Jesuit Novitiate in 1937 in Oregon, was ordained for the priesthood in 1948, and received his first degree in 1949, as Licentiate in Sacred Theology, from Weston College in Massachusetts. In 1955 the University of St. Louis granted him his doctorate and five years later the Marquette University Press published his dissertation, *The Principle of Sufficient Reason in Some Scholastic Systems 1750-1900*. The 196-page text is thoroughly researched, closely reasoned, and every bit as tedious to read as its title implies.

Photo 19.3.1a Father Jack
Father John Edwin Gurr
Photo from the cover of his 1959 book
"Principle of Sufficient Reason
in Some Scholastic Systems."

From 1955 to 1960 Father Jack was a philosophy professor at Seattle University and for three years the school's academic vice president. **Photo 19.3.1a** is Father Jack c. 1959.

In the early 1960s Father Jack taught philosophy at the Jesuit order's Mount St. Michael's Scholastic in Spokane and often visited his Spokane relatives. It was his life-long practice to keep in contact with the Gurr families on travels, through voluminous correspondence, and by newsletters about his pastoral work in Alaska. The flow of communications increased after he was posted to the Fairbanks Diocese of northern Alaska as Vicar General in 1965. In 1967-68, he served as rector of the Cathedral of the North in Fairbanks before moving on to the city of Bethel near the western coast of Alaska, where he was the supervising priest of the Eskimo missions in the lower Yukon-Kuskokwim River region. In 1974 he served as "pipe-line chaplain," his "parish" consisting of construction camps along the northern part of the 850 mile long Aleysha pipe-line that was being built from Prudhoe Bay on the Arctic Ocean to Valdez on the Inside Passage. He conducted services at camps between the Arctic terminal and the Brooks Range, travelling by "planes, helicopters, trucks or whatever happened to be going in his direction."

Father Jack had significant impact on the lives of some of his relatives. He persuaded his uncle and aunt, Robert and Anne Gurr that their sons, Ted and Dave, should begin primary schooling in parochial schools. In Spokane those schools accepted children up to a year younger than those entering public schools and offered more rigorous instruction – backed up by nuns quick to use rulers to slap the hands of miscreants. As author Ted recalls:

> They (the parochial schools) gave my brother and me a welcome head start. Jack never proselytized for his Church and accepted our Anglican commitments. I recall with some amusement a visit he and I made to the Baha'i Temple in Wilmette, Illinois, on one of his 1970s visits to the lower 48. Father Jack never wore clerical garb when travelling, so far as I recall, and we were approached by a Baha'i who was all too eager to interest us in conversion to his faith. Jack politely rejected the importunities but said nothing at all about his own faith or works.

From 1975 to 1980 Father Jack was back tending missions near the Bering Sea, this time based at the settlement of Kotzebue. A parishioner later recalled that he was "a slightly bent and elderly man...hard of hearing but his pious and friendly manner endeared him to all." We can speculate about why a Jesuit theologian, who seemed to be ascending the Order's hierarchy, should spend most of his later life in the Alaskan wilderness. Family members were told that he was posted to Fairbanks as Coadjutor Bishop, that is as the diocese's administrative officer and Bishop Theodore Boileau's likely successor. But Father Jack also said that he had a falling out with the bishop, and so was sent to the remote missions. He did not regret a move that others might consider a demotion, because he wanted to serve there. His letters are filled with accounts that reflect his love of mission life and its challenges.

19.3.1b Father Jack, A Man of Character

What was Father Jack's dispute with Bishop Theodore Boileau all about?

In 1965 Father Jules Convert, who was General Superior of the Jesuits in Alaska, wrote a series of letters to Vicar General Father Jack urging the Church to dismiss one Joseph Lundowski as a volunteer. Later accounts showed that Lundowski enjoyed the protection of a Father Endal, both of whom repeatedly molested Eskimo and Indian children, some as young as 6 or 7. Father Convert was dismayed that Bishop Bolieau had moved Lundowski from one mission to another and said the Bishop should have gotten rid of him "a long time ago." Father Jack in turn asked why Father Convert could not take action, asking "What would you do if it involved a woman? You should try to bring the scandal to an end."

Ken Roos is an Anchorage attorney who years later represented 240 adults who had been molested as children, 112 of whom identified Lundowski as their abuser. "To sum it up," he said in a Public Broadcasting System interview:

> What really happened between 1960 and 1975 was, for a 15-or 16-year period, Father Endal and Joe Lundowski moved through a series of Alaska villages, always in very remote parts of the state, always with no one there to supervise them except themselves... And the way I read it is that the abuse of children by both of them became more and more blatant, more and more egregious, more and more violent and vile, until it got the point where there was almost nothing that wasn't being done. And they were doing it with complete impunity.

But in 1965 Father Convert and Father Jack concluded that neither of them had the authority to remove Lundowski and that only the Bishop could do so. [310] We can envisage a scenario in which Father Jack urged the Bishop once too often to dismiss Lundowski at a time when the Church chose to conceal sexual predation by its priests [311], and being told by the Bishop that he should go to the missions and deal with such issues first hand. This is inference, of course, but on several occasions he tried to persuade author Ted and his first wife to spend summers in Kotzebue as lay teachers – perhaps because he trusted us over others. We note, in sad conclusion, that the missions where Father Jack served were distant from those where Father Endal and Lundowski were posted, so he was no position to check their abuses of children that, we now know, continued for another decade.

In the early 1980s Father Jack was suffering from what the author Ted's brother David Gurr has said appeared to be Alzheimers and in 1983 he went to Portland for medical help. He returned to Spokane in 1986 and died there, at the Jesuit House Chapel near Gonzaga University, on February 28, 1994.

---

[310] Most of this information, including quotations, is from a chronology of the Catholic Church's failure to deal with reports of sexual predation in Alaska, retrieved from www.pbs.org/wagbh/pages/frontline/the-silence/timeline. The site includes the full transcript of the interview with Ken Roosa. Quotes are from correspondence between Father Convert and Father Jack summarized in the chronology, and later offered on eBay in 2013.

[311] In 2003, CBS News obtained a confidential Vatican document written in 1962, that allegedly laid out a church policy on sexual abuse by priests. The document calls for absolute secrecy when it comes to these cases, warning that anyone who speaks out could be thrown out of the church. The U.S. Conference of Bishops later said that the document was being taken out of context.

19.3.2 Cecelia Frances Gurr, Sister Cecelia

We know about Sister Cecelia's career mostly from her obituary. [312] She earned her BA from Marylhurst College in 1940 and later an MA from Seattle University and in 1946, at the age of 32, she entered the Novitiate of the Sisters of the Holy Names at Marylhurst in Clackamas County in Oregon. Before that she had worked at the Portland Public Library and in the Child Welfare Department of Clackamas County, and was an elementary school teacher for a year. No doubt her older brother encouraged and supported her religious commitment.

Most of Cecelia's life in the order was devoted to teaching at Catholic high schools in Seattle and in Eugene and Medford, Oregon. From 1956 to 1960 she was Principal at St. Mary's Academy in Portland. In later years, according to her obituary, she was Educational Consultant, Secondary Supervisor and Director of Studies for the Oregon Province of the Sisters of the Holy Names. She was also a member of the Provincial Council for seven years. In 1976 her health began to decline and she retired to the Order's Convent at Marylhurst. In the last few years of her life she, like her brother, appears to have suffered from Alzheimers. She died in the Marylhurst Care Center on May 16, 1989 and is buried in the Convent's cemetery where nuns of the Sisters of the Holy Names are interred.

Family members recalled that she visited in Spokane, when she could. She is mentioned in her Uncle Will's probated will of 1977 as Sister Luelia (a typing error) Gurr of Marylhurst, Oregon. And there is an occasional reference to her in family correspondence – thus we know that she attended the memorial service for her Aunt Eileen in Mount Shasta in January 1975.

19.4 The Gurr Children of Chelan

These are the vital statistics of the five children of Reverend Henry Jonathan and Mabel Gurr:

Eileen, born in Chicago, Apr. 13, 1899, died in Mount Shasta, CA, Jan. 1, 1975
Robert Lucas, born in Chelan, Sept. 25, 1905, died in Evanston, IL, Jan. 20, 1980
John Bennett, born in Chelan, Sept. 4, 1907, died in Contra Costa, CA, Aug. 30, 1971
Henrietta (Harriet), born in Chelan, Dec. 23, 1908, died in Spokane, Feb. 12, 1985
Helene Florine, born in Chelan, Aug. 25, 1910, died in Glendale, California, Jun. 25, 1989

19.4.1 Eileen Gurr Wood

Eileen had the most interesting and unconventional life of Henry's five children of Chelan. We know that her mother was already pregnant with Eileen in the fall of 1898 when the Reverend Gurr began his futile attempts to sail from San Francisco to Alaska. Mabel went by train back to Chicago, no doubt to her parents' home, where Eileen was born. A year or two later mother and daughter rejoined the Reverend Gurr in Juneau. Several photos of Eileen learning to walk are in the Reverend Gurr's Alaska albums, including **Photo 19.4.1** on the following page.

In Chelan Eileen attended the First Creek School, a four- to five-mile walk from Gurrland. She is listed in school censuses for 1913-14 and 1914-15 but the census taken in May

---

[312] With thanks to Sarah Cantor, archivist for the Sisters of the Holy Names at Marylhurst, Oregon, who found the obituary in the Order's records.

1917 notes that she was away in college. According to family accounts she was sent to an Episcopal boarding school in Spokane with some of her expenses paid from the sale of one of Gurrland's small herd of cows. She studied nursing, where we do not know, and spent more than half a century as a Registered Nurse – in parallel to the careers of several of her cousins from Alfred Richard's family in Merced. At the time nursing was one of the few professions open to young women who hoped to be something more than elementary school teachers, clerks, and housewives.

In 1925 Eileen was living in Spokane at the West Dean rectory and employed as a nurse. At some time that year she married a 48-year-old physician, Dr. David Thompson Wood, and by 1930 was living with him and his four children by a previous marriage in Corpus Christi, Texas. One of the four was a daughter, Marjorie. Eileen remained close to her stepdaughter all her life, as we know from her correspondence and the fact that Marjorie was a principal beneficiary of Eileen's will. Eileen followed Dr. Wood to Animas, Colorado,

Photo 19.4.1 Mabel with Eileen Learning to Walk
Henry J. Gurr Album

where she worked as nurse. The marriage ended in divorce, probably in 1938-39, because - it was rumored in the family - he had deviant sexual preferences that she rejected. Whatever the truth of this, the author remembers vividly that in the early 1940s she drove an impressive cream colored 1940 Hudson convertible, probably part of a divorce settlement.

By 1940 Eileen was back in Spokane, resident at the West Dean residence along with her younger sister Helen. Their mother Mabel died on March 18 of that year and the census was taken on April 10. Eileen probably was in Spokane to attend her failing mother and stayed to settle her affairs. She then went to work at a Spokane hospital, until in January 1946 she left on route to Hawaii. In early 1946 she wrote letters from the *SS Aleutian* out of San Francisco and bound for Honolulu. According to family accounts she served first at the colony for victims of Hansen's Disease (leprosy) on Moloka'i, but we have no way of verifying that. The same accounts say that later she was school nurse at the Kamehameha School for Boys in Honolulu, a school established in 1887 for native Hawaiians. The school's records show that she was on the staff from 1947 to 1951, but without a note about her position.

Back on the mainland, it became increasingly evident that she was an enthusiastic convert to the Theosophical IAM Movement, forerunner of several latter-day New Age religious movements. The IAM Movement was founded in the early 1930s by engineer Guy Ballard and his wife Edna and in its early years attracted as many as one million adherents who followed the teachings of the Ascended Masters, Jesus and Saint Germain among them. Eileen was one of them and abided by several of the Movement's day-to-day tenets: she became, for example, a strict vegetarian and eschewed the use of the color red. She tried to interest her brother Robert in the movement and Ted Robert Gurr's childhood home was cluttered with IAM pamphlets in the Movement's approved lilac and pale green and yellow colors.

Edna Ballard, who long outlived her husband, was the Movement's charismatic leader until shortly before her death in 1971. She was chronically ill in later life and Eileen became her personal nurse, though we do not know where and how this happened. Eileen may have been with her at the movement's Santa Fe residence, and in Chicago at the Saint Germain Foundation's headquarters. Officials at the Foundation recently verified that Eileen cared for Mrs. Ballard at Shasta Springs and she probably was with Edna Ballard when she died in February 1971 at the Movement's Royal Teton Retreat, in Wyoming. Eileen's later life in Mount Shasta was also linked to the Movement. It was there that Guy Ballard said that, while hiking, he met Saint Germain, an Ascended Master from the 18th century who inspired him to establish the Movement. Mount Shasta remains an icon for followers of the IAM doctrine, and is the site of a reading room and an annual pageant. And it was there that Eileen lived and worked during the last years of her life.

Eileen's obituary says that she had worked as a registered nurse in Colorado, Arizona, Washington State, and Hawaii as well as five hospitals and convalescent homes in northern California. Her last will and testament, written a decade before her death on New Year's Day, 1975 was a source of difficulties, especially for her stepdaughter Marjorie Wood Sirchia, then residing in San Gabriel. She was to receive several tracts of land in Mount Shasta and in Chelan. But by the time of her death only one could be transferred, the others had either been sold to pay Eileen's expenses or given to the IAM Movement. Eileen's executor, Walter C. Laird, who also represented IAM interests, insisted that household goods including a collection of silver spoons be given to the Movement. Her estate was valued at $24,176 after expenses and, after a few monetary bequests were paid out to relatives, the residual of $20,493 was given to the Saint Germain Foundation. On June 29, 1975 Marjorie wrote Robert and Anne Gurr, after her go-rounds with the executor, "I'm hoping I never hear about the "I Am Activity" again – if they are a charitable organization, perhaps the 'Mafia' could qualify. These people were like a bunch of vultures...."

19.4.2 Robert Lucas Gurr

Robert was the first son born to Henry and Mabel Gurr and was the favorite of his maternal grandmother, Mary Amanda Lucas. His education was limited by the constraints of life at Gurrland and the long walk to the First Creek School. In 1913-14 a school census showed he attended school 76 of the possible 155 days and in 1914-15 only 42 days. We can surmise that his low attendance was partly due to bad winter weather, and perhaps also because in these years the Reverend Gurr required his help running the family's sawmill operation on Bear Mountain. After the family moved to Spokane in 1921, when Robert was 16, he attended North Central High School but dropped out in his junior year.

Robert met author Ted's mother, Anne Juliette Cook, when the Reverend Gurr was affiliated with Holy Trinity Church in Spokane and living at its rectory on West Dean. Anne was the last of 18 children of an immigrant English mason, John Cook, whose family lived nearby and worshiped at Holy Trinity. Though her father was illiterate, Anne was a high school graduate (she attended against her father's express wishes) and had a lifelong love of literature and history. She also had a knack for accounting and already as a teenager helped manage the Church accounts. She was active in the congregation's youth group, nearly 100 strong, through which she met Robert. **Photo 19.4.2** is an informal photo showing the extended Gurr family together on the porch of the West Dean house.

Photo 19.4.2 Gurr Family in Spokane 1920's
Front row from left: H.J. Gurr's children, John, Helen,
wife Mabel Ethel Lucas, son Robert Lucas, his fiance Anne Cook
and the Rev. H.J. Gurr.   Back row: daughter Harriett,
holding unidentified child, Mabel's mother Mary Amanda Lucas.
From Anne Cook Gurr Album

In his early teens Robert was a busboy at the Campbell Hotel in Chelan and after he dropped out of high school he reportedly worked at a logging camp. But for almost all his adult life he worked with trucks and autos – which he said fascinated him as a boy when the first cars arrived in Chelan. So from the mid-1920s onward he worked at places like the City Ramp Garage in Spokane and at dealerships for Desoto-Plymouth, Packard, and Ford before taking a lease on a Texaco service station in the Spokane valley. During World War II he avoided conscription by servicing heavy construction machinery at military installations being built in northern Idaho and in central Washington, at what became the Hanford Nuclear Production facility. Meanwhile his family in Spokane participated with varying degrees of enthusiasm in the Victory Garden movement, scrap drives, and collecting stamps to buy Savings Bonds.

Robert's household, in addition to Anne, consisted of two sons and an ever-changing menagerie of dogs, cats, rabbits, goats and chickens. In an echo of his boyhood at Gurrland, he purchased a parcel of land north of Spokane in 1951, inspired by a Rodale Press book on how a family of four could feed itself by intensely cultivating an acre tract. And so the family did, as closely as possible. Ted, born in 1936, and David, born in 1940, learned how to do everything from cultivating vegetables, picking fruit and scything alfalfa to milking goats and plucking freshly-killed chickens. David also learned how to overhaul auto engines and went on to become an enthusiastic hot-rodder as well as an early Peace Corps volunteer in Ethiopia, followed by 36 years as an official of anti-poverty programs in New York and Washington, DC. Ted buried his nose in books, whenever he could find a few minutes to spare, and pursued an academic career that has been chronicled elsewhere. [313]

In 1970 Robert retired and he and Anne joined Ted and his first wife, Erika, in the Thames-side village of Wargrave, Berkshire UK, where Ted was on leave from Princeton en route to a more senior position at Northwestern University. It was Robert and Anne's first trip to Europe and for seven months they traveled in Britain and on the Continent. After a few years more in Spokane, Robert's heart began to weaken so they sold the acre tract and moved to Evanston, Illinois to be closer to Ted and his family. Robert died on January 20, 1980 and his ashes were interred at St. Andrew's Episcopal Church on Staten Island, where his son David then lived with his wife Barbara. Anne lived on, at Episcopal Church residences in the Washington, DC area until June 23, 1998 when she died at the age of 96, long after all her siblings and most of her nieces and nephews had died. She is buried at Lakemont Memorial Gardens near Annapolis, Maryland, where Ted and his second wife Barbara resided. Attempts to transfer Robert's remains to the same plot, in the shadow of an 18th century Episcopal chapel, came to naught because Robert's urn could not be found beneath his grave marker in Staten Island, not even with a metal detector. So Robert Gurr has two headstones, in locales where he did not live, and his remains are not to be found beneath either one.

19.4.3 John Bennett and Helene Florine Gurr

We group these two siblings, for what little we know of them consists of a few glimpses of their childhood at Gurrland. John and his older brother Robert may be two of the boys in **Photo 19.4.3a** on the following page, obtained from one of their father's albums. The house in the background probably is their homestead – the Gurrs' two-wheeled gig is visible behind the house at the left. Captain Lucas mentions in his 1911 diary that two-year-old Helen suffered a concussion when she fell from her highchair and did not recover for a week. The school censuses, referred to above, list John at age 7 in attendance for 140 days in 1914-15 but only 42 days the following year and 99 days in 1916-17. Helen did not begin school until the latter year, when she was 6, and attended 92 of 144 days. It should be kept in mind that the children were

---

[313] David J. Eyre, (2012). *'Times is Good Here and We Be Alrite': A History of John Lavis Cook and Harriet Exworthy Cook.* The lives of John Cook, his wife Harriet, their 18 children and 36 grandchildren – the last and only ones still living in 2013 being the author Ted Robert Gurr and his brother David Gurr. Privately published and available from the author at eyremount@aol.com. Ted's professional career is summarized in his Ted Robert Gurr, Wikipedia entry.

attending the one-room school house at First Creek, which pretty much ruled out grade-specific instruction.

Photo 19.4.3a Group of Boys, Chelan Farmhouse
Left rear: Robert Lucas Gurr, Right front: Edward Lucas Gurr
Henry J. Gurr Album

Photo 19.4.3b John Bennett Gurr and Family
Visiting Anne and Robert Lucas Gurr
John between sons Dennis and Kenneth
Wife Lorrie, daughter Luana, Anne and Robert
Anne Cook Gurr Album

We can track the outlines of John Bennett's life through census records, city directories, and Democratic Party voters' lists. In 1930 he was living at the West Dean house with his parents and his sister Harriet, and was working as an auto salesman. A year later he is probably the John Gurr who was crew member on a ship sailing from Vancouver to San Francisco, working as an oiler. From 1932 to 1943 he lived in San Francisco and then Oakland, employed as a truck driver. Sometime between 1944 and 1946 his first marriage ended – we do not know how –and he married Lorraine Frances Byrnes, eight years his junior, with whom he had three children. Their twin boys were born in 1946 and a daughter two years later. **Photo 19.4.3b** shows John and his family on a rare visit to Robert and Anne Gurr in Spokane in 1959. John died in 1971 at the relatively young age of 64. His older sister Eileen specified that Jack Gurr of Valley View, Orange County - perhaps one of his sons -- should receive all her father's photo albums and family pictures. And so they were disbursed by her executor, to the chagrin of all in the family who would have liked to see more of the Reverend Gurr's many albums.

Helen Gurr lived in Spokane at the West Dean residence until she was 30. She graduated in 1931 from North Central High School – her older brother Robert had dropped out of the same school a few years earlier. For the next decade she is listed in city directories, sometimes as a clerk or saleswoman, and later as a credit bureau reporter. She married a Mike Mathison, though we do not know when or where. In April 1951 they were living in San Gabriel, California and we know from one surviving letter that she was five months pregnant. The child was a daughter, Christine, and family correspondence from the 1970s says she was a burden for her mother, who was by now either divorced or widowed. Christine's problems were well enough known that no one thought it necessary to explain what they were. Letters also refer to their poverty. Eileen's will, probated in 1975, leaves $100 to Helen and $1000 to Christine, and Will Gurr in 1977 bequeathed $200 to Helen – but only $1 each to Robert and Harriet Gurr. In 1971 Helen attended her brother John's funeral in Oakland, and according to a news account she was then living in Glendale, in greater Los Angeles. One family recollection is that Christine committed suicide. Helen died in Glendale in 1989 at the age of 79.

19.4.4 Harriet Gurr

Harriet was characterized as retarded, an explanation for being different that was in vogue in the first half of the 20th century. She was in some ways "intellectually disabled", to use the modern term for her debility. The family's explanation was that she suffered brain damage at birth. Whatever the cause of her debility she was able to attend the First Creek School during the same years as Robert, John, and Helen and for about the same numbers of days. In 1921 she accompanied Henry and Mabel Gurr to Spokane and was still living in the West Dean rectory in 1937.

Harriet had no regular occupation that we know of, though one city directory entry says she was a sorter for a seed company and another that she was a nurse. In 1937 she married Walt Wallace, a mail carrier thirteen years older than her, with whom she had children named James and Barbara. Spokane Directories in the mid 1950s list Harriet and Walt at different addresses. We don't know what happened to that marriage, although author Ted's brother David recalls a 1951 meeting at the family's cottage where Harriet was accompanied by someone by the name of Price. Also a letter to Harriet from her sister Helen dated 1951 asks if she is still using the name Wallace. In 1965 she remarried a widower named Newton Cole. The probate record for Will

Gurr's will in 1977 gives her name as Harriet Gurr Cole and her residence as a Spokane nursing home.

During the 1940s and 1950s the Robert Gurr family occasionally visited Aunt Harriet and her children Jim and Barbara, neither of whom seemed handicapped in any way, though Ted and David got the impression that the visits were mostly acts of social obligation. Ted does not recall that Aunt Harriet or her children were ever invited to family or holiday celebrations at their home. One poignant letter from Aunt Harriet survives, written in 1975 to Eileen's stepdaughter Marjorie after Eileen's death. Harriet rambles in a scarcely literate way about Eileen's money, asking repeatedly whether "the county" (Siskiyou County in northern California) took it all. She mentions that "my sweetheart died a week ago, money went to his children, heart trouble." She adds that he was "86 years old a railroad man" and she therefore had to move to a different apartment, helped by Jim and Barbara. And she mentioned that she was $180 in debt, which she seemed to think might come to her from California. Newton Cole would have been 78 in 1975 and did not die until 1986, so she may have separated from him by then. But we have no way of knowing the identity of her 86-year-old sweetheart. Two years later Harriet was living in a nursing home and probably remained there until her death in 1985.

19.5   Some Observations on Education

The Reverend Henry Gurr may have been a "restless and not very practical man," as one of his Chelan parishioners recalled, but in retrospect his greatest failing was that he did not provide well for his children's education. His sons by his first marriage had episodes of schooling in a half-dozen or more towns, but evidently none at all during their two years in a boys' home. There's no evidence in his son Will's memoirs that their father encouraged or valued their education. The children who grew up in Gurrland fared little better. Their ranch was built because of its spectacular views, probably with no thought to the fact that the nearest school – with one room – was four or more miles' walk away. When the children were in their early teens the family moved to Chelan town and access to school was easier, but probably not enough to make up for an inadequate start on Bear Mountain. Eileen was sent away to boarding school and became a nurse. Only one of her siblings, Helen, is known to have completed secondary school.

This is all the more difficult to understand because the Reverend Gurr, along with his older brother, Alfred Richard (and probably his younger brother Edwin) received exceptionally good early education in mid-Victorian London. Their attendance at more or less elite schools was a rare advantage by comparison with the opportunities afforded most children of working and lower middle class London families. Henry Gurr was able to build on that foundation by completing three years of advanced education at the Seabury Divinity School where he mastered a rigorous classical and theological curriculum.

It is often said that some personal traits and talents "skip generations," which could be invoked to explain the fact that some of Henry Gurr's grandchildren became teachers, scholars, professors and civil servants. But that doesn't fit well with the generational evidence. A second-generation inheritance of intellectual potential was evident in Will and Alf, Eileen and Helen. What was lacking for them and most of the third generation as well was encouragement and example. The accomplished children of the second generation received that, not from their grandparents, but from the parochial schools of the Roman Catholic Church, for Jack and Cecilia, and from Anne Gurr for her sons Ted and David.

Chapter 20
Descendants of Edwin Robert Gurr

20.1   Pedigree, Marriage and Children

First Wife

Alfred James Gurr b. Oct 1823 d. 29 Jun 1874	Mary Ann Bennett b. 06 Dec 1819 d. 1884	Natural: Urban Santer Adoptive Father Herbert Santer	Natural: Mother Unknown Adoptive Mother Ann Wilmott Santer
Married 21 Mar 1846		Married Date Unknown	
4th child of 8		Order Unknown	
Edwin Robert Gurr b. 15 Jan 1855 d. 07 Feb 1929		Alice Santer b. 15 Sep 1864 d. 04 Jan 1894	
Married 15 Sept 1887, Islington			
Children of Edwin Robert and Alice Gurr			
George Herbert Edwin b. 18 Jul 1888 d. 12 Jan 1974	Harold Wilfred b. 12 Aug 1889 d. 12 Dec 1965	Arthur Ernest b. 16 May 1891 d. 1891	

Second Wife

Alfred James Gurr b. Oct 1823 d. 29 Jun 1874	Mary Ann Bennett b. 06 Dec 1819 d. 1884	Joseph Hall b. c. 1827 d. After 1911	Frances Unknown b. c. 1828 d. After 1911
Married 21 Mar 1846		Married c. 1847	
4th child of 8		4th child of about 9	
Edwin Robert Gurr b. 15 Jan 1855 d. 07 Feb 1929		Ada Alice Augusta Hall b. 04 Nov 1855 d. 18 Nov 1934	
Married Sept 1903, Portsmouth			
No Issue			

20.2   Early Family Life

All three of Edwin's and Alice's sons were born in Brentford which was part of Ealing in the late 19th century. Alice had a difficult third pregnancy and their third son Arthur died within a few months of his birth in 1891. Alice never quite recovered from the ordeal and her post partum difficulties are probably related to her death in January of 1894, although this is speculative. Still, her condition was such that Edwin provided her with a nurse and a housekeeper (Emily M. Card) throughout 1891 and most of 1892.

Whether or not the move from London to Merced was in part the promise of a more moderate climate and cleaner air, as family members have suggested, the couple did in fact immigrate to America with their two surviving children in the fall of 1892. The family of four sailed to New York on the 4225 ton *Richmond Hill*, Saloon Class, arriving September 21st. Emily Card went with them to look after Alice and the two children, and is listed as a nurse on the ship manifest. This may be further evidence that all was not well with Alice. It is interesting that Edwin gave his occupation as manufacturer rather than the usual milk contractor.

From New York, the family continued on to California where both of Edwin's brothers were living at the time; Alfred Richard in Merced and Reverend Henry Jonathan in the Bay area. Edwin returned alone to England a few weeks after their arrival in Merced, but re-crossed the Atlantic on the *Aurania*, arriving in New York on December 5th 1892. We do not know why he made this return trip.

It is almost certain that Edwin planned on settling permanently in Merced. We believe, but have not yet obtained proof, that he bought land on Gurr Road near his brother's poultry farm, but he applied for landed immigrant status in 1893. Unfortunately, at this time his brother Reverend Henry was having marital problems and during that year Henry instituted divorce proceedings against his second wife and eventually left California for Chicago. A few months later Edwin's wife Alice's condition worsened and she died in Merced January 4th, 1894.

Edwin immediately returned to London with his two sons, arriving in Southampton on Feb 7, 1894, aboard the *City of Paris* out of New York. It was only for a short stay and probably his intention was to grieve with Alice's family, and possibly to bring her remains back to England. Whatever his motive had been in returning home, he headed back to New York less than a month after his arrival in England, with both sons in tow, arriving on the *Majestic*, First Class on the 15th of March 1894. We are certain that it was intention to remain in America for he has given his destination in the United States as California and for a protracted stay.

We know nothing more about Edwin and his two sons movements until the early April recording of the British 1901 census. During that census widower Edwin is living in Tonbridge (south of London) with George and Harold and the boys are attending a commercial [314] school. His occupation during the census is once again listed as milk contractor. On Sept 9th of that year, the two boys were placed in a residential school [315] (Ivydale Road School) in Southwark, and Edwin's address is given as 81 Ryehill Park in the same neighborhood.

There is little doubt that Edwin's two sons spent much of their young lives in a number of different boarding schools in England following the death of their mother. The two received at least a college entry level by the time their father immigrated to the United States, passing through Canada in 1906. George Herbert may even have spent a few months at Oxford or another school of higher learning, or so family tradition suggests, for we know that when he arrived in Canada he had never been employed and had never been out of an academic environment.

---

[314] This probably means that it was a fee-paying school.

[315] The information was recorded on the Ivydale Road School's admission papers for the two boys in Sept 1901.

Edwin married his second wife Ada Alice Hall in Portsmouth, Hampshire in September of 1903. Ada was the daughter of a London stonemason and bricklayer, Joseph Hall and his wife Frances. Joseph is listed in the 1881 census as a construction manager and the couple appear to have been financially comfortable. They had at least nine children in the 1850s and 1860s. They retired at a relatively early age, first to Bexhill (1891 census) and later moving to Portsmouth (both 1901 and 1911 censuses).

Ada (Adelaide) Alice Augusta Hall was born in December of 1855 and baptized in January of 1856. During the 1891 census she was single and living with her retired parents in Bexhill, East Sussex where her occupation was private school teacher. Her parents Joseph and Frances eventually moved to Portsmouth in the 1890s. Ada was not residing with them when the 1901 census was taken, nor can we find any listing for Ada in that census. We believe she may have married and then separated, divorced or been widowed between 1891 and September of 1903 when she and Edwin were married. This belief is based on a rumor in Chelan in 1917 that Ada obtained a passport to return from Washington to England to settle family affairs, perhaps related to children she had from an earlier marriage. However, it is more probable that she returned (as her passport application states) to settle two estates, likely those of her parents, who died sometime after the 1911 census.

Ada's July 1917 passport application declares her intention of returning to England via Liverpool on the passenger ship *S.S. St. Paul* departing New York on Sept 1, 1917. We do not know is she took passage on that ship, although we are certain that she reached England before the end of WWI. [316] The United States had entered the war less than three months prior to Ada's passport application, and the unprepared nation was being mobilized throughout the balance of 1917. There was a great deal of confusion as the lives of millions of Americans changed with short notice as over 2,800,000 troops were drafted, trained and shipped overseas. The entry of the United States into the war was instrumental in bringing it to an earlier than anticipated end.

20.3 To North America

After having made several crossings to North America landing in New York, in 1905 Edwin brought his family to the continent through the port of Montreal via Halifax, Canada. One reason for this may be that, at the turn of the 20th century, being a British subject meant that you were entitled to enter the Dominion of Canada [317] without a visa. Although Edwin probably had a legal status in the United States by this time, the same could not be said for his new wife nor even his children who were 16 and 17 years of age in 1905.

---

[316] The United States entered WWI on April 6, 1917, following the sinking of seven US merchant ships after Germany began unrestricted submarine warfare in January of 1917. Ada's plans may have changed, because of the US entry into the war, for the St. Paul was officially taken over by the U.S. Navy on October 27, 1917 and used as a troop carrier, and we cannot find any evidence of the St. Paul crossing the Atlantic in the two months preceding her commissioning.

[317] The debate about the relationship between Canada and Britain after Canada became an independent nation under Confederation in 1867 included the possible designation of Canada as a Colony, a Kingdom or a Dominion. The term : "a member of the British Commonwealth of Nations" was suggested in 1884, and was adopted after the Balfour Declaration of 1926 at a conference of British Nations.

Whatever the reason for their passing through Canada, we find Ada, with stepsons George and Harold in Winnipeg, Manitoba during the June 30, 1906 census and they list their date of immigration to Canada as 1905. In fact, Edwin and George arrived in Canada on April 5th, 1905 aboard the *Bavarian* [318] out of Liverpool, travelling steerage class. On the ship's manifest Edwin lists his occupation as dairyman from Middlesex, and his destination as Winnipeg. Neither Ada nor Harold is on that ship. Their date of arrival in Canada is unknown.

Why Winnipeg? All rail traffic to Western Canada must pass through Winnipeg, the gateway to the Canadian West, for north of Winnipeg there are over 100,000 lakes including two of the largest inland lakes on the planet, and to this day there are no railroads or highways through that region. But in 1905, Winnipeg was also the northern terminus of a major route into the United States via the south to north flowing Red River [319] and the Northern Pacific Railway had a branch from Winnipeg that connected to the Western United States. The United States also had a consulate in Winnipeg and this and the geography made it a major point of entry for immigrants to the United States.

Alone, Edwin entered the United States through Winnipeg sometime in late 1905 or early 1906, leaving Ada and his two sons behind. Since Edwin had already established his residency in the United States in the 1890s, it seems logical that he proceeded to the family's final destination on his own to prepare for their arrival. Immigration to the United States was being restricted more than it had in past years and it is probable that the rest of Edwin's family was awaiting entry visas.

Edwin applied for homestead acreage on Chelan Valley's Bear Mountain adjacent to his brother's property in 1906 and Ada joined him there in 1907, according to her naturalization papers. George and Harold did not continue on to Chelan, at least we can find no evidence of their having done so. Some details of the brothers' subsequent lives makes up the balance of this chapter.

20.4 George Herbert Edwin Gurr

20.4.1 Memories of my grandfather [320]:

When I began looking into my family genealogy following my retirement in 2007, I must admit to being almost completely ignorant of my mother's lineage. Her father, George Herbert Edwin Gurr, came in and out of our lives during my childhood, for he separated from my grandmother when my mother was only six and her brother and sister were not yet ten years old. All I knew of George Herbert Gurr's background (Pop to the family) was that he was born in England, and was reputedly expelled from a prestigious college there when he was about seventeen, just before he came to Canada. I once heard

---

[318] The Bavarian went aground near Montreal in Nov. of 1905 and was salvaged for scrap in 1907.

[319] The Red River is one of the very few rivers that flow in that direction, emptying into Lake Winnipeg, which with Lake Manitoba are the remnants of the vast pre-historic glacial Lake Agassiz, the result of the melting of the glaciers of the most recent ice-age.

[320] By Paul Magel, great-grandson of Edwin.

that this black sheep of the family had a brother Harold, but I never knew Pop's parents names or where they came from.

My mother grew up during the 1920s, and her memories of her father, Pop, were of a successful entrepreneur who amassed and squandered a small fortune, while enjoying the company of many women, as his children lived in abject poverty. She spoke of him infrequently and then with unabashed disdain, if not hatred. On the other hand, my mother's sister, my Aunt Dorothy, remained in contact with Pop throughout the years that he was absent from the family (I found hundreds of letters and postcards he had sent to her tucked away in her closet when she died in 2008). Dorothy always spoke about Pop respectfully, despite the fact that she once admitted to me that she thought him a bit of a scoundrel.

The depression of the early thirties brought hard times for the somewhat gregarious George Gurr. Although he was never averse to hard work in his early years, he appears to have developed a determination to follow an easy and carefree life. Though he tried his hand at many different occupations during the 1930s, 1940s and 1950s (he worked in a munitions plant in Winnipeg during WWII), perhaps the occupation that most defines him is as a "carnie" running the darts concession for the Conklin and E.J Casey Shows, two carnival groups that travelled the Canadian West during the mid-1900s. I visited Pop at his concession one summer in the early 1950s. He wanted to assure me that his dart game was honest, unlike many other concessions, but warned me that I should stay away from most of the others because fraud and short-changing customers were common practices.

We usually saw Pop only at Christmas, and I have memories of his entertaining us with sleight of hand card tricks and recall that he claimed to have had a magic act on one occasion [321]. During the winter months he often worked as a travelling salesman, and in his later years he was proud of his success selling a product called All-Sew from the Canadian Lakehead all the way to Vancouver.

When my grandmother (Nana) became ill in the late 1950s, to his credit, but probably because he was aging and alone, he came home to Nana, who was living with my Aunt Dorothy, and he cared for the wife he had treated so badly in earlier years, until her death in 1963.

He had been a relative stranger to me for most of my life, but in those latter years of his life, I learned a little about the man he was, if not his history. I found him to be affable, good-hearted, and well mannered. Always well-dressed [322] and well-manicured, he met people with ease and was always polite and I never once heard him swear or show temper. He enjoyed playing cards, he loved card tricks and he enjoyed cooking, but showed no interest in sports or televised drama. He was well-read and appeared interested in world events. A bit of a rogue, perhaps, he was at the same time charming and fascinating, loved being with people and never spoke badly of anyone.

---

[321] He evidently performed in a Winnipeg theatre in the mid-1910s, but in one letter to his wife in 1919 wonders that they haven't called him back recently and wonders if it is because of hard times.

[322] He was always well dressed and usually wore a suit and tie. In the 1940s and 1950s I still recall him wearing spats in the stylish English fashion of the turn of the century (spats are made of cloth or felt and button around the ankle to protect socks from mud and moisture).

20.4.2 A Canadian in the Gurr Family

George Herbert Edwin Gurr was born in England in 1888 and by April of 1894, he had crossed the Atlantic to America and returned to England twice with his father Edwin and brother Harold. George was back in England for the 1901 census and we believe he spent the next few years in various boarding schools before his father brought him to Canada in the spring of 1905. The fact that documentation shows he arrived in Canada with his father aboard the *Bavarian* (and without his brother and stepmother) lends credibility to a family tradition that his father Edwin had to return to England to bring him to Canada following his expulsion from a British school of higher learning (possibly Oxford).

When Edwin and Ada immigrated to Washington State in 1906-1907, not yet 18-year old George Gurr decided to remain in Winnipeg. Why George did not join his parents in the United States is a mystery, but since his brother Harold, who was only sixteen, also appears to have selected the option of staying behind with George, we suspect that there was little affection between father and sons at this stage in their lives. Harold eventually returned to England, and to our knowledge never saw his father again.

George would spend the rest of his life centered in Winnipeg. He married Ellen Mabel Wilton in 1909 and they had three children between 1909 and 1913. In the 1911 Federal Census George was recorded as the manager of an Express Company, and it may be that he was working for the Canadian Pacific Railway, for a few years later we know this was the case. The Gurr family was not prosperous, but comfortable and George was considered a good father and husband and his wife and children loved him. In 1919 George and his family went to the Chelan Valley in the State of Washington. There George would see his father Edwin for the last time and the visit ended with the separation of George and his wife.

20.5 Washington Bound

In the spring of 1919 George was working for the Canadian Pacific Railway as an Express Agent. The war in Europe in which Canada had been fully involved was over and tens of thousands of troops were still on their way home [323], many bringing war brides with them. The cost of the war had led to a huge national debt, high unemployment and calls for a more socialistic approach to the people's welfare. Another worrisome factor was the Spanish flu pandemic which was still spreading around the globe with a death ratio that would leave an estimated 100,000,000 or 2% of the world's population dead. For many Canadians in 1919, the future held little promise.

With the professed intention of emigrating from Canada to the United States, George sent his wife Mabel and his three children to Chelan in May of 1919, promising to follow shortly. What transpired over the next twelve months leaves us wondering about his real intentions from the start. However, the correspondence between the two during the months that he delayed

---

[323] The population of Canada was just under 8 million, but the Expeditionary Army numbered about 650,000 or almost 9% of the total population. Approximately 65,000 military personnel died in the conflict and there were another 170,000 casualties.

leaving Winnipeg to join her (which Mable kept as long as she lived) suggests they were still a loving couple.

Winnipeg was a major center of unrest at this time, although many other countries were experiencing similar post-war problems. On one occasion, the situation in Winnipeg even prompted the *New York Times* to run this headline: "Bolshevism Invades Canada." [324]

George stalled his departure to Washington, claiming that he was held up by strike events and the desperate need of the CPR company for his services in these chaotic circumstances. He also felt he should not leave for fear of being ineligible for his holiday pay. While these reasons may be valid, there is also some evidence that he was enjoying the separation from his family, for in some of his correspondence he mentions visits to the beaches north of Winnipeg. Almost four months after Mabel's departure from Winnipeg, George finally arrived in Chelan in late August.

Photo 20.5.1 George Herbert Edwin and Edwin Robert Gurr,
Son and Father in Chelan, 1919
Paul Magel Collection

---

[324] The Winnipeg General Strike which began May 15th, 1919 was one of the most influential strikes in Canadian history, and became the platform for future labor reform. The reason for the strike: the end of WWI resulted in an influx of returning soldiers looking for work and jobs were scarce. At the same time unemployment was rising with new immigrants flowing in, factories being shut down after the war, inflation rampant and wages already poor and dropping. Several worker's unions banded together to form a Central Strike Committee calling for better wages, better working conditions and other reforms. Strikes and unrest continued the rest of May and most of June.

On June 21, 1919 about 25,000 strikers assembled for a demonstration at Market Square in downtown Winnipeg, and under threat and fearing violence the mayor read the Riot Act and called in the Mounties. They rode in with clubs, firing weapons into the air and scattering the crowd. Two people were killed and many more injured, and arrests followed. This Bloody Saturday, as it came to be known, left Winnipeg under something akin to military occupation. A few days later the Central Strike Committee which included members of the combined unions officially called off the strike and people began to return to work.

We have no idea how the reunion of father and son turned out. **Photo 20.5.1** on the previous page was taken of Edwin and George somewhere in the Chelan Valley in August of 1919 and both men are smiling and look comfortable in the setting. They had not laid eyes on one another for almost 13 years, nor had there been much in the way of correspondence. But George would soon discover that his father Edwin's circumstances did not allow Edwin to offer assistance to George and his family, and in fact Edwin was having some trouble supporting himself. The immediate need for George to find a way to support his own family when he arrived changed his plans. George might have stayed on in Washington and taken over the Chelan homestead from his father, for both Edwin and his brother Reverend Henry would soon abandon the property known as Gurrland, but the hard life on the mountain trying to eke out a living as an orchardist would certainly have held no attraction for the urbane London-born gentleman, George Gurr.

August was apple season and everyone was expected to tissue-wrap and box the apples from Edwin's orchard so that they could be sold or bartered for food. But this activity could not give George sufficient income, so he soon went to nearby Winesap, in the hope of finding gainful work, leaving his family with his father. The relationship between George and Mabel could not have been more strained. Through much of September, October and into November Mabel did not receive much in the way of support money from George and in mid-November she sent an inquiry to officials at Winesap asking about recourse. George immediately sent a mis-addressed note to Mabel telling her that a money order was on the way. Mable was desperate. She later received correspondence from officials at Winesap suggesting that she take court action, and the district attorney sent a letter to George advising him of his parental obligations and the legal implications of desertion.

20.6   Separation

Under this pressure, George eventually packed up his few belongings and left his wife and two of the children behind. Surprisingly, and for some unknown reason, he took his eldest daughter, Dorothy [325], with him and moved back to Winnipeg. He and Dorothy lived with a Mrs. Knight (a mistress?) for a short time, but soon George put Dorothy in the Sacred Heart Convent in St. Charles, Winnipeg.

Abandoned, penniless and alone in a foreign environment Mabel spent a long winter not knowing exactly where her husband and daughter had gone. She communicated her plight to her father and friends in Winnipeg, and in April of 1920 received correspondence responding to her many inquiries about Dorothy's whereabouts. The Sister Directress of Sacred Heart Convent confirmed rumors by mail disclosing that George had indeed placed their daughter in the convent's care and enclosed a letter written by eight-year-old Dorothy to her mother. In that moving letter Dorothy wrote that she hated Daddy and the greedy Mrs. Knight and asked if her mother still loved her and if she could come and get her and her clothes from the convent. Mabel returned from Chelan soon after, accompanied by her other two children and eventually rescued

---

[325] As previously mentioned, there appears to have been a special bond between father and daughter all their lives.

her daughter. She and her three children were re-united, but George and Mabel were separated for the next forty years.

The story of George and Mabel and their separation is factual, for we have most of the correspondence between the two from 1919 to 1920, as well as the corroboration of Dorothy before her passing in 2008. These are the facts, and we are saddened by the disintegration of a family. But a century later we can only guess at what transpired between two people who seemed happy together before something or someone came between them, and we are understandably reluctant to play judge as to where the fault lay.

20.7   George in Later Years

George was never one to be idle and according to his daughter Dorothy he was engaged in several different occupations and always appeared successful. He was definitely entrepreneurial. We have documented the fact that he operated a successful shoe repair shop for several years in the 1920s. He also did some catering and baked and sold cakes which were in high demand among the more privileged citizens of Winnipeg, for they were elaborate and relatively expensive.

George suffered from hardening of the arteries and eventually lost circulation to his legs. Gangrene set in and both legs were amputated below the knee in 1972. He spent his last two years under constant care, but seemed cheerful enough when the author occasionally brought him out of the care center for a weekend. George died in 1974 and was buried alongside Mabel. I know that's what she would have wanted, for she once told the author that "you never stop loving someone you really love."

20.8   Census and Other Records:

Birth: July 18, 1888 in Ealing, Middlesex, England

Marriage: Jan 25, 1909 in Winnipeg, MB Canada to Ellen (Mabel) Pimlott Wilton (born 07 Aug 1882 in Hampton, Surrey, died Apr 1, 1963 in Winnipeg)

Separation: Began 1919-1920, divorce was not an option to Mabel.

1901 UK and Wales Census: Scholar living in Tonbridge, southeast of London with father and brother and attending boarding school

Emigration: From England to Canada landing April 5, 1905

1906 Manitoba and Saskatchewan Census: living in Winnipeg with stepmother Ada and brother Harold on June 30, 1906

1911 Canada Census: living in a suite at 370 Aikins Ave in Winnipeg with wife Mabel and son George Edgar Gurr and working as a foreman for an express company

1919 Residence: 782 Spence St. Winnipeg

1919 Border Crossing: Aug 19th from Winnipeg. Destination Washington State

Directories: Winnipeg Business Directory 1926: leased 747 Wellington Ave for $120.00 per month). Winnipeg City Directory 1928: Canadian Shoe Repair Shop, 747 Wellington Ave, proprietor George Gurr.

Photo 20.9.1a
George Edgar Gurr
c. 1930
Paul Magel Collection

Photo 20.9.1b
George Edgar Gurr
1970

Paul Magel Collection

Photo 20.9.1c Dorothy Gurr, 1938
Paul Magel Collection

Photo 20.9.1d Connie Gurr 1940
Paul Magel Collection

20.9.1 Children of George Herbert and Mabel Wilton Gurr

George Edgar Robert Gurr, **Photos 20.9.1a and 20.9.1b**. Born Nov 6, 1909 Winnipeg MB, died Dec 20, 1974 Osoyoos British Columbia

Dorothy Gurr (born Apr 7, 1912 Winnipeg MB, died Aug 13, 2008 Winnipeg, MB), **Photo 20.9.1c.**

Constance Elizabeth Gurr (born Sep 18, 1913 Winnipeg MB, died Dec 27, 1989 Miami FL), **Photo 20.9..**

James Leslie Gurr (born Sep 15, 1924 Winnipeg MB) and adopted by Ellen Mabel Gurr in the 1920's. Les is still living and a much loved member of the extended family.

20.9.2 Notes from the Author Paul Magel's Interview with Dorothy Gurr in 2007

When asked about Chelan:

I remember going to Chelan but I recall very little about it. I do remember that I spent a great deal of time wrapping apples and putting them in a box. We had to do this just so, and I must have been good at it, because I did a lot of boxes and was complemented on how well I worked.

I remember men, but I don't remember who they were, chasing a deer down the mountain side. It may have been a doe with its fawn. They killed it (them) and served venison for dinner one night. Connie and I knew that they were putting that deer on our table and we wouldn't touch it. They were pretty mean about it and wouldn't let us leave the table until we ate it. I didn't eat mine and everyone was mad at me. I don't know whether Connie gave in or not, but I sure didn't. (Connie was six, Dot was seven.)

Pop followed us down there and there was a lot of arguing. Mom told me later that I wanted to go home with Pop when he left, but I don't believe I wanted to go. Maybe I didn't like where I was. Pop brought me back to Winnipeg - just me and him, but I don't remember when.

When we got back he was living with another woman - he always had another woman - and I don't think they wanted me around. I took gum out of my mouth once and that woman got very angry with me for doing such a bad-mannered thing. It wasn't long after that Pop put me in a convent. When Mom came back to Winnipeg and found out where I was she was beside herself, but had a hard time getting me out of that convent.

When asked about her early life:

We were living at 431 Parkview in St. James. I remember we used to walk down to Donnely's Food Store, about four blocks away. Donnely's was on Silver near King Edward. Once in a while we would get a nickel for candy. That was quite a treat, because we were very poor. Mom had to pay $13.00 a month for the house. The owner was a nice man. He wanted to sell Mom the house for $1300.00, but there was no way she could buy it.

Pop wouldn't give us a dollar without a fight. Grandpa Wilton must have been paying the bills. Mom would do dressmaking, cook cakes and make things to sell, but she never got much more than a dollar for anything. We use to get handouts of used clothes from well-meaning people, but we only resented them for it.

Mom would sometimes send us down to Pop's shoe shop to get money. We would ride the street car. Tickets were eight for $0.25. His shop was called Wellington Shoe Store. It was somewhere on Wellington, but I think near Arlington. His clients were all well to dos from River Heights. He was very mean about giving us money. He would make us wait for hours while he went about his business. When he did give us money, he would often throw it at us. He was nasty, but I don't know why he was so nasty. Usually, he would give us about five dollars. Once he only gave us a two dollar bill. When we got home Mom cried. She took the money and threw it in the stove. Connie and I were so upset. We had spent the whole day getting that two dollars and Mom burned it.

I remember a friend, Vivian Henderson. She was a black girl and she liked me for some reason. We were in grade six or seven. That was when I went to work at the *Country Guide*. [326]. I was with that company for over 60 years. We worked five days a week and a half day Saturday. We'd all go to lunch together at places like Picardy's and another place farther down and across from Eatons. I started buying Royal Daultons. I just loved them. I would put a dollar down and pay a dollar or so a week until they were paid for and mine. I bought my first one at Johnson and Hutchinson Jewelers - near the old Lyceum Theatre.

What about boyfriends? She began by talking about her brother.

Edgar's Winnipeg girl friend's name was Ruby and there was some question of his having done something not quite acceptable (illegal) that caused him to run away in the night, for fear of being arrested and charged. Edgar left home in Sept. 1930, penniless. He rode the rails to Vancouver and found work at an undertakers, for board and room. Times were tough for everyone. Connie couldn't find work and barely avoided arrest when she started shoplifting.

When pressed about boyfriends !

I don't remember what we did for fun. We may have gone dancing at the Roseland on Sherbrook near Harman's Drug Store.

First beau was Bill Dyck – wouldn't talk about him. She did tell me that she and Bill bought a car together c. 1930.

Second beau was Joe Schmidt – wouln't talk about him. He died suddenly in 1938 of natural causes. They were engaged to be married.

20.9.3 George (Edgar) Gurr, son of George Herbert Gurr

Edgar (as he was known in childhood) is of interest for having accomplishments that rivaled those of his cousin Will Gurr of Chelan (see Chapter 17). Edgar actually met and probably spent time with Will (his father's first cousin) when then nine-year-old Edgar was at school in Chelan during the winter of 1919-1920. However, to our knowledge the two never met again for the rest of their lives.

---

[326] *The Country Guide* was a popular farm magazine produced by the Public Press, headquartered in Winnipeg. For years, Dorothy headed up the circulation department. She was gifted with a remarkable memory and could recall minute details about every subscriber the magazine ever had.

In May of 1920, Edgar returned to Winnipeg from a year in Chelan with his mother and sister Connie and his mother began the search for his sister Dorothy. During the next several years Edgar would finish high school and find employment at a Winnipeg department store.

He became enamored with a young lady by the name of Ruby and although she was from a well-to-do family whose parents scolded her for her involvement with Edgar who likely had no way of keeping her in the style to which she was accustomed, the two fell in love. Whatever the truth of the matter, Ruby's parents blamed Edgar for theft of an article they claimed was missing and threatened to call the police. A despondent Edgar fled the city and a month later, travelling by rail he reached Vancouver. He "rode the rails" hiding out in empty boxcars and sometimes clinging to the underside of railcars, often narrowly escaping capture by the railroad cops (bulls or bulleys with clubs). It was "the thirties" and so many people were out of work and homeless that there were camps (hobo jungles) near the rail yards where people of no means gathered in support of one another, many waiting for the opportunity to catch a car to the next stop looking for work. Edgar's letters home are full of stories about his adventures.

When he arrived in Vancouver he was unable to find work anywhere. He ended up in Victoria where he finally did find work in a funeral home as an undertaker's helper in exchange for his board and room. This served him well for this experience enabled him to find paid work a year or so later. He contacted Ruby and she joined him in Vancouver. The couple were planning marriage but things were not what they had been and Ruby decided to end the relationship.

Soon afterward Edgar married and he and his wife Nell eventually settled in Princeton, British Columbia in 1941 where he worked for a funeral home (the Princeton Mortuary) which he eventually arranged to purchase. Princeton is just east of the Cascade Mountains, and just west of the Okanogan Valley about 140 air-miles north-north-east of Chelan, where Edgar had spent the winter of 1919-1920, and where Will was still living. From the time Edgar arrived in Princeton he asked to be called by his first name, George.

Like Will Gurr, George Edgar Gurr was entrepreneurial. He bought a grocery store. He bought a share in a sawmill which he spent a great deal of time developing. The author recalls riding down a mountainside on a timber truck loaded with logs to the mill below and watching while workers debarked the logs and cut them into cants, that is, pieces that could be used for further reduction into different types of lumber. He invested in an insurance company. He started a freight service. He formed a construction company and his company built 21 miles of the Trans-Canada Highway near Roger's Pass.

Edgar served on the Princeton Village Council, and was Past Master of a Masonic Lodge and a Rotarian. He was a magistrate and judge in Princeton for twelve years before his death.

Compare George Edgar's life with that of Will Gurr in Chapter 17. It is interesting that these two cousins, in similar geographic surroundings, without any communication between them, and with so little in the way of attention from their respective fathers, should lead such extraordinary lives.

20.10 Harold Wilfred Gurr

After their father Edwin and stepmother Ada left Winnipeg for Chelan (Ada left in 1907), George and Harold both remained behind for reasons that may have been visa related. Harold was only 17 when Ada left. He was back in London by the time of the 1911 census, but we have no idea of when he returned there, or how he occupied himself in the intervening years.

His occupation in 1911 is listed as dairy worker living in Bournemouth (Hampshire). That he ended up working in the dairy industry on his return is not surprising. There is little doubt that, as the nephew [327] of Sir George Barham, he would have had little difficulty getting employed in some capacity in his great uncle's thriving dairy empire.

He served as a private in the Hampshire Regiment during WWI. The first Battalion saw almost immediate service in France, but it seems unlikely that he was in the army at the beginning of the war. The second Battalion was in India in August 1914, returned to England, was then transferred to Gallipoli and Egypt before heading back to France in 1916. Again, it is unlikely that a new recruit would be added to this regular service unit. The third Battalion, a training depot at the start of the war, was held in reserve. There were also six Battalions in the Territorial Force, and these served in India and other parts of the Empire. There were many other Battalions formed during the war, but many saw only home service. Without knowing which Battalion Harold was in we cannot know where he served.

Harold Gurr (of Bournemouth, Hampshire) married Ida Muriel Stanton in the county of Dorset on Dec 12, 1919. Harold was living on Grange Road in Ealing in 1934 (Electoral Register). He married Dorothy May Rogers in Middlesex in the summer of 1942. Harold Wilfred Gurr died on December 12, 1965 at Middlesex Hospital, St. Marylebone London, leaving an estate valued at £677.00 to Dorothy May Gurr, his widow.

---

[327] The 1911 census form which Harold filled out and signed clearly states his relationship to the head as nephew without elaborating. He is probably resident at one of his great uncle Sir George Barham's homes. The entry was later changed to Head, so he may have been living alone in a property belonging to an uncle.

Chapter 21

Some Observations

21.1 Conclusions

We have chronicled all that we have been able to learn about the lives and travels of our Gurr ancestors from rural Sussex to the American West and the Canadian Plains. We have not found any wealthy or titled or famous ancestors, nor did we expect to do so. Our earliest known ancestors were Sussex farmers at the end of the 18th century. We surmise that they were descended from a Norman soldier in the service of a 14th century Anglo-Normal lord, and the family surname Gurr almost certainly derives from the Old French and Middle English words for soldier.

Our recent male ancestors became part of two great migrations of the 19th century, first from rural to urban England, and the next generation from London to North America. Some of these men became entrepreneurs, first in London, later in Canada and Washington State. Others were farm laborers, streetcar conductors, electricians and engineers, store clerks, priests, government officials, auto mechanics, professors…. the list of occupations is very long.

As for the women, one of our great aunts married into an English family of physicians and three generations of her descendants followed in that profession. Three of our cousins and one aunt became registered nurses in the Western United States. And what about the spouses of our male cousins? Most were mothers and housewives about whose lives we know very little (typical for women until the mid 20th century).

Most but not all our ancestors and their descendants were hard-working, responsible people, but one of our direct ancestors was something of a charming scoundrel who abandoned his family, while another was an inveterate adventurer who provided his children with little nurture or education. Yet the family survived, and thrived.

Whenever possible, in an account that spans two centuries and encompasses nearly one hundred individuals, we have sought to reconstruct our ancestors' lives and times – so this is a social history, in so far as documents permit. But for many of our ancestors, down through the late 20th century in North America, we have little information other than public records of births, marriages, occupations and deaths. Some of this may make for dull reading, little more than genealogical outlines. But at the same time there are fascinating and detailed stories of adventuresome lives in interesting places, from Victorian London to Merced, California to Gold Rush Alaska to Chelan, Washington.

21.2 Some Simple Guidelines

The authors do not presume to have professional expertise as genealogists but we have learned a great deal about where and how to look for information about our English ancestors and in the following paragraphs we offer a few simple guidelines, hopeful that in some limited way, our experience may help others discover theirs.

21.2.1 Sources and Guidebooks

The wealth of information that has been made available on line by *Family Search,* [328] *London Metropolitan Archives* [329], *Ancestry.com* and other genealogical sources has allowed the North American authors [330] of this book to compile concrete evidence concerning their English ancestors. This evidence would most certainly have been out of reach of our resources a decade or two ago. In addition to these sources, there are also several guides available to those seeking information about their ancestry that describe in detail how to go about finding it. Personally, we recommend *Your English Ancestry, A Guide for North Americans,* by Sherry Irvine and *A Genealogist's Guide to Discovering Your English Ancestors* by Paul Milner and Linda Jones.

21.2.2 Historic Societies

To help you find individuals who lived in previous centuries and to understand who they were, and why and how they did what they did, you should know some of the history and geography of where they lived, and you must also know something of the laws and customs that shaped their lives.

The first three chapters of *A Gurr Family Odyssey* will provide those of you with English ancestors and especially those whose English ancestors came from Sussex or Kent with some basic information on the history, laws and customs of south-eastern England, many of which apply to England generally. For those of you searching for ancestors in other counties of England, we recommend that you research this information in those counties. A good way to start is by checking on-line to see if the county or a municipality in that county has established a website. Many towns and some villages in England show pride in their history and the people who have developed that history and the number of municipal websites boasting historic and genealogical information is steadily growing.

21.2.3 Surnames

Our search for our English ancestors began with very limited information and we started with little more than the Gurr surname. Oral tradition was that our grandparents were born in England, probably London, and that they had come to North America sometime before the end of the 19th century. We knew our grandparents' surnames and given names but we had no information on their parents' names, nor on their parents' lives and ancestry.

We were fortunate that the surname Gurr is relatively rare, which is a great advantage compared to those searching UK records for a Smith, Jones, Taylor, Brown or Williams, five of the most common British surnames. However we found that the name was sometimes recorded as Gurr, but often Gurre, Guere, Gur, Gun and even Green. So, a word of caution: there are

---

[328] A great starting point for those with a limited budget is www.familysearch.org.

[329] Another source of free information at www.cityoflondon.gov.uk under London Metropolitan Archives.

[330] One born in Manitoba, the other in Washington State.

often slight variations of any particular surname. Be prepared to search all spelling variations of your surname and other ancestral names you encounter and even their phonetic possibilities. Moreover, keep in mind that surnames were not in common use in Britain until about the 14th century and not mandatory until the reign of Henry the VIII. In the 11th and 12th centuries "Brits" [331] were almost exclusively known by their given names, with their occupation or location added to clarify. Thus John the tailor could become John Taylor and often his descendant would be tailors.

21.2.4 Given Names

Obviously, searching for an individual with a given name that is distinctive, or better still one having two given names, is advantageous. Unfortunately, the number of given names in use in Britain was small, and the use of two given names was unusual until about the mid-19th century. Historically, British given names were Anglo-Saxon (Alfred, Edwin, Edgar, Matilda, Hilda and Emma were common) or biblical (Thomas, John, Peter, Mary, Sarah and Rebecca and others from both the New and the Old testament). 17th century Puritanism brought more unusual, often biblical names into use (Benjamin, Samuel, Ezra, Hannah, Faith, Hope). Name changes within British families were gradual, for it was traditional to honor a parent or other family member by giving a new-born the name of a close relative. In some families the first-born male was always named after the father or grandfather, and the first-born daughter after the mother or grandmother. One author's only grandson, born in London in 2004, is named Jonathan Gurr Lavan and his mother, cultural anthropologist Lisa Anne Gurr, says she had no knowledge that his great-great-great-great grandfather, born in Sussex in 1800, was also named Jonathan. We have also found many instances where a newborn was given the same name as an earlier deceased brother or sister. To the genealogic researcher, one advantage of this traditional use of given names is that it helps tracking one generation to the next, for a sudden change in given names in a family is unusual.

21.2.5 Records

As we prepare this manuscript in 2013, *Ancestry.com* and other sources have census results for the United States as recent as 1940 and as early as 1790, Canada 1911 and earlier (with some Provincial censuses 1916), and the United Kingdom 1911 and as early as 1841. In addition, day by day, additional information comes from on line records such as baptisms, marriages, births, deaths, wills, immigration records, ship manifests, city and trade directories and a host of other data too numerous to mention. This information must be used with some caution, keeping in mind that some of the originals that provided the information are scarcely readable or the enumerators' writing barely legible, so there are, understandably, transcription errors. Also, there are often many individuals with the same name (Thomas Jones, for example – for whom there are thousands of records) so don't assume that you've found your ancestor without confirming evidence such as matching spousal or vital statistics. On the other hand, when you do discover a

---

[331] Although we don't know when this term came into use, it was common for emigrants from England to refer to themselves and others from the British Isles as Brits by the beginning of the twentieth century.

record that may be pertinent, but are uncertain, carefully log the record and the source in a notebook or electronic record for future reference, for a confirming match may be a day or a month away, and finding the original discovery without such a log can be time consuming.

21.2.6 Getting Started

We recommend that you begin with a hard-cover log book or a retrievable electronic file and use it as a diary to record what you've done on any day as well as the information you've found and where you found it. This will allow you to review your progress at any future date. Log what you know of your pedigree, recording your parents' names, dates of birth, baptism, marriage, and death, education and the location at which each occurred. Ditto this for your grandparents and great grandparents, as far back as is possible. Ask family members for their input and consult family bibles or diaries if available. You can also search city and other directories at your local library. *Family Search* and, for those of you with English ancestors, the *London Metropolitan Archives* are free sources of information, and both are well worth looking into early in your preparation stage.

Second, take out a trial subscription to a genealogy site such as *Ancestry.com* and verify your known data. You will be able to enter your data and put it in a family tree format, and compare with other family trees on the site. Verification is important, for it is always possible that your original information is in error, regardless of the source. Always record the information found being careful to include source citations. If you are satisfied with your trial subscription you can extend your membership.

Warning: Even with a simple four letter name such as Gurr, we found transcription errors Gun, Gunn, Green etc. that were in fact Gurrs (*Ancestry.com* eventually corrects these or annotates them with the alternative, once errors are reported to them).

Warning: Be sure to gather irrefutable source documentation. From census and other records you may be convinced that you have made a discovery of a new ancestor, but you need to confirm the accuracy of that discovery – in other words, VERIFY.

The authors' example of a successful progression in finding English ancestors:

- A Henry Gurr and an Edwin Gurr were enumerated in the 1910 US Federal Census living in Chelan, Washington. That Henry was known to be the grandfather of Ted Robert Gurr, one of the authors, and family tradition suggested that Henry had a brother Ted Robert, after whom the author was named.

- Uncertain whether the enumerated Edwin Gurr was Ted, the authors searched the UK censuses looking for a Henry and an Edwin Gurr in the same family. We were fortunate to find an Alfred James Gurr in the 1871 UK census who was the father of two sons Henry Gurr and Edwin Gurr.

- We then searched for census, marriage and birth information on Alfred James Gurr and discovered a record existed for the marriage of an Alfred James Gurr to a Mary Ann Bennett. By purchasing a copy of that 1846 marriage record direct from *Vital England*, we found Jonathan Gurr, Publican, recorded as the father of the groom. Jonathan Gurr now appeared to be the next male Gurr ancestor in our pedigree.

- Using *Family Search* we found that a Jonathan Gurr married a Mary Barham in 1823, which led us to the *Society of Genealogists* in Clerkenwell, London, where we found records of the couple's eight children, which gave us additional information on Jonathan's son, Alfred James Gurr.

- We eventually established a connection between Jonathan and John Gurr of Salehurst, now confirmed as our earliest known Gurr ancestor. We then re-traced the connection back to Alfred James Gurr and to our Washington Gurrs. One difficulty we encountered was finding evidence of Jonathan's passing, because the *Gurr* surname was transcribed from the original records as *Gun*.

21.2.7 Personal Records

The ability to reconstruct the lives of our ancestors and their dependents depends first on public records of births, marriages, and deaths: those delineate the outlines of their lives. But if we want to know how they lived then we need to ask whether they wrote and were written about – in other words their letters and memoirs, publications and news accounts. Some of the subjects of this book lived within the authors' lifetimes, or the lifetimes of other relatives in families that have kept in touch. So we have been able to use some of our own and others' recollections to flesh out the sketches here. And sometimes in the course of our research we have found more distant relatives who also are reconstructing family history. For example we learned a great deal about Ellen Gurr, youngest sister of Henry and Edwin, and her physician descendants from memoirs compiled by her great grandson, Col. Hugh Stott of East Sussex.

The farther back in time, the less likely are personal correspondence or diaries to have survived – if they were written all. Time and again we have found frustratingly indirect evidence of relevant documents that have been lost or discarded, for example the Reverend Henry J. Gurr's unpublished memoirs and his letters to his brothers in London that persuaded them to emigrate.

So here are two keys to those who hope to reconstruct family lives of the recent and more distant past. One is to track down their diaries, correspondence, photos, and memorabilia from other family members, however distant. The other is to record memories and conversations, because they are windows on the past that provide far more color and depth than the cold script or print of public records.

Appendices

Appendix A
Data Relevant to Gurr Emigration from England

A1 Gurr Households in the English Speaking World

In a 1990 survey of Gurrs in the English-speaking world, 1281 Gurr households are identified from city and telephone directories, almost half of them in Great Britain. Contemporary households with the surname Gurr number about 1300 and are distributed today across all the English-speaking countries. **Table A1** shows the distribution as of 1990.

Appendix A Table A1:
Distribution of Gurr Households in the English Speaking World [332]

Country	Great Britain	United States	Australia	Canada	New Zealand
Households	610	317	165	156	35

A survey based on city and telephone directories is likely less complete than census data, which could explain the shrinkage in numbers of Gurr households in Great Britain between 1891 and 1990. Alternatively, many of them may have emigrated as the authors' ancestors did.

We have also found evidence of Gurrs of English heritage in Ireland (including McGurr), Bermuda, the South Pacific and in non-English locations, including Mexico.[333] The Gurrs of Mexico probably include descendants of Enoch Eldredge Gurr, who is mentioned elsewhere in this work. The countries covered in this survey undoubtedly include Gurrs households of German decent. For those living in the United States and Canada this is definitely the case, and data confirming this may be found in Chapter 10, where in Table 10.5b we find that of 168 individuals with the surname Gurr recorded in the 1880 United States Federal Census, 34 were born outside the USA: 23 England, 5 Europe (Germany), 5 Australia, 1 Phillipines: another 2 were of unknown origin. Incidentally, the Australians enumerated are known to be of English ancestry.

---

[332] From *The World Book of Gurrs, Halbert's Family Heritage*, (1990), Section V. A survey based on city and telephone directories is likely less complete than census data, which could explain the shrinkage in numbers of Gurr households in Great Britain between 1891 and 1990. Alternatively, many of them may have emigrated as the authors' ancestors did.

[333] Mormon colonies in northern Mexico were established by members of the Church of Jesus Christ of Latter-day Saints beginning in the 1880s, but only two are active today. The Edmunds Act of 1882 made polygamy a felony and the Federal Government of the United States was determined to end polygamy in America. The Mexican colonies prospered at first, but in the summer of 1912 they were evacuated because of anti-American sentiment during the Mexican Revolution and many of the colonists returned to the United States, including George Romney, (father of United States Presidential hopeful, Mitt Romney) who was born in one of the Mexican colonies.

A2   United States Federal Census, 1910

The US Federal Census of 1910 shows 469 records for the Gurr name (exact spelling only) of which 26 were born in England, 3 in Canada, 404 in the USA*, 19 in Germany and 22 in other (including Russia, China, Mexico and Italy).

*Voluntary migration from England to the USA was high during the middle of the 19th century as part of the great movement westward. A large percentage of the 404 listed as born in the USA in the 1910 US Federal Census were descendants of those English migrants.

A3   Canadian Federal Census, 1910

The Canadian Federal Census of 1910 shows 61 records for the Gurr name (exact spelling only) of which 46 were born in England*, 11 in Canada, 3 in USA, none in Germany and 1 in China.

*English Gurrs were usually farmers or farm workers and those emigrating from England would naturally head for regions were they could farm. The Canadian west was not opened up until after Confederation in 1867, and prior to that date there was a very limited amount of farmland or farm work available for immigrants. Except for a few small communities, the Western Canadian prairies were largely unsettled until the turn of the 20th century, when English and German immigrants were attracted by offers of 40 acres of free land. All of Paul Magel's English and German ancestors arrived in Western Canada during this period (1899-1906).

A4   US Immigration Data [334]

Tables A4a and A4b on the following page show that emigrants from Germany, Ireland and Great Britain accounted for almost 80% of the European immigrants to the United States between 1841 and 1890. Of the over 12,200,000 listed about 4,300,000 (35%) were from Germany, 3,200,000 (26%) from Ireland and 2,200,000 (18%) from Great Britain (predominantly from England).

---

[334] US Immigration Files (Homeland Security). Retrieved from http://www.latinamericanstudies.org/immigration-statistics.htm

Appendix A TABLE A4a	Main Sources of European Immigration To the United States, 1841 - 1860	
Country	1841-1850	1851-1860
Belgium	5,074	4,738
Denmark	539	3,749
France	77,262	76,358
Germany	434,626	951,667
Great Britain		
England	32,092	247,125
Scotland	3,712	38,331
Unspecified	229,979	132,199
Ireland	780,719	914,119
Netherlands	8,251	10,789
Norway & Sweden	13,903	20,931
Switzerland	4,644	25,011
Totals	1,590,801	2,425,017

Appendix A TABLE A4b	Main Sources of Immigration To the United States, 1861 - 1890		
Country	1861-1870	1871-1880	1881-1890
Austria-Hungary	7,800	72,969	353,719
Denmark	17,094	31,771	88,132
France	35,986	72,206	50,464
Germany	787,468	718,182	1,452,970
Great Britain			
England	222,277	437,706	644,680
Scotland	38,769	87,564	149,869
Unspecified			
Ireland	435,778	436,871	655,482
Italy	11,725	55,759	307,309
Norway	71,631	95,323	176,586
Sweden	37,667	115,922	391,76
Switzerland	23,286	28,293	81,988
USSR	2,512	39,284	213,282
China	64,301	123,201	61,711
Canada & Newfoundland	153,878	383,640	393,304
Totals	1,910,172	2,698,691	4,629,496

Appendix B
Miscellaneous Information

B1   An Example of Language Change [335]

Appendix B **Table B1** on the following page is a middle English selection of literature that was written by Chaucer in the late 14th century and is presented here to illustrate how a name such as Guerrier could become Gurr over several centuries.

It shows how the English language changed after the Conquest. Note that many words are identical to modern English, such as the following: *that, with, March, to, the, every, of, which, is, in, and, open, eye, folk, for, from, they,* and *were*. But also note that two of the English dialects in use in England in Chaucer's day are inter-mixed in this selection: the Scandinavian form "they", "their" and "them" and the London form "hi/they", "hir/their" and "hem/them." The Chancery Standard (c 1430) would standardize on the Scandinavian form, probably because the London forms might easily be confused with "he", "her" and "him" also in common use.

Many words end with an "e", including *roote, sonne, melodye, ende, wende, seeke, olde,* and it is known that in earlier times the letter "e" was pronounced, as were all written vowels. By Chaucer's time, the final "e" had become silent in normal speech, although it could optionally be pronounced in verse as the meter required, and it was normally silent when the next word began with a vowel. Chaucer followed these conventions: "e" is silent in "kowthe" and "Thanne", but is pronounced in "straunge", "ferne", "ende", etc.   Engelond is, of course, England but it is significant that the middle "e" is dropped in standardization as were most "e's" not sounded in the spoken language of the day.

Appendix B Table B1 illustrates how it is possible that the family name Gurr was shortened from the Old French "Guerrier" (warrior or foot soldier) to Gurre between the time of the Norman invasion and the introduction of the Chancery Standard, as there is some evidence that the middle "e" was not pronounced, and the "ier" was softened in the spoken language, as it is in modern French. Finally, the trailing "e" was dropped with the introduction of the Chancery Standard.

Chancery records with the name "Gurr" have been found dated as early as 1504-1515. [336]

B2 Details of the Alfred Richard Family in America

All of Alfred Richards Gurrs twelve children were born in England. **Tables B2a, B2b and B2c** on the following pages provides a few details about their births/deaths, education, marriage and/or divorce, and how they earned their livelihood in America. In addition these tables also identify their children and occasionally their grandchildren as well as a few facts about those descendants.

---

[335] Chaucer, Geoffrey: An excerpt from the prologue to *The Canterbury Tales*, written between 1387 and 1400.

[336] British Chancery Records, 1386-1558; Volume 4, Bundle 316, Page 242.

Appendix B Table B1: Prologue to the Canterbury Tales	
Whan that Aprill, with his <u>shoures soote</u>	shoures soote = showers sweet
The <u>droghte</u> of March hath perced to the roote	droghte = drought; perced = pierced roote = root
And bathed every <u>veyne</u> in <u>swich</u> licour,	veyne = vein; swich = such
Of which vertu engendred is the flour;	vertu = virtue; flour = flower
Whan <u>Zephirus</u> <u>eek</u> with his sweete breeth	Zephirus = west wind; eek = also
Inspired hath in every holt and heeth	
The tendre <u>croppes</u>, and the yonge <u>sonne</u>	croppes = crops; sonne = sun
Hath in the Ram his halfe cours yronne,	half course run
And <u>smale</u> <u>foweles</u> maken melodye,	smale foweles = little birds
That slepen al the nyght with open eye	Slepen = sleep
(So <u>priketh</u> <u>hem</u> Nature in hir <u>corages</u>);	priketh = pierce; hem = them hir = their; corages = feelings
Thanne longen folk to goon on pilgrimages	
And <u>palmeres</u> for to seken <u>straunge</u> <u>strondes</u>	palmeres = pilgrims; straunge = strange strondes = places
To <u>ferne halwes</u>, <u>kowthe</u> in <u>sondry londes</u>;	ferne = distant, foreign halwes = shrines, hallowed places Kowthe = known; sondry londes = sundry lands
And specially from every shires ende	
Of Engelond, to Caunterbury they wende,	
The <u>hooly</u> <u>blisful</u> martir for to <u>seke</u>	hooly = holy; blissful = blessed; seke = seek
That <u>hem</u> hath holpen, whan that they were <u>seeke</u>.	hem = them; seeke = sick

Table B2a Alfred Richard Gurr's Family in America 1900 - 1940

Name (Nickname) Spouse Name (From)	Birthdates	Death	1900	1910	1920	1930	1940	Married Single
Alfred Richard Gurr **Emily Hunter**	Mar 13, 1851 May 8, 1854	Apr 5, 1944 Sep 12, 1940	Merced	Merced	Merced San Mateo	San Mateo	San Mateo San Mateo	1872
Alfred James (James) Daisey (Oregon)	Jul 14, 1873 1872	Dec 21, 1961	Madera	Merced	Merced Robla	Santa Clara	Los Altos Santa Clara	M
Henry Robert (Harry)	Feb 1, 1875	Aug 21, 1948	Merced	Merced	Merced	San Mateo	Unknown	S
Edwin (Ted) Steta McKenzie (Illinois)	Jan 28, 1876 Aug, 1879	Jan 3, 1960	Merced Alt.	Merced Alt.	Merced Alt.	Merced	Merced	M 1899
Emily May (Queenie)	Mar 3 1877	Oct 1969	Merced	San Fran	San Fran	San Mateo	San Mateo Nurse*	S
William Hedwig Noschka	Mar 24, 1878 Jan 7, 1885	1965 Dec 29, 1971	Merced	Alameda	Alameda	San Mateo	San Mateo	M
Mary Maude Madison Crookshanks	Oct 3, 1879 1866	Jul 17, 1967 1959	Unknown	Unknown	Exeter, Tulare	Exeter, Tulare	San Jose	M c.1900
Ellen (Nellie) Frederick C. Dewar	Mar 15, 1881 1871	Feb 12, 1967	Merced	San Fran Nurse	San Fran Nurse	San Fran Nurse*	Palo Alto	M 1924
David Jessie (Michigan)	Aug 30, 1882 1894	Aug 1, 1925	Merced	San Fran (+ Nell)	Nevada, Mason	Electrocuted 1925		M
Ethel Elizabeth Cornelius D. DeJongh	Mar 20, 1884 ?	Oct 14, 1965	Merced	San Fran	San Fran	San Fran	Nurse* San Fran	M 1908
Gordon Florence (New Jersey)	Nov 28, 1885 Aug 9, 1901	Jan 1933 Jun 30, 1970	Merced	Imp. Valley	Imp. Valley	Chula Vista Laborer	Chula Vista	M
Beatrice (Bea) Alvin E. Weaver	Jul 1, 1887 Sep 13, 1891	Jan 11, 1985 Sep 27, 1982	Merced	Merced	Merced	Merced	Merced (Flo)	c.1917
Ernest Bertha C	Oct 11, 1888 Feb 18, 1886	Aug 19, 1980 1957-58	Merced	Merced	Merced	Merced 1932	Merced	M 1917

Table Continued as Table B2b

Table B2b Alfred Richard Gurr's Family in America 1900 – 1940 (Continued from Table B2a)

Name (Nickname) Spouse Name (From)	Grandchildren of Alfred and Emily	Notes
Alfred Richard Gurr / Emily Hunter		Alfred Richard and Emily arrived in America on 4th November 1889 aboard the Etruria sailing from Liverpool to New York, then travelling by rail to Merced, CA.
Alfred James (James) / Daisey (Oregon)	Married, but no family	Daisey is next of kin in 1917 Draft. Alfred works for Gurr Co.
Henry Robert (Harry)	Unmarried, but has same box no. as Ernest and Bertha in 1938.	
Edwin (Ted) / Steta McKenzie (Illinois)	Edwin Donovan (b 31 Mar 1903, d 17 Oct 1983) Melvin L. (b. 1907); Kenneth William (b 1914, d ?)	Edwin D's children include Marvin D born in 1929 and John Edwin (b circa 1940)
Emily May (Queenie)	Unmarried	
William / Hedwig Noschka	Jack E. (b. 1916, d. ?); William A. (b. 1918, d. ?)	Conductor in Oakland -Draft Reg. Sept 1918
Mary Maude / Madison Crookshanks	A. Robert (b.1901, d. 1976); M. Thelma (b. 1903); Donald P. (b. 1905); Mildred M. (b. 1907); Evelyn E. (b. 1913); Ivan C. (b. 1916, d. 2004)	Divorced in 1920's, Madison living apart as a lodger in 1930.
Ellen (Nellie) / Frederick C. Dewar	Married, no family	Passport issued Aug. 1919 - travel to China via Japan dep. Oct 16, 1919. Returned Hong Kong-San Fran Dec 3, 1920 (the Venezuela).
David / Jessie (Michigan)	Married, Details unknown; No family	Electrician, Manager of Light and Water Co, Mason, Lyon NV for draft reg. Sept. 1918
Ethel Elizabeth / Cornelius D. DeJongh	Henry R. DeLongh (b. 1921) Emily M. DeLongh (b. 1922)	Couple and Daughter in 1942 Frisco phone book. C.D. was a bank bookkeeper
Gordon / Florence (New Jersey)	Richard P. (b. 1928); Emily M. (b. 1925)	Gordon works in Cotton Mill (laborer) Flo was a hotel Maid in 40's (widow).
Beatrice (Bea) / Alvin E. Weaver	Emily D. Weaver (b. 1918, d. ?); Barbara Weaver (b. 1921, d. ?)	Ernest Living with Beatrice in 1930, as is Emily M. DeLongh (niece).
Ernest / Bertha C	Married to Bertha? who has same box no. in Merced in 30's, 40's, 50's) No indication of offspring.	Ernest living with Beatrice in 1930, but no Bertha mentioned. Last Soc. Sec. to Oregon. Mar. Lempi Hakala or Kohonen Jan 1961?

Table Continued as Table B2c

Table B2c Alfred Richard Gurr's Family in America 1900 – 1940 (Continued From Table B2b)[1]	
* Graduate Nurses of St. Luke's Hospital School of Nursing (est. 1889 as St. Luke's Training School). Diplomas received: Ellen (1906), Ethel (1909), Queenie (1909). *SF Genealogy.*	
St. Lukes's Hospital destroyed in 1906 quake, but staff assigned to the Red Cross relief effort (including Ellen). Almost all San Francisco hospitals were destroyed by the quake or subsequent fires.	
Edwin Donovan Gurr married Helen in 1928.	
Was there a Nellie May Jackson married to an Edwin Donovan in year ? as suggested in an unconfirmed Jackson family history - since withdrawn).	
John Edwin married Margaret Thompson in ?.	
Henry R. was living with Alfred Richard, and Emily M. was living with Beatrice at the 1930 census	
Barbara married Frank Beames in ?.	
There are at least three Ernest Gurrs in California in the first half of the 20th century (two in Oakland directory in 1920's) - exercise caution in assuming relationships. Mar. Lempi Hakala or Kohonen Jan 1961.	
Merced County	In 1900, Township 2, Alfred R. In 1910, Township 2, both Alfred R and Edwin (Alt. site) farming separately.
Santa Clara County	In 1926, 481 Pettis, Mountain View, Alfred J and Daisey. 1938 Los Altos, Mtn View
San Mateo County	1922, Township 3, Bay Rd (Redwood City) Alfred R., Emily, Harry, Miss Emily May. In 1932 at 545 Clark St. (and in 1940 2261, Clark St.) East Palo Alto, Alfred R., Emily, Miss Emily

---

[1] Compiled from Federal Census, State Voter Registration, and Draft Registration Records, also entries in Alfred Richard and Emily Gurr's family bible.

Made in the USA
Lexington, KY
17 February 2017